TWO
SISTERS

Also by Åsne Seierstad

With Their Backs to the World

The Bookseller of Kabul

A Hundred and One Days

The Angel of Grozny

One of Us

TWO SISTERS

INTO THE SYRIAN JIHAD

ÅSNE SEIERSTAD

TRANSLATED BY SEÁN KINSELLA

VIRAGO

First published in Norway in 2016 by Kagge
First published in Great Britain in 2018 by Virago Press

1 3 5 7 9 10 8 6 4 2

Copyright © Åsne Seierstad, 2016
Translation Copyright © Seán Kinsella, 2018

The moral right of the author has been asserted.

A CIP catalogue record for this book
is available from the British Library.

Hardback ISBN 978-0-349-00905-6
C-Format ISBN 978-0-349-00904-9

Typeset in Perpetua by M Rules
Printed and bound in Great Britain by
Clays Ltd, St Ives plc

Papers used by Virago are from well-managed forests
and other responsible sources.

MIX
Paper from
responsible sources
FSC® C104740

Virago Press
An imprint of
Little, Brown Book Group
Carmelite House
50 Victoria Embankment
London EC4Y 0DZ

An Hachette UK Company
www.hachette.co.uk

www.virago.co.uk

Contents

Author's Note

This is a documentary account.

It is based on testimony. I constructed scenes on the basis of what those who were present related. Some scenes have several sources, others have only one.

I based descriptions of a person's thoughts upon what that person said he or she thought in a given situation.

Some individuals chose not to contribute to this book. They are described according to their actions, written sources, and what others related about them.

For Arabic words, I use a simplified version of the *Journal of Middle Eastern Studies* transcription system. I depart from this in the case of some proper nouns with established spellings in Western languages.

For the most part I printed e-mails and texts without correction. In these I reproduce the sender's spelling of Arabic words and names.

A comprehensive review of working methods is provided in the afterword. A glossary of Islamic words and expressions and a list of published sources appear at the back of the book.

Part I

The Prophet said of the martyrs:

Their souls reside in green birds, nesting in lanterns
hung from the throne of the Almighty, roaming
freely to eat the fruits of Paradise. Their Lord
looked upon them and asked did they wish for
anything. They said: What more shall we desire? We
eat the fruit of Paradise from wherever we please.
The Lord asked them again, and when He asked for
the third time, they said: Lord, we wish that thou
return our souls to our bodies so we may again offer
our lives for your sake. When God saw that they
were not in need of anything, He let them stay in
Paradise.

—Imparted by Abdallah ibn Masud,
died c. 650

We will all return to Allah when we die, but let us
all strive to return to Allah while still alive.

—Umm Hudayfah aka Ayan,
October 10, 2013

1

The Rupture

The bunk bed was in the center of the room. A white metal rail ensured that whoever lay on top did not roll off. The bed divided the room in two and was made up with colorful bedclothes. By the door there were a desk, a chair, and a wardrobe. On the other side, a chest of drawers and a window with a view of a reddish brick housing block, identical to their own. The window ledge was so low that you could easily swing your legs over it and drop down onto the grass. Notes were taped to the furniture, neatly written letters, first drafted in pencil, then gone over in blue marker: Bed. Window. Chair. Desk. Door. The wallpaper above the chest of drawers was covered in them. Big, small, high, low, warm, cold. The Arabic script was carefully rendered, although obviously the work of a beginner, as several of the letters were mixed up. The translations into Norwegian were spelled correctly but written sloppily in faint pencil.

The younger sister, the one who slept in the top bunk, had put up the notes. They not only adorned the girls' room but also hung around the rest of the apartment: Lamp. Sofa. Curtain. Shelf. The course in Arabic began with worldly things, but the purpose was spiritual – to read and understand the Koran as it was revealed to the Prophet Muhammad.

I. He. We. I am. He is. We are. *Allahu Akbar.* God is great. God is greater. *Guide us to the straight path!*

That October morning, Leila had climbed down from the top bunk earlier than usual. She put on a floor-length dress and joined her mother in the kitchen, which was adjacent to the girls' room. Sara was the one in the family who woke first. She would steal out of bed, placing her feet carefully on the floor so she wouldn't wake Sadiq. It was not until he missed her warmth, until the bed had cooled and he noticed he was freezing, that he would get up.

Sara stood at the breakfast table, lost in her own thoughts. She looked up in surprise at her daughter, who had turned sixteen the week before. Leila resembled her father – slender, tall, and long-limbed.

'I can help you get the boys ready,' she said.

'Don't you have school today?' her mother asked.

'Yeah, I just thought you could use a hand . . . '

'No, you get yourself organized, I can take care of the boys myself.'

In contrast to her big sister, who had taken on several of the household duties, Leila did not usually offer to help out. 'Her royal laziness,' her father often called her.

Sara softly roused six-year-old Isaq and eleven-year-old Jibril. She helped Isaq get dressed and hurried the boys into the kitchen.

Sadiq was already standing by the stove.

The brown beans had been prepared the previous evening. Now he sautéed diced onion in oil, added a couple of crushed garlic cloves, a little more oil, then strips of red pepper and spices, until it all took on a darker color. He added the beans and simmered the mixture, then blended it all with a hand mixer. He poured the purée onto a large plate, drizzling olive oil to make golden circles in the brown.

Isaq and Jibril were still drowsy as they plunked down on their chairs. They dipped pieces of bread into the bean stew and popped them in their mouths. Isaq made a mess as usual. Jibril hardly let a crumb fall outside his plate.

Leila hovered around the table, where a pot of black tea with cardamom seeds had been placed.

'Aren't you going to sit down?' her father asked.

'No, Ayan and I are fasting,' the sixteen-year-old replied.

Her father did not pursue the topic. Leila and her big sister, Ayan, who was in the bathroom, were strict when it came to fasting. Women were not permitted to perform religious rituals while unclean, and the girls wanted to catch up on the days they had missed as soon as possible. Mondays and Thursdays were the best days, when the Prophet Muhammad fasted. Today was Thursday.

Ramadan had been an ordeal. This year the fasting month had fallen in July, when the sun did not go down until after ten o'clock at night and rose just a few hours later. It was long to go without food and drink. Now, during Dhu al-Hijjah – the month of the pilgrimage – the girls were fasting again and had intensified their daily prayer. It was the most sacred period in the Islamic calendar, the best time for the *hajj*, to travel as a pilgrim to Mecca. Good deeds counted for more now than at other times of the year.

Ismael, the third brother, who was between Ayan and Leila in age, entered the kitchen with a towel wrapped around his waist. He was on his way to the bathroom, where Ayan had just finished. If he encountered his sisters when strutting around half-naked, he usually lurched into them for fun. 'Don't!' they would shout. 'Mom, he's annoying us!'

The three teenagers – Ayan, who was nineteen years old; Ismael, eighteen; and Leila, sixteen – had drifted apart. The sisters complained that their brother was only interested in working out, hanging around with friends, and playing computer games. His lack of attendance at the mosque did not go unnoticed. It was embarrassing. 'You're not a Muslim!' Ayan had recently shouted at him, and had gone on to urge her mother to throw him out. She could not live with someone who did not pray.

'He's just confused!' their mother had said in his defense.

'Kick him out!'

'In the summer,' their mother said, trying to mollify her, 'I will take him to a sheikh in Hargeisa, ask him to pray over him, talk to him . . . '

Ayan had been vociferous in these arguments; Leila had merely followed her lead. The previous evening, when Ismael came home from training, Leila had rushed over and thrown her arms around his neck.

'Oh, Ismael! I've missed you!'

'Huh? I've only been gone a couple of hours . . . '

'Where were you?'

'At the gym.'

'How was the workout?'

'Eh . . . I was working on my upper body. Chest and arms.'

Girls. Seriously. Leila had been mad at him for ages, and then suddenly she was all sweetness and light.

Ismael put on jeans and a shirt and joined the others for breakfast. He opened the refrigerator door, where alongside the note bearing the word *thallaja* – refrigerator in Arabic – the girls had stuck up words of wisdom from the Islamic Cultural Centre of Norway. On a green sticker, torn at the edges as though someone had tried to peel it off, was written, *Allah does not see your wealth and property, He sees your heart and your actions.* A purple sticker read, *Let he who believes in Allah and the Last Day treat his neighbor with kindness, be generous to his guests and speak the truth, which is good, or remain silent (e.g., refrain from improper and impure talk, slander, lies, spreading rumors etc.).*

Ismael stood at the counter spreading mackerel in tomato sauce on three slices of wholemeal bread. The eighteen-year-old was particular about his protein intake and thought his parents used too much oil in their cooking, as well as boiling food too long and frying things to a crisp. He wanted pure, healthy, simple food and disliked Somali seasonings and spices.

He joined the others at the table, bumping playfully into his little brothers as he sat down. Isaq responded by punching him on the arm; Jibril merely squirmed and asked him to stop.

'Let the boys eat,' Sara said.

*

The day was slow to break; it would still be a while before the sun appeared over the roofs of the apartment blocks in the east.

Sadiq was on sick leave. He had injured his shoulder when a crate fell on him at the Coca-Cola warehouse. Next week he was going to a physiotherapist he had been referred to by NAV, the Norwegian welfare authority. Thoughts flew through his mind. It was a long time since he had heard from his mother in Somaliland. Was she sick? He would make sure to call her later today.

From the girls' room he heard a wardrobe door slam and something heavy being moved. Ayan had left secondary school in the spring and was working as an on-call employee for an agency offering personal assistants to elderly people who, as it stated in her contract, required practical assistance in everyday life. It was a sort of gap year before she went to college.

She came out of the bedroom with a suitcase.

'What are you doing with that?' Sadiq asked.

'Aisha is borrowing it,' Ayan replied. 'She's taking a trip.'

The girls and their friend often borrowed things from one another. Aisha lived a few streets away. The sisters sometimes asked their father to drive them over. On one such trip he had asked what they carried in the plastic bags they had taken back and forth. Aisha's washing machine was broken, they explained, and they were doing her laundry. Aisha was a couple of years older than Ayan; when her husband left her, she had moved back in with her mother and sisters, along with her baby.

Ayan dragged the suitcase behind her down the hall. At the front door she stopped by the mirror and wrapped her curly hair in a *hijab*.

The elder daughter had inherited her mother's features: a curved forehead, soft, round cheeks, and deep-set eyes. She tightened the hijab until there was not a single strand of hair showing, pulled a *jilbab*, a sort of hooded tunic, over it, and finally a loose cloak. The hallway was filling up; Jibril was standing ready to go, while Isaq was trying to get his foot into a shoe.

'You have to unlace it,' Sadiq told him.

'I can't,' the boy moaned.

The same rule goes for everything in life, his father said: 'Use your brain, not your brawn!'

The youngest boy was built like Sara and Ayan, compact and stout. Sadiq crouched to loosen the tangle of laces.

Ayan was the first to leave. 'Bye!' she said, smiling to them.

The door slammed behind her. There was more space in the hallway once she and the suitcase disappeared. Leila took her turn in front of the mirror and copied her sister's movements. When the garments were on, she remained standing, her schoolbag on her back.

'Do you want a lift?' her father asked. He was still struggling with Isaq's laces.

On days Leila started class at the same time as her younger siblings, she usually joined them in the car, even though her school lay just a short walk away.

'No thanks,' she replied.

Her father looked up in surprise.

'I need to lose some weight, get more exercise,' she explained.

'You? You've no fat on you! You're a stick!' Sara said, rolling her eyes.

Leila just smiled and gave both her parents a hug.

'I love you, Dad,' she whispered in her father's ear. 'I love you, Mom,' she whispered to her mother.

The declarations of love were in Somali. The siblings always spoke Somali to their mother. With their father it varied, and between themselves Norwegian was most common.

'Will we walk together?' Ismael asked.

They both attended Rud Upper Secondary School. Leila was in the first year of the health and social curriculum; he was in his third year, studying electronics. They rarely accompanied each other in the morning, but since she had been 'her old self' the previous evening, it seemed strange not to go to school together, as they had always done in childhood.

'No, I've got to . . . ' Leila replied.

Her brother did not catch her answer, just noticed her disappearing out the door with her rucksack.

Finally the rest of the family was all set. The smaller boys ran up the steps, Jibril first, followed by Isaq. The terraced block of flats was built on a steep slope. In order to exit the upper side of the building, they had to ascend three flights of stairs.

Kolsås ridge, rising up like a dark wall behind the housing estate, was shrouded in a layer of fog. Sadiq unlocked the car while the boys argued about who would sit in front.

'Okay, okay, okay,' their father chided them. 'How was it last time? Jibril was in the passenger seat; now it's Isaq's turn.'

They waited for the car to warm up, then Sadiq swung out from the parking lot, much too sharply, much too fast, as usual.

At Bryn School, Jibril, who was in his sixth year, wanted his father to leave right away; being seen with Daddy was embarrassing. But Isaq, who had just started school two months before, asked their father to walk him into the schoolyard.

When the bell rang, Sadiq drove home to collect Sara and take her to a doctor's appointment. Lately she had been suffering from headaches, pains in her neck, fingers, wrists, legs, and feet. She was often tired and run-down, felt cold and clammy. Were there any remedies? Maybe iron supplements would help? Calcium? Vitamin D? She had begun taking fish oil capsules, but they had not helped. 'What I need is hot camel milk,' she used to say. That would make the pains go away. She was living in a country at a time of year when the sun did not warm her up, scarcely gave off light. She was not made for this.

They drove to the local shopping center and found a spot with free parking for three hours, then they walked to the Bærum Health Clinic. When the family came to Norway, they were settled in Bærum, an affluent neighborhood nine miles southwest of Oslo. At the clinic, their family GP listened to Sadiq's translation of his wife's problems, posed a few questions, examined her, and came to the conclusion that what she needed was not more pills but a change in lifestyle. Sara had to exercise more and start walking, and she should lose a considerable amount of weight.

After the appointment, Sadiq drove his wife back home. She lay down to rest, as she often did during the day.

The boys were finished with school at half past one. Leila usually got home shortly after them. She would take off her hijab and floor-length cloak, wash, pray, and eat a little something before going into the room she shared with Ayan. There, she would turn on her PC to do homework or listen to sermons and Koran recitals. The girls spent a lot of time in their room. 'Don't come in!' they called out, irritated, if anyone tried the door handle.

While other mothers fretted about their daughters having boyfriends or dressing indecently, Sara had nothing to worry about. Her daughters always did as she told them. They asked permission for everything, even to knock on the neighbors' doors, she boasted to her friends. It was gratifying that they did not melt too much into Norwegian ways. Ismael, on the other hand, was a source of concern. He was slipping away from his Somali background, she felt, and was in danger of becoming *too Norwegian.*

The minute hand on the clock passed three. Ismael had come home early from school, having promised to help his little brothers with their homework. They were lagging behind in a number of subjects. The three of them were sitting around the kitchen table. Strange that Leila was not home yet.

Sara tried calling her. Her mobile phone was turned off. Ayan did not pick up either. Maybe the girls had something scheduled for the afternoon that she had not been aware of.

She waited awhile before phoning again. First Leila. Then Ayan. Finally Sadiq. None of them took the call. She asked Ismael to send a text message. Something must have happened. Why else would Leila be late?

Sara was prone to thinking the worst. Perhaps somebody had assaulted her daughter? She knew there were Norwegians who did not like those with darker skin, or Muslims, at any rate, and Leila had said she'd been harassed by a gang of boys once.

Finally Ayan answered her telephone.

'Where are you?' her mother burst out. 'I'm very anxious about Leila, she hasn't come home yet!'

'Don't worry. Leila is with me,' Ayan replied.

'Ahh!' Sara exclaimed, relieved. 'That's good!'

As long as they were together, everything was all right. She took a few cuts of lamb from the refrigerator and filled a saucepan with enough water to boil rice for seven.

Sadiq was sitting in the library in Sandvika, the center of Bærum municipality, reading *Science Illustrated*. His shoulder ached; it was going to be a while before he would be able to return to work at Coca-Cola. He wanted another job. Once, he had dreamed of being an engineer and had attended an evening course in Oslo to obtain the qualifications needed for serious study – but he had given up.

He loved this library. He came here nearly every day. The first thing he did was pluck his favorite magazine off the shelf, peruse it, and then go online.

Sadiq went outside to have a cigarette and noticed the missed calls.

'The girls are out doing something,' his wife told him. 'Can you call them and say you'll pick them up? Then you all come home for dinner.'

He pressed Ayan's number, then Leila's. They might be at the Rahma Mosque nearby or at Aisha's. Leila's telephone was turned off. Ayan did not answer. Could they have gone to the Tawfiiq Mosque in Oslo?

He went back into the library and chatted for a while with a friend. Around five o'clock he left for home. He took off his shoes in the hall before heading straight for the living room and the sofa. He wanted to lie down while he waited for dinner.

The sofa, in black imitation leather, was across from the TV. On the wall behind him hung a picture of Mecca. In the corner, over toward the balcony, were a few carpets and an old exercise machine. Otherwise the living room was empty, sparsely furnished à la Somali.

Sara asked him to try to call the girls again.

'Where are they? I don't have time for this!' he exclaimed.

A little after six o'clock, Ayan answered her telephone.

'Calm down, Dad,' she said. Then she waited a moment, as though to give him time, before continuing. '*Abo*, sit down.' Her voice was slightly hoarse. 'We've sent you an e-mail. Read it.'

She hung up.

Sadiq fetched the laptop from his backpack, found his glasses, and opened his e-mail. There was an unread message at the top, sent at 17:49, October 17, 2013.

'Peace, God's mercy and blessings upon you, Mom and Dad,' it said in Somali. The text continued in Norwegian.

We love you both sooo much and you have given us everything in life. We are eternally grateful for everything ♥.

Sadiq read on.

We ask your forgiveness for all the pain we have caused you. We love you both sooo much, would do anything for you, and would never do anything to purposely hurt you, and is it not then fair and proper that we do everything for ALLAH *swt*'s sake and are grateful for what he has given us by following his rules, laws, and commands.

Muslims are under attack from all quarters, and we need to do something. We want so much to help Muslims, and the only way we can really do that is by being with them in both suffering and joy. Sitting home and sending money is no longer enough. With this in mind we have decided to travel to Syria and help out down there as best we can. We know this sounds absurd but it is *haqq* and we must go. We fear what ALLAH swt will say to us on the day of judgment.

The blood drained from Sadiq's head. Everything went black. All his energy left him. While he continued to read, the air around him thickened. This had to be a joke. They were messing around with him.

Abo you know this is *fard al ayn* not only for men but also for women and whoever is able.

Sadiq quickly scanned the e-mail to find an explanation for all this nonsense. He knew *fard al-ayn* – the obligations of each individual, like prayer, fasting, charity, and traveling to Mecca.

We have now left and will soon arrive *inshallah*. Please do not be cross with us, it was sooo hard for us to leave without saying goodbye in the way you both deserve. Forgive us inshallah, when we made this choice we did so with what was best for our *ummah* in mind, but also what was best for our family, and it might be difficult to understand now, but inshallah this decision will help us all on the day of judgment inshallah.

We love you both sooo much and hope you will not break off ties with us, inshallah we will send a message when we arrive at the hotel and then you can call inshallah.

We want to tell you again that we love you with all of our hearts and are sorry you had to find out this way, we have already asked too much of you but we have to ask a favor: for both our safety and yours no one outside the family can know we have left, this cannot be stressed enough. Please try to understand our actions inshallah.

Praise be to Allah, the lord of the worlds ♥. Ayan & Leila ♥.

Sadiq held his hands in front of his face.

'What does it say?' Sara stood leaning over his shoulder, her gaze switching between the black letters on the screen and her husband.

'Ismael, come here!' Sadiq called out.

In his room, Ismael, hearing his father's unsteady voice, wondered what he had done wrong now.

'Read it aloud,' Sadiq said when his son entered the room.

After a few lines, Ismael's voice began to quiver.

'What? What?' Sara shouted. Ismael read first in Norwegian and then translated into Somali for his mother.

' . . . We have decided to travel to Syria . . . ' he read.

'*Illahayow i awi!* Allah, help me!' Sara cried, and fell to the floor.

Sadiq tried to help her up but tumbled down himself. He remained sitting there, his arms around his wife, rocking her.

'I can't believe it,' he mumbled. 'It's not possible.'

The smaller boys stared at them. Isaq came over, crept close to his parents.

'Daddy, where have they gone?' Jibril asked.

'I don't know,' Sadiq replied.

He tried to gather the chaos in his mind. They could not have taken off just like that, without warning, no, he did not believe it. There were three possibilities. One, they were joking. Two, someone else had written the e-mail. Three, he had not read it correctly.

The police operations center logged the call at 9:54 p.m. The caller had 'received an e-mail from two daughters where they informed him they had left for Syria to take part in jihad.'

Sadiq implored the police to track the girls' telephones to find out where they were.

'Someone has kidnapped them!' Sara exclaimed.

Sadiq called and called. The girls could not have gotten far! Finally he heard a click on the other end of the line.

'Abo—'

He interrupted his daughter, cleared his throat, and tried to calm down.

'Ayan, stop where you are, it doesn't matter where, stay there, I'm on my way, I'll put gas in the tank, please, wherever you are, just wait there and—'

'Dad, listen to me—'

'I'm coming to pick you up, I'm taking the car, where are you?'

'In Sweden.'

'Wait for me. I'll drive, or no, I'll fly, I'll take a plane!'

'Forget about it, Dad.'

'Think about this, both of you, we need to talk. Who are you with?'

The line went dead. When Sadiq rang back, he was told the number he was trying to call had no network coverage.

He rang the police operations center again. The operator logged the girls' location as 'an unidentified hotel in Sweden.'

Suddenly Ismael shouted something from his room and came into the living room pointing at his laptop.

'Ayan is online, she's on Facebook!'

Sadiq saw a name he recognized, his daughter's middle name: *Fatima Abdallah.*

He sat down and wrote to her: 'My child, tell me where you are so I can come and meet you, or answer the telephone. You're causing the family huge problems. Don't make things worse. My dear chiiiiild, please, my chiiiild, talk to me.'

He sat staring at the screen. Ayan's voice had been firm. Obdurate. They *had* to go to Syria. To *help*. The people there were in *need*. It was their *duty*.

The decisiveness Sadiq had mustered when he called the police was gone.

Sara was talking to a friend on the telephone.

'Oh, you poor things,' her friend said. 'I heard about some girls from England who went to Syria and . . . '

There was a smell of burning coming from the kitchen. The rice lay black in the bottom of the saucepan.

Isaq seemed to have become a part of Sadiq's body, clinging to his father like a baby animal. Sadiq let him be. Jibril circled them both, anxiously, vigilantly.

Ayan usually put the boys to bed, read to them from the Koran, then told them about the life of Muhammad or talked to them about the day that had been.

That night they went to bed without the blessings of the Prophet.

At 10:47 p.m. a reply ticked in from Fatima Abdallah aka Ayan. She used Facebook Messenger.

'Abo, you all need to relax. It's better to speak when everyone has calmed down and had a chance to think.'

'Okay, talk to me now,' her father answered.

'Can't we talk tomorrow?' she suggested. 'Whatever you do, for all our sakes, don't tell anyone.'

'My child, you are stronger than to allow yourself to be brainwashed. I believe you are my little Ayan who used to listen to me. Your mother is in a coma. The house is full of policemen. Child Welfare are here.'

'Why did you call them? We told you not to do that!'

'My child, did either of you tell *us* anything?'

'You would never have let us go.'

'Ayyyaaaan, fear God if you truly believe in Him. You are not allowed to travel without a male guardian. Name one sheikh who has permitted this so that he can convince me with theological evidence. I'll go blind if I don't find you!'

'Abo, relax! I'll send you an entire book.'

'My daughters, we will never forgive what you have done, not now or in eternity. And neither will you receive any divine reward for this.'

'Dad, don't say things you will regret. Everyone is worn out, we're very tired, can we talk tomorrow?'

'Paradise lies at the feet of your mother. That is a *hadith*, my child – the word of the Prophet. Your mother's in the hospital, lying in a coma. How will you succeed? Where will the divine reward you seek come from? My child, do not invest in hell!'

'You have two small children to take care of, be strong for their sakes. We're safe and can look after ourselves,' Ayan assured him.

'Don't be naïve!' Sadiq wrote, and repeated that paradise was at their mother's feet. 'Have you forgotten that?' he asked his elder daughter.

'Paradise comes with the grace of Allah,' Ayan replied. She logged off Messenger.

A picture appeared on Ismael's mobile phone, on Snapchat: a large steak on a plate, a white tablecloth, nice cutlery.

'Last meal in Europe!' it said beneath the photo, which disappeared after a few seconds.

The text had been sent via Viber. Ismael clicked on the message. What his sister did not know was that the message app automatically showed your whereabouts if you had not disabled that function.

Seyhan, Adana, Turkey, it read. He clicked again. A map came up, and a blue dot. He zoomed in and saw an intersection, streets.

'They're in Turkey!' Ismael came rushing in to show his parents the dot. 'I can see exactly where they are! Call the police, they need to get in touch with the Turkish police, they can arrest them, there in the restaurant. They're eating there right now!'

Sadiq called the police and gave them the information his daughter had unwittingly provided. It was past eleven o'clock at night.

'We're in a desperate situation. You need to help us right now. Find them before it is too late!' Sadiq urged.

His words were taken down in the operations center and the information forwarded to the local department of PST, the Norwegian Police Security Service.

The message lay there, unread, in an unopened e-mail, all night, while the girls settled down to sleep at the Grand Hotel in Adana, where they had checked in using their own passports and under their full names.

Half an hour before midnight, Sadiq's laptop notified him an e-mail message had been received. It was from Ayan. It contained no greeting, no dear Mom and Dad, but got straight to the point.

Read the ENTIRE book and find out who the author is before replying, we have planned and thought this through for almost an ENTIRE year, we would never do something like this on impulse. Yours sincerely Ayan

Sadiq opened the attachment. It was a book manuscript and on the first page it read:

DEFENSE OF THE MUSLIM LANDS
The First Obligation After Iman
By Dr Abdullah Azzam
(May Allah accept him as Shaheed)

It started with a quotation from Muhammad: ' . . . But those who are killed in the Way of Allah, he will never let their deeds be lost.'

Sadiq remained seated and read. Ismael shut the door to his room. He lay on the bed with the phone in his hand, staring at the ceiling. It all felt unreal. He logged on to Facebook, scrolled, clicked, and his mind whirled. Suddenly he saw that *Fatima Abdallah* was back online again.

'Ayan. It's Ismael,' he typed. 'I know you have left. What are you planning to do there? Like, actually do. When do you land in Syria?'

His big sister replied right away. 'First, what's happening at home? Are the police there? Are child services there?'

'No. No.'

'Thank God! Is Mom in a coma?'

'She's crying. Is miserable. Your turn.'

'Well, we're going to do what we need to do.'

'What do you mean by that exactly?'

'Everything from fetching water for the sick to working in refugee camps.'

'Mom thinks you're going to get married. With men waging jihad in order to satisfy them. Lol. Mom thinks you're going to be raped.'

'God forbid. You know we're not like that.'

'I'm not sure what I know anymore.'

'What do you think I am, a whore?'

'I don't know,' answered Ismael, adding a sad emoji. 'Thought you trusted me more. You could have at least said something to me.'

'You would have stopped us!' his sister wrote. 'Tell Mom we're sorry for the worry we've caused, but Allah comes first, before anyone else.'

'She's mad at you, in her coma.'

'She's not in a coma.'

'She can just about manage to speak, and she's crying. What would you call that?'

'If she's crying then she's not in a coma. Don't lie to us about things like that.'

'Hmm, I exaggerated, I can make a video of her.'

'Nooo.'

'How did you get the money?'

'I worked.'

'How much money do you have?'

'We have enough. Anyway, ask Dad to read the whole book I e-mailed him.'

She handed the telephone to her sister.

'Ismael, dear Ismael, it's Leila. I love Mom more than anything on earth, but when it comes to ALLAH and the Prophet, I fear what ALLAH will ask me on the day of judgment. I know I am hurting a lot of people here in dunya, but I am not thinking of dunya at the moment. I'm doing this because I love my mother and father and my whole family sooo much, it's not just for my akhirah but for all of yours too. I'm not a particularly good daughter and I don't give my parents what they REALLY deserve, but this is my chance to make up for that by being of help to them in akhirah. Please try to understand. If you had the chance to help your parents on judgment day at the expense of maybe hurting them in dunya but in so doing help get them into Jannah, wouldn't you also do EVERYTHING in your power for that chance?'

The message came in bits. Leila was pressing Send line by line as she wrote. Ismael knew enough about Islam to understand the content. *Dunya* was life here on earth, *akhirah* was the afterlife, and *Jannah* was paradise.

'Are you coming back? Like, ever?' Ismael wrote from his bed.

'We don't know for sure, but we have no wish to,' Leila answered.

'So we're probably never going to see each other again?' Ismael included a crying emoji.

'Don't ever think that, we always have Skype, haha.'

'But in real life?'

'You never know.'

Ismael sent a disappointed emoji and added, 'Oh, well.'

'How are you?' his little sister asked.

'Feel weird. Dunno. Sad.'

'It hasn't sunk in yet for us either. Don't be sad, we're not dead and we're doing fine. Try to think positive. Think pink ☺ Remember in the spring? You said I would NEVER do anything like this because I was too cowardly?'

'Yeah, you win. Can you come home now?'

Leila did not reply right away, so he added quickly: 'Haha. Have fun. Do what you think is right.'

'We will.'

'I'm cool,' answered Ismael.

'Good night.'

Leila sent a smiley and a heart.

She logged off.

Ismael lay in bed with the phone in his hand. Tears trickled down his cheeks.

In the living room, Sadiq was reading *Defense of the Muslim Lands* while keeping an eye on his mobile phone and Facebook account in case his daughters texted him or went online.

'There is no Caliphate,' the text began. 'A glorious empire the world once feared. A people entrusted with the final revelation of God. The religion destined for the whole of humanity. Where is it today?' asked the writer. 'The unclean have duped the dull masses of Muslims by installing their wooden-headed puppets as false figureheads of states that remain under their control. Colonialism has taken a new face. They have come from every horizon to share us among them like callers to a feast. There is no greater humiliation for the people expected to lead humanity to redemption. How will they recognize the gravity of the situation? Their house is crumbling and their neighbors are laughing.'

Sadiq skimmed the text. Muslims had to unite under one caliph. That had to be fought for by the sword.

Abdullah Azzam was the father of modern jihadism. He had become acquainted with Osama bin Laden while teaching in Saudi Arabia in the early 1980s, and was a driving force behind the Saudi businessman's financing of *mujahideen* – the holy warriors who fought against the Soviets in Afghanistan. There his friendship with bin Laden deepened and he set down a *fatwa* concerning the rules for when jihad was an individual obligation – *fard al-ayn* – and when you could let others fight for you – *fard kifaya*.

'To offer prayer – as opposed to waging jihad on the battlefield – is like the trifling of children,' Azzam wrote in contempt for what he perceived as cowardice. 'For every tear you have shed upon your cheek, we have shed in its place blood, on our chests. You are jesting with your worship; while you worshippers offer your worship, mujahideen offer their blood and person.'

The Palestinian scholar wrote that if a piece of Muslim land, even the size of a hand span, was infringed upon, then jihad became fard al-ayn for all Muslims, male and female. 'The child shall march forward without the permission of its parents and the wife without the permission of the husband.'

This was what the girls wanted him to know from this book – that their obligations to the Muslim ummah meant they could depart without his consent, that the teachings of the learned supported them. Sadiq closed the document.

Jihad.

Caliphate.

Martyrdom.

Nonsense.

Read the ENTIRE book before replying. And the part that hurt the most: *We have planned and thought this through for almost an ENTIRE year.*

Sadiq did not sleep that night.

The heavens had come crashing down.

2

Veiled

A new day broke.

As soon as he woke up, Ismael checked Viber, Facebook, Messenger, WhatsApp. Nothing.

'Ayan, Leila, are you alive?' he wrote beneath the thread from the previous night.

Sara was crying. 'Someone must have tricked them into going!'

'Brainwashed them,' Sadiq said.

Although Ismael was no longer trembling as he had been the night before, the shock lingered in his body, like a punch he had been unprepared for. He blamed himself for not having seen this coming. The hours on YouTube listening to clerics and preachers. Their anger that he did not attend the mosque. The accusations. Their abhorrence of *kuffar* – unbelievers.

'Don't use that word!' their parents had admonished them. 'It's disrespectful.'

The girls had refrained, for a while, but their contempt for infidels returned. It was as though they could not be pure enough when everything around them only grew dirtier.

Leila had often spoken about the day of judgment, when only the true believers would be spared God's wrath. This life was a test, she said. Real life came afterward, in paradise, but only if you followed God's teachings. Then you would live in a garden where every kind of delicious fruit grew, by a river of milk, have everything you desired, and experience intense well-being. All your emotions would be beautiful and pure. You would never feel anger, sadness, pain, or regret. Only perfect harmony, happiness, and sheer joy. You would walk on floors of diamonds in houses with walls of gold. The angels would sing and you would sense the presence of God at all times.

When Ismael expressed his doubts about all this, Leila grew annoyed.

'What do *you* think happens when you die, then?' she had asked.

'I think you die, you're buried, and then . . . well, that's it.'

'No,' Leila corrected him. 'Either you go to paradise or you're cast into hell. Ismael, believe me, it's not too late. Let me help you. I can show you the right path.'

To question the word of God was blasphemy, she pointed out. And the rightful punishment for it was death.

He realized how extreme they had become. How could he not have seen where they were headed?

Ismael reread the long message Leila had sent the night before. She had written that being able to answer to God on judgment day was more important than worrying about hurting people in the here and now. 'I'm not a particularly good daughter and I don't give my parents what they really deserve, but this is my chance to make up for that by being of help to them in the afterlife.' By enlisting in holy war, she would save them all from hell. If you died as a martyr, you could choose seventy family members to join you in paradise. She had sacrificed herself *for them*.

Later that morning, Sadiq received a phone call from the district division of the PST, the Police Security Service, where somebody had finally read the message about the girls being in Turkey. The policeman asked several questions about the girls, places they frequented, whom they socialized with, if the parents could think of anyone who might know something, if they had any leads.

In order for the police to issue a bulletin, they said, the family had to report the girls missing.

Sadiq put down the phone. The two smaller boys came padding into the living room. Sara had not roused them from sleep this morning. Sadiq was not going to struggle to lace their shoes. There would be no arguments about who sat in the front seat because no one could summon the energy to take them to school.

'Was it wrong of them to go?' Isaq asked.

'Yes,' Sadiq answered.

The boys looked at him, then sat down to play computer games.

Who could know something? Who had known? Sadiq attempted to unearth some clue, some trace, anything. During the night he had racked his brain, trying to understand. By early morning he realized he had no idea what his daughters had been doing or whom they had spent their time with over the past year. Sometimes he had driven them to the Tawfiiq Mosque in Oslo city center, Norway's biggest Somali mosque. They had gone in the women's entrance, that was all he knew. He had also driven them to meetings of Islam Net, as well as to a mosque in Sandvika. But whom had they met there? The Koran teacher, had he encouraged them? Hadn't he been a holy warrior in Mauritania? Sadiq could not quite remember, was perhaps mixing him up with somebody else. He had not been paying attention, he understood that now. He had to go to the mosques and find out. He had to ask Aisha if she knew anything. Didn't Ayan say that the suitcase was for her? He needed to drive over there and investigate.

But he did not. He continued mulling things over.

Sadiq and Sara had been so satisfied, even self-satisfied, when it came to their daughters. He remembered the first time the girls talked about attending an evening meeting. 'It starts at eight o'clock,' they had said. He and Sara had laughed when they realized they actually were going to a meeting at the mosque; it was not a ploy to go out in the city on a Friday night. And yet here he was, unable to remember one single name, call to mind one single face, of any of the people they had mixed with in the past year.

The day before they had left, Ayan had asked him to help her run some errands.

'Can we take the car?' she had inquired. Of course they could, he was on sick leave, after all, and had no plans for the day. He was actually glad to be asked; she had been so distant lately, avoided contact, almost stopped speaking to him. It had bothered him, because of everyone in the family, Ayan was the one most like him. He often had problems understanding Leila, but Ayan was a kindred spirit, someone who enjoyed discussions, figuring things out. She had always asked his advice, but as time had gone on, she had formed her own opinions, and they had begun to disagree. Eventually their discussions had ceased altogether.

Ayan wanted to go to a few shops by the Rabita Mosque in Oslo. Aisha was going on a trip, she had said, and needed help buying things. He had not asked any more; he was simply happy his daughter wanted to have him along.

For most of the drive, they had sat in silence. He had tried to initiate a conversation, but something hung in the air between them. Upon arriving in the city center, he had gone to a café by the Gunerius shopping center while Ayan went shopping.

Now it cut him to the very core. He had driven her around so she could buy what she needed for the girls' trip. It must have been Ayan who had planned it. Of the two sisters, she was the boss, the one who led the way. The second-in-command, Sadiq used to call her. After Sara.

When they got home with all the bags, she had hugged him and said, 'Thank you so much, Dad!'

They dulled us with hugs, Sadiq thought. They had milked his love, they had blinded him.

Later that night, Ayan had come out of her room and asked to borrow his Visa card. Hers had expired, she said, and she needed to make a purchase online. 'I've hardly any money on my card,' he had replied, less than 1,000 kroner. She had seemed stressed. 'Can you drive me to the bank in Sandvika? Then I can put the money into your account. I have cash.'

'The bank closed ages ago, can't it wait until tomorrow?'

Ayan had insisted on driving there with him to see, but he was right, the bank was shut. What had she intended to buy? Tickets? No, they must have already had them. Who had in fact organized the tickets, the whole trip? *Who* had encouraged them to travel at all?

Leila had stayed in the bedroom nearly the entire evening.

'Are you sick?' he had asked. Leila had just shaken her head. Then she'd given him a playful dig in the stomach, like in the old days. 'I'll knock all that fat off you, Dad,' she had said, smiling. And when Ismael came home from the gym, she had thrown her arms around him.

After the shopping and the trip to the bank, Ayan had gone into her room. She had logged on to Twitter and written: 'Kindness is the language which even the deaf can hear and the blind can see.' On the previous day she had tweeted: 'Shaytan is the virus & Islam is the cure.' *Shaytan* was Arabic for Satan.

Her profile picture was a bird with shiny green feathers. The Prophet had said that if you died in *jihad*, Allah would allow your soul to reside in the body of a green bird that would fly to paradise. There it would build a nest in the lanterns hanging from the throne of the Almighty.

The police received the report of missing persons at 12:30 p.m. Only then was an international bulletin sent out via Interpol. According to the official log, the following measures were taken: 'Invocation of the legal principle of necessity and appeals for information sent out to banks, telecommunications companies, airlines, and border stations.'

At the Asker and Bærum station, the local police had put a man from the missing persons unit on the case. He made contact with Sadiq.

'Are you sending people down to find them?' Sadiq asked.

'We have informed the Ministry of Foreign Affairs, and the embassy in Ankara is on the case. We're also cooperating with the Turkish police.'

'So what are they doing?'

'We'll keep you informed,' the policeman promised.

'But how could you let them leave the country? Why weren't they stopped at the airport? Leila is a minor . . . and . . . '

Sadiq was given no answer. Instead he was told a car would be sent to pick up the family and bring them to the station.

'If it had been Norwegian children who had been reported missing, they would have reacted differently,' Sara said. 'It's because we're Somalis! The police don't take us seriously.'

Sara felt that a part of her had been torn away. The loss left a lump in her stomach.

They were shown into an office at the police station. First Sadiq, then Sara.

'What will I tell them?' she asked Sadiq.

'Just answer their questions. Leila has just turned sixteen. Ayan is scarcely an adult. They're Norwegian citizens. The police will do everything in their power to track them down,' he assured her.

There were two men present during the questioning, one from the missing persons unit and another from the local PST.

Finally it was Ismael's turn.

'How are things with you?' they asked. 'Have you gone to the Koran school as well?'

'Do you attend the mosque?'

'What are you going to do next year? Do you have plans?'

'Have you applied for college, or are you going traveling?'

'Did you know what your sisters were planning?'

'Were they forced to travel?'

'What did your parents know?'

'Are you also a radical?'

The questions annoyed the eighteen-year-old. It seemed that the interviewers' aim was to determine if he was ideologically close to his sisters and might follow them, and if they formed part of a larger network. For Ismael, however, stopping his sisters was the priority. As he spoke, he established one point for the investigators that Sadiq had not made clear: The sisters had traveled of their own free will.

In the car on the way home, Sadiq was dejected.

'They see us as a danger,' he said, 'not as a family who've reported two daughters missing. We asked them for help and they're treating us like criminals!'

At around five o'clock that day, the doorbell rang.

There were three policemen standing outside, two in uniform and one in plain clothes.

'We have a search warrant,' one of the officers said.

First they searched the girls' room. The men in uniform opened wardrobes and drawers while the plainclothes officer took notes. They gathered papers, notebooks, and everything computer-related, then moved on to the other rooms. They looked through closets, shelves, and boxes.

Isaq was clinging to Sadiq again. 'Daddy, give me your hand,' he softly pleaded, while looking at the men.

The family was asked to remain in the living room, and when Sadiq got up to see what the police were doing, he was bluntly instructed to keep his distance.

'Are we terrorists?!' Sara exclaimed in Somali, pacing the living room. 'Are you going to terrorize us instead of helping us?'

'Sit down, calm yourself. It's their job,' Sadiq told her.

'God help me! God help me!' Sara cried out.

Distressed after all the questioning at the station and now the ransacking of her home, she phoned a friend. But she did not find much solace.

'What! You got in touch with the police? That was a big mistake! They're not going to do anything for Somalis! Find the girls yourself; don't expect the Norwegian police to help you.'

Ismael couldn't take any more of his mother's crying and his father's agitation. He went to his room and shut the door. He had not received any answer to the message he'd sent that morning.

At seven o'clock he sent a new text: 'Hello. Answer pls.'

Eight o'clock: 'Hello.'

Nine o'clock: 'Ayan?'

*

That same morning, the girls had checked out of the Grand Hotel in Adana. They retrieved the passports they had handed in at reception. Then they headed south, toward the Syrian border. In the afternoon, they no longer appeared on the Turkish telecom network.

Sadiq was frantic, afraid of what might happen to them. There was something else: The girls had humiliated him, the police had trampled over him, he had lost face; he had not been in control.

Now, Sadiq, show what you are made of, a voice in his head said.

I am Sadiq, a man in charge of my family.

According to the Viber message about their 'last meal in Europe,' the girls' last known stop had been Adana. He could not sit around waiting for them to show up, for them to change their minds, or for the police to track them down. He had to stop them before it was too late.

Sara made the decision for him. 'Go find them!' she commanded from the sofa.

He was suddenly in a hurry. He had found a direction. Now all he needed to do was plot a course.

Turkish Airlines operated daily departures from Oslo to Istanbul. He booked a ticket for the next day, threw some clothes in a bag, and borrowed money from a friend. At the airport he changed everything into dollars, taking a couple of thousand. His flight left just after noon.

Three days after his daughters left, he was traveling the same route.

Please turn off all electronic devices. For three hours he would not be checking his telephone every minute. He found himself alone with his thoughts.

It was just after the summer holidays that he had noticed Ayan change, become quieter, reticent, but it had occurred gradually. He had attributed her behavior to boy trouble.

Sara had brushed it aside. 'She's a teenager, it'll pass. Leave her be.' Sara was usually the strict one. She had put her foot down when Ayan developed a crush on a boy she had met at Islam Net a couple of years ago. He was Somali like her, and one day Ayan had announced that she wanted to get engaged. Sara had reluctantly agreed for them to meet but still maintained they were way too young to marry.

'I don't care, I'll do what I want,' Ayan had responded. Ismael had been impressed. He would never have dared take that tone with his mother. Once Ayan was granted permission to spend time with the boy, the fantasy shattered and she lost interest.

Could it have been some new flame who had gotten his daughter mixed up in this?

The first time he had seen the girls dabble in fundamentalism had been about two years earlier. Leila was fourteen years old and Ayan was seventeen.

'We're going into Oslo with some friends, but we're broke,' Ayan had said.

Sadiq usually gave them some money for a kebab, an ice cream, or something small. That day he had no cash, so handed over his Visa card and gave them the PIN.

'You're allowed to use five hundred kroner max.'

'And if that isn't enough?'

'It will be.'

He replayed the scene in his head. Ayan had given him a hug, Leila too. They returned that evening with several shopping bags.

'We spent six hundred,' Ayan said, curtsying apologetically.

He tried to adopt a stern demeanor. 'Don't do that again. We agreed on a sum, a deal is a deal.'

They had gone to their room. A short time later, they came back out. Or rather, two figures in black tents reappeared in the living room.

Sara's reaction was immediate. 'Get those off!'

The girls merely laughed. The folds of their clothing shook.

'Do as your mother says,' their father ordered. 'You both look like devils!'

Only their eyes were visible. They stared out in defiance. Their noses protruded like black beaks beneath the material.

'Who put that idea in your heads?' Sadiq asked.

'We did.'

But they had returned obediently to their room, taken off the *niqabs*, folded them, and placed them in the wardrobe. When they came back out they were sulky. Islam required women to cover themselves.

'The niqab has nothing to do with Islam,' Sadiq said. 'It's culture, not religion, and Arabic culture at that, not Somali.'

'Women wore the niqab in the time of the Prophet,' the girls said. 'God bade the Prophet tell his wives and daughters to cover themselves to guard their modesty from the gaze of strangers.'

'Don't lecture me on Muhammad,' Sadiq exclaimed. 'I know the Koran better than you. I could recite the first *sura* by heart by the time I was eight years old!' The Prophet never told his wife or daughters to cover their faces, he went on, while the teenagers insisted that at the very least the Prophet's favorite wife, young Aisha, had worn a niqab in the presence of strangers.

'That still doesn't mean that the two of you should do it!'

'We saw lots of women in Somalia in the summer wearing it!'

'Well, that's nothing to do with us,' their father replied. 'We're not like that. Where did you buy them, anyway?'

'At Hijab House. By Rabita Mosque. They have clothes for Muslim women there, niqabs, lots of nice stuff.'

They thought they had gotten value for money; in addition to the niqabs, they had purchased two floor-length cloaks and several new hijabs.

Some time would pass before Sadiq saw the niqabs again. But Sara had come across the veils in different places on the shelves of their wardrobe when putting away laundry.

Not long after that, the girls had again broached the subject. Ayan was bothered by the looks men gave her. Leila agreed.

'They stare at us,' they complained. 'It's *haram*. We want to cover ourselves.'

'Of course the boys at school look at you. Small wonder when you're both so beautiful,' Sadiq quipped.

'No, it's not them. It's Somali men in Oslo, in the city, grown men in Grønland who stare at us when we're on our way to the mosque. They try to flirt with us.'

'Then you just tell them to mind their own business. Let them know you're the daughters of Sadiq *gabayaa* – Sadiq the poet – that'll soon shut them up!' In Somaliland, Sadiq had been a member of a circle of poets. They had met at cafés in Hargeisa, reciting poetry and engaging in discussion until the war broke out and they were scattered to the four winds. Years after the conflict, some of them had made contact on the net. Verses and thoughts flew online between Hargeisa, Naples, Gothenburg, and Bærum. Sadiq often took part in Somali cultural events in Oslo, reciting his own poetry or playing the drums. That gave him a certain status and position among the liberals within the group. The more religious types looked down upon the drummer. 'Musician' was, for them, a term of abuse. Music, and everything that came with it, was sinful.

Somalis in Oslo upheld a strict code of honor. People kept an eye on one another. Especially in the downtown neigborhood of Grønland in Oslo – coined 'Little Somalia' – where most of Norway's thirty-six thousand Somalis lived. The Somali community had just surpassed the Pakistani to become the country's largest non-Western minority.

Even though Sadiq had studied in Saudi Arabia and was fluent in classical Arabic, making him more highly educated than most of his compatriots, many criticized him for not holding Islam and Islamic tradition in high enough regard. 'He thinks he's a Norwegian,' they said behind his back. Many of the young were more observant and stricter in their interpretation of the Koran than the previous generation.

The girls had been so single-minded. They had always been good at arguing a case. Sadiq had given in: 'Okay, fine, when you're in Grønland, then, put them on if you want, but don't wear them here in Bærum and never in school!'

He knew that Norwegian society viewed covered women as

oppressed. That was something the poet and musician was not going to be associated with.

Not long after, he and Sara were called in to Leila's school for a meeting. Sadiq was the one who went. The pupil was also to be present.

'We're having trouble recognizing her,' the teacher said. 'We need to have eye contact, have to be able to make out facial expressions. That's not easy when someone is wearing a niqab.'

Sadiq looked at his daughter. 'Didn't we agree you wouldn't wear the niqab at school?'

Leila did not reply.

'You have to conform to school rules. If the school doesn't allow you to cover your face, then that's how it is,' he continued, looking back and forth between her and the teacher.

'Okay, Dad.'

Chicken or beef?

Sadiq looked up at the Turkish Air flight attendant and then down at the tray. His stomach tensed as he chewed the first bite of chicken. He put down the plastic fork. Outside, the sky was blue and some downy clouds swept by. Thoughts drifted through his mind. Was it his fault? Had he not been strict enough? Had he let everything slide? Been too occupied with his own concerns? The drumming? The poetry?

He took a cup of tea with sugar. It tasted metallic.

How had he not seen this coming?!

But who could imagine his little girls wanting to wage jihad?

They dulled us with hugs. They milked my love.

His little girls. The only ones.

The plane entered Turkish airspace.

At home, Sara, too, was at a loss. She was trying to piece together whatever she could from memory.

The girls had begun to live by strict rules sometime back. Prayer, attire, food, behavior – everything was to be right and pure. They stopped wearing makeup and jewelry. Perfume containing alcohol was thrown out, and then all perfume was disposed of. It was haram – it could attract men.

The girls had downloaded lists of E numbers, the codes for food additives that appeared on food packaging in Europe, and examined packets and cans, checking the ingredients against the lists to see if the product was fit to be consumed by Muslims. Several household foodstuffs were deemed unacceptable. Eventually Sadiq had grown angry. 'Where in the Koran does it say anything about E numbers?'

One day Sara had opened the family photo album and found that several pictures had been ripped out. Some had been removed completely, while heads and bodies had been cut out of others. Ayan and Leila had been expunged from the album.

Sara had been furious.

'But we're not covered, Mom! Imagine if someone outside the family saw us. It's haram!'

The memories were gone. She had mourned the loss of those photos.

She went into the girls' room. Stood looking around. No, it was too painful. She went out again. They had left. Without saying goodbye. 'We love you both sooo much, would do anything for you, and would never do anything to purposely hurt you,' they had written. So come home, then!

Years ago, she used to scold Ayan for having become too Norwegian. Back then she had been afraid of losing her. Her elder daughter had begun going to parties, and one night Sadiq had seen a packet of snus fall out of her pocket.

Ayan had dressed like her friends, in tight jeans and close-fitting T-shirts. One unusually hot summer evening, Ayan had invited some classmates over for samosas. They had entered the kitchen in low-cut tops, all bare midriffs and white thighs. 'My God, they're naked!' Sara had exclaimed in Somali.

'Get over it, Mom, let people be how they want,' her teenage daughter had replied.

'As long as you promise me *never* to walk around like that!'

Sara said. Ayan had glared at her before turning to her friends and laughing.

Only now did Sara try to recall the last time the girls from the class had visited. She could not remember. She herself had only Somali friends and did not consider it out of the ordinary for Ayan to lose touch with her classmates.

When she and the children came to Norway, Ayan was six, Ismael five, and Leila three years old. They should never have come! They should never have left home! Then this would not have happened and she would have had her daughters with her. She had never actually wanted to leave Somaliland; it was Sadiq who was convinced they would get a better life in the West.

While she had been pregnant with Leila, Sadiq had bought a passport, got a tourist visa to Denmark, and flown from Addis Ababa to Copenhagen. A friend there told him he should go to Norway, that it was the best place for Somalis. Sadiq traveled on to Oslo, where he went to the police and told them that if he returned home he would be killed, as both his father and his brother had been. He related that when he was fourteen years old, all the men in his neighborhood had been rounded up. Those who had supported the rebellion against the dictator Siad Barre were to be put to death. He had been taken along with the men, but his mother had come screaming: 'He's only a child! He's only a child!'

That was what saved him, he told the asylum authorities. While all the others, including his father, were killed in front of his eyes. 'Avenge him!' his mother had later said. He had taken a weapon from a body in the street, he told the authorities, and had joined the rebel forces.

The rebellion was successful but peace was short-lived. The victors began fighting among themselves for control. Two clans, formerly part of the opposition army, from opposite sides of the river running through Hargeisa, both wanted to rule and again took up arms. This was not a war worth dying for, so he left.

Sadiq was sent to the Tanum reception center for asylum seekers in Bærum, after which he was transferred some 350 miles north to

Levanger, spending six months there before being sent south again, to Klemetsrud reception center in Oslo. He told them he had been arrested and held prisoner aboard the family's small cargo boat, together with his brother and the rest of the crew, while it was used to transport weapons. His brother had been killed but Sadiq had been released.

'I'm a dangerous man,' he had told the police upon arrival. The reception center arranged for him to see a psychologist to treat his war trauma. As time went on, his anger lessened, and he calmed down. It was time to bring over his family. But first he needed to be granted asylum. Time dragged on. In May 1998, after two years in Norway, he received an answer.

'The Norwegian Directorate of Immigration (UDI) is not of the view that the statements of the applicant justify his belief in persecution, in respect of pertinent laws and conventions, upon return to his home country. The civil war and the overall difficulty of the situation in Somalia do not in themselves form a basis for asylum.'

UDI's opinion was that the capture of the family boat bore the hallmarks of a random criminal act. In addition, the incident had occurred some considerable time ago, yet the applicant had resided in his home country without problems since then. Neither did the authorities attach much importance to the applicant's claims of belonging to a small clan without influence. 'The applicant is nevertheless granted permission to seek and engage in employment,' the letter went on. This work permit was valid 'throughout the country' for one year and could be renewed. The most important part came at the end: 'This permission can form the basis for permanent residence.'

Sadiq immediately applied for family reunification. He filled out forms, wrote letters, and chased up responses. It dragged on. Two years after he had been granted the residence permit, he faxed a handwritten letter to the Norwegian embassy in Ethiopia, where Sara and the children were waiting to emigrate. 'My family has no relatives in Addis Ababa and no means of support so it is a hell there.'

He added that his wife and children were sick. 'I ask therefore you will give my family priority first before you go on holiday.'

That same autumn, Sara and the children were flown to Norway as part of a UN family reunification program and settled in Bærum, the Norwegian municipality with the highest percentage of millionaires and the greatest divide between rich and poor. Ismael and Leila were enrolled in the kindergarten, and Ayan entered a class where newly arrived refugee children were given a year to learn Norwegian prior to being placed in regular schools. From her first day of school, Ayan wore a headscarf, which her classmates learned was called a hijab. She had different ones, with lace, with trimming, in various colors and patterns. The first time she got into a fight over the headscarf it was the bully, a fair-haired boy, who wound up in tears. If someone said something she did not like, she let fly. Physically at first, in time with words. No one was a match for Ayan's verbal attacks. As soon as the language barrier was broken, the teachers at Evje Primary School began to notice how clever she was. She knew about things her classmates had no knowledge of, and she loved telling stories. The only pupil from Africa in the class was simply pretty impressive.

A year after they arrived in Norway, Sara became pregnant, and in 2002 Jibril was born. Isaq came along five years later. As the family grew in size, the Bærum authorities allocated them larger apartments. For a long time they lived in Hamangskogen, a development of high-rises with lots of space between them. The area was crowded with children. The girls jumped rope, ran around in the playground, went to the beach, and learned how to swim at the pool. Leila's chief desire was to follow her big sister no matter what she did or where she went. Sometimes she was allowed; more often she wasn't.

Ismael played football every chance he got. Football was the last thing he thought about before going to sleep and the first thing on his mind when he woke up, and he asked his father to put his name down for a team. He dreamed of having a kit with BÆRUM SPORTS-KLUBB across the front, dreamed about playing in matches, going to cup competitions, telling people about the goals he scored, and of having a coach. He pestered his father. To no avail. Busy with his own life, Sadiq would say 'next year' every new season, while Ismael went on playing ball between the blocks.

From the day she arrived, Sara felt lonely and yearned for her family in Hargeisa. She pushed little Isaq around in the buggy and complained that people criticized her no matter what she did. She never knew what she was doing wrong because she didn't understand what the elderly in the neighborhood were saying to her. Did she go to the wrong places? Did they not like the color of her skin, her wearing a headscarf, or her covered-up body?

Even after thirteen years in Norway, her soul was still in Somaliland.

Now it was torn apart.

Sara went into the bedroom and lay down on her unmade bed. Her mobile phone lay beside her with the ring volume on full. In case.

She and the girls had their share of quarrels, of course, but they used to be able to talk about things. And the girls always asked permission . . . *even if it was only to knock on the neighbors' doors.*

Sadiq wandered around Atatürk Airport at a loss, struggling to find his way out of the international terminal. When he eventually reached passport control, he was denied entry because he didn't have a visa. He joined a new line in front of a cashier's window, where he bought one and then rejoined the passport queue. Finally he made it out of the enormous terminal and walked over to the run-down hall where the domestic flights departed from.

He bought a ticket to Adana, the place Ayan had inadvertently given as the girls' location when she sent her message about the 'last meal in Europe.'

He would catch up with them.

While he flew south, larger machinery was being set in motion. A direct line of communication had been established between the leaders of the investigation, the Norwegian Ministry of Foreign Affairs, and Kripos, the criminal investigation service of the Norwegian police, which were in touch with Interpol. The Norwegian embassy in Ankara had contacted local police and border stations in the south of Turkey requesting that the girls, if they were identified, be taken into custody.

As Sadiq landed in Adana, a message from the police appeared on his phone. The girls had most likely traveled to Antakya in the south. This was a presumption, because there had not been any activity on their mobile phones in the past twenty-four hours.

Antakya? Where was that?

'You can get there by bus,' he was told at the information desk.

That Saturday night, rumors started flying. From Sandvika in the west to Grønland in the heart of Oslo, via the valley in the east and along the fjord back again to Bærum. *Have you heard? Surely not? Is it really true?*

Word reached the newspaper street of Akersgata, and by Sunday morning, the same day Sadiq had left, reporters from *VG*, the country's biggest tabloid, rang the doorbell. Ismael opened the door and told them that yes, my sisters said they were going to Syria. No, they are not picking up when we call, but my dad has gone after them. We hope they have not crossed the border into Syria. No, our family is not particularly religious but my sisters have become more radical lately. Among other things, they have both started wearing a niqab. Mom was very opposed to that and they argued about it.

Ismael told all this to the journalists but appealed to them not to reveal their names or where they lived.

That night, *VG* was the first newspaper to break the story: 'Sixteen-year-old travels with big sister to help Muslims in Syria.' Below the headline, in slightly smaller print, it read: 'International search' and 'Police Security Service raise alarm.'

'The family, who reside in Akershus county, fear that two teenage daughters aged sixteen and nineteen traveled to Syria just before the weekend to play their part in the war currently ravishing the country,' the story began, citing the anonymous brother as the main source. It went on to say that a small group of investigators were working round the clock to try to determine the girls' exact whereabouts abroad.

Martin Bernsen, the head of media relations in PST, was quoted as saying, 'Since last summer we've been seeing an increase in the number of people traveling to conflict areas, especially Syria. Many of these are young. We suspect, and fear, that some of them intend to fight alongside al-Qaida-linked groups in Syria. This is a source of concern. Moreover, it is dangerous. We are aware of several people from Norway who have lost their lives. We're also concerned at the prospect of people with extremist views having experience of war and then one day returning to Norway, still suffering perhaps from postconflict stress and trauma.'

In his room in a house in Bærum, a sixteen-year-old boy sat reading the story about the 'two sisters from a small urban area in Akershus county.' He immediately posted the link to a discussion group run by Leila's former classmates.

'This is too tragic to be true,' Joakim wrote beneath the link. 'The rumors weren't bogus . . . crazy stuff.'

The first comments came right away.

Alexander: Leila . . . .
Sofie: HOLYSHITTHISISBAD
Emilie: Really is it Leila?
Alexander: it's genuine
Joakim: It's fucking worse than bad.
Emilie: Does it say it's her?
Sofie: of course it's her
Silje: wow
Sofie: she is 16 AND she had a big sister aged 19, she and
   the sister both went around in hijabs
Emilie: omg the poor family!
Henrik: fuck me, I knew something like this would happen . . .

she was a member of some kind of organization in oslo,
    they were probably the ones put her up to it . . .
Synne: shit that is completely nuts
Theodor: she did say she was going to Somalia when she
    turned 18
Henrik: somalia is in syria now is it?
Emilie: don't diss each other pls
Alexander: what is she trying to achieve? How is a 16 year
    old going to help in an actual war?
Emilie: she must have thought it was so horrible seeing all
    those people being killed that she felt she had to do more
    than just send money . . .

The comments streamed in, with exclamation marks and capital letters, questions and replies tumbling through the thread as more people logged on.

Storm: Leila wasn't quite right in the head and her religious
    beliefs were not altogether healthy, we could see that
    in class.
Synne: I think writing that kind of thing shows a lack of
    respect, we are all passionate about different things in our
    lives! I think it's a brave thing to do. But scary. Imagine
    something happens to Leila?
Alexander: She's made her own choice. It's the family I feel
    sorry for not her, not in any way.
Joakim: I'm pretty sure it can only end badly for Leila . . . we
    need to prepare for the worst!
Alexander: seems so
Ulrik: She is an extremist though
Synne: a person is missing? and you guys talk shit about her.
    Wow you all need to get real
Alexander: saying she is an extremist is not talking shit about
    her. Just because she is missing doesn't mean people
    should suddenly have a load of respect for her

Theodor: This was unbelievably not thought through, it's a
fucking war. It's not going to be like 'hi will you help carry
the wounded,' she'll be lucky not to end up as one of
them . . .

Around midnight the comments abated. Monday was a school day for the sixteen-year-olds. The discussions would continue in the schoolyard.

3

Blind Man's Buff

A stench hit him as he stepped down off the bus. It was still dark, the night air was humid, and his skin felt clammy. Once he was standing on the asphalt, exhaust fumes replaced the rank breeze that had initially assailed him. He straightened up, searched through his pockets, and found a cigarette.

The trip had taken half the night. Finally, he drove through darkened suburbs, then in toward the city center where the lights were on, street after street, so many places to hide.

He inhaled the nicotine as people hurried past, lugging large rucksacks and suitcases, as bus drivers called out their destinations. The passengers moved along like ants, struggling with their burdens, crisscrossing one another, knowing well where they were going. He himself had no route to take.

He did not know a word of Turkish, but surely here on the border to Syria there must be people who spoke Arabic. He collected his thoughts, put out the cigarette, hailed a taxi, and asked the driver to take him to the Arab part of town.

'I want a hotel that's cheap and clean,' he said.

'How cheap?' the driver shot back. The cheapest rooms cost from twenty lira up, he said, 'but they're not clean.'

Sadiq tried to work it out in dollars, dividing by three. 'Find me one for forty,' he said.

The backpack with the laptop lay safely on his thighs, the small suitcase with wheels on the seat beside him. He pulled his baggage closer.

The taxi pulled up at a narrow doorway. The sign above read SEKER PALAS – Sugar Palace. Sadiq paid the driver and clambered up a steep flight of stairs. At the top he came to a pay window, behind which a man sat sleeping. Sadiq knocked at the glass. The hatch was opened.

Room. Bed. Now. He did not place great demands on the receptionist's language abilities. He was handed a key.

So this is where you'll stay, he said to himself as he lay down on the bed. Outside, the sun was rising, but he had to sleep, just for a little while.

He awoke with a start, drenched in sweat. It was Monday morning, eleven o'clock. He called Sara, who was impatient for an update.

'Have you found them?'

No, he told her dejectedly.

'You were asleep? You're not a tourist! Get outside and look!'

Back home, the media had laid siege, at least that was how it felt. Neither Sara nor Ismael could face going out the front door. As a result, the boys had not gone to school.

Sara had been berated over the telephone, even by people she scarcely knew, calling to say the family had brought shame upon Somalis.

You shouldn't have contacted the Norwegian authorities, we're Muslims and you're not going to get any help from them.

You're crazy! Cooperating with the media! With the police! Naïve!

On Somali online debate forums and social media, the verdict was harsh. The family had lost control over their daughters because the mother had not brought them up properly and the father had neglected them.

Sara's friends tried to console her. 'They will soon come back of their own accord, you'll see. How long do you think they'll be able to stick it out in a war zone?'

Not long, Sara thought.

Sadiq had to stop them before they got that far.

He listened to his wife. He needed to hear her voice. They had to be together on this.

'I'll find them,' he promised.

Do not lose your way. That will only make things worse.

Sadiq walked as far as he dared in one direction, turned, then went back toward the hotel and walked as far as he thought he could risk in the opposite direction. Back and forth, farther and farther afield. He made a note of places before turning around, then took a different route, always using the hotel as his starting point. In this slow, laborious manner he gradually increased his familiarity with the city.

My objective is invisible, my objective is unknown. Lines of verse tumbled through his mind.

It was hot. He needed to drink something. He bought some water. His head whirled. He ate lentil soup with bread. Drank more water.

He began approaching passersby.

Girls?

Here?

People shook their heads. Somali girls? In niqabs? No . . .

A photocopy of their passport pictures was the only visual aid he had found at home. Leila had been looking into the camera in a pink hijab. Ayan was wearing a black one.

In the photocopy everything was gray.

He focused on women in niqabs. Some walked alone, others in groups. In the early evening, when the worst of the heat abated, more of them were out on the streets. *There, there, there!* His daughters might be in the crowd, but they never were. Could he have passed them without noticing? No, he would have recognized them by their gait, their height and posture, the way they held their heads, high and proud, like him. They were different from the women here, who either scurried along almost nervously, or puffed and panted underneath the black folds of material.

He walked toward the high mountain bounding the city to the east. Finding two girls in a city was . . . impossible. He turned, walked back to the hotel, and sat down at the nearest bar, which was called Gulp. He drank strong Turkish coffee. The flavor was so sharp he felt it cut him in his mouth. He collapsed onto the bed at midnight. He needed a change of strategy. Searching haphazardly was a waste of time.

There were several taxi drivers who hung around outside the hotel, one of whom had given him a card when he had arrived. 'I'm Mehmut. If you need a car, call me.' After a humid, oppressive night, Sadiq rang the number on the card. They arranged to meet.

'Why are you so stressed out?' Mehmut asked.

Sadiq shifted his weight from one foot to the other. 'Let's go find a table in Gulp and I'll tell you everything.'

The taxi driver had the build of a boxer, with powerful upper arms and a bull neck. His front teeth were false and he had a gold implant. He sat silently while Sadiq told him his story.

When he had heard everything, he said, 'I'm here for you. You're my friend.'

Sadiq liked what he saw in his eyes.

Mehmut drove him around all day, and although more effective than walking, it seemed equally aimless.

Sara rang a number of times.

'Have you found them? Have they called?'

The next morning Mehmut suggested they go to the police. 'You won't find them the way you're going about it.'

Mehmut drove him to police headquarters, a stately redbrick building with tendrils of pink flowers climbing wild up white railings. Turkey's flag, red with the white star and crescent, flew on the roof.

The two men went inside. Sadiq recounted his story. Mehmut translated.

'My daughters have traveled from Norway and are planning to cross into Syria. Can you help me?'

The local police were forthcoming, but they needed to be officially petitioned, they said. They required a request from the Norwegian police.

'The girls are on Interpol's missing persons list,' Sadiq said.

'They haven't committed any offenses here, so there's nothing we can do. Ask the Norwegian police to get in touch with us, and we'll keep our eyes open.'

It was hopeless. Hopeless. Hopeless.

The Norwegian authorities had actually dispatched a police liaison who worked for the Scandinavian embassies in Ankara to act as an intermediary between the Turkish police and the police back in Norway. He had called Sadiq, who had not understood what he said because the policeman was speaking in Danish. Eventually Sadiq just hung up.

After another visit to Gulp, he collapsed on the bed once more. He was fumbling in the dark.

Sara called: *Well? Well? Well?*

He answered: *Unfortunately. Sadly. Sorry.*

The following morning, after a cup of strong tea and a breakfast of beans, olives, and yogurt, he asked the hotel receptionist, 'Is there a meeting place for people who want to get into Syria?'

The receptionist looked him up and down. 'There's a park,' he said, his voice lowered. 'They meet there. Make deals. They can get you in.'

Sadiq had met two Somali youths from Gothenburg at the hotel. They had returned from Syria. One had been wounded in the back and wanted to get home to Sweden for treatment. Hatay province was a way station for jihadists. They flew in, or came by bus, staying for a few days while waiting to be smuggled into Syria. Some of them traveled straight from the airport to the border and crossed over within a matter of hours. Or they returned from the war zone to Antakya, which Syrians called Hatay after the surrounding province, to gather their strength, rest up after seeing action, meet their families, and stock up on supplies.

'Take a left when you go out the door,' the receptionist motioned. 'Follow the pavement until you reach a main road, then take a left, walk over the bridge, then take a left again at the first set of traffic lights across the river, then continue on until you come to a park . . . '

He could make out the tops of the trees from a distance, tall palms and Mediterranean conifers. Drawing closer, he saw trails and walkways crisscrossing one another, shaded patches between the trees, playground equipment, and a kiosk selling soft drinks. Nothing happens there until after dark, the receptionist had added as Sadiq had made ready to leave. He sat and waited.

In the playground, women sat chatting. The squeals of the children livened up the drowsy atmosphere. Elderly men rested in low chairs in the shade, smoking and engaging in quiet conversation as the late afternoon turned to evening. Large fir cones lay strewn all around.

A mother wheeling a buggy exited the park, a couple of young men entered. An old man with a cane rose unsteadily to his feet, two bearded men took his place. So it continued, until the sun went down.

The game began. Money, notes, telephones, and messages changed hands. Conversations were carried out in low voices, with common knowledge implied, and alternated between Turkish and Arabic. Most of the smugglers were Arabs of Syrian extraction.

Hatay province mirrors the ethnic distinctions in Syria. Here live Alawites, Sunnis, Kurds, Circassians, Armenians, and Christians. Family ties to Syria are common.

Under Ottoman rule, Hatay was the hinterland of the powerful trading city of Aleppo. With the breakup of the Ottoman Empire after the First World War, the spoils of victory were distributed among the Western powers, which drew up new borders – so-called spheres of influence – in the Middle East, in accordance with the Sykes-Picot Agreement. Hatay was incorporated into the French Mandate for Syria. In the 1920s and '30s, the province avoided Kemal Atatürk's campaign to impose a unitary national identity, since Turkish annexation did not take place until 1939. Syria protested, to no avail. But the Assad regime still included Hatay within Syria on official maps. The two countries had attempted to find an amicable solution and planned a Friendship Dam to create a reservoir on the Orontes River, which formed part of their mutual border. But that was before the uprising in Syria changed everything.

The Turkish authorities feared that the civil war, which was creating ever greater divisions among Syria's ethnic and religious groups, would spill over the border. At the same time, they turned a blind eye to the smuggling of weapons and influx of fighters. Every day jihadists from all over the world were landing at Turkish airports to make their way into Syria.

Sadiq had found an underworld. Smugglers who drove people into Syria for money. Or were paid to get them out. People slipped in and out, to kill or be killed.

The park was merely the gateway. The real black market was on the outskirts of town. The smell of gasoline from drums of oil drawn from Assad's wells filled the air. Everything could be bought here. Weapons, what type? Ammunition, how much? Drugs, any kind you like. A woman, for an hour, a night, or as long as you wanted.

Whom the weapons would be aimed at, no one cared. What the woman's name was, only she knew. No one asked about your beliefs, your doubts. Here, the price was everything.

Are you looking for a son or a daughter? he was asked.

Two daughters.

One thousand dollars first. That will get you an answer. If they're alive, it costs three thousand each to get them out. If you want both of them, it'll be six thousand.

There were no guarantees. Sadiq's instinct was to take matters into his own hands.

Still, there *were* young people being extricated. One wounded boy was to be taken out, paid for by his family, he told Sara. Parents from Kuwait, Qatar, the UK, had come looking, he recounted. Hunched figures. Desperation in their eyes. Wringing hands. Shoulders stooped.

Because when your child is missing, it shows.

Then there were those who did not get their children. Instead they only received word: *He's dead. He died there. Your son, forget about him. Your daughter, forget about her.*

One day he was driven to a place to negotiate. He sat in the backseat almost passing out, every turn or bump was nauseating. Out of the car, up a staircase, he found himself in an apartment.

Let me see my daughters, then I'll pay you six thousand dollars.

No, the money first.

I have a large family, I can't throw away money.

No payment, no girls.

The middleman said, *Okay, just give us one thousand now, then a thousand afterward.*

The next day he was told: *Your daughters arrived here last Friday.*

They stayed in an apartment, along with several other girls, never stepping outside, until they all traveled over together.

They had been here a week. At the same time as him.

They crossed the border yesterday.

4

In

Mehmut whispered, 'Good luck . . . '

Sadiq got ready.

He sprinted toward the barbed wire. It tore into skin and flesh. Searchlights swept slowly across no-man's-land, leaving pitch darkness behind. He forced his way through the hole in the fence. *Do not get caught. Do not stumble. Do not fall.*

He ran.

Beyond the border lay a two-mile-wide unoccupied zone. Parts of this stretch were dug up, as though defensive trenches had been planned. On either side of the ditches lay fields and flatland.

He heard shots. His body tensed, an acrid taste of blood in his mouth. *Do not fall now, do not fall.*

In places the terrain was flat, and it was like running along a straight road. In others there was gravel and sand, and you could stumble on a loose stone, run into a barrier, get entangled in barbed wire.

A man panted alongside him, another was gaining ground behind. *Do not lose control. Do not panic.*

Somebody groaned in the darkness.

Allahu Akbar!

A fresh burst of gunfire. Was he running in the right direction?
Had the girls run through here too?

When he'd heard that the girls had crossed into Syria, he had
broken down.

He had dragged himself back to the hotel, hauled himself past the
receptionist behind the glass, and trudged up the stairs to his room
on the third floor. Then he had lain down on the bed.

His mind was whirling. Everything seemed hazy. It grew dark.
The sun came up. Then night fell once more.

He had not called Sara. What would he say?

He stayed in bed, getting up now and again only to gulp water
from the tap. He had failed as a father and as a man.

When the sun came up for the second time, he began to pull
himself together. He talked to himself, an old habit.

I am not a father if I don't keep on searching.

I am not Sadiq if I return home now.

Then he had called Sara.

'Don't go over, yes, go over, no, come home,' she said. And
eventually: 'Find them.'

He had then called up Asker and Bærum police station.

'We would strongly advise against that,' was the message.

Sadiq called Mehmut. 'Can you drive me to the border?'

They left at sunset. Thistle and stiff grass grew along the roadside,
with fields beyond. It was the end of October. The crops had already
been harvested. The earth looked like hard-packed sand.

The landscape was illuminated in a final glimmer of pink before
fading into dim hues of brown and gray. Then darkness fell.

Mehmut had initially asked him to reconsider.

'I have to know what's happened to my daughters. I have to.'

'Okay. I'll help you. I have friends there.'

He rang back and told Sadiq to be ready that same afternoon.

'I have a friend called Osman,' Mehmut said, when they were
in the car. He placed emphasis on the name. 'Osman can help you.

When he gives his word, you can count on him to the bitter end. Don't trust anybody else. Remember that.'

They stopped outside a village by the border.

There were others skulking around the area. They had arrived by car, by moped, and on buses. Bearded types with Gulf accents. North Africans. Brits. Clean-shaven Turks. And him. The Norwegian. The Somali.

Hundreds of people crossed no-man's-land illegally every day. The frontier was fenced, but there were many holes in the fence. Mehmut had driven several jihadists to this spot, including, only recently, three Norwegians, he told Sadiq. Two had traveled together, one was on his own. Sometimes he picked people up at the airport and drove them directly here. Often these tasks would come from Osman. Once again he stressed: 'Don't trust anyone but him. Not there, not here. Osman is expecting you on the other side. He'll be waiting there, in an olive grove.'

You could be driven through the border station at Bab al-Hawa and be in Syria in a matter of minutes. But it was expensive – the smuggler wanted money, the driver needed to be paid, the border guard had to be bribed.

The other option was to run.

That alternative cost $200. You paid half on the Turkish side and, if you got over, the rest in Syria.

He heard sand being kicked up, voices. Someone was running in the opposite direction, toward him. Out. Away from the war.

Suddenly he was surrounded by people, flashlights, shadows. He came to a halt, panting, gasping for breath, sweat pouring off him.

From the light of a beam he could discern trees: crooked, dark branches, the gleam of leaves. There were a group of men in front of him. He could hear and feel their proximity. They had Kalashnikovs slung over their shoulders and were wearing flak jackets and balaclavas. Sadiq peered around, at a loss. A flashlight was pointed at him. A hefty man approached.

Then something was being pulled over his head. He raised his hands to resist and lost his glasses. Someone clutched him by the throat.

'Calm down!' a voice said. 'It's only a hood!'

'Keep away from me!' Sadiq shouted.

'All newcomers have to have one on. I'm Osman,' the voice said calmly. Peering through the hole in his hood, Sadiq could see a broad man in the semidarkness.

The foreign fighters wore hoods so they would not be identified. They were often smuggled over the border in groups by the same network, so if one were seen and recognized, the others could be found. Sadiq had taken the same route as the jihadists and had to abide by the same rules. He picked up his glasses and squinted through the eyeholes. The man speaking was in his thirties. He was tall, heavyset, with fair skin and a large beard.

'You're one of us now,' he said, handing Sadiq an AK-47 and an ammunition belt. 'There are twenty-six rounds in the magazine,' he told him.

Sadiq had not held a weapon for many years. He judged the heft of it in his hand, ran his fingers across it.

'No, it holds twenty-five,' Sadiq said.

'Twenty-six.'

Sadiq pointed the gun in the air and fired off a shot.

'Are you crazy?' Osman hissed.

'Had to check if it worked,' Sadiq replied. 'And you were right, there were twenty-six bullets, one was already in the chamber.'

Gunfire crackled between the trees.

'Out of here! Now!' someone said. They clambered into a light-colored Škoda pickup.

'What's going on?' Sadiq asked.

'It's not about us,' he was told in reply, as he sat squeezed between fighters in the backseat.

Not us. Who were we?

'*Man nahnu?*' he asked. Who are we?

'We're Jabhat al-Nusra.'
Al-Qaida's men in Syria.

The truck sped along at a furious pace over the potholed back road,
then swerved onto a roundabout and veered off down darkened
streets. Shooting could still be heard when the car stopped. Sadiq
had switched to soldier mode, an identity he thought was gone.
But no, his brain was already programmed, all it needed was to
be reactivated. The gunfire took him back to the war that had
formed him.

He reverted to the mind-set of the teenager who has joined the
struggle against a dictator. He collected himself. A good soldier
needed to remain calm amid chaos.

He had enlisted in the National Movement without ever having
held a weapon. As a boy, he had known no fear. If government
soldiers were in front of him, he ran straight at them. After being
wounded in a firefight, he was sent to Saudi Arabia for treatment.
During his time there they had discovered how poor his eyesight
was and given him glasses. He was delighted. But on his return he
found he was no longer as brave – because now he could see. On
the other hand, his aim was much improved. In time he was placed
alongside the marksmen. It was in their ranks that he had learned
how to control a pounding heart.

He was in the zone. He felt at home, among friends, warmed up,
fired up almost, and he awaited orders.

'No, no, not now, there are two other groups fighting, and that,'
Osman said, pointing to the machine gun, 'is only to defend yourself
with, just in case. The war is around us. Everywhere. At all times.
Anything can happen.'

His blood pumped more slowly. No, he was not going to fire.
Because this is not my war.

I have come to save my daughters. *I'm just a father.*

'Ismael, we're alive *Alhamdulillah!*'
Twelve days had passed since they had left.

'Everything is fine with us,' the sisters wrote on Messenger and apologized for not having been in touch sooner.

'We have found out that you have reported us missing, which makes it hard to stay in touch. We have so much news to share and would really like to talk more but it is difficult. You don't need to worry, we are safe and sound Alhamdulillah. We now have a place to stay and everyone makes us feel very welcome. Everything here is like in Somalia hehe, broken toilets, electricity and water on the blink and zero traffic rules, but Alhamdulillah we are content. Dad, if you are still in Turkey, go home. We are far away and it is of no use to any of you not to be together as a family at this difficult time. Tell Mom we're so very sorry for the pain you are going through, but stay strong and pray to Allah that everything turns out for the best. Tell Jibril and Isaq that we miss them. Btw they can have the iPad.'

The message was a declaration of independence and a vindication.

'We are aware that many people think what we did was wrong but we have spoken to an *alim* [Islamic legal scholar] down here and he approved of our actions. In order for us to tell you more and stay in touch you need to keep this to yourselves. We never wanted anybody besides our family to know we left, so dearest ones whom we love so much, forgive us and have *sabr* [patience].'

Ismael responded right away.

'Hi. Happy you keep in touch.'

The girls clarified their message: 'Tell Dad to go home! It is not safe for him here!!'

'Dad is not planning to come home,' Ismael replied. ' He says he would rather die down there.'

'We are not anywhere he can get to us and no one knows who we are apart from the people we have told. Handing money over to people who claim they can help him is not going to make him find us.'

'Do you want to speak to Mom?' Ismael asked, sitting in his room. 'She thinks what you have done is wrong and she wants Leila to come home.'

'We cannot talk on the phone at the moment.'

'Are you planning on coming back?'

There was no answer.

'Mom says both of you promised never to leave her!' Ismael continued.

The sisters logged off.

Sadiq lay sleeping in Osman's backyard.

The previous night he had been led through a blue door, across a courtyard, toward a small lean-to by the wall. He had fallen asleep instantly on a narrow bed.

At the crack of dawn he was awoken by a husky voice: 'Abu Ismael, Abu Ismael . . . '

He looked around. An old man was looking in at him.

'Will you join me for tea?'

Abu Ismael was the name Mehmut had given the smugglers. It meant Ismael's father. In the Arab world, it was common to be known by the name of your firstborn son.

The only thing Abu Ismael wanted at that moment was to continue sleeping. He had finally been in a heavy, dreamless slumber. But he could not refuse, so he got up to drink tea with Osman's father – Abu Omar, after his eldest son.

The old man rolled two cigarettes, gave one to Sadiq, and lit up both. It was his own homegrown tobacco.

'Osman has good contacts, he can help you,' the older man said, clearing his throat.

Sadiq began to cough. He assuaged the pungent taste with strong, sweet tea.

Each time they were finished smoking, Abu Omar set about rolling two more. And so it continued.

Eventually he heard a door opening and a sink being filled with water. The rest of the household was stirring. Now they would head out and find his daughters. According to the smugglers in Hatay, they had most likely been driven precisely to where Sadiq now found himself – in Atmeh.

Osman joined them around ten. In daylight, Sadiq could see he had light brown freckles and an auburn beard, a typical northern Syrian.

A platter of eggs, olives, cheese, and zatar, a purée made from fresh thyme, sesame seeds, sumac, and oil, was carried in by Osman's younger brothers. Warm bread and more tea were also brought in.

It was time to negotiate. Sadiq had to pay for a car, men, and the rent of the Kalashnikov. He needed two minders, the price was $10 a day plus expenses per man. He would get the Kalashnikov for $20 a day. Without people to guard him, he could not go outside. Because Sadiq too could fetch a price. There were criminal gangs among the ranks of the militias, who kidnapped foreigners and handed them over to Assad or the Islamists. If you were alive, Osman told him, they would throw you in a cell and demand $5,000 from your family or government for your release; if you were dead, they would ask for only $2,000. In that case, you would be placed in a freezer, your corpse stacked on top of others, until they received payment for you.

'Hence the guards,' Osman said. 'But you need to be on the lookout too, keep an eye on everything going on, these are troubled times.' He sighed. 'But you're safe here in Atmeh. Everybody knows us here.'

His father, a retired colonel from Assad's air force, looked at his son in silence. Then shook his head.

'No one is safe in Syria.'

The land of fear, the country was called. For many Syrians fear had become a part of themselves; impossible to separate from. Present as every breath they took and every beat of their hearts; lodged in their minds and in their stomachs. It lay deep in their souls. And the older you became, the more afraid you were.

Typically, it had been the young who had gone into the streets to demonstrate when the protests against the dictatorships in the Arab world broke out. Older people had been more skeptical. Disobedience would be punished as it always had been. They did not possess the fearlessness of the young. They had seen too much.

For decades, Syrians had lived under the Assad family. When Hafez was born in 1930, his father had already been given the nickname *al-Asad* – 'the Lion' – for his early opposition to French rule, and later to the Syrian authorities. Hafez was brought up in a poor village inhabited by the Alawite minority, leaving at the age of nine to become the first of his family to be educated beyond primary school. He sought out milieus where Alawites were accepted, developing an early hatred for the Muslim Brotherhood, whose members in Syria came from affluent, conservative families. As a sixteen-year-old, he joined the Baath Party, whose motto was 'unity, liberty, socialism,' and began networking. He made friends among poor Sunni Muslims and Christians, united in their opposition to the bourgeoisie who ruled the country. The army and the party were good career paths for ambitious young men of modest means. Hafez rose quickly through the ranks at the military academy in Homs, which offered free room and board, a grant, and pilot training.

Hafez al-Assad was in his midthirties in 1966, when the Baath Party staged a successful coup, in the wake of which he was appointed minister of defense. Following a fierce power struggle between the military and civilian wings of the party, the former proved victorious, and in 1970 Hafez al-Assad seized all power in a new coup. He demonstrated particular brutality against religious opposition; Islamists were tortured and killed.

There had been clashes between the regime and Islamists from the beginning of the 1960s. Over the course of the '70s, the Muslim Brotherhood abandoned peaceful opposition and adopted guerrilla tactics. Representatives of the regime were killed in a series of car bomb attacks. One morning the duty officer at the military academy in Aleppo called all the Alawite cadets to a meeting, whereupon the unarmed young men were massacred by the officer and his accomplices. The following year, in 1980, Assad narrowly avoided a similar fate in a grenade attack, when one of his bodyguards sacrificed himself in the blast. The president's revenge was merciless. Members of the Brotherhood were executed by the hundreds, the organization was banned, and membership was punishable by death.

The attacks on the military and local Baathist Party supporters continued. In early 1982, Islamists declared the Sunni-dominated city of Hama 'liberated.' The regime decided to crush opposition once and for all. In the space of a few weeks, the army, under the leadership of Hafez's brother Rifaat, razed the city to the ground. Twenty, perhaps thirty thousand people were slaughtered, but no exact figures and no pictures of the killings exist. Only afterward did rumors about what had happened leak out.

Assad and his clique ruled, but Sunnis, Shias, Christians, Islamists, Kurds, and Druse all formed the apparatus of power, sharing privileges as well as guilt. The tactical alliance with the Sunni middle class in Damascus and Aleppo was of particular importance. The Alawites, who made up scarcely 11 percent of the population and were regarded by dogmatic Sunni Muslims as infidels, had never previously held political power. Avoiding favoritism toward any of the main religious groups was the strategy, and in so doing Assad created a relatively secular state.

Islamists ended up in cells and torture chambers. Intellectuals laid down their pens, their voices silenced. Because people want to live.

Their hope lay in the Lion's successors loosening the grip.

Hafez's firstborn son, Bassel, was groomed to take over the throne. One January morning in 1994, he crashed his sports car at a roundabout on his way to Damascus Airport and was killed instantly. Consequently, his brother Bashar, studying ophthalmology in London, had to undertake an intensive course in military training and political instruction. There were many who doubted Bashar was strong enough to carry on the regime.

When Hafez died of a heart attack in 2000, the intellectuals, as well as the Islamists, saw a glimmer of hope. The young eye doctor opened the door for a debate that would never have been tolerated under his father – the Damascus Spring. In the absence of a free media, the discussions were carried out in the salons – *muntadayat* – of private houses. These discussions resulted in a demand for reforms. The Statement of 99 was a manifesto drawn up by ninety-nine Syrian intellectuals demanding political diversity and a state governed by the rule of law that would allow freedom of expression and the right to organize. In January 2001, the Statement of 1,000 went even further, demanding democracy and a multiparty system.

Then came the Damascus Winter. Pressure from the army and the old guard in the Baath Party led to a reverse in the thaw, and leaders of the reform movement were jailed.

All other parties were to remain banned. Homage was to be shown to the new president. His image was hung on walls and lampposts, in bazaars, in offices, schools, and hospitals. Everywhere you turned, Bashar al-Assad looked down upon you, just as the face of his father before him, the old pilot, once had. The only update from his father's time was that the young Assad posed in sunglasses à la *Top Gun*.

Osman had just turned nineteen when Bashar took power. Osman had left his parents in Atmeh to train in Aleppo as an electrician.

Syria had become a backwater. The barren areas in the north were stagnant, there was hardly any industry; people lived off what the land could offer – beans, lentils, and chickpeas. But things were stable. You had a fair idea how the autumn harvest would turn out and knew the price of a goat and what news would be broadcast on TV. The new president promised reforms in his Five-Year Plans, but the benefits of any economic growth were concentrated in the hands of the few, the hands of those holding Bashar's.

One Syrian man in four was unemployed. Osman figured out there was more money in being a trader than an out-of-work electrician. Cheap Syrian products fetched a good price in Turkey; likewise, you could buy goods that were hard to find in Syria for a reasonable sum in the neighboring country. He got married and moved back in with his parents in Atmeh, who owned an olive grove close to the Turkish border. It was this proximity to the border that created the conditions for profit: Income was earned from legitimate trade, from more dubious dealings, and from smuggling.

The border guards looked the other way as long as their palms were greased; otherwise Osman made use of herding tracks and crossed the border on foot. As living standards increased in Turkey and stagnated in Syria, there was more money to be made each year. The price of a carton of cigarettes was many times higher across the border, and there was good money to be made in the diesel trade.

In Atmeh, the identity of the smugglers was an open secret. Nobody was making a fortune. There were too many at it for that. Every family had one member involved in 'the business,' while the rest toiled in the olive groves, worked the barren earth, or just sat around.

Then everything changed. Syria, as people knew it, would disappear forever.

One late afternoon in February 2011, after school was finished, a group of boys in Dar'aa, a city in the far south of the country, met up to play football. Afterward they sat around talking. One of them got an idea – to write a message of protest against the president on the wall of the school. *Iyak al-dawr ya, doktor* the fifteen-year-old spray-painted on the wall before they all ran home. *Soon it will be your turn, Doctor.* The headmaster read it the following morning and called the police. The pupils were taken in for interrogation in groups of ten. After one of those accused of being complicit, a fourteen-year-old, was beaten bloody, he named the others involved.

The boys were arrested. And disappeared. Their parents went to the police, who merely shrugged. Gradually people began to gather outside the police station to demand the release of the boys. When the fathers again marched in to see the police, they were told to forget their children. 'Send your wives and we'll make some new children for you,' was the response of one of the station chiefs.

The demands for the children to be returned escalated into protests. The security forces opened fire. The first two lives in the rebellion that would later claim hundreds of thousands were lost in Dar'aa.

After a month in prison, the boys were released. Their school-bags along with their schoolbooks were returned to them, and they were informed that the president – *al-Doktor* – was granting them an amnesty because it was Mother's Day. The boys came out with a vacant look in their eyes. They had been burned, cut, beaten; some of them were missing fingernails.

This was how it began. With the letters of a child on a wall.

The protests did not spread as they had in Tunisia, Egypt, and Libya, where public disorder took place in the capital cities. Damascus was controlled too effectively for that. Informants and plainclothes policemen were everywhere, and any form of protest would be reported within seconds and put a stop to within minutes. Buses carrying men from the security forces drove around the city, the men ready to spring into action at a moment's notice.

In satellite towns and provincial cities, where levels of preparedness were not as high, people raised their voices. They did not demand Bashar step down – that was too dangerous – but they did demand reform, liberty and democracy. With the exception of Friday prayers, gathering in groups in Syria was forbidden. Consequently, the first demonstrations began after congregated prayer, with men marching in silence. As time went on, they began chanting slogans.

Some rallies became celebrations. Local singers entertained on makeshift stages, poets stood aloft on ladders among the crowd and recited verse, little girls swayed on their parents' shoulders, and women stood on balconies waving their shawls, all on a high of emotion.

Extremism came later, jihadism came later, as did the weapons. First came the dream of freedom.

War began as it often does, with scattered skirmishes. One person killed, one family grieved. Two people killed, the people continued dancing. Three killed, they will never break us. Four killed, the women stayed indoors; five killed, the children disappeared from the demonstrations; six killed, the singing stopped; seven killed, funerals turned into protest marches; eight killed, the dead had to be avenged; nine killed, young men took up arms; ten killed, they learned to kill.

Then the slaughter began.

The murder of the demonstrators throughout 2011 was carried out with a brutality that stirred the collective memory of the Syrians and brought to mind the massacre in Hama a generation before. The difference now was that it was being captured on camera, people filmed it with their mobile phones, recordings were smuggled out and spread on the internet. The Assad regime was no longer able to kill in the darkness. Not that the international community lifted a finger. Although world leaders condemned the violence, it was left up to the Syrians themselves to oppose it. In response to the regime meeting demonstrators with tanks, the Free Syrian Army, FSA, was formed.

At the beginning the rebel army was composed of soldiers, officers, and a few generals who refused to open fire on their own people. These deserters wanted the Arab Spring to come to Syria – an end to the Assad regime. As new demonstrators were killed, more civilians joined the armed resistance. Poets no longer regaled the crowds; they learned how to fire live rounds. Barbers no longer shaved; they let their beards grow and cleaned their weapons. Engineers manufactured bombs and medical students mixed Molotov cocktails. The Free Syrian Army was open to all: Sunnis, Shias, Alawites, and Christians. It had no program other than a free, democratic, secular state.

The regime's response was to steer the conflict onto a sectarian track, in order to foster division within the disparate coalition. Bashar's strategy was to pitch extremists, who had little support in Syria, against the moderates, who represented the majority of the population. The eye doctor feared democracy more than Islamism.

State propaganda consistently referred to the revolutionaries as terrorists, and as early as spring 2011, when the revolt was in its infancy, the authorities released hundreds of militant Islamists from Sednaya prison outside Damascus. They soon formed militias and demonstrated their gratitude – prisoners often didn't get out alive – by refraining from attacking the soldiers of the regime, training their weapons instead on the armed, secular opposition. A new front was opened against the FSA – jihadists funded by the oil wealth in the Gulf.

The forces fighting for democracy implored the West for arms support. Europe's leaders were irresolute. Obama was reluctant. The world looked away.

*

The border town of Atmeh, where Osman lived with his parents, wife, and two daughters when the civil war broke out, was conquered by the Free Syrian Army in October 2011. Owing to its location on a strip of Syrian land jutting into Turkey, the town had been spared Assad's air strikes. Their long-range rockets were imprecise and the Syrian regime did not want to run the risk of hitting a NATO member. The town became a revolving door for foreign combatants, fired up on the way in, wounded on the way out. Trucks carrying weapons from Turkey came through, while oil from the fields the militias had taken over was driven out.

When Sadiq arrived at the end of October 2013, Atmeh was split between the FSA and a motley assortment of Islamists, with Jabhat al-Nusra and two other militias, Ahrar al-Sham and Suqur al-Islam, the biggest actors. The front lines between the militias were fluid, hence the constant exchanges of fire. Young men wearing different headbands, always armed with loaded weapons, glowered at one another in a fight for territory. Fuses were short and hostility ran high. If one side fired a shot, the other side responded. *Here we are! This is ours! Keep out of our way!*

Atmeh, once a sedate village surrounded by olive groves, was on speed.

In Osman's living room, morning turned to afternoon. Eventually they agreed on a price for the minders, the weapon, and the vehicle, the same Škoda pickup from the night before.

'You are my guest,' Osman said, grinning, because no one's lodgings came free. The first order of business was to bring Sadiq around and introduce him. The war had its own bureaucracy; foreigners could not be in Syria without belonging to a group, somebody had to vouch for you. If you operated on your own or delayed in choosing a side, you could easily be suspected of being a spy.

They went first to Jabhat al-Nusra. Al-Qaida's branch in Syria was the most powerful militia in the area and took its orders from the leaders of the terror organization. Their income was derived from oil trading, hostage taking, looting, smuggling, donations, taxes, and appropriation of property. At their headquarters, one of the Assad regime's public buildings, Osman and Sadiq were met by Abu Islam, a young man with thick glasses and a plump, pear-shaped body.

They placed their shoes outside and walked barefoot into a carpeted room where some commanders were having a discussion over glasses of tea.

Sadiq related his story. Unfortunately, Abu Islam had not heard of any Somali girls. Foreigners usually passed straight through the area and traveled farther on, he told them.

'Farther on to where?'

'Al-Dawla al-Islamiya fi al-Iraq wa al-Sham,' he replied. 'Daesh.'

He elaborated for Sadiq: 'They're the ones who recruit women. Not us.'

Daesh is used as the derogatory name for the Islamic State in Iraq and *al-Sham* – Greater Syria – an area also comprising parts of Jordan, Israel, Lebanon, and Turkey, historically referred to in the West as the Levant. ISIS and ISIL are different names for the same organization as the al-Sham often translates as *the Levant*.

Daesh and al-Nusra, having both arisen from the same source – al-Qaida – were theologically similar. When the war in Syria began, the Islamic State in Iraq (ISI) dispatched a group into the country to start the offshoot Jabhat al-Nusra. Then ISI itself entered Syria. After asserting its independence, the group was expelled from al-Qaida and, under the leadership of Abu Bakr al-Baghdadi, renamed itself ISIS. They had created al-Nusra and now they demanded the group's reincorporation. Jabhat al-Nusra refused. They preferred to remain with al-Qaida.

The recruitment of women was one bone of contention. Al-Qaida's men would welcome women in Syria, but only when the war was over and the true caliphate established. ISIS wanted them to come right away.

Abu Islam showed the visitors to the door, nodding all the while, promising, 'We'll keep an eye out.'

Their next port of call was Ahrar al-Sham, an Islamist militia that was more moderate than al-Nusra and had no connections to al-Qaida. Ahrar al-Sham also wanted an Islamic state but rejected global jihad and a caliphate beyond Syria's borders. Their sole aim was *sharia* in Syria.

The leaders of the organization had spent years in Sednaya prison being subjected to brutal torture. When Assad opened the gates, the prison comrades formed a militia. They set themselves apart from more hard-core Salafists by promising to protect religious minorities and cooperate with secular forces. They were labeled closet pragmatists.

'Do you have any inkling where the girls might be?' the commander, Abu Utham al-Atar, asked.

'Only that they're in Syria, I don't know where,' Sadiq replied. 'They've likely passed through this area. Someone may have kidnapped them.'

'A father who comes to a war zone to get his daughters. Respect,' the commander said, and promised to keep a lookout.

Sadiq showed him the worn photocopy of their passport pictures. But the photos were probably of little use; the girls were likely now wearing niqabs.

The headquarters of the Free Syrian Army was just a few minutes' drive away, at the local police station. The force, having initially wrested control of the town from Assad, was losing territory. The FSA had support from both the United States and Saudi Arabia, but the Assad regime, with its heavy artillery and air force, and the Islamists, with their superior weaponry and greater number of vehicles, had both intensified their attacks on the group. Many young fighters, persuaded by the Islamists' aggressive propaganda or tempted by the resources available, had defected from the secular side to their ranks. In addition, the FSA was weakened by internal divisions. The army had also been infiltrated by bands looting in their name, and popular support was waning. This stood in contrast to Jabhat al-Nusra and Ahrar al-Sham, which were winning over the local population with acts of charity.

The smell of cigarettes hit Sadiq as he entered their headquarters. Finally he could light up. Osman took one too. The atmosphere at the FSA was otherwise gloomy. They had been attacked the previous night, and Sadiq and Osman now had to wait for the brigade leader to finish a meeting. After they'd waited long enough to smoke several more cigarettes, a tall, thin man in his sixties with a walrus mustache approached them.

'Sad, very sad,' Abu Alush said, upon hearing Sadiq's story. The colonel had been among the first to desert Assad's army.

'There are a lot of bad things happening that are out of our hands, but I'll let you know if I hear anything.'

'They're almost certainly being held hostage,' Sadiq said. 'Most likely by a criminal gang.'

The colonel nodded. 'Yes, yes, no doubt, but you have to leave now.'

There was one group left: the Islamic State in Iraq and Syria.

Their headquarters was in a villa once owned by an Assad general, situated behind high walls and a large gate. The building was surrounded by a desiccated garden in which only a few almond trees had survived untended. Inside, there was a homey smell – a couple of young boys were preparing dinner, lentil soup with black beans and bread.

They were welcomed by a tall *emir*, Abu Saad al-Tunisi, the last part of his name indicating his country of origin. Sadiq put great effort into choosing the right words. By this stage he had fashioned a good story, emphasizing the parts that had made an impression on his previous listeners, leaving out the weaker points. He focused on his daughters being kidnapped and held against their will.

Abu Saad offered food, but no promises. Trays were brought in. Sadiq could hear the sound of several others eating in the adjacent room. The sounds of men in high spirits, their weapons put down but not, as he remembered from his time as a soldier, far out of reach. He recalled how you held your gun close, like a girlfriend, if you became unsure, checked it was loaded, that the safety catch was not on. Putting the safety off took three seconds, but in that time you could be dead.

Abu Islam, the pear-shaped Islamist they had met at the Jabhat al-Nusra base, was the one who had arranged for them to meet with ISIS. He now entered the room and greeted them briefly before leaving the villa. Even though the two jihadist armies were able to share a meal and enter into tactical alliances prior to a battle, their relationship was tense. The power struggle between their leaders was bitter and uncompromising; instead of pointing their weapons in the same direction – against the Syrian army – the jihadist groups had been fighting that summer for control of Syria's northern areas.

Green headbands were replaced with black ones. Men shifted their loyalties to those they received the most from. After a few months, ISIS began attacking their hosts: the ones who had given them everything – even their daughters – in the hope of forging lasting alliances.

The days passed. Wait. Pay. Wait.

Until his wallet was empty and he no longer had protection.

'Go to Hatay and take out money,' Osman said.

In war, cash is king, money in the bank is worth nothing. Sadiq had to make the run again, two miles over, two miles back.

He called Mehmut. The taxi driver promised to be waiting on the other side.

The sun was about to set. There were several others ready to try to make it across. A few of them tried but turned back, discouraged by the many patrols. Eventually Mehmut called him from the Turkish side. 'Sadiq, don't try it tonight, the guards are out in force.' One Egyptian took a chance and was caught, as were a few others. A Turkish prison awaited them. A crestfallen Sadiq returned to Osman and was given a day's board and lodging on credit.

The following night he ran. Mehmut had arranged for him to be picked up by a motorcycle halfway across. He hopped on and rode pillion while the driver, a youth, drove as fast as he could over the gravel and stones. The mile on the back of the motorbike cost him twenty Turkish lira. He dearly hoped that NAV had put his rehabilitation allowance for November into his account.

The ATM dispensed the cash. He returned to the border, paid, and, for the second time, ran into the war zone.

Back in Idlib province, Osman continued to help him with his inquiries, at brigade after brigade, village after village. Sadiq described his daughters. Tall. Proud posture. Probably wearing niqabs. He shared his story with whoever would listen. By now he was becoming a familiar figure to the people in Atmeh. There goes the father looking for his daughters, they would say.

'We need to start looking beyond this province,' Osman said to him one day. 'But that's not going to be cheap.'

For a third time, Sadiq had to get his hands on money. The following day was a public holiday for the Turks, Osman told him, so crossing over would be no problem. He was right. Sadiq ran over, was picked up by Mehmut, emptied his account from the ATM in Hatay, and went to pick up the belongings he had left at the Sugar Palace. Suddenly Osman himself showed up in town, saying he had pressing business to attend to.

'For a few dollars, I can ensure your return journey is a lot more pleasant,' he promised.

A car picked them up and drove toward the Bab al-Hawa border station. The barrier was raised for them to go straight through without being checked or searched. They were back in Atmeh by dinnertime.

Osman had secured himself safe conduct across the border. He had leased out to a foreign aid organization a parcel of the family's olive grove where Sadiq had first met him. In addition to money for the land and free passage across the border, he had seen to it that his relations got jobs at the camp, which had increased the population of Atmeh tenfold. Thirty thousand people lived in and around the olive grove: those who didn't have the hundred dollars required for the run across the frontier.

The electrician from Aleppo cashed in on all this misery, making sure the wheels of war were kept in motion by smuggling even more jihadists into Syria.

He took Sadiq south. Refugees were moving in the opposite

direction. Women, men, the elderly, children. On foot, in carts, and in cars. Headed toward the camp in the olive grove, toward the Turkish border, anywhere, just away. By autumn 2013, two million Syrians had fled the country. Many more were internally displaced and sought refuge in areas on the peripheries of the fighting.

Sadiq was downhearted. Bombed-out buildings. Fresh graves. Rubble. People. All the time, more people.

The regime had launched a new offensive in an effort to regain strategic areas around Aleppo, and opposition forces were now suffering heavy losses. Aleppo had long been a fighting ground for hundreds of jihadist factions, secular militias, and Salafist armies. Efforts were under way to unite and mobilize against the regime; several groups were on the way from the front at Raqqa and from Idlib.

The men stopped at every camp to ask if anyone had seen the girls. No one had. Who would be looking for girls when a war was raging around them?

Foreign fighters from Europe had arrived in the thousands that autumn. Their number had tripled since the summer. Some came to fight against Assad, others to abet the fulfillment of the prophecy that the final battle before judgment day would take place in the Syrian town of Dabiq.

ISIS used Assad's abuses of the civilian population as a means of recruitment. When a thousand human beings slowly choked to death in a chemical weapon attack carried out by the regime that same summer, they exploited it in their propaganda. ISIS was the most open to taking in random foreigners. Other militias were more selective, preferring experienced soldiers, not cannon fodder.

Speaking to local Syrians, Sadiq got the impression they were fed up with jihadists coming to wage war in their country. They arrived with their own customs and ways from European cities or moneyed backgrounds in the Gulf. They were arrogant, boorish, and cruel, and set about trying to create their own state, a divine state on earth. On Syrian soil.

Sadiq pondered the nature of war. Everyone was sure that *they* had the right to the land and the *others* should be forced to leave. That they had God on their side while the others were in league with the devil. Everyone believed they owned the truth, and everyone seemed thirsty for blood. At night, words echoed through his mind. *Kill, behead, avenge.*

Like combatants, Sadiq and Osman sheltered in abandoned buildings. They had to look up, at the holes in the roof, at the concrete left hanging around the exposed reinforcing steel. Would the roof hold for one more night? Would the house stand for yet another day?

Sadiq couldn't get used to it, settling down for the night in a deserted house, a home a family had left behind, taking their children by the hand and fleeing.

He inquired, he despaired. The front line had moved. Carrying on along the road would mean driving into territory under regime control. They had to leave the truck and negotiate the rugged terrain away from the road in order to avoid the regime soldiers. Osman suggested hiring donkeys.

'Abu Ismael, can you ride a donkey?'

A small boy showed him how to get the donkey moving. The gangly Somali mounted the animal, which refused to shift from the spot.

'No, not like that. Look. Slap here. Kick there!'

To think it could be so hard! He had ridden camels and dromedaries and had been a goatherd for his grandfather. He asked the boy how old he was.

'Eight.'

Isaq will soon be eight, Sadiq thought. *My son, who cannot walk to school alone or tie his shoelaces.*

The Syrian boy had holes in his trousers and no shoes.

'Like so, sit this way,' he continued patiently.

Sadiq slid off.

Eventually he let the donkey carry his rucksack and weapon while he trudged alongside. He lagged behind. The $10-a-day minders followed the ridge of the hill, he kept farther down.

Suddenly there was a crackle of gunfire. They had wandered into a firefight. Bursts of shots from various calibers of weapon sounded. Sadiq stayed flat on the ground among the scrub. He tried to control his breathing. If he managed to slow it down, he could get a good aim. He had two full magazines. This was how he had survived the civil war in Somalia, by being a better shot than the enemy.

His throat was dry. He began crawling away from the sound of firing. His arms and legs on the ground, he felt he was in free fall, a feeling of first hanging poised in the air, then crashing down, as if a parachute did not open. *I have no control over my life, over the situation, nothing.* Now, all he had to do was keep his head down. He tried to figure out where he was in relation to the landmarks Osman had pointed out. That is where they are, and we are here, the Syrian had explained. But Sadiq had had enough on his plate with the donkey. He was angry with himself for relying blindly on Osman instead of attempting to gain an overview on his own.

Assad's soldiers would mistake him for an Islamist if they came across him, there were many Somalis among their ranks. He heard low voices.

'Alhamdulillah,' said Osman. 'Are you in one piece?'

'Yes, thankfully,' Sadiq answered.

'Keep your head down,' Osman said. 'If they see us, they'll take aim.'

Syria is big. Sadiq began to lose hope.

They were on the outskirts of Aleppo. The once splendid city stank. The smell in the rebel-controlled areas was overpowering. Corpses lay beneath the ruins. He could not dwell on it, he had to keep going. *Find them!* was the last thing Sara had said to him.

In some neighborhoods hardly a building was left undamaged. One more round and they would collapse. The structures were built close together, most of them with shared walls, and there were holes in those walls that allowed the rebels to move from house to house, as though through a tunnel, to the front, which was nothing more than a street or corner. A place where schoolchildren had walked, young couples had necked.

Now death visited daily.

When darkness fell, they took refuge in an apartment block.

Sadiq looked around. This would once have been a very nice apartment, he thought. It was only partially destroyed, though the façade was missing, like in a doll's house. There were plates in the cupboard, saucepans you could use to soak beans in or make *foul*, and dried onionskins in a basket. There were books on the shelves and clothes hanging in the wardrobes.

A framed wedding photograph hung on the wall. The couple had gleaming eyes and were beautiful in the way happy people are. She was powdered, made up, wore a long white dress, and had flowers in her hair. He was clean-shaven, in a white shirt and dark suit. The style of the clothing suggested the wedding had not been long ago, they seemed so modern, so contemporary. *They are still young*, he thought. *This is happening in our time.*

Where could they be now? Among the people they met along the road, dragging themselves onward, trudging over sandy, muddy, stony surfaces?

Standing there, in front of the beautiful couple, in the ashes of their happiness, he could not hold the tears back.

So many shattered dreams.

He grew furious at his daughters. He cried out loud. The Syrians did not need more people coming here to fight! Not girls and boys from the West! They needed peace! He slammed his hand against the wall. A hollow thud sounded in response. He searched his pockets for a cigarette. Found none. Left the living room.

There was a double bed in one of the rooms. He threw himself down on it, then stiffened. *Their* bed. He had lain down on *their* marital bed.

He sobbed loudly.

Why did my girls come here?

Ayan! Leila! What is wrong with you?!

Part II

Seven Steps to Radicalization

1. Otherization: I am of one group, they are from another.
2. Collectivization: They are all the same.
3. Oppression narrative: They are oppressing us.
4. Collective guilt: They are all complicit in oppressing us.
5. Supremacism narrative: We are better than them.
6. Self-defense: We have to retaliate against their aggression.
7. The idea of violence: Violence is the only way.

—@iyad_elbaghdadi,
Arab Spring activist, 2015

5

Early Teens

Gjettum Lower Secondary School was situated on Bærum's east–west divide. On the east side, the houses were larger and the fortunes fatter; in the west, row houses and average incomes dominated.

The school claimed the student body was diverse, but the pupils were for the most part blond, blue-eyed, and Norwegian through and through. The girls were preppy, shopped as a hobby, and wore Uggs, leggings, checked shirts, and yachting jackets. They had long blond hair, wore pale, subtle makeup and lip gloss.

Three girls stood out among the thirteen-year-olds starting at the school in autumn 2006. Ivana had an emo style, dressing completely in black. Ela wore oversized Red Hot Chili Peppers and KISS T-shirts. Ayan wore turquoise shawls, large earrings, and skinny jeans. All three had jet-black hair.

Their outsider status drew them together. They were known as the immigrant gang. Ivana was a refugee from Croatia. Ela's parents had come from China, and Ayan was, as in primary school, the only African in her class. The girls spoke Croatian, Mandarin, and Somali at home. Ivana was Catholic, Ela was a member of the Chinese congregation in Oslo, while Ayan regularly attended Koran school.

They discussed their faiths, the similarities and differences. God. Life after death. Heaven and hell. Sex. Homosexuality. Abortion. Those kinds of things. When Ela had her confirmation, Ayan and Ivana were invited to the family gathering as a matter of course. All three would say they owed their lives to Norway; Ayan and Ivana had fled from civil war, while Ela had eluded China's one-child policy. The youngest of three, she would not have come into the world had her parents not left. Her father had been a masseur at a Beijing hotel when one day the Norwegian billionaire Stein Erik Hagen was a customer. The supermarket magnate was so pleased with the treatment that he arranged for Ela's father to move to Norway.

All three girls were certain, however, that when they grew up they would leave Norway. 'I want to live in Australia,' Ivana said. 'Norway is cold and boring.' She disliked the winters intensely. As did Ayan. 'The sun in Norway is like a flashlight,' she said, 'only light, no heat!' She wanted to be a diplomat, work at the UN, and fight injustice and poverty. Ela, whom the class referred to as 'our little Christian Chinese piano player,' wanted to sing in a rock band and tour the world.

Everything they did for the first time, they did together.

They went to parties.

They developed crushes.

They squeezed pimples. Ate tortilla chips. Put on weight. Began jogging. Measured their waistlines. Synchronized periods. Shared lip gloss, feelings, and the details of their romantic conquests.

They went from thirteen to fourteen to fifteen together.

The Juma family belonged to the lowest economic tier in Bærum and lived in council housing. Sadiq worked at times, before returning to the welfare rolls and training courses, all the while dreaming of becoming an engineer. Sara had been enrolled in a Norwegian course but couldn't focus. When Isaq began kindergarten, she was still at home and had not learned the language.

But Ayan had discovered books. Knut Hamsun was her favorite author. 'In neo-romanticism the first-person takes center stage,' she wrote in an essay about *Hunger*. 'Everything is about what *I* think, what *I* feel, and the human psyche is all-important. Neo-romanticism is not concerned with religion or nationality, but with imagination, with matters mystical, irrational and inexplicable.' She describes the end of *Hunger*, where the main character lingers around in Kristiania, that later changed its name to Oslo. 'He views himself as a loser, then on impulse boards a ship to escape the misery of Kristiania, the city that no one leaves before it has set its mark upon him.'

Ayan was impatient, as well as prone to acting on a whim, which came through in her writing. Punctuation and spelling were secondary to making her opinion clear. She could produce the wildest compositions, like the time they were to write 'a short story where a change for the better occurs.' The first sentence was supplied in the assignment: 'Finally! Her eyes shone!' Ayan called her story 'Heart Beat,' a title the teacher 'corrected' to 'Heartbeat.' It was about Oda, who had once had 'eyes like a beautiful night sky filled with sparkling stars, but that now more closely resembled two bottomless holes,' because Oda had become a prostitute. A man employed at the local mortuary becomes a customer. 'They were supposed to have sex on one of the examination tables at his workplace the first time she was with him. But things got a little hot and heavy, causing a corpse to fall down on top of her, prompting him to ask her to have sex with it. He paid her very well so she went along with the idea and has met him once a week since.' One night Oda sleeps over at the customer's place and 'lies thinking about how nice it is to wake up in the arms of a man you love. *A man I love*, she mouthed quietly to herself, and realized they had in a way a good relationship. He had been kind to her from the beginning and she had stayed over with him several times when she had no place else to go. Just the thought that she was in love with him made her whole body tingle, and a warm, peculiar feeling built up and grew the more she thought about it. A life with him would not be so bad, he had a job and earned good money.'

The short story ended with the customer taking a business trip to

Germany and asking Oda to come along. 'The offer left her stunned, then he came out with the most shocking thing of all: I love you, Oda, come with me. She thought about it carefully – did she have anything to lose? No, there was nothing for her in Norway, so why not take the chance?'

Ayan received a B–. Her teacher said the piece was 'well thought out with good depictions as well as the use of literary devices to underscore the plot' but gave it a 'minus for a load of homonymic errors, incorrect punctuation for quoted speech, and failure to combine compound words.'

In her next essay, she wrote from the perspective of Torvald Helmer, Nora's husband in Henrik Ibsen's *A Doll's House*. '23.9.1890. Dear diary, today I was promoted to manager of the bank. What glorious news, my dear darling Nora was delighted on my behalf. But no matter what I do, I cannot refrain from worrying, there is something she is not telling me. I can see it in her sad dove's eyes, such a wonderful little lark ought not look so melancholy.'

In another composition, she imagined she was an American soldier in Vietnam. The year was 1966. 'Dear diary. Today is my eighteenth birthday. I feel terrible and cannot even look at myself in the little shard of glass I use as a mirror. We were on night patrol doing a recon. Those sly gooks could be hiding just about anywhere. We were ordered to stay out of sight until the sun rose once again, removing the dark blanket that lay over all the bodies, covering all the blood.' The soldier described massacres he had taken part in, where women and children were tied up and oil was poured over them and set alight. 'How can the sky be so beautiful when the world is so sickening? How can the stars twinkle and sparkle when the earth is on fire?' the soldier asked. Six months later, he simply writes: 'Dear diary. I wonder if there is a God.'

From the age of fifteen, romance loomed large.

'I feel like DYING,' Ayan wrote to Ela in the winter. They were in their third year at Gjettum. 'I found out he has a girlfriend. (But that's just the way it is, he can live happily with her :)'

Ela responded, 'Awwwwwh poor you . . . but it's good you accept it and are happy for him. THERE ARE PLENTY MORE FISH IN THE SEA!!!!!!!! I'll be there for you, NO MATTER WHAT!!!!!! LOVE YOU LOADS BABE!!!!!!'

The text messages flitting among three housing blocks in Bærum were strewn with hearts and smileys, emojis crying and weeping tears of laughter. During the summer holidays, text messages flew back and forth between Europe and Africa, from the Dalmatian coast to the Chinese congregation's youth camp all the way to Somaliland.

'Tons of cute boys here, but I can't even hit on them,' Ayan wrote to Ela in the summer between third and fourth year. 'It's roasting here, but I bought Snapple so now I'm happy. I haven't seen a single cockroach so far, happy about that, and Granny is coming from Djibouti soon, can't wait! Have you heard from Ivana?'

'Yo bitch,' Ela wrote back. 'The weather here in Norway is amazing (hoping to work a little more on my tan, I'm so pale-.-!) I've been hanging around with the people from the church a lot lately and summer camp is in two weeks. I can't wait.'

'Whoa!' Ayan replied. Ela's experiences at camp were the highlight of her summer, and this year her camp was in Stockholm. As for what was happening in Somaliland, Ayan could tell her: 'I have good news and bad news. I have cut my hair a lot shorter, phew, what a relief!!!! There's a guy here I'm soooo into but he is such a charmor (think I spelled that wrong) and the bad news is he is the kind of guy all the girls are after but he flirts so much with me (which feels amazing btw) I don't know what to do. He tried to kiss me four times last night, but we kept getting interrupted, I almost died!!! And today he came over, sat down beside me and kissed me on the cheek. But then some people came into the room so we didn't get a chance to do anything else ☹☹☹. I like him but I don't want to get hurt, not now or when I leave, I feel so strange when he's not around and can't manage to eat or sleep, my aunt is worried about me, Mom too!!!'

Life was one big delightful drama.

*

Ayan came across as tough and self-confident. She was indignant at the oppression of women, the focus on body image, and was critical of fashion magazines for reinforcing girls' insecurities. 'Are you unhappy about the way you look? Stressed out? How many boys looked at you tonight? When did you last have sex? All these sly questions that make you feel like an outdoor toilet in India,' she wrote, in an essay called 'Women's Liberation.' 'And what's worse, we have to give birth to little rat males who we look after and hold dear, right up until they turn from boys into men who in turn go on to oppress yet another woman.'

She was prone to digression in her writing, often failing to bring her reasoning to a satisfactory conclusion. 'Explain!' the teacher wrote in the margin. 'Where does this fit in?' or 'Disjointed!' But also 'Well put!' or 'Good!'

'In the distant past in Saudi Arabia, the brutal oppression of women was such that if you gave birth to a girl, she was buried alive,' Ayan wrote. 'Then the Prophet Muhammad came, the man of the Muslims, and ensured that women were treated equally to men. After his death the oppression of women began afresh, and still exists, but in the wake of the Second World War more and more women grew tired of being seen as housewives.'

Ayan concluded 'Women's Liberation' by paying tribute to those who had paved the way: 'Even though you were stoned, called witches and often killed. Thank you for telling the truth and setting us free.' She got an average mark along with the comments that she had made several good points but the text was somewhat rambling and the paragraph division questionable.

It was in religion class that Ayan excelled. She was not only knowledgeable about several faiths but also made her own critical evaluations. There was a lot about Islam she disliked, she declared, especially how the religion was used to subjugate women. They did not hold the same position as men or have the same rights. But she was not going to stand for it, she informed the class, because if it continued, then she would not be a part of that religion!

When she graduated lower secondary, her diploma contained

an equal number of A—'s and Bs. She made an ambitious choice and applied to one of the most prestigious schools in the county – Nesbru Upper Secondary – in the hope of being accepted in their International Baccalaureate program. The school described the course of study as academically challenging, and one of 'the best programs in the world for university preparation.' The instruction was in English in all subjects except Norwegian and foreign languages – appropriate for an aspiring diplomat.

Ayan was accepted into the first year. During the summer, however, she began to regret her choice. At Nesbru she would not hang out with her friends anymore; they had applied to vocational school in Rud. Ela was to attend the music program and Ivana was doing the drama course.

Ayan wrote to their little Christian Chinese piano player, who was at a camp in Toronto. 'Hello, Norway calling ☺ Heard you got yourself a dude ☺ you GO girl ☺ bored out of mind here and dreading starting school have heard lots of shit about Nesbru ☹ and I miss my little yellow friend. Try to have a bit of fun, even though it's a Christian arrangement, be a little bad!'

Her first year's results would determine whether or not she could continue on in the IB program, which would open the doors to the big wide world. She could become the first person in her family to go far academically.

Nesbru included Nesøya in its catchment area, an island renowned for the wealth of its inhabitants and the mansions with a view of Oslo Fjord. Ayan did not know anyone, did not resemble anyone; she was different – a girl with golden skin, soft round cheeks, a high forehead, and a sparkle in her eyes. She cut an upright, proud figure and dressed in tight jeans and colorful hijabs.

English had been her favorite subject in lower secondary, which now stood her in good stead, but her form teacher, Knut Gundersen, was surprised at the discrepancy between her oral and written skills and suspected she had mild dyslexia. Her economics teacher, a woman of Iranian descent who had been educated in the United States and had herself learned Norwegian as an adult, attributed

Ayan's spelling mistakes to a lack of grounding in her mother tongue. 'She knows a string of languages,' the teacher said, 'but not *one* for real.'

Gundersen believed Ayan had an aptitude for considered thought and reflection that many of her classmates lacked. She was able to relate what they discussed in class to her own experiences in an interesting and thought-provoking manner. She was simply on another level.

In the autumn, each pupil was to attend a parent-teacher meeting with the form teacher. Ayan came with her father. The teacher told Sadiq that Ayan was a pleasure to have in the class and that she was hardworking and well-informed. 'That's what we like to hear!' Sadiq smiled.

They resemble each other, the teacher thought. *Both of them are cheery, laugh a lot, it is obvious that they get along. Strong family ties*, he concluded.

Gundersen, who taught Norwegian, rarely gave his students creative assignments, viewing them as not particularly successful, but he sometimes allowed the pupils the freedom to write whatever they wanted. Ayan wrote a piece titled 'Journey into the Unknown.'

There were once two young girls who wanted to go out into the world and find themselves. At home they had always got everything they wanted, attended the best school, worn the newest clothes, but had never been given the opportunity to decide anything for themselves, something young women strongly desire. For a long time they had planned a trip, or rather they had planned how they were going to get away, because where they were headed they did not know. Late one summer evening, when their parents were not at home, they wrote a text message: 'Mom, Dad, we're going out for a while, don't wait up.'

The sisters came to a taxi stand. A number of handsome drivers offered them a lift, an old crone wanted to trick them, and then they met a 'peculiar man.' Finally they made it to the airport and took a flight to Turkey, a land 'west of the sun and east of the moon.' They traveled far, as far as can be, before they finally arrived. They had terrible jet lag, but they had to continue on until they saw three suns and three moons and then take a right by the abyss of lost souls. When they got there, they found their journey was at an end. Whether or not they had found themselves we do not know, but they lived there happily for the rest of their lives.

Knut Gundersen awarded her a B and wrote in green ballpoint: 'a fine story, with a lot of good points, but a rather unsatisfactory ending & some grammatical errors (you haven't quite got your dyslexia under control yet).'

He paused, pondered for a moment. Granted, the story was confused and rambling, but was it saying something else, something deeper, something he did not comprehend?

6

The Mission

That first autumn at upper secondary, Ayan was introduced to a new religious phenomenon: a Muslim youth organization based on puritanical principles. The preaching was charismatic; feelings were to be awakened, thoughts would follow, life was to be pure and true.

Islam Net held a series of lectures at Oslo University College. They began simply enough, with the Five Pillars of Islam. She knew about that, about the Prophet's life and teachings, his successors, it was familiar stuff.

But still it was exciting, the people were cool, and it felt right. Plus, there were *a lot* of cute boys there.

Over the course of the evening lectures, where girls and boys sat on separate rows of benches, a foursome developed: Aisha, Emira, Dilal, and Ayan.

Aisha was the driving force. She was energetic and engaged but could be slightly brusque, making hurtful comments. Proud and sometimes aloof, she'd adopted the habit of holding her head slightly back with her chin up when speaking to people.

In Dilal's opinion she was actually kind, just not really in tune with people's feelings, owing to the fact that from a young age she had closed herself off from her own, to protect herself from an abusive father.

Like Aisha, Emira had problems at home. Her parents had already planned her wedding. Her husband-to-be was from the countryside in Pakistan. Emira begged to get out of it, to choose a husband herself, but her parents stood firm. She asked to at least have the wedding postponed until she was finished with her studies. Her parents had gone along with that, for the time being. Emira was a dedicated student, and wanted to be a computer engineer. Her passion was soccer. She was an important player on the Holmlia team – exercised a lot and wore mostly athletic shoes and sports gear.

Dilal was a Kurd from Iran, who had lived in Iraq until the family moved to Bærum when she was small. She looked like a Middle Eastern model, with made-up almond-shaped eyes, powdered skin, and a little aquiline nose. She was hooked on exercise, mostly yoga, Pilates, and light weight lifting. She would chastise Aisha, with whom she had attended lower secondary, for eating junk food and having a *trashy* lifestyle that was ruining her skin and figure. Aisha responded that what was on the inside counted and admonished Dilal in turn for not covering her hair. Islam required it, she said. Dilal disagreed. Both of them found verses of the Koran to back up their views.

Together they all grew strong. A four-leaf clover with one stalk.

Islam Net had started out as a Facebook page two years previously, in 2008. Ten or so engineering students at Oslo University College were behind it.

The wave that gave the engineering students direction, and that they would continue to surf, was Salafism. Salafists emulate *al-salaf al-salih* – the first three pious generations after the Prophet Muhammad.

Salafism is ultraconservative, seeking radical change and looking to the past for inspiration. Islamic practice is to be built upon the foundations of Islam – upon the Koran and hadith. One should strive to follow the messages and maxims of the Prophet literally and rise above the local culture and more recent handed-down exegetical traditions. The roots of the movement are deep, but its growth worldwide has occurred in the last fifty years.

In the 1950s, Saudi Arabia began its efforts to Islamize nearby regions. Over time, the kingdom financed a global missionary network to carry out *dawa*, which means 'to invite' and is used in the sense of 'to proselytize.' The movement's mode of thought and interpretations streamed out of the Arabian desert, financed by oil money. Mosques and madrasas the world over accrued generous gifts. Stipends and scholarships to study in Mecca and Medina were granted to obedient young men.

The organizers of Islam Net did not term themselves Salafists, but said they were Muslims who were 'guided by the four major schools of Sunni Islam.' Salafism had received negative attention in the wake of the September 11 attacks, and the students wanted to avoid that label.

When their Facebook page proved a success, the engineering students decided to make a web page. They discussed the possible content.

Someone had already blazed a trail for them. Their icon was Zakir Naik, a Salafi-oriented Muslim televangelist close to the Saudi royal family. One of the students suggested that they copy the concept from his book *Answers to Non-Muslims' Common Questions About Islam*, which aimed to 'clear up misunderstandings about Islam.' Naik's speeches, which were available on YouTube, were put on Islam Net's home page. On his channel, Peace TV, the young men were discovering new preachers all the time. Their message seemed fresh, new – and true.

The students now had friends on Facebook and followers on their home page. During a conversation in the prayer room at the university, one of them suggested expanding. In order to recruit more people, they had to hold get-togethers where people could meet.

A couple hundred people attended the first gathering, where Norwegian-Pakistani Zulqarnain Madani was the guest speaker. The imam, who had studied at the University of Medina, was invited to lambaste the Dutch politician and activist Geert Wilders's film *Fitna*, but the question that caused the most debate was: Who was behind September 11? Madani argued that the attacks were planned by the Jews and the U.S. government.

After holding a handful of meetings, Islam Net swelled to several hundred paying members. The leaders wanted the organization to grow even larger and suggested that a Peace Conference would ensure this. The concept had originated in Mumbai, where for many years charismatic preachers had been awakening the Indian masses with rhetoric steeped in religious fervor.

In Norway, Islam Net illustrated a generation gap. The students were opposed to the tradition of ethnically divided mosques. When the first Muslims arrived in Norway in the 1970s, mosques were not considered a priority, as the immigrants' stay seemed destined to be short. Only during the '80s, when it became apparent most of them would be permanent residents, did the need arise. People wanted settings for the rituals of life – births, weddings, funerals – and a place to seek guidance when life proved difficult.

The older generation had used apartments, basements, and disused factory floors, consecrating them as places of worship. The mosques became venues to gather for Friday prayer and to meet one's compatriots. The students viewed their parents as having blended culture with religion, continuing to pray as they had in the Punjab or in Mogadishu. For them it was more about tradition than having a conscious attitude toward Allah. The students believed that mosques divided along national lines did little to contribute to the collective interests of Muslims. If the cultural veils of these mosques were drawn away, true religion would form the framework. Then, the students felt, Islam would stand center stage.

They were second-generation immigrants, born and raised in Norway. Some members of this generation felt outside mainstream Norwegian society and did not believe they were given the same opportunities as ethnic Norwegians. No matter how much of an effort they made, they would never be wholly accepted.

Some protested their parents' modest, traditional lifestyles by adopting a life of hedonism, with everything that went along with it and was haram in Islam. Others gave society the finger – if you don't want me, then I don't want you – and became gang members. Young men with Muslim backgrounds were overrepresented in crime statistics.

But most found an identity allowing them to stand with one foot planted in each culture, deciding which values they would take from their parents and which they would adopt from their own country of birth. Some attempted to claim their place among those seen as Norwegian through and through – first in education, then in the workplace – and succeeded. Others leaned to one side, lifted a foot, and balanced on one leg. They found Western secular values incompatible with Islam.

In the wake of the terror attacks of September 11, there were many who felt being Muslim became more difficult. Islam consti-tuted the new image of the enemy. Fear of immigrants spilled over into criticism of Islam. The need to stand together with others grew stronger. Muslim identity gained in importance.

Some teenagers stuffed all their setbacks and growing pains in the same bag: *It's because I'm a Muslim.* They believed the media were against them, that they were being met with misunderstanding and prejudice, and Western society wanted to offend them. The debate over the car-toons of Muhammad in a Danish newspaper exploded when the leaders of Islam Net were teenagers. They needed some form of defense.

Why be a second-class Norwegian when you can be a first-class Muslim?

Girls usually had stricter upbringings, and many entered traditionally male fields and enrolled in law and medical schools. Others were inspired by the revivalist wave and held the Koran aloft as an instruc-tion manual. The ideal of chaste womanhood grew in popularity, even among girls at professional schools. The hijab came into fashion.

Dilal was given none-too-subtle hints. 'You're distracting boys at the meetings,' a girl whispered to her, 'you should dress more modestly.' Dilal ignored the suggestion. Emira, on the other hand, began wearing a hijab, even while playing football. She went from sporty to Muslim sporty to just Muslim. Later that autumn she took to wearing a jilbab, also known as a Somali burqa – a covering for the head and neck that descended into a long enveloping garment. She quit the soccer team.

Joining Islam Net could be a rebellion against family traditions. The demand to marry a cousin from your homeland felt like a burden for many. Islam Net encouraged girls to choose a partner for life from the whole ummah – among all strict Muslims. Islam should serve to unite them, it shouldn't matter where their family hailed from or what nationality or ethnicity they had. In that respect, Islam Net was color-blind.

Emira was particularly receptive to the teachings on this matter. Her father had agreed to her marriage to his brother's son when the children were small, a so-called import marriage, so that one more member of the family could have a future in Norway. Her single life was nearing an end. She implored her father, she begged him. But he was unyielding. She was to do as the family said.

The computer engineer wanted to make her own choice. And she already had. She was in love, she whispered to Dilal one day.

'With who?'

'I can't tell you.'

'Enjoy it while you can,' Dilal said.

'He's gorgeous,' Emira added. 'And very religious.'

Aisha surprised her friends when she showed up at a talk in a full niqab. Only her eyes were visible.

'Brace yourself for a reaction!' Dilal said drily. 'I don't think Norway is ready for that.'

Emira quizzed her about the impracticality of being enveloped in so much material, while Ayan was fascinated. She covered only her head and wore regular clothes.

Now Aisha could see everyone and no one could see her. It made her seem even tougher, invulnerable in a way, now that she could only be heard. The niqab gave an impression of militant piety, of moral superiority.

Aisha's sharp religious shift had come after a family stay in the UK, where her father had enrolled her and her sisters in a strict Muslim school.

'You're doing your daughters a disservice. That education will render them unsuited to employment in Norway,' Ikhlaque Chan, a childhood friend who worked with integration services in Bærum, told him.

'Is that so?' Aisha's father replied, and let the girls remain at the school.

The pressure on Dilal increased. One of the leaders approached her. 'You should cover your hair,' he said, in a friendly tone.

Dilal looked up from under mascaraed lashes and affected a smile.

'I'm taking things one step at a time, bit by bit, okay?'

One evening, instructions about how they could increase the membership of Islam Net were distributed. *He who submits to Allah and proselytizes shall be rewarded by Him.*

First impressions were important. You had to alter your approach depending on whom you were talking to. If the person was a practicing Muslim, you were to stress the missionary aspect of Islam Net. 'Inform them how it is obligatory for Muslims to have a group engaging in this type of work in every society. Tell them about the rewards the job brings. Talk about our activities and the results we have achieved in so short a time. Let them know we are just students and doing this only for Allah swt and that is why we need their support. Tell them we are sacrificing a lot, that our most active members have quit their jobs and failed exams because they are dedicating so much of their time to this work.'

When it came to nonpracticing Muslims, you needed to be more persistent. 'Tell them about how the media are portraying Islam and Muslims as extremists and terrorists. How the media are giving the impression of Islam being a faith that oppresses women, and that we are working to clear up misconceptions about Islam.'

To non-Muslims, you were to say, 'We try to build bridges between different ethnic and religious groups. We work to span diverse worldviews in order to facilitate understanding and contact between people with different religious affiliations.' You were not to mention anything about sacrificing yourself, but should use words like 'equality' and 'dialogue' and invite them to come along for a chat, preferably at Islam Net's information stand on Karl Johans Gate. 'Do not make any reference to people converting,' was written on the sheet.

Ayan began with the people she knew. Ivana and Ela, the Catholic and the Protestant. She sent an identical message to both a couple of weeks before Christmas 2010: 'Hi you, a little debate that's taking place, maybe you'd like to come along?' She attached an invitation to a meeting at Islam Net.

Ivana was busy with her drama program, Ela was following her dream and had started a band with her classmates Alex and Håkon, who had been in Ayan's class all through primary and lower secondary. They were now in the music program with Ela and had big plans for their band – Kid Astray.

Ayan invited the whole band to the meetings at Islam Net. None of them went. She continued sending invites.

Håkon swiped through the material that kept on coming in on his mobile phone and mailbox. He went onto Islam Net's home page and quickly decided it was not for him. He was struck in particular by what was written about homosexuals, premarital sex, and the covering up of women. He was surprised that tough, stand-up-for-your-rights Ayan had become a member of something like that. He could not get his head around it. Alex agreed. What had happened to Ayan? Then they forgot about it, did not have time to mull it over. They were making new friends and new girlfriends, and in time the invitations from Ayan felt pretty much like spam. If anyone was Kid Astray, it was her.

At Nesbru, Ayan handed out invites in class, pinned them up on bulletin boards, and taped them onto lampposts. In spring 2011, as her first year drew to a close, she told Knut Gundersen she had joined a Muslim youth group and was wondering if some of the leaders could come to the school to give a presentation. Certainly, the form teacher replied, always happy to see pupils taking an active interest in things. 'Just ask them to e-mail me and we can work something out.'

Islam Net promptly got in touch with him to arrange a suitable time. Gundersen thought he ought to find out about the organization. He went online and the first hit he got was an article in the tabloid *VG*, accusing Islam Net of running an intolerant 'convert school' that branded those who disagreed with them as infidels. The organization had also faced criticism for inviting controversial imams accused of radicalizing young Norwegian Muslims. Gundersen continued reading.

'Islam Net is taking Norway in a dangerous direction,' warned Abid Raja, a lawyer and leader of the centrist Liberal Party. 'They want to assume ownership of how Muslims think and act.' The Norwegian Pakistani, who had been awarded the Fritt Ord freedom of speech award the same year, claimed that a number of the speakers supported the death penalty for lapsed Muslims, praised holy war, defended violence against women, and were in favor of the stoning of homosexuals. Akhtar Chaudhry, a Socialist Left Party politician and the first non-Western deputy speaker of the Norwegian Parliament, agreed: 'Young Muslims should interpret our religion in line with the democratic and humane values of Norwegian society.'

Older Muslims were skeptical. Established mosques did not welcome the growth of Islam Net. Knut Gundersen got cold feet. In addition to the two politicians' warnings about Islam Net, there was something in the tone of the e-mails he got from Islam Net that rubbed him the wrong way, that did not sit well with the open, international atmosphere of the school.

Islam Net never came to Nesbru.

7

Eating with the Devil

The Somali mothers in Bærum were dissatisfied with the Koran instruction their children were receiving. Sometimes Sadiq would give lessons, other times one of the other fathers. They taught some verses from the holy book, a little about Muhammad, a few Arab words, before letting the children go outside to play, perhaps eat a bit. It was, the mothers felt, too slapdash. *All they do is play.*

Sara and a couple of the others had learned of a popular Koran teacher from someone at the Tawfiiq Mosque in the city. They agreed to ask him to meet with them. Mustafa was young, not yet twenty years old, but already a respected and sought-after teacher. He spoke in a calm, mellow voice, came across as knowledgeable, and made the mothers feel he understood what they wanted, that he was on their side. He promised a stricter framework for the teaching. The handsome young man, who concealed the early onset of baldness beneath a prayer cap, charmed them. They decided to divide his fee among them. Money from social security, paychecks, and housekeeping budgets went into the kitty for the new Koran tutor. Classes would take place on Sundays, at their homes, on a rotational basis. The mothers would provide food but would not be involved otherwise.

Around the same time Islam Net began to develop, the fathers who'd been doing the teaching until then met the new tutor.

'Weak in Arabic grammar,' Sadiq concluded.

'Extremist,' the other father said.

But when it came to the children, Somali tradition favored the mothers' decision.

At the first lesson, Mustafa asked the youngsters to form a ring around him on the floor, boys on one side, girls on the other. A couple of the pupils grabbed cushions from the sofa. He gave them a blunt reprimand.

'This isn't about being comfortable. You're here to work hard and suffer in order to benefit in the future.'

The mothers had been right. Mustafa really was out of the ordinary. When he held forth, Islam became exciting, even appealing. He created a private place where only they were in the know, a room with space only for them. Others remained outside, unaware, uninitiated.

The Koran teacher told them about the life of the Prophet in a way that brought him to life, he taught them hadith and *iman* – belief in Allah, belief in the angels, belief in the prophets, belief in judgment day, belief in destiny.

Fate was divided into three, Mustafa explained. 'Everything that is written for you from the day you are born. Everything that happens in the Koran. The destiny you make yourself.'

His voice would put you in mind of Morgan Freeman, Ismael thought. No matter what he said, you would believe it.

Ayan made notes in round, slightly untidy writing in an exercise book: 'Intention is the foundation of every action. Three things are required for an intention to be pure: 1. Reverence for Allah. 2. Timidity toward Allah. 3. Desire for Paradise.'

To live in accordance with true Islam required that you give thought to many practical matters. They learned when you should brush your teeth and perform *wudu* – the ritual washing before prayer. In the Koran it said, according to Ayan's notes, 'You who believe, when you rise to prayer, wash your faces and your forearms to the elbows. Wipe over your heads and wash your feet to the ankles.' 'Remember the correct order,' Ayan commented in the margin. She wrote rules for visits to the lavatory, like how you should not be facing Kaaba, the sacred shrine containing the holy black stone in Mecca, while seated on the toilet. Preferably, you sit with your back toward Kaaba, but your back must not face the sun or the moon. If you inadvertently 'scratched your bottom through your clothes' or brushed against a man from outside the family, drank alcohol, smoked, came in contact with your privates, fainted, or slept, you were to cleanse yourself anew. It was important to use your right hand when eating because 'if you eat with your left hand you are eating with the devil.' Furthermore, the food eaten with the left hand gave only half the nourishment.

Mustafa hammered into them what was *halal* – permitted – and what was not, and could lose himself in detailing the punishment for the forbidden. The Juma children knew most of this from before, but some things were new to them. 'Kitchen utensils in gold or silver are not allowed!' was written on a line by itself in Ayan's exercise book. The pages were filled with exhortations and rules about what was Correct! Proper! Clean!

Sometimes Mustafa's rules for living were based on the Koran and sharia, other times on traditional belief. When one of the boys tripped over a shoe in the hallway, causing it to lie upside down, Mustafa shouted, 'Turn it over! A shoe must never lie with the sole upward!' When he was asked why, he told them you must never show the sole of your shoe to Allah. The sole is dirty, you never know what you might have stepped in. If a shoe lay that way, angels would not enter the house, leading Allah to ignore it.

Mustafa was strict about pronunciation when they read verses of the Koran, picky and exacting when it came to reading aloud Arabic words. At each session, he chose some pupils to recite the week's lesson to the others. The three Juma siblings had been fairly average when their father was teaching. Now Ayan and Leila were studying with a newfound intensity, which pleased their mother, while Ismael was beginning to lag behind, which bothered her.

As the weeks passed, the pupils were introduced to several of the
central concepts of Islam, such as the different types of holy war:
the internal *jihad al-nafs* – jihad with the soul, the struggle against
evil ideas and desires, where you strive to live as God wants; and the
external *jihad bi'l-sayf* – jihad with the sword, where you do battle
against the infidels. There was jihad against hypocrites, traitors, and
oppressive leaders. It could be waged in different ways – with the
heart, the tongue, the hand, the pen, money, or your entire being.
The highest form of jihad was to risk your life fighting.

'Those who wage this last type of jihad,' Mustafa said, 'are
allowed to sit beneath God's throne in paradise.'

Ismael began to dislike the Koran teacher. He thought he took
himself too seriously and that his wispy beard that refused to grow
looked ridiculous. Ayan and Leila's fascination grew.

Death was a major theme for Mustafa. In the texts he chose, death
was beautiful; martyrs died with a smile on their faces and a scent
of sweet musk upon them.

'We Muslims view death as the start,' he said in his dulcet voice.
Only then did life begin.

Ismael was critical. 'He's romanticizing death!' he said to his
sisters.

They united in ignoring their brother's protests. The tenets in
Ayan's notebooks were adorned with beautiful trimming. One
sentence in particular had been carefully decorated: 'The prophet
said we are instructed to kill all people until they make *Shahada* [the
Islamic declaration of faith], until they pray, and to continue until
they give *zakat* [alms], and only then to let them go.'

Ismael thought what they were learning was becoming increasingly unpleasant. He asked Mustafa, 'Do you mean you should kill
those who are not Muslims?'

'It is a quote from the Prophet,' Mustafa responded. 'It was
recounted by Abdullah bin Umar, brother-in-law of the Prophet,
and later written down. He is a reliable source.' He went on to quote
Abu Hurayra, one of the Prophet's companions: 'The people before
us asked too many questions and were opposed to their prophet.'

Ismael took this as a reprimand.

He had stopped taking notes. These men, born in the seventh century on the Arabian Peninsula, filled up the pages of Ayan's notebook but they meant absolutely nothing to him. One of them, Abdallah ibn Masud, a contemporary of the Prophet said to have resembled him, was a particular favorite of Mustafa's, and he often quoted him: 'It is not halal to spill the blood of a Muslim except in three instances . . . The married person who has committed adultery is to be flogged on Thursday, with one hundred lashes, and on Friday he or she is to be killed. He who murders, shall be killed, a life for a life. And lastly, he who forsakes Islam shall die.'

A girl asked if leaving Islam really meant death. 'I'm only quoting the close friend of the Prophet,' Mustafa replied. 'And he was quoting Muhammad. Remember! Muhammad received his revelations directly from Allah.'

'I've heard that only God can be the judge in the question of apostasy, that people cannot punish someone for leaving Islam,' the girl countered.

The teacher clarified: 'When a person commits *ridda* – abandons Islam – his blood can be shed. He can be executed according to the law, because the Prophet has said: "If somebody discards his religion, kill him."'

Ismael just wanted to get away.

Mustafa added that someone who leaves Islam is not to be washed before burial, no prayers are to be read over him, and he is not to be buried with other Muslims.

The preaching struck an ever-darkening chord. What they heard in the class echoed around their minds and took root. Withdrawal. Distance. Discord. After each lesson, they were that little bit more detached from their immediate surroundings, from Bærum.

Ayan made a note in turquoise ink on the squared paper of her notebook: 'Remember Allah DAILY! If you put your trust in Allah, you will be tested by fear, hunger, loss of wealth, injury, but those who are patient will earn a place in paradise. Their reward will be infinite.'

The walls around the room the Koran teacher had built grew thicker, the ceiling lower, the windows smaller. It was oppressive to some, appealing to others.

Ismael wanted out.

Ayan wanted to go further in.

8

Norway, Thine Is Our Devotion

All of the Juma family were by now Norwegian citizens. They had passports, voting rights, and PINs for public services. Nevertheless, their nationality was hyphenated: Norwegian-Somali.

The children had all of their schooling in Norway, had learned the national anthem, 'Norway, Thine Is Our Devotion,' and other songs espousing love for the flag and the country, such as 'Norway in Red, White and Blue,' written in response to the German occupation during the Second World War. On May 17, Constitution Day, they put on their best clothes and waved flags at the children's parade like everyone else. In 2011, Ayan sent a text message to Ela, whom she had not seen in ages. 'Hi you, happy constitution day☺'

Ela sent good wishes and a smiley face in return. She and her family were celebrating with the Chinese congregation in Oslo. Ayan and Leila had gone along with their little brothers to the local school, where Jibril was taking part in sack races, egg-and-spoon races, and a tin can toss.

Aisha had stopped celebrating National Day. There was debate on Islam Net's web pages about whether a practicing Muslim could celebrate the Norwegian Constitution, which after all was not based on sharia. Opinion was divided. According to some, it was no big deal, the Constitution was not so bad. In Aisha's view, however, it was haram to mark the national day of a Christian country, especially one whose flag was adorned with a cross.

Aisha had written an essay that was going to be published that same month. The Aschehoug publishing house had approached a number of Muslim girls, asking them to write about their life and faith for a book called *Uncovered*. Aisha Shezadi was one of the few in Norway who dressed in full niqab; the editor had found her via the debate pages on Islam Net and asked if she might consider writing something. She would. The piece was given the title 'You, me, and niqab':

'I was born and raised in Norway. If there is one thing I have learned, it is that respect, tolerance, equality, solidarity and unity are important values in Norwegian society,' Aisha wrote. 'But is it respectful when people ascribe opinions to me and associate me with something criminal? And subsequently degrade me by saying I support the oppression of women and the murder of innocent people? Accuse me of having attitudes I in no way have and tell me I am brainwashed and indoctrinated? What then of tolerance? I do not mind a lack of support or acceptance, but surely a little broad-mindedness is not too much to ask in a country that is supposed to value the thoughts and attitudes of others so highly.'

A reviewer of the book in *Dagbladet* was hesitantly positive. *Uncovered* provided 'an adequate number of new insights' to make up for 'the many passages of ruminating truisms.' With regard to Aisha's contribution, he was not convinced. 'It is obviously a political choice, a strong marker, and for those of us on the outside it is difficult to understand Aisha Shezadi when she says that "the niqab has made me happier than I ever have been."'

At the same time that people were reading and discussing Aisha's chapter, her life was falling apart around her. She wanted to run away from home. All their lives, Aisha and her sisters had seen their father beat their mother against the wall, against the furniture, and to the floor. She had been scratched, slapped, and punched, struck with belts and objects. Their father was on partial disability benefits after a car crash and was taking antidepressants. His wife, a cousin he had brought to Norway in the 1980s, was the first to suffer when his mood darkened. In time he also directed his ire at his five daughters, to whom he didn't hesitate to say he would have liked to swap for sons. They tried to avoid arousing his anger, for fear he would break things, strike out, take their mother in a stranglehold, or drag her around by her hair. Sometimes they had to throw themselves over him in order to save her.

Their mother made sure there were as few breakable objects as possible in the house, as few items of any kind, in fact, because the father could fly into a rage when he didn't find something he was looking for, so it was best to keep things tidy.

Aisha was used to hearing her father scream and shout *Whore! Dog! Pig!* at her mother. The children were told they were piglets.

By the time she was twelve, Aisha could not take any more. During a quarrel between her parents, she had stood in front of her mother to prevent her father from hitting her. He punched his eldest daughter in the face instead, pushed her out of the way, and let loose on his wife. But her daughter's protest seemed to give the mother strength. For the first time, after fifteen years in Norway, after fifteen years of abuse, she called the police. A patrol car came around. But nothing changed. The following year, while her husband pushed her to the ground, straddled her, and beat her head against the floor until she thought she would die, while her youngest daughters cried, she made up her mind that if she survived she would report him. The case went before the Mediation Service, where it was noted with regard to Aisha's father that 'he promises never to be violent to his wife again. He will try to understand her better and give her more time. He promises to refrain from swearing – in particular to abstain from references to pigs.'

But nothing changed. One evening, the father was alone with his daughters and, enraged by their bickering, began hitting one of the younger girls while shouting that it was their own fault that he beat them. The children ran to the bathroom to escape his blows but their father chased them. Aisha blocked the doorway, and he first beat her and then her sisters. Aisha's fingers got caught in the door, and were injured badly enough to require hospital treatment.

When her hand healed, she wrote the text for *Uncovered*.

Aisha had become a writer, and Ayan and Emira were rising through the ranks of Islam Net. In the summer of 2011 they were appointed to the group's organizing committee.

At the first meeting, on a hot, drowsy Wednesday in July, a handful of students sat planning the following year's big event — the Peace Conference. Who was going to speak? Where would it be held? The previous year's conference had been held at Sentrum Scene, a concert hall downtown, but holding it at such a central location was expensive. The farther out of the city you went, the cheaper the premises. On the other hand, the more central it was, the more chance of walk-ins. The first two days of last year's event had been aimed at non-Muslims, who paid no entrance fee. Islam Net was ambitious with regard to conversion of Norwegian youngsters.

Two days after the meeting of the organizing committee, a twenty-thousand-pound bomb detonated outside the government buildings in Oslo. The immediate reaction was that it was the work of Islamic terrorists. Speculation centered around al-Qaida. Two hours after the bomb went off, a blond man dressed in a police uniform shot his first victim on the island of Utøya, where the youth wing of the Labor Party was holding its summer camp. During the course of the evening, it became clear that it was not a foreign terror organization behind the attacks, but Anders Behring Breivik, a Norwegian right-wing extremist. The terrorist act resulted in the deaths of seventy-seven people.

In his manifesto, which was available online, Breivik demanded the eradication of Islam in Europe; all mosques were to be demolished, all traces of Muslim cultural heritage needed to be destroyed, and all Muslims had to either convert, be deported, or face their allotted punishment: death. Arabic, Urdu, Somali, and Farsi were to be banned, converted Muslims had to adopt Christian names, no

Muslim was to have any contact with relations in their home state if that country's population was over 20 percent Muslim, and they were not allowed to have more than two children.

In spite of his declarations of hatred of Muslims, it was the Labor Party the terrorist attacked, not a mosque or Islam Net. The powers that be were the traitors. They were the ones who had let the Muslims in. The act of terror would force them to see the error of their ways and stem the tide of Muslim immigration.

Norway was in shock. People reached out to one another.

'Hi Ela, how are you and your loved ones?!' Ayan wrote straight after the attack. The friends, who had been so close at one time, had not seen each other since lower secondary school. The circumstances that had brought them together in the immigrant gang in Gjettum had dissipated when they no longer needed one another. They had taken separate paths, developed and cultivated new sides of themselves. Sides that no longer seemed compatible.

'Hi you, I'm fine ☺,' Ela replied. 'No one I know was hurt. You?'

'Good to hear, I don't know, haven't heard of anyone I know so far.'

'Ahh, that's good!' Ela wrote. 'Hey, we have to get together soon! When is good for you?'

'Ehhhh I can meet up any day except Wednesdays and Fridays, hehe ☺'

'What about tomorrow then?'

'Good stuff, what will we do?'

'We can head over to Sandvika, buy strawberries and sit on the quay? Or go shopping?'

'Haven't been to the mall in ages but I wouldn't say no to strawberries,' Ayan said.

They arranged to meet at Ela's. The sun was shining, people were walking around wearing hardly anything.

Ela was taken aback when she opened the door. But she did not say anything other than 'Ayaaaaan!'

'Is your father home?' Ayan asked when she came inside.

Ela shook her head.

'What about your brothers?'

There was nobody else in the house. She removed all her veils and eventually she was standing in a sleeveless top and light trousers. She was drenched in sweat. Ela looked at her. Ah, it was good to see her! Both began to laugh, threw their arms around each other, and hugged.

'Remember? Allahajaja! Haram, Haram!!'

'And you laughing!'

'Islam & Black Hair forever!'

They joked and reminisced. They found their way back to the strings of their friendship. On Ela's terrace, the sun warmed parts of Ayan's body that she did not reveal to anyone, they ate sweet straw-berries, looked at each other, and laughed. The seventeen-year-olds did not get around to shopping or make it to the quay. They merely needed to be together, just like everyone else in Norway those days.

For some time, a few weeks, maybe a few months, the words 'unity' and 'love' had real meaning. But for Ayan and Ela, as for others, that solidarity would not prevail.

It was to be the last time they met.

'Unless otherwise specified, any e-mails from me require a response within twenty-four hours!'

Five days after the terror attack, the leader of Islam Net was demanding increased discipline from the organizing committee.

'Who of you have gone through all the documents I sent and asked you to read?' Fahad Qureshi inquired.

The committee was discussing how to make more money and agreed to organize a fund-raising dinner. 'Everyone must ensure they sign up five wealthy people. Nafeesa needs to make sure one hundred women attend, and Saad must get one hundred men, inshallah,' the leader demanded. His anger was due to his not being kept abreast of the marketing of a Way to Paradise event. Emira was supposed to make the invitations and Ayan was to supervise her. 'Nadia needs to make sure Ayan does her job' read the minutes of the meeting. 'Has Ayan found sisters to come to the event?

Promotion on Facebook MUST improve. There have to be seven hundred participants confirmed on Facebook by Friday.'

Ayan was assigned responsibility for poster design. 'Has the lettering for the heading been decided upon? No. Nadia needs to remember to ask Ayan about this and Ayan needs to give it thought. When you are working with events planning you have to keep your mind on the event the entire time in order to stay alert to things that need fixing.'

Fahad Qureshi was the undisputed leader of Islam Net. The student of construction engineering ruled the organization like an Arabian kingdom – where he, together with his brother, made all the important decisions. Other family members had central roles; Fahad's wife, Madia, was queen of the women at court. Democracy was nonexistent, total loyalty expected.

This authoritarian style did not suit everybody. There were those who attended a couple of meetings, had a taste, found it unappealing, and disappeared. But more people were flocking to the organization than leaving it. Within the space of a few years, Islam Net had become the most important Salafist movement in Norway and claimed to have two thousand paid-up members. The goal was to be even bigger.

The committee was planning an event to recruit more girls. 'When can Ayan get the flyers designed?' the leader asked. 'Ayan needs to ask me to send her the logo for Islam Net. We need ten sisters to work on fund-raising. Ayan has to find these but they have to be approved by Madia because it is of the UTMOST importance that they understand the job 100%.' Ayan put four exclamation marks in the margin beside this last point.

A week prior to the beginning of the school term, Fahad tightened the reins: 'The minutes of meetings are to be sent out to everyone the same day the meeting takes place. Ayan needs to remember this. Meetings are mandatory. If one person does not show up it is detrimental to the group as a whole. If this were a paying job everyone would turn up on time. We are doing this for Allah and it is more important than paid work.'

Fahad was not pleased with ticket sales. 'Ayan was responsible for recruiting sisters and for promotion online. Ayan, do we have ten sisters to work on fund-raising?'

Summer ushered in a change in Ayan's style of dress. She showed up for the first class of the new term in dark clothing that covered her from head to toe.

The American-educated economics teacher presumed her parents were putting pressure on her. As soon as the opportunity arose, she asked her.

'Why are you dressing like this? Why black? Why brown? Why not green or blue or pink?'

'Ah, my mother says the same thing!' Ayan replied.

The teacher was surprised by her answer. Was the mother not the one responsible for her covering up? Surely the parents must be behind it. In Somali culture, Ayan would have been considered marriageable for some time. Ayan had caught the teacher's eye in the hallways the year before, because she thought Ayan was so stylish in her colorful shawls and modern jeans. She had admired how her head scarves always matched whatever she was wearing.

One day Ayan showed up wearing all black.

'Is everything all right?' the teacher inquired.

'I'm going to the mosque, it's Friday,' Ayan answered.

The teacher took her aside and asked, 'Does your mother wear this?'

'No, but she soon will,' Ayan replied. 'And my sister already does.'

Ayan then asked if it would be possible for her to leave a little early in order to make it to prayers. A request she from now on would make every Friday.

Her parents were called in for a meeting. Sadiq showed up alone.

'What exactly is going on?' the teacher asked.

Ayan's attire was not the only thing that concerned her. She seemed to have stopped doing schoolwork entirely. She was not delivering assignments and was showing up to class unprepared. The International Baccalaureate program required pupils to put in a lot of work on their own time, the economics teacher stressed.

Sadiq was surprised. He had not been aware of this. It seemed to him that Ayan was busy with schoolwork all the time. He apologized, admitting he was perhaps too preoccupied with his own studies. He was studying to be an engineer, he added.

The teacher looked at him sternly. Pupils needed to apply themselves. She herself had gotten where she was through strict self-discipline.

Ayan spent most of her time on the computer in her room, Sadiq went on.

'Yeah, exactly, she has the computer on in class too,' the teacher exclaimed.

At times she had to go over to Ayan and close it. 'There's nothing on there of relevance to this class!' she had told her once when Ayan had an Islam Net web page open.

The minutes of the next organizing committee meeting warned of an even more rigid regime.

'Madia and I have experienced communication problems with the committee. People are not answering e-mails, are not taking responsibility and things are not getting done. This cannot go on if we are to reach the goals we have for Islam Net.' Fahad Qureshi emphasized that the committee was supposed to operate as the right hand of the board. He had hit upon an idea. 'As of today we are implementing a system of fines. Every assignment will have a deadline and failure to carry it out within the time limit will incur a penalty. Everyone needs to respond to e-mails from me and the other board members within 24 hours or face a fine. Status reports have to be sent in before 3 a.m. on Saturday every week. If they are late there will be a fine and deadline number two is Sunday at noon. Fine number one will be 100 kroner and fine number two 200 kroner, a total of 300 kroner if neither deadline is met. A new deadline and fresh fine will be determined in each individual case.'

Sanctions were the new whip.

There were only a handful of rank-and-file members on the committee, so each individual had a lot resting on his or her shoulders.

Ayan was assigned the task of directing fund-raising for the Peace Conference 2012. She was given a deadline of two weeks to collect 50,000 kroner and place advertisements in two local newspapers, send in the logos, and get contracts with a mobile phone company signed. The committee was still looking for somewhere to hold the conference. Unfortunately many of the places had the 'drawback of not being allowed to actively separate men and women.'

Emira was given the job of applying for public funding for the conference. 'By next Wednesday she needs to have found relevant subsidies and started on the application process as well as learned how to keep accounts,' the minutes stated.

At the end of September, Ayan received her first fine. She had failed to place an advertisement in one of the local newspapers and the minutes drily recorded: 'Deadline not met, Ayan fined 100 kroner, has this been paid?'

The committee was planning an event involving the Egyptian preacher Fadel Soliman. Its aim was to improve Islam Net's missionary work. 'Presentation skills, public speaking skills, presenting Islamic beliefs & rituals, questions of non-Muslims' would all be looked at. Admission was free for members of Islam Net. 'Fahad organizes brothers to volunteer, Ayan organizes sisters,' the minutes stated.

Soliman was controversial. He had said that it was 'fine to hit a wife who doesn't please you.' A slap was okay, as was a stick, a small stick, mind you. His views were acceptable as far as Islam Net was concerned, but the leader was not happy with the preparations for his visit. 'Ayan was to arrange sisters to work. Madia needs to know who they are beforehand, not on the day itself. She also feels the people Ayan *has* gotten hold of are not competent. Ayan is fined due to my not receiving a list of the forums Emira has promoted the event on. New deadline: tomorrow!'

The form teacher noticed that Ayan was wearing a new ring, a thin band of golden metal, which she fidgeted with in class. Was it an engagement ring? The teacher called her parents in again. Her father came.

'What are your plans for Ayan?'

When Sadiq hesitated, the teacher spoke plainly. 'Are you marrying her off?'

'Nononono,' Sadiq replied, adding, 'We are not radicals.'

The thought that they were extremists had not crossed the teacher's mind; she was merely concerned that they were pressuring Ayan
into a cloistered, traditional woman's role.

As autumn went on, the teacher found herself driven to distraction by Ayan's failure to pay attention in class. One morning she was
explaining the concept of supply and demand in economics when she
noticed Ayan's lips moving rapidly and silently while her fingers counted
invisible prayer beads. She had a contemplative look in her eyes.

The teacher slammed her hand down on Ayan's desk. 'You cannot
do this in front of me!'

It was not the first time she had told Ayan to refrain from praying
during lessons. In addition to viewing it as an affront, it ruined her
concentration and demonstrated a lack of respect. She asked Ayan
to leave the classroom if she wanted to pray.

The following day the teacher decided it was time for a serious
chat. She wanted to find out what exactly was going on in her pupil's
life. The teacher inquired about the lack of effort Ayan was putting
into her schoolwork.

'You are so far behind! The whole year will be wasted. Pull yourself together,' she implored.

The program was demanding. Perhaps Ayan wanted to transfer to the normal course of study to have a chance of making up
lost ground?

'I'll think about it,' Ayan replied.

It was early November and morning frost lay white over Bærum
as the first class of the day was starting. Ayan was wrapped in several
layers of clothing, both on top of and beneath her cloak. When she
tried to remove the outer layer, the shawls bunched up, trapping her
arms over her head. A classmate came to her aid and Ayan eventually
managed to remove what she was trying to take off and pull back
down what she wanted on.

'Why are you wearing all that stuff?' a boy asked.

'Because I want people to see my intellect, not my body,' Ayan answered.

'Why shouldn't they see your body?' he asked.

'Because you should be interested in my brain.'

'In that case, you better start putting it to use, so there is something to get to know there!' the economics teacher quipped.

That was Ayan's last day at Nesbru.

9

This Outfit

BE THE CHANGE YOU WISH TO SEE IN THE WORLD.

The quotation, wrongly attributed to Mahatma Gandhi, stood in black letters on the wall inside the door of Dønski Upper Secondary School. Beside it was a quote from Monty Python: *Always look on the bright side of life.*

'Welcome' was written in several languages with different characters and alphabets next to posters warning of the dangers of drug use. From the entry, a stairway led to the second floor, where there were classrooms and the library at one end and the principal's office and staff rooms at the other. A glass door divided the corridor in between. It had previously been left open, until a pupil had helped himself to teachers' handbags, mobile phones, and laptops, whereupon a lock with a key card and code had been fitted.

This was Ayan's new school.

In early November 2011, Ayan had notified the counselor at Nesbru that she wanted to transfer to Dønski. All her friends were there, she said.

From the train station close to the school she could get into Oslo city center in just a half hour. She was quick to adjust. The academic standards at Dønski were lower, routines more lax. That freed up more time for Islam Net.

By late November the tasks assigned by Islam Net had piled up. 'Ayan was to go around shops in Oslo to find sponsorships. Was this done as of the last meeting? If not a fine is imposed. If not done by today that means another fine. There is very little time left until the final date for funding and Ayan has not managed to put a single sponsor in place, has this been carried out? If not she is fined.'

On her own copy of the minutes, Ayan wrote: 'Talk to Madia!!!' and 'Get in touch with Madia! Ask Fahad!'

Under the heading *Miscellaneous*, the minutes read: 'The deadline for payment of fines is one week after they have been issued. Fine and new deadline of tomorrow for those who have not sent in the reports from courses in which they have participated.' The minutes ended: 'Have all of you paid each of your fines?'

On Sundays, Koran school in Bærum continued.

Mustafa's worldview was similar to Islam Net's. Living a pure life was impossible if you got caught up in Norwegian society, with all its decadence and immorality. A Western lifestyle meant nightclubs, drugs, and sex. It led straight to hell.

The leaders of Islam Net indulged in the same rhetoric. 'Norwegians are bored from Monday to Friday, the weekend comes as a release and is filled with drunkenness and wild sex,' Fahad Qureshi told an audience of teenagers. Most Norwegians suffer from depression, he claimed, and 'the more preoccupied we become with this world, the more depressed we get.'

In order to find salvation, you had to live according to the rules of Islam, as strictly interpreted by Sunni Islam. That meant women covering up, not shaking hands with men, avoiding eye contact, and never being alone with a man who was not a family member, because then the devil was always present.

The Koran lessons were sometimes held in the home of the Juma family; then Ismael found it difficult to skip them. The more his sisters got caught up in Mustafa's outlook on life, the more repelled he became. He found the undertones of the Koran teacher's tirades troubling. Mustafa was promoting terror groups, 'sponsored by Mom and the other mothers,' Ismael said to Ayan. The Koran teacher paid tribute to the sacrifice of those involved. *God would approve. Martyrdom is beautiful.*

Ismael asked him straight out if he supported al-Qaida. Mustafa would not answer.

'What about the terrorist group al-Shabaab?' Ismael asked.

Mustafa offered a cryptic reply. 'I have nothing bad to say about them.'

Ismael was appalled and told his mother that the teacher refused to condemn these terror organizations.

'You must have heard wrong,' was all Sara said. She shooed her son away, thinking he was only trying to wangle his way out of the Sunday lessons.

Sara did not care for al-Shabaab. But she had respect for authority and had made her mind up that she liked the Koran teacher.

Mustafa, in Ismael's view, was pushing his pupils, the youngest of whom was around twelve years old, into the camp of hatred. He was creating an image of the enemy and reinforcing the idea of mistrust in their minds: The media were in league with security institutions in the West, which were in cahoots with those whose goal was to destroy Islam.

'I need to find out if I can trust you all,' the Koran teacher said one day. 'Let's say that I've done something against the West, and the CIA or FBI comes to get me. I've hidden in that closet over there and the agents enter the room fully armed and ask you, "Where is Mustafa? Where is he?" Would you tell them where I am?'

The youngsters looked at him mutely, some of them shook their heads.

That did not suffice.

'Put up your hand! Put up your hand if you would tell them I was in the closet!'

No one raised a hand. Not even Ismael. He could not be bothered.

*

Aisha had become Norway's first niqab-wearing celebrity, a voice worth listening to. Her contribution to the *Uncovered* anthology had attracted the interest of Association !Read, a state-funded organization whose aim was to promote reading and literacy among children and adolescents; they sent out texts from the anthology to secondary schools and offered to facilitate visits from the authors. Aisha accepted the invitations that came. If she managed to convert anyone on the tour, which was sponsored by the Norwegian Non-Fiction Writers and Translators Association, it would get her lots of *ajr* – extra points in heaven.

Criticism was not long in coming. The outfit is political, Professor Kjell Lars Berge of the University of Oslo claimed, and not an existential or private choice.

'It testifies to a religious conviction that is extreme and connected to a political program leaning in a Fascist direction. We know well what these groups represent and it has no place in the classroom,' he told *Klassekampen* newspaper in January 2012.

In protest, the author Morten Skårdal returned a prize he had been awarded by Association !Read. The culture editor of the *Bergens Tidende* newspaper, Hilde Sandvik, drew a parallel between Aisha Shezadi and the right-wing extremist Anders Behring Breivik, and claimed that supporters of the talks in the schools were legitimizing violence. Her colleague in Norway's newspaper of record, *Aftenposten*, Knut Olav Åmås, warned against equating the niqab with extremism. 'Should a niqab-wearing Norwegian youth from Bærum be prevented from touring schools because nearly everyone hates what she stands for? No.' He asserted that society needed more openness and debate after the terrorist attacks of July 22, 2011, as a strategy against those forces that did *not* want either of those things.

The tour of schools had not drawn much attention until Aisha had expressed support for the Taliban's attacks on Norwegian soldiers. Beneath a photograph of an international coalition soldier and a Taliban fighter on her Facebook page she wrote: 'No matter how much equipment they have they will never eliminate the lions of Allah.' She encouraged people to protest, and on another Facebook event page titled 'Demonstration: Norwegian soldiers out of Afghanistan,' she wrote, 'Inshallah, the demo will be a success . . . the more attention it attracts the better – it will mean more people pay attention and we inshallah can show what we are good for.' On a discussion thread supporting the introduction of sharia in Norway, she wrote, 'What is the point of democracy anyway when we have sharia?'

The main speaker at the demonstration was Arfan Bhatti, a charismatic man in his midthirties, with deep-set dark eyes, a long beard, and agile steps. He was of medium height, broad shouldered, and feared for his aggressiveness. After serving several prison sentences for acts of violence, he had drifted from the criminal underworld into the group of extremist Islamists, reinventing himself as an emir, a Muslim commander.

'The people of Norway need to know that their security is in danger as long as Norway has soldiers in Afghanistan. This is not a threat. It is a warning for your own good!' Arfan Bhatti shouted to the assembled demonstrators. This de facto leader of the Islamists, a man who mixed newly learned hadiths with street slang, said the country was at war with Islam and therefore with all Muslims. He called Norwegian soldiers terrorists and promised revenge.

Aisha, in her niqab outside the Parliament building that January day, approved of what she heard and what she saw.

This outfit was unequivocally political.

10

It's All About the Heart

On December 25, 2011, Ayan turned eighteen. She could obtain a passport, apply for a credit card, order things online, qualify for a driver's license, and vote. The school could no longer contact her parents with any concerns they had, as attendance was now her own responsibility.

In January she opened a Twitter account. Her debut of 140 characters was a quotation by a man her Koran teacher often referred to, Muhammad al-Tirmidhi: 'Know that victory comes with patience, relief with affliction, and ease with hardship.'

Ayan's profile, in contrast with Aisha's, contained nothing hateful or extreme. She posted links to interviews and talks, such as one in which the American journalist Glenn Greenwald spoke of how meaningless the terms 'terror' and 'terrorism' were, and she wrote, 'The U.S. is kicking out 1000 immigrants a day. Not bad for a people who stole the land in the first place.'

She was interested in her own African identity. 'Being black is not easy *wallahi* [I swear to God]! How the world is against black people at times!! I praise Allah for Islam.' She added, 'Especially in countries like Norway! But Alhamdulillah for Islam!'

*

The Arab Spring was entering its second year. It was a year since the Tunisian dictator Ben Ali had fled to Saudi Arabia in the wake of mass demonstrations. Hosni Mubarak was in prison in Cairo, and a few months earlier Muammar Gaddafi had been dragged from a drainage pipe, beaten bloody, sodomized with a bayonet, and shot in the head before his corpse was placed on display at a militia head-quarters in Misrata until the stench made them remove him.

In Syria, Bashar al-Assad was still in power. Ayan followed developments from afar, waging jihad with her heart, tongue, and keyboard. 'Ugliest dog in the world dies – what a misleading title, I thought they finally killed Bashar,' she tweeted in March 2012.

Western leaders declined to support the Syrian uprising as they had backed Libya's. They sat on the fence when the Assad regime attacked peaceful demonstrators, and when the demonstrators took up arms they were left to fend for themselves. An intervention in Syria would involve an entirely different set of challenges. The Syrian military was far stronger and possessed advanced Russian-produced antiaircraft systems. In addition, the regime was supported by Iran, and any intervention would motivate Iran to assist Assad more directly and further undermine American interests in Iraq, in turn jeopardizing Iran's continuing involvement in the negotiations for a deal regarding their nuclear program. It was simply not worth it.

Western leaders turned a blind eye as the first foreign fighters from Europe entered the theater of war. For a time they were viewed as something akin to aid workers and freedom fighters. Although a few enlisted in the Free Syrian Army in the hope of introducing democracy to the country, most were jihadists and joined al-Qaida's Syrian branch.

With Islam Net's Peace Conference approaching, Ayan's activity on Twitter intensified. As a member of the organizing committee, she exchanged text messages with several of the speakers. The tone was personal and confident; she usually addressed them as *akhi* – my brother. The conference was the highlight of the year for the young Salafists. It was to open at the start of Easter week, when most Norwegians were packing their rucksacks and heading to the mountains.

At Ekeberghallen, an indoor sports arena just south of Oslo city center, where the organizing committee had eventually managed to land a good deal, two entrances were planned, one for boys, one for girls. There would be segregated rest areas where samosas, cakes, and soft drinks could be purchased.

At a table in the women's section, some of the girls Ayan had recruited were to distribute dawa literature. Books that had been sent by a publisher in Egypt were handed out free of charge. There were pink brochures on 'Women's Rights in Islam – respected, honored, cherished,' peppered with quotations from the Koran, mostly framed in hearts: 'And the male is not like the female. Does not the one who created you know?' Still, men and women needed each other. 'They are clothing for you and you are clothing for them.'

Ayan and Leila skipped school to be at the opening on Friday morning. Easter fell late, it was already the end of April. Crocuses and tulips were in bloom in the gardens of the villas in Bærum, the cherry trees blossoming. Ayan took a picture of a lustrous birch tree against a bright blue sky on a verdant slope and posted it on Twitter: 'Cause after every rainfall a rainbow must come! #springinnorway #alhamdulillah!'

The sisters got on the bus in Bærum wearing long black dresses. They put on niqabs before arriving at the square in front of Oslo Central Station, where they boarded the bus that would take them to Ekeberg. The closer they got to their stop, the more people in similar attire got on the bus. They were all going the same way: *fi sabil Allah* – God's way.

The sisters bypassed the women's queue; after all, Ayan was a member of the organizing committee. Behind tables at the entrance where you checked in and were given a stamp sat the girls she had recruited to work Admission.

The seats slowly filled up, boys in front, girls at the back. Youngsters made their way, alone or in groups, to the back of the hall to pray. White athletic shoes, high-heeled pumps, boots, and sandals were removed, while they washed. They bowed in prayer – *There is no God but God, and Muhammad is his messenger* – before returning to fill up the rows of chairs.

After several hours, due to the lengthy, detailed registration process, Fahad Qureshi welcomed everyone. He was wearing a tight-fitting dark suit and a white shirt. Atop his head he wore a *kufi* – a brimless prayer cap. According to *sunna*, the teachings of Muhammad, the kufi went back to the time of the Prophet. Fahad's was striped.

The Norwegian Pakistani basked in the limelight and the glory of the big names soon to take the stage. The purpose of the weekend was to convey the true message in order to stem fear, prejudice, and hatred. Perhaps the tragedy of the right-wing July 22 terror attacks could have been avoided, he suggested, if society had more knowledge of Islam?

People were freezing. The hall was ice-cold. Girls drew shawls and cloaks tighter around them. Some wore niqabs, most merely hijabs in a variety of styles: leopard print, gold, glitter, striped, baby pink, earth tones. Covering up and bling were in no way incompatible.

The big name was the British convert Abdur-Raheem Green. He had been born in Tanzania, where his father had worked as a colonial administrator. He spent his childhood in Catholic boarding schools before opening the Koran at age twenty-four and subsequently converting.

Dressed in a long beige tunic, Green resembled a Viking right out of central casting: tall, powerfully built, with pale blue eyes and an impressive blond beard. He was banned from speaking in Canada, denied entry to Australia, as well as barred from the Emirates stadium, home of Arsenal F.C., for statements such as 'Muslims and Westerners cannot live peaceably together' and that 'to die while fighting jihad is one of the surest ways to paradise and Allah's good pleasure.' He had been caught on camera at Hyde Park Corner in London shouting for a man wearing a Jewish kippa on his head to be removed: 'Why don't you take the *Yahudi* over there far away so his stench doesn't disturb us?'

Islam Net deemed his views acceptable. His lecture was titled 'Empty Hearts, Crazy Lives.'

'Let's look at the nature of the heart,' he said, after uttering the customary Islamic greetings. 'A piece of flesh. The Prophet, peace be upon him, said when this piece of flesh is sound, the whole body is sound. When it is corrupt the whole body is corrupt.'

What the heart contained came out through the mouth. 'You've heard the expression *You are what you eat*. If you keep eating rubbish for long enough, you'll become rubbish and you'll become so addicted to rubbish, you can't even eat anything else.' People had become like rats, feeding themselves junk food. And that meant, Green was keen to stress, you were not getting the nutrition you needed, that your soul needed – God.

The heart hungered to know Allah, to obey Allah, to worship Him, adore Him. This was what gave life to the heart. 'You need to look inside your heart, examine yourself. What motivates me, what is the purpose? Is it because I want fame? To get my picture taken? The admiration? Being seen on Facebook?'

While he was speaking, people in the back rows were chatting and children were playing. Green did not let this affect him, however, and began listing all the things that were detrimental.

'Music fills your heart, it does, it fills it. You feel happy for a bit while you're listening to music, but when it's gone, when you're alone, your iPod broken, then you realize how empty your heart is. It's the same with movies, it's the same with recreational sex, it's just a way to fill the empty heart. I need something to distract me, marijuana, acid, coke, heroin, alcohol, the same thing.' The results of this were increased promiscuity, alcoholism, drug addiction, violence, depression, suicides.

Fortunately, there was a cure.

'Read the Koran! This is a book that Allah has sent down so that we can know Him! Pray! Pray with your heart! Understand what you are saying. *Allahu Akbar!* What does that mean? It doesn't mean God is great, no, God is the greatest, no. It literally means *Allah is greater*. It's almost an unfinished thought. Whatever you can think of, Allah is *greater*.'

He had been speaking continuously for almost an hour. It was time for questions from the floor. A young man asked Green how he knew that Allah was the only proper thing to fill the heart with.

'That's the nature God gave to the heart . . . How do we know Islam is true? . . . The Koran teaches us that this universe has a creator and this creator is unique, the creator is not like the creation and not one thing in the creation is similar to the creator. Nothing in the universe is similar to God.'

There was a system and logic to the universe. Like an iPad. It was created. It did not merely come about through a series of random events, by things being thrown around, shaken and mixed. 'Although Christianity has a similar concept of God, Christianity confuses this by saying that Jesus is God. That doesn't make sense. It is not rational.'

When the boys finished posing their questions, the girls were allowed their turn. One of them stood up. 'I've seen Muslims fill their hearts with hate, seen them kill one another, Salafists have attacked Sufi mosques while shouting about how they will get to paradise and eat with the Prophet. How can we prevent the hatred spreading between Muslims? How can we prevent the heart being filled with hate instead of love when we get rid of the rubbish?'

Green replied that it was a good question and one his talk on Sunday would answer.

'Any more questions?' he asked.

Another girl spoke up. In the wake of the terror attacks on July 22, songs had played an important part in the grieving process and in bringing people together. Were songs also haram? she wondered.

Green did not know what she meant, so she had to elaborate. Could not songs create unity and harmony as opposed to what he had said about music creating empty hearts? Green still did not understand what she was referring to. Nervously, she repeated the question for the third time, again making reference to the terror attacks in Oslo, of which the speaker declared his utter ignorance.

He still answered the question. 'Some may say scientists have proven that a glass of red wine a day actually makes you more healthy, it is full of antioxidants and has health benefits,' but the harm, he said, far outweighed the benefits. It was the same with music. 'Music may have some therapeutic benefit,' but that did not make up for all the harm that came with it.

Ayan listened when she had time. There were things to take care of. She was up there now, rubbing shoulders with the leadership. A person of note in Islam Net. She swept graciously around the hall, disappearing into the women's section. Reemerged, straightened up.

Aisha and Emira also had tasks to carry out during the Peace Conference. Ayan had added Dilal's name to the list of volunteers, but the Kurdish girl was rejected by Madia when she turned up. 'If you want to play any part in our organization, you'll have to cover up,' she said. Those were the rules. Dilal insisted the hijab was not obligatory in Islam. Queen Madia had no interest in a debate and asked Dilal to find a seat in the hall.

Exquisitely dressed and made up, she sat as an ordinary member of the audience while her friends filled important positions in long tunics and head scarves.

When Dilal went over to them at a break and said that Madia was 'pigheaded,' Aisha held up her palm. 'You can't say that! You can't use the word "pig"! And certainly not about a Muslim.'

Dilal shrugged, she was used to Aisha telling her off.

The lectures were to continue after the break. The hall had finally begun to warm up. Emira was anxious and keeping an eye on the men's entrance door. She had told Dilal whom she was in love with, a man she was meeting in secret.

'He's coming later. Or maybe tomorrow. I'll tell you when I see him, but I can't talk to him here.'

He was Pakistani, she whispered. 'He's called Arslan.'

Dilal shrugged. 'Who is he?'

His name was Arslan Maroof Hussain, but he had recently changed it to Ubaydullah, which meant 'Allah's little slave' – the one who submits to God. The sweet-faced man, a former football referee, worked for the toll road company in Oslo but dreamed of being a full-time Islamist.

The final speaker on Friday evening was one of Ayan's favorites, Moroccan-born Riad Ouarzazi from Canada. The tone of their communications on Twitter was flirtatious. She hinted that she might be too busy to catch his lectures.

'Why? Are you planning to come in late to some of my events????' the preacher replied.

'So do you have a punishment for being late ready?!' Ayan asked, to which he quickly responded, 'not in this type of event.' Ayan answered: 'I am one of the leaders for the event, so hopefully no, it would be fun to see live ☺'

She made it, of course, and took pictures of him onstage that she posted along with the text: 'The Sheikh in action!'

Ouarzazi lowered and raised his voice as though in a memorized dance; he shouted, whispered, smiled, and hissed. 'The angels are here, right here, they come down and surround us. If we were to see them we would faint.'

The lecture was about mercy. 'One day the Prophet was crying so Allah sent Gabriel to ask him, oh Prophet of Allah, why are you crying? The Prophet said *Ummati, ummati*, my people, my people, I want Allah to save my people.'

Ouarzazi fought back tears as he related what God had commanded the archangel: 'Go and tell him we shall please him and please his people!'

The eyes of the young people in the audience, however, were dry. They had, after all, grown up in Norway, where public displays of emotion were not commonplace.

The speaker lowered his head, concentrating as he approached the high point: Muhammad on his deathbed, accompanied by his wife Aisha. 'Now the Prophet is sixty-three years old. Gray hair.' His voice failed him again.

He concluded with a declaration of love to Muhammad and asked if the young people in the audience loved the Prophet as much as he did.

'Do you love him? Do you really? How much do you love him? How much are you willing to sacrifice for him?' he called out.

Ayan took photographs of the weeping preacher and posted them on Twitter. He had dried up and wrote a terse reply saying they were kind of blurry.

A group of men turned up toward the end of the three-day conference. They were dressed in traditional Salafi garb: short, wide trousers ending just above their ankles, and *qamis* – tunics – as the Prophet was said to have worn. They sported beards but no mustaches, because the Prophet had said that no hair must touch the mouth. Some of them wore *keffiyehs* – Arabic scarves worn around the neck and head.

The men had checkered pasts. A number had been in gangs and some had criminal records, while others had grown up under the supervision of Child Welfare Services.

One of them was Hisham Hussain Ahmed, who had attended Dønski a few years before Ayan. Together they had manned Islam Net's dawa stand on Karl Johans Gate, the main street in Oslo, where Ayan had approached nonbelievers and Muslims of varying degrees of faith according to the instruction sheet they had been issued. Smiling broadly in the pedestrian area, she had tried to give people a taste of Islam, while Hisham had stood watching for the most part, lacking the courage to engage with people directly, content to merely hand out brochures. They had also met clambering up and down ladders stocktaking for IKEA, a work detail Islam Net had organized to raise funds. They had hit it off.

Hisham had arrived in Norway in 2003, three years after Ayan. While she had been flown in as part of a UN family reunification program, Hisham had traveled alone from Eritrea. He gave his age as thirteen upon arrival, was registered as an underage asylum seeker, and was placed with a foster family in Bærum. He quickly made friends and spent his time playing football. They had never had a more harmonious foster child, the family said.

After a year in the reception class, and after completing lower secondary, he was accepted on the sports program at Dønski. He was a skillful football player, a talented athlete on the whole, in fact, and had the biggest, whitest smile in the class. In a school photograph from Dønski, he is lying across the girls' laps, like a mascot.

What he had not told the authorities when he arrived was that his family was in Oslo. He had uncles and cousins living in the city. He led two lives. One in Bærum, one with his uncles.

He had changed since Ayan saw him at the IKEA fund-raiser. His beard was longer. His features were hard where before they had been soft. He wore the clothes of the Prophet. Something else had changed, she discovered: his civil status. Hisham had married.

It was time for the concluding lecture. The theme was the day of judgment.

'Dear brothers and sisters,' Muhammad Abdul Jabbar began. He was the leader of a large missionary organization in Birmingham.

The end is near! was the message. Earth would break up and be smashed to pieces, the oceans would burn, people would try to escape but there would be nowhere to hide. The stars would be extinguished and fall from the sky, darkness would descend as the universe reached its end. Everyone would perish prior to resurrection to face God's judgment.

Ayan had set up a profile on YouTube where she posted links to websites and religious channels. Jabbar's speech, 'The Soul of a Believer,' had the same message as the one he conveyed at the Peace Conference: 'These are dark times, there is no denying. The end is near!'

The special effects showing the apocalypse were Hollywood inspired. There were thunder, lightning, flames, people burning, screaming, and falling before the deep voice of the preacher resounded: 'Is this the end? No, it's just the beginning . . . ' The angel of death will appear, flames coming from his eyes, his nostrils, his mouth, to take the sinners with him. Behind him an abundance of angels will stand with glowing faces and bouquets of flowers in their hands to welcome the chosen ones.

Those who had obeyed Allah and lived a life subject to his rules would be raised up. Because God had said, 'They who believe and do righteous deeds – those are the companions of paradise.'

The others would be destroyed: 'The drug dealers. Pimps. The wine dealers. Junkies. Crackheads.' All of them would go down, but others as well. The men who fooled women, who made women do things they did not want to do. Those who did not pray, who did not fast. The adulterers. The ones who stole, lied, and killed! No one would escape judgment. Unbelievers would die as unbelievers. An agonizing punishment awaited them, and they would have no one to help them. Because God had said, 'If anyone seeks a religion other than Islam, it will never be accepted, and in the next world he will be among the losers.'

The omens for the approaching day of judgment stood written in the Koran. These signs included a proliferation of murders and killings, oppressive world leaders, almost everyone drinking wine, and children making decisions instead of their parents. In addition, people would stop believing in God and begin to believe in the stars, song and music would be everywhere, suicide and death wishes would be commonplace, time would move quickly, and false prophets would appear.

The next portents would be great earthquakes, one in the east, one in the west, as well as one in Arabia, which, according to the Prophet, was the center of the world. A wind would blow across the whole of the globe, the sun would rise in the west, and there would be a great fire in Yemen. Once these signs appeared, repentance and conversion to Islam would no longer be possible. By then it would be too late.

Jabbar was reaching the end of his talk. The Muslims of the world were appalled at Western culture, he thundered. Role models like Lady Gaga, Snoop Dogg, and 50 Cent had taken the place of the Prophet. He urged those in the audience to do as al-salaf al-salih – the true believing forefathers – and invest in akhirah, life after death. A perfect segue into the money collection. Buckets were passed around. Donating money to Islam Net was an 'investment for Allah's sake' and would give extra points on the day of judgment, the audience was reminded.

'For those of you who are not members, you'll find registration forms on the floor beneath your chairs. You can fill them in and pay at the tables over there!' boomed a voice throughout the hall.

The collection turned into an auction, where you raised your hand depending on the sum you wanted to donate. It was important to stake money on paradise while still in this world, one of the preachers who had been flown in called out. Alms would wash away sins and help against illness. Words of warning and blame were called out.

The bearded men in the clothes of the Prophet had already left. They raised money for their own causes and some of them were often seen with collection boxes at the metro station in Grønland and outside the mosques. Emergency aid, they said. For the children in Syria. And for the widows.

The differences between these rougher-looking types and the leadership of Islam Net could appear slight from a purely religious point of view. They all wanted a society based on sharia, all believed in the day of judgment, and all laid claim to follow the Prophet. The style of dress differed, but what set them apart was something far more important. Where Islam Net followed the Prophet's instruction to spread the word, those who had left the hall wanted to go in the footsteps of warrior Muhammad and conquer the world by the sword – jihad bi'l-sayf.

What set them apart was the belief in violence.

11

Valentine's Ummah

Aisha was having a rough time.

When criticism rained down in the Norwegian media, she was left on her own to weather the storm. She wanted Islam Net to back her up in the niqab debate and had approached Fahad Qureshi for support. That was something the board would have to consider, he replied.

It took time.

Aisha had told him about being assaulted by a man, one of those motionless, statuelike men painted gold who stand on the street and hardly blink. She had been walking past him by Parliament, when he had suddenly reached out and pulled off her veil.

The board was in favor of women wearing the niqab in public, both in school and in the workplace, but was now the right time to pursue the issue? And was Aisha the right one to front it?

Aisha had a tendency to be brusque, not a quality held in high regard by the board. She was subservient to God alone, not men in general. Feminism was, in her words, about 'fighting for the right to cover up.' The niqab served as protection against the world; it was not about her letting someone else make decisions for her.

Islam Net was also uncomfortable with the powerful rhetoric the former extortionist Arfan Bhatti had used in the speech he'd

given at the demonstration against Norwegian military engagement. The group was further distressed by a video that had been
made to promote the rally, a video that Aisha had shown support
for. The director was Bastian Vasquez, born to parents of Chilean
ancestry in Skien, a couple of hours' drive south of Oslo. The short,
slightly overweight, but strong convert had made a video about the
Norwegian forces in Afghanistan, featuring footage of Crown Prince
Haakon, Prime Minister Jens Stoltenberg, and Foreign Minister
Jonas Gahr Støre, followed by the threat: 'Oh, Allah, destroy them
and let it be painful!'

A few hours after Bastian posted it online to advertise the demonstration, the police were at his house. He opened the door wearing only
a towel around his waist. They followed him into the bedroom while
he got dressed, and began searching the room. One of the officers saw
him put something in his mouth and heard it hit hard against his teeth.
The policeman put him in a headlock to prevent him from swallowing.
Bastian was eventually forced to spit it out – a memory stick containing the film, bomb-making instructions, and footage of hundreds of
beheadings and torture methods signed by al-Qaida.

One of the first things Bastian Vasquez demanded when he was
placed in custody was that Arfan Bhatti, the former leader of the
underworld, be notified. He never asked for his wife.

According to police interview notes, Bastian had set up a new
online profile 'a couple of weeks ago with the intention of finding
a second Muslim wife.' The notes recorded that 'the accused is
married but polygamy is permissible in Islam.' He had also created
an online profile under the name Mohammad Jundullah in order to
'network and make as many friends as possible online.' The notes
went on to say that 'the accused has been a member of Islam Net
and views proselytizing as an important task.'

Bastian confirmed that he and Arfan Bhatti had arranged the
demonstration and elaborated on his relationship to his infamous
co-arranger. 'The accused perceives it as special to be together with
Bhatti and in making the video he had hoped to gain his recognition.
The accused hoped that people would think he was cool. He realizes

how idiotic this sounds but the accused was bullied while growing up and thinks this might explain it.'

Bastian denied having threatened anyone, and when he was asked what he meant by 'Oh, Allah, destroy them and let it be painful!' he answered 'that, like, Allah would punish them ones and get them out of Norway . . . out of Afghanistan.'

'Who are "them ones"?' his interviewer asked.

'Norwegian soldiers killing innocent people.'

'How would they be punished?'

'By a fever or something, or . . . dunno . . . illness, something that would make them leave in any case.'

With regard to the question of how he had chosen the people in the video, he replied that he had picked Prime Minister Stoltenberg 'solely on account of the NATO symbol in the background.' He had no idea who the crown prince was, he said, and had 'only seen him as a man in a photograph greeting a Norwegian soldier in Afghanistan.' He said he thought the foreign minister was a general or had 'something to do with the army.'

By 'destroy them,' he had meant that he hoped the soldiers would suffer psychological problems upon returning home.

The type of guys Aisha admired were all on the PST watchlist, a list Islam Net did not want to be included on.

The board discussed her case. Any greater focus on the niqab issue at the moment would only whet critics' appetites; in the worst case, they feared, it could lead to a niqab ban. Then Aisha would be damaging both 'the situation of the niqab and of Muslims.' The board voted not to publicly support Aisha.

Later Fahad Qureshi took Aisha aside. 'It's sad you're at the receiving end of so much criticism,' he told her. 'May the man who pulled off your veil get his rightful punishment.' But Norway was not ready for the niqab, he explained, Norwegians did not accept people who were different. Inshallah their attitude would soon become more inclusive.

At home, the trouble continued. The family lived in a small

basement apartment in Bærum. Aisha and her sisters were at their
wits' end. One night, one of them was pleading, tearfully, with
their parents to stop arguing; when her father pushed her aside
and stormed out, she lost her temper. She swept everything on the
table onto the floor, followed by everything on the shelves and on
the worktops. 'I'm only doing the same as Dad!' she shouted. She
smashed the TV and her father's cameras. She flung his laptop at the
wall and then threw everything into a pile.

When their father came home, all hell broke loose. He beat his
daughter around the head several times, then pushed her mother
onto the floor and kicked her. One of the sisters bit his hand to stop
him from hitting them. Aisha took the three youngest sisters into
another room, locked the door, and phoned the police. A patrol car
arrived, arrested their father, and charged him with assault. It led to
a fresh meeting at the Mediation Service. 'He has promised not to
lay his hands on his wife and children,' the report drily stated. The
father moved out and the parents separated. Following one more
violent episode, a restraining order was taken out against the father
in the spring of 2012. Aisha vowed never to see him again.

Beatings, intimidation, fear. She had switched off her emotions in
order to survive. Once she was free of her father's influence, she was
eager to fill the void with something beautiful, something strong,
something of her own.

Men wearing the clothing of the Prophet caught Aisha's attention.
Who could be more dependable and true than a man who followed
Muhammad?

The bearded men who had turned up at the Peace Conference
did not have a solid hierarchical organization with positions and
membership lists, but they nominated a leader – emir – and a ruling
council – shura. They wanted Norway to become an Islamic state
governed by sharia, but they disagreed on how best to achieve that
goal. For the time being they made do with preaching on the streets
and demonstrations.

There was no ideological guiding light to decide on the matter in dispute, but there were several strong personalities who ruled along the same lines as in gang culture, employing bonds of loyalty. The group often bickered about theology, which the open discussions online testified to. The language could appear somewhat schizophrenic, neofundamentalism mixed with criminal code and gangster slang.

Some immersed themselves in the Koran. Study circles were held at a mosque in Grønland until the religious leader there, fearing problems with the authorities, asked them to leave. They borrowed other premises or met at one another's homes.

When the videomaker Bastian Vasquez was released from custody, Arfan Bhatti was there to pick him up. The convert with the Catholic background was not an academic Islamist and reading frustrated him. 'This isn't the time to dust off old books, it's the time for action,' he wrote in an e-mail to another in the group after having sneered his way through a meeting. It was the first and last study circle the convert would attend. With his video he had accomplished part of his goal – recognition from Arfan Bhatti. The two of them now hung out together almost every day.

While some in the milieu attempted to be scholarly, others preferred to discuss the use of terror. Following the reprinting of the Muhammad cartoons in Norwegian newspapers and in protest against Norwegian military involvement in Afghanistan, the most militant believed that attacks against targets in Norway were legitimate. The killing of Muslims in other parts of the world had to be avenged.

An eye for an eye, the principle of retributive justice, was central.

A number of the young men discussed possible targets and settled on the best location to attack: Aker Brygge, a high-end residential and retail area on the waterfront in Oslo. In the evenings, there would be no children or strict Muslims around, only financial employees in its restaurants and bars, along with bumpkins on a visit to the city.

They also agreed that Parliament was not such a bad target either. However, after lengthy discussions, the shura decided that

Norwegian civilians could not be targeted, even in a country where the population was responsible for its own leaders. After all, some of the victims of the terror attack might not have voted for the war-mongers. It would be better to attack an army barracks.

Perhaps they had too much to lose. Perhaps the little country they lived in was not bad enough. In any case, the most militant among them found a new arena to fight in, one with far more appeal than an attack on a domestic military base.

'To offer prayer – as opposed to waging jihad on the battlefield – is like the trifling of children,' Abdullah Azzam had written. The mujahideen were to offer their blood when Muslim lands were attacked. In Syria they could fight for an Islamic state alongside real brothers, and then Islam could spread northward from there.

Some were attracted by the adventure. Some by the camaraderie. Others by the promise of getting their sins washed away. One thing was certain – Syria gave them a direction in life, a feeling of doing the right thing. And if you were killed, you were guaranteed a place right beneath God's throne.

The methods used to stir people into action were familiar terror-ist recruitment. Gruesome images of dead and wounded children in Afghanistan and Syria were contrasted directly with the Norwegian military effort. Selective quotations from the Koran, reinforcing the message that the West was at war with Islam, offered further back-ing. The myth that Europe wanted to wipe out Islam also proved effective propaganda. That Norwegians did not like Muslims was an established fact. Muslims were repressed and discriminated against. Supporting jihad was an act of self-defense.

The milieu had a love-hate relationship with the media. They both sought publicity and shied away from the public eye, but were adept at getting their points of view across. At the same time as some journalists were being threatened – shots were even fired through the windows of one's home – the suspect, the infamous Arfan Bhatti, was conducting a secret romance with a blond and blue-eyed TV reporter.

*

Aisha announced she wanted to get married.

'To an emir,' she told Dilal.

'Who?' Dilal asked in surprise.

'His name is Ubaydullah Hussain.' Aisha showed her a picture of him online. He was smiling into the camera, looked cute with curly hair and a roundish face.

Isn't that the same guy Emira had a secret relationship with? Dilal wondered.

That's over, Aisha was quick to counter, and went on to tell her she had asked a go-between to propose for her.

Dilal was astonished. '*You* proposed?'

Aisha nodded. She had never spoken to the object of her affections but had seen him with a microphone in his hand while dressed like the Prophet and liked what she saw. The baby-faced Islamist was a good public speaker. Besides, he was *hafiz*, someone who knew the Koran by heart.

The matchmaker, a Norwegian Iraqi from Larvik, was one of the foremost figures among the new wave of Islamists. Mohyeldeen Mohammad entered the public eye when he held a rally in Oslo against the Muhammad caricatures: 'When will the Norwegian authorities and their media understand how serious this is?' he said. 'Maybe not before it's too late. Maybe not before there is a September 11th on Norwegian soil. This is not a threat but a warning.'

The demonstration had led to Mohyeldeen's expulsion from the Islamic University in Medina. The institution decided he was an agitator. He was placed under arrest by the Saudi Arabian security police upon his return to the country and deported back to Norway.

The answer Aisha was waiting for was slow in coming. Every time she inquired, Mohyeldeen told her he had yet to hear anything.

Dilal followed from the sidelines. To think that Aisha had proposed herself! Taking what had always been the man's privilege as her own – it could be viewed as a feminist act. Breaking with convention in a radical way. Aisha was unconventional in a sense, seemingly unconcerned about what people said. When she wanted something, she went at it like a freight train. Now she wanted the spokesman for extremism in Norway, the man PST would in time suspect of being the central figure in the radicalization and recruitment of Norwegian Muslims to go fight in Syria.

Dilal was aware of the lack of a father and a safe base in Aisha's life, and it seemed to her that what her friend now sought was status and respect rather than love. She wanted to be the wife of one of the leaders in the Islamist milieu, which had become her new home. Here she found a sense of belonging, support, and sentiments she identified with: *We are different, they are oppressing us, we must retaliate.*

The proposal eventually reached the ears of the recipient. Ubaydullah asked around to find out more about the young woman behind the straightforward offer. What he heard led him to reject it. *She wasn't very pretty*, he was told. *A bit chubby*, someone whispered in his ear. In short, *no deal.*

Rejection proved no hindrance to Aisha; she merely set her sights higher, on an even more prominent figure. She could not use Mohyeldeen again, though, and taking matters into her own hands, she set up an e-mail account under an alias and made contact with the new target – a man fifteen years her senior, who had spent more of his adult years inside a prison than outside, and who, among other charges, was convicted of shooting at the synagogue in Oslo, but acquitted on terrorism charges – Arfan Bhatti himself.

He was already married, but that was no impediment.

There were several parts to her plan.

'I'm contacting you on behalf of a friend,' Aisha wrote. 'She is very religious and wishes to know if you would be interested in marriage. She is willing to become your second wife.'

Yes, indeed, Bhatti was interested in marriage.

What to do next? Aisha wondered. She asked Dilal.

'I suppose you have to show up as that friend on your own e-mail address,' Dilal suggested. 'But are you sure *he* is the one you want?'

Aisha had never been so sure of anything.

Arfan Bhatti's criminal career had begun at the age of thirteen, when he joined the gang Young Guns. When he was fifteen, he stabbed a shop owner in central Oslo with a kitchen knife after having hit him over the head with a bottle. For that, he received his first conviction. His boyhood years were spent between primary school in Norway and stays with his extended family in Pakistan. Child Welfare took increasing care of him and he was placed in an institution. His teenage years were characterized by gang criminality and time spent in and out of prison. He acquired a reputation in Oslo for violent extortion, and at twenty-one he was placed under preventative detention for having shot a person during debt collection. The court-appointed psychiatrist, Berthold Grünfeld, determined that he had 'insufficiently developed mental capacities,' and in two later court cases the experts diagnosed an 'antisocial personality disorder.' He demonstrated 'deficiency in his sense of responsibility and respect for social norms and obligations, apathy toward the feelings of others and the absence of an ability to feel guilt.'

Aisha pretended she'd been contacted by her fictitious alter ego and got back in touch with Arfan as herself. They began chatting on Facebook. They exchanged messages and talked on the telephone. She had seen him at the demonstration in January, which he had attended with his little sons in tow. He had never seen her and she offered to send him a picture. He refused. He wanted things to proceed in the proper way, in the Islamic way.

Dilal gave her friend some well-intentioned advice to facilitate Arfan falling for her.

'You have to do yourself up, Aisha. Put on some makeup. Fix your hair. Buy some nicer clothes!'

Beneath all the layers of veils, Aisha usually wore sweaters and loose-fitting jogging pants. Dilal felt obliged to offer some instruction: 'Remember, you *are* going to remove your niqab when the two of you are alone together!'

'Allah doesn't see the exterior, only what is within,' Aisha replied.

'But you aren't marrying Allah!'

'Don't blaspheme!'

'Some deodorant, or perfume even, and you should—'

'That is haram,' Aisha responded.

*

Aisha came in through the women's door. Arfan strode in the main entrance. He was dressed in traditional Pakistani garb. She wore a niqab. He had procured a man to conduct the marriage ceremony, as well as two witnesses and a guardian – a *wali* – for her, a well-known Islamist belonging to the old guard.

It was a *nikah* marriage, one conducted according to Muslim law.

A couple of minutes later they were husband and wife.

The missed calls from her mother had accumulated on her telephone. She knew that her mother would never have gone along with her marrying Bhatti. She had confided only in her closest friends. Eventually, while sitting beside one of Norway's most feared men in the passenger seat of the car en route to her honeymoon, she called her mother back and informed her she was on the way up the mountains with her husband.

She did not bother to tell her father. He later heard about the marriage via an acquaintance.

The honeymoon was to be spent in Hafjell, a posh ski resort a few hours' drive north of Oslo where downhill skiing events had been held during the Winter Olympics of 1994. Arfan had rented a cabin. The newlyweds stopped along the way to buy food. They were really going to have a fine time of it.

When they got to the cabin, Aisha took off her veils.

The honeymoon was a disaster. In the car on the way home they scarcely exchanged a word.

The Islamist had tired of her almost immediately. Back in Oslo, Aisha lay on the sofa in their apartment in Stovner in the eastern suburbs and cried. Arfan had told her he regretted the marriage, he was not attracted to her. 'You're not how I thought you'd be,' was all he said.

'What will I do?' she sobbed over the telephone.

Dilal was at a loss for ideas, searching her repertoire.

'What about dolling yourself up a little?'

Aisha's reply was inaudible.

'Have you got anything other than jogging bottoms?'

She had a pretty Pakistani dress, Aisha replied meekly.

'Put that on, apply some makeup, prepare some good food, and greet him at the front door with a kiss!'

It was to no avail. He walked straight past her when he came home. They already slept in separate rooms.

Arfan had neglected to inform his first wife of his new bride. She heard the news from someone else after a couple of weeks. It resulted in a row where she threw a clothes iron at him and he hit her. He was later convicted of domestic violence. He termed it 'smacking,' akin to what he did to his sons when they failed do their Koran lessons properly. The charges cited blows to the face, head, and back.

In the summer of 2012, he relinquished custody of his children and began making plans to travel to the tribal areas between Pakistan and Afghanistan. He had 'so much damned hate' in his heart, he told a journalist, the very thought of the authorities made him so angry that he could cry. Living in the West was no longer an option. He had to go ahead and blaze a trail so his children would not grow up being too influenced by Norwegian culture.

'When I get back, I want you gone from here,' he told Aisha before leaving. But he ended up throwing her out in the middle of the night prior to his departure.

In the early hours, Aisha called the man regarded as the kindest among the Islamists – the Kosovo Albanian Egzon Avdyli, a former troublemaker from Dønski. Sitting in the stairwell outside Arfan's apartment, she asked him to come and collect her. He brought along his mother and drove Aisha home to Bærum.

Arfan Bhatti left the country a short time later. He wrote online that he was taking part in action against the international forces in Afghanistan. From the tribal areas he sent a text that read: '*Talaq. Talaq. Talaq.*'

It was over. A nikah marriage could be dissolved by the man saying *talaq* – I divorce – three times.

But by then Aisha was already pregnant.

12

Target Practice

'My reasons for leaving are not based on religious grounds,' Ayan wrote to Fahad Qureshi. She sent her letter of resignation at the end of August 2012, just after she began her final year in school.

'I feel I have given what I can for the moment. Perhaps in the future when I have more knowledge I will have something more to contribute, inshallah. Thank you for everything you have taught me and for allowing me this opportunity. I truly felt Islam Net allowed me to grow but then something changed, and I no longer feel needed. Yours sincerely, Ayan.'

In response, Qureshi wrote, 'I hope one day inshallah you return, more skilled, motivated, disciplined and purposeful.'

Emira also had left the organization. The reason for her departure had been more clearly outlined.

'I have a different understanding of the faith,' she told Islam Net. The board was aware of the rumors of a secret affair between Emira and Ubaydullah Hussain and believed he had influenced her decision to leave. Talk, gossip, as well as people flowed back and forth between the two milieus. Islam Net regretted the loss of her computer skills.

Emira had repeatedly denounced the West to a member of the organization she was now leaving.

'You mean you support terrorism against civilian targets?' he had asked.

At first Emira would not answer.

'Like a café, for example?' the young man went on.

Emira had grinned.

Aisha had departed the organization in disappointment. Ayan had politely taken her leave. Emira had moved on, Dilal too. She had never felt particularly welcome in Islam Net in any case.

Besides, they all had new heroes.

At the end of September 2012, several hundred people gathered outside the American embassy in Oslo. They had come to demonstrate against the film *Innocence of Muslims*, which they believed was offensive to Muhammad. On the pavement between the Palace Park and the triangular embassy building, black flags with the Islamic creed inscribed contrasted sharply with the blue sky.

'Obama, Obama, we are all Osama!' was chanted loudly.

The police filmed the demonstrators, who included militant Islamists, convicted violent offenders, renegades from Islam Net, and twenty or so well-covered women. There had been an internal discussion about whether or not women could participate in the demonstrations and it was decided they could, as long as there was no 'mixing with the opposite sex.' A young man calling himself Abu Muaz had put up the rules for demonstrations on a secret Facebook group page: 'Brothers and sisters shall stand separately. Brothers in front and sisters behind, with some brothers forming a guard who will ensure compliance and that sisters/mothers are not exposed to scorn from the enemies of Islam.'

The group now had a name: the Prophet's Ummah.

Ubaydullah Hussain addressed the crowd. 'Nothing is more beloved to us Muslims than the Prophet! We thirst for revenge!' The punishment for slighting Islam is death, he said. 'The world needs a new Osama bin Laden!'

Some of the people standing on Henrik Ibsens Gate that autumn day were occupied with thoughts of traveling to Syria to take part in jihad – a duty ordered by God when Muslims were under attack.

One of them was Hisham Hussain Ahmed, who had come alone from Eritrea to Norway as a minor, had been settled in the Juma family's neighborhood and had manned the mission stand with Ayan on Oslo's main street the previous year, too timid and polite to approach passersby.

Hisham had escaped from war when he was thirteen years old.

Now he had war on his mind once again.

His life had been without direction recently. He was working as a deliveryman for a crooked employee in a transport company, a midlevel manager taking on jobs off the books. Some of the money was winding up in Hisham's pockets.

The good thing about a cash-in-hand job was that he could also receive unemployment benefits. It allowed him more time to do what he liked best, fishing. He was free to go to Sandvikselva, the premier trout river in the Oslo area, with a friend in the middle of the day and stay until midnight. Or he could get out of bed at three or four in the morning, the summer sun already up, grab his fishing equipment, find a nice spot, cast a line, and lose himself in a reverie.

He had never been in his element before. Barely literate when he arrived in Norway, he had struggled in many subjects at school. English, which he had not a word of, had proved particularly challenging. Compounding his failure was the fact that he refused to do any homework. He gave up easily when something bored him. The teachers were kind and awarded him a pass, often with the lowest grade. His gym teacher tipped him off about Wild X, a multicultural outdoor activity organization for immigrants and other 'asphalt kids,' as the organizer, Tor Bach, called them. Hisham was invited along to canoe and fish. This was a relief from the interminable hours spent cross-country skiing in gym class. On skiing days, he did not complete the course until hours after the first finishers, since he had neither grown up skiing nor learned how. Toward the end of secondary school, his life began going downhill drastically. He started hanging around with the Kosovar bad boy Egzon Avdyli, smoking hash, drinking, and partying. Nonattendance was common.

In the company of Wild X, he could both relax and challenge himself. He learned how to read a map and use a compass, and how to light a campfire. In the winter they built snow caves and spent the night in them, and the participants who passed the hunting license test were allowed to go on a grouse hunt.

When school finished for the day, he worked at an institution for people with disabilities. He was popular with both colleagues and those in his care, more for his ability to entertain than his hard work. When the time came to make plans for life after school, a guidance counselor suggested that since he had enjoyed his time working at the institution, he should consider qualifying as a social worker and take a degree in health and social work.

'Society needs competent social workers who understand how mental and social problems arise and how to offer help in a professional manner,' read the description of the social worker degree. Despite his appalling grades, he was accepted by Volda University College.

Volda is a beautiful spot, situated by a fjord, with houses spreading up the mountainside. When the summer sun shines, the sea and landscape glitter in blue and green, against a backdrop of sharply outlined snow-covered peaks reaching skyward. Perfect for everything he enjoyed – mountain hikes, fishing trips, and grouse hunts.

But autumn came and things turned gray, cold, and gradually black. The safe surroundings of secondary school were gone, he was not prepared for further studies, still barely able to write in Norwegian.

His roommates in the student block noticed that he sequestered himself with a book. But it was not a course book he was absorbed in. It was the Koran.

Before the first semester came to an end, he had dropped out. On returning to Oslo, he got a job as a parking lot attendant. One of his colleagues was Ubaydullah Hussain.

*

In late winter 2012, Tor Bach of Wild X received a call from Hisham. They had not seen each other in three or four years, and Bach was pleasantly surprised to hear from his former hiking companion.

'It's been ages!' he said, and told him to drop by.

Tor Bach was a sturdy fellow, open and nonjudgmental. He was also behind a left-leaning website called the Wasp, which had as its stated goal to engage in 'investigative journalism about violent, racist, totalitarian and anti-democratic groups and milieus.' His eyes widened when the pike fisherman, as they had called Hisham in Wild X, came in with three pals, all bearded, as jihadist fashion required.

The last time he had seen Hisham, he was a slight teenager. Now he was pumped up from lifting weights.

'You look like al-Shabaab!' Tor Bach chuckled.

His comment did not raise even the hint of a smile from Hisham. Wannabe jihadists displayed a total lack of self-irony, Bach thought.

There was hardness in Hisham's eyes, or was he just putting on a tough guy act? What had happened? He remembered that Hisham had a penchant at times for some pretty bizarre conspiracy theories, but this . . . ?

The stern-faced visitors wasted no time on small talk and got right down to business. They wanted places in the hunting course.

Bach was silent. He looked at them, hesitating before enumerating the practical details. First there were classes in theory, nine in total, three evenings a week for three weeks. The title of the first class was Humane Hunting and Ethics. After that was Practical Shooting and Hunting Techniques. They would learn rules and regulations, animal species, and weapon safety. They would be taught about the different breeds of hunting dog and given an introduction on how to deal with downed game. After the courses, they could take the official hunting license test arranged by the local authorities.

Passing the exam granted a firearms license.

'When does the course start?' Hisham asked.

When the three Islamists had left, Bach called PST.

'We can't stop anyone from taking the hunting exam course as long as they haven't committed any crime,' the police told him. 'But we will keep an eye on them.'

The answer did not put Tor Bach's mind at ease.

Bach registered their enrollment. The course started. Hisham and his friends were a lot more interested in weapons than in grouse and deer. One of the other participants told Bach he had overheard the bearded guys talking about hunting Yahud – Jews.

By the time the theoretical element was completed, Easter was over and the spring sun had melted the snow. It was time for shooting practice at a firing range. Tor Bach took everyone by the hand and informed them of the rules. The course participants were then allowed to start shooting.

'Allahu Akbar!' Hisham and the others called out when they hit the target.

Tor Bach stood silently and watched. On the other side of the fence was a white car with two men inside. It was the PST observing and taking photographs.

The date for the exam was approaching. What the hell was he supposed to do?

He called PST again.

'We can't intervene and we can't stop them from taking the exam,' was the response.

But Tor Bach could. He broke the adult education laws and neglected to enroll them. When Hisham got in touch to ask when they could take the exam, he told him, 'There's something wrong here. I don't get it, but I can't seem to put your names down.'

Hisham called him up again, angrier this time. 'What's going on?! When is the exam?'

Tor Bach told him he didn't have the foggiest clue, but the system refused to let him register their names.

'Could it possibly be due to a criminal record of some kind?' Bach asked.

Hisham did not make contact again.

*

Hisham's wife was at home, nearing the end of her pregnancy. The child was due in December.

The couple disagreed about where they should live. Hisham believed it was haram to reside in a non-Muslim country. He wanted to travel to Syria and outlined a life in prayer and battle, in loyalty to God on sacred soil. He wanted them to go together, have the child there, and live in a righteous Islamic way. If they were killed, they'd be guaranteed a place in paradise.

The mother-to-be did not find the idea appealing. Her life was right here. She worked at a kindergarten and argued that they could live good Muslim lives in Norway, just as they were already doing.

Her husband was stubborn. Jihad was more important than anything else, than him, than her, than them. It was for God.

A friend thought Hisham's plan was rash. 'You need to know Islam through and through before you travel. Only then can you make the right decision,' he told him.

In spite of everything he had read in the holy book, Hisham had only a passing, and highly selective, knowledge of Islam.

'I'm just not made for studying, for reading,' Hisham responded. 'As long as I manage to fulfill my obligation to pray every day, then that's enough for me.'

Another friend was also skeptical. 'You lack purpose in life. You go to bed and get up when you want, fish at night and sleep in the daytime. Now you want to take your family to Syria, without even knowing why. Read the Koran first, put off traveling.'

Hisham responded to both pieces of advice with what had become the mantra of the ummah collective: 'We are not people of knowledge, we are people of war.'

He left Norway in November 2012, a few weeks prior to his wife's due date. She was left on her own to experience the heartbeats and kicks of the child, the worry and anxiety about the birth; she was alone when the contractions began, and when the child came into the world.

After the birth, she had a tough time. She moved back in with her parents, could hardly face getting out of bed, stayed indoors, and rejected her child. Postpartum depression had set in, interrupted only by intense panic attacks. She might be possessed by the devil, the parents feared, observing her angst-ridden attacks. Her parents tried to calm her by reading the Koran to her.

In Syria, Hisham joined Jabhat al-Nusra. Several others from the Prophet's Ummah followed in his wake. Among them was the Chilean Bastian, who had not traveled empty-handed. He had collected money for the Islamist relief organization Al-Furqan in Grønland. People had put large sums of money into the collection boxes; sometimes the volunteers were handed thick envelopes filled with cash. *Zakat* – alms – is one of the Five Pillars of Islam, and Al-Furqan's charity drive had led to substantial donations being made to the organization after Friday prayers.

A number of criteria had to be met before you could collect money for Al-Furqan. You had to swear *baya* – loyalty – to the emir of the organization, be a practicing Muslim, train in martial arts, and support Muslims who were on haqq – the true and righteous path – and all the oppressed. Beyond that, Allah was the only one you need answer to. 'Allah is our auditor,' was the mantra.

Bastian did not answer to anyone but himself. When he left for Syria, he took all the money he had collected with him. The head of Al-Furqan was furious. The swindler would answer to Allah on the day of judgment. But Bastian said the money would be put to best use where he found himself, because when Al-Furqan sent aid to refugees, they also risked helping sinners, yes, even 'people who smoked.' So his helping himself to the money was legitimate.

Like Hisham, Bastian also left a child behind. He had married a Somali teenager in a Muslim ceremony about a year earlier. The girl had escaped from the marriage after becoming pregnant and moved home with her parents when he had turned violent and domineering. She reported him to the police, who wrote in their report, 'He beat her, kept her confined, refused to allow her to go outside unless she dressed in clothing covering her head/face completely – nikab.' He continued to try to see her, so she obtained a restraining order. This report said: 'She was certain that the reason Bastian wanted them to live together was not because he loved her, but in order to have control over the child. He has told her that he wishes the child to be brought up in a Muslim country and furthermore had planned to raise the child to perform a suicide mission.'

Another woman soon joined Bastian. Emira – the student of computer engineering – left behind college, her parents, and her planned wedding. The former soccer-playing girl threw everything overboard for what she viewed as her freedom – Syria. In Turkey, Emira was met by Bastian, who had taken the name Abu Safiyya. They married before crossing the border together.

Hisham also wanted another wife. If his first wife changed her mind, took their child, and followed him, that would be no problem; in Syria he could have four wives. He spoke neither Arabic nor English and there were few Eritrean women in Syria, so he figured his best option was to follow Bastian's example and bring a wife from Norway.

He asked around.

Emira sent constant updates to her friends. Things were good, Alhamdulillah. She had been allocated a place to stay together with Bastian, a large house with a garden and a backyard.

Her parents were devastated – they had lost a daughter. Her cousin in Pakistan was disappointed; he had lost his admission ticket to the West.

Aisha also wanted to go. She had been the prime mover in the gang, after all. But her pregnancy held her back. She told Dilal, who was studying nursing at Oslo University College, of her frustration.

'Are you mad?' her friend exclaimed. 'That's no place for a baby! Not for you either.'

But Dilal was also drifting toward the rugged men in the Prophet's Ummah. A Norwegian girlfriend who had converted had introduced her to the milieu. She had said that they were a bit wild, but that the leader was handsome and intriguing.

Dilal asked to join the private Facebook page of the Prophet's Ummah. Membership was controlled by the handsome and intriguing leader himself – Ubaydullah Hussain, the man Emira had at one time had a crush on and whom Aisha had proposed to before she married Arfan Bhatti. He had to ensure that those seeking admission were strict Muslims and not journalists, researchers, or working for PST.

A short time after Dilal asked to become a member of the group, she received a reply on Messenger. It was from Ubaydullah Hussain.

'You're not wearing a hijab on your profile picture. Why?'

Dilal answered that she was not ready.

'Why do you want to join?'

'To learn. I'm curious.'

'You're not a Shia, are you?'

'No.'

Silence. That was the end of the exchange.

Was it due to her not being covered up? The fact she was a Kurd? Who did this guy think he was?

A couple of days later her younger brother received an SMS and exclaimed, 'What the . . . ? Ubaydullah Hussain has sent me a text. He's asking if I'm Shia. What does that terrorist want with me?'

Dilal pretended not to know but was secretly pleased. Ubaydullah must have looked through her profile and come across her brother. That meant he was taking her seriously. Her brother, who was in the same year as Ayan at Dønski, realized something was going on. 'I hope you know what you're doing,' he warned her.

The next time she logged on to Facebook, she found a notification that she had been accepted into the private group. She began reading the posts and comments.

Ubaydullah got in touch again before too long. He wanted to act as her personal guide. Dilal was flattered. Although she disagreed with most of what he wrote, there was something about him she found appealing. They chatted online more and more often, in the daytime and evenings. At some point she let go of her own opinions. What he said had to be true. It must be right. He had read the whole Koran. He knew it by heart. How could she contradict him?

In no time, everything he said was the obvious, unadorned truth.

'Can we get to know each other?' he asked one day.

They arranged to go for a walk. Dilal was nervous. He was in a relationship, he told her, but was in the process of breaking up. They strolled for several hours. Along the way he halted abruptly and asked her, 'What is it you want?'

She was silent, her eyes downcast, and then he asked, 'Do you want to meet me again?'

Yes, she would like that.

After their first meeting she missed him all the time. Wanted only to be with him. He sent her a succession of messages. First she fell for the words. The beautiful, pure, logical way he put things. Or was it his power? Did his notoriety, his being in the public eye, lend him charisma? Ubaydullah and the other leaders in the Prophet's Ummah had an almost magical power of attraction on the women in the milieu. There were many who wanted a man on the warpath. Jihad, whether waged physically or by the pen, made little difference, as long as it was for Allah.

'I miss you!' he wrote.

'I miss you too!' she replied.

Strange that a guy like that can be such a pussycat. To think I am the one who has brought out this soft side, Dilal marveled. The thought of him made her tingle. They met at his place by the horse race tracks at Bjerke and sometimes at Arfan Bhatti's flat in the eastern suburb of Stovner. Eventually she was staying over more and more, telling her parents she was at a friend's and spending the night with him.

'We have to get married,' he told her. 'We've done this, that, and the other. You have to marry me.'

'I can't. My family will never go along with it. My brothers would kill you.'

'If your family won't accept me, then they must be infidels. They can't deny you a Muslim husband. There's no logical reason to refuse.'

No, no logical reason. They were bound together by invisible ties.

His flat in Bjerke began to define her world. Ubaydullah confiscated her mobile phone, wallet, bank card, ID cards, and laptop.

He would not allow her to continue her college studies, get in touch with her family, or go outside without him.

The West was at war with Islam.

The West is against us.

Norway is a land of infidels.

Its people are going to hell.

They are the enemy.

They mean us harm.

They scorn us.

We need to fight back.

We have to stick together in our ummah.

We are brothers and sisters.

We are going to paradise!

After Arfan Bhatti left for Pakistan, Ubaydullah was chosen as the new emir of the Prophet's Ummah.

Dilal was sent to the kitchen when the sheikh who was to wed them arrived. She sat on one of the three chairs there was space for and waited. The kitchen was spotless, Allah's little slave kept things spick-and-span. He mopped the floor at the appearance of the slightest speck of dirt. Now he, the sheikh, two witnesses, and her wali sat in the living room. Dilal had not caught his name – Abu something or other. He was the same man who had acted as wali for Aisha. It was a role her father should have filled. Failing that, the eldest brother should act as guardian, and if he was unable, the next eldest, and if you had no brothers it fell upon a grandfather, an uncle, a cousin, and so on through the extended family. But none of them had been asked.

She could hear the muffled sound of voices from the living room. The door handle moved. Abu something or other entered the kitchen. She looked up.

'Look down,' he ordered.

She lowered her gaze.

'Listen. You have two things to do,' he said. 'Look down and say yes.' She sat in silence, staring down at her hands. He asked her if what Ubaydullah had said was correct, that her family was opposed to the marriage merely on the grounds that he was Pakistani. She answered yes. According to the Koran, a father could not refuse his daughter's hand to a good man as long as he was a practicing Muslim. Differences in race, nationality, culture, or tradition were not acceptable reasons.

The elderly man asked in a solemn voice if she accepted Ubaydullah as her husband.

She replied yes.

He read some verses from the Koran. Ubaydullah gave her an item of jewelry. They were now wed.

Dilal's family was outraged. Their only daughter had left them. There was talk of revenge.

The way Ubaydullah had ridden roughshod over the family, not asking for Dilal's hand, led to discord in the Prophet's Ummah. His lifestyle on the whole was a divisive theme within the group. He had been involved in many conflicts and scandals and left a trail of broken hearts in his wake. Many disliked the negative headlines he generated. He had thundered against the Norwegian state for demanding taxes from Muslims while at the same time engaging in war against Islam. The only problem was that he himself lived off that same state, which others paid taxes to, even as he was receiving 19,000 kroner, almost $3,000, a month in welfare payments after resigning from his job. His Facebook page was filled with outbursts against different groups. On the subject of Jews who felt threatened and expressed a desire for police protection, he wrote, 'I'll give them protection all right, inshallah. As soon as I pass the hunting exam and get my hands on an AK-47.'

Arguments and interpersonal conflicts threatened to destroy the unity of the group, and in early March 2013 Ubaydullah stepped down as leader. On Facebook he offered numerous reasons: 'Among other things there has been too much focus on me personally and not enough on the ideology and message of the group.' He added that even though elements within the Prophet's Ummah had clearly been opposed to his style of leadership and to him personally, they were all brothers in Islam, as long as they worked in accordance with the Koran.

Their reputation as righteous Muslims had been tarnished due to the Islamists' philandering and casual attitude to marriage: a proposal, a few verses from the Koran, followed by cohabitation for a week, or a month or maybe two. Then everything ended in a straightforward divorce by the husband saying, *Talaq* – 'I divorce' – three times.

One of the members who had been particularly opposed to this womanizing was Egzon, the leading Kosovo Albanian of the group. Dilal's brothers had been good friends with him while growing up. He let them know how angry he was: 'If it was my sister Ubaydullah had taken, I'd have killed him.'

He warned the members against these hasty marriages and quickie divorces.

'An Islamic marriage is a beautiful thing and is not to be treated as a Shia mutah marriage that is declared null and void in the face of a little adversity,' Egzon wrote, using his online moniker of Abu Ibrahim, and received a host of likes and hearts, as well as comments like 'agree' and 'not a disposable toy' in response.

Mutah, which Egzon referred to, literally means 'pleasure,' and *nikah al-mutah* is used in Shia Islam to denote a temporary marriage that is not fixed for any particular period of time, long or short. The woman must be chaste but not necessarily a virgin. Some deem the practice religiously approved prostitution. The Prophet, who himself had twelve wives, was said to have been opposed to it, and fourteen centuries after his death the debate still continued in Oslo.

Several of the Islamists' former girlfriends felt affronted, used, and fooled. Some, like Emira, had been secret lovers, led along by promises of marriage. Others, like Aisha, had wed in the Muslim way, without the knowledge of their parents and then been dumped. Some, like Hisham's pregnant wife, had just been abandoned.

'Brothers! Treat your wives as you would want your sisters and daughters to be treated,' wrote Abu Khurosan, aka Arfan Bhatti.

'And do not marry in secret, it is meant to be a joyful day to be shared, not kept under wraps.'

They called themselves the Prophet's Ummah but followed the Prophet only when it suited them.

13

Halal Dating

The classes with the Koran teacher grew ever more intense. Sundays were filled with death and the wrath of God. Bliss and salvation would come later.

Due to Mustafa's increasing popularity, the Somali mothers had looked around for larger premises. They had managed to borrow Rykkinn recreation center, a house owned by the local authorities in Bærum. The Somali Women's Association was listed as the group using the facilities. The contract explicitly stated that the premises were to be used for cultural activities and not religious or political purposes. The Women's Association gambled that no one would check.

There were now around twenty students in the class. In addition, Mustafa tutored some of them at their homes in the afternoons. He gave lessons over the entire city now. His reputation was growing.

He drew students close. They admired him. He made them feel special when he turned his attention to them, one after the other, and picked holes in their pronunciation of Arabic words. He repeated himself constantly. Now and again someone had to stay behind after the lesson because Mustafa had been unhappy with a recital. The two of them would then practice alone.

Those selected felt fortunate.

'Just think, he's taking the time to read with me on my own,' a girl said before her extra lesson.

When the others left, the two of them remained behind. A Koran teacher was the only male outside of a family member who could be alone with a young girl without rumors starting.

Ayan was among the most dedicated of students. Besides the Koran recitations, she read about the Syrian rebel force Jabhat al-Nusra. She watched what the group had posted and viewed videos of Assad's assaults. She excelled in fasting and prayer, covering up and virtue. But what really interested her was something quite different: getting a boyfriend.

Salafism required that a woman wait to be set up with someone, and that was difficult. But online she was free. She added a video to her YouTube playlist called *Halal Dating*. It was in five parts. A handsome young man in a freshly ironed tunic and crocheted kufi sat behind a desk, smiling into the camera. A shelved wall of books with golden script on thick spines provided the background.

He spoke about being called up by a young man who asked, 'How am I going to meet a girl when you people put up walls between us? How can I know whether we are compatible or not if we don't talk?'

The preacher, who appeared to be in his midtwenties, was named Saed Rageah and he was from Somalia. He had studied in Saudi Arabia before immigrating to the United States and later to Canada. In fluent English, he reassured the boy in question that if he just followed sharia, everything would be fine.

'Sharia is geared toward what will benefit you. It protects you from what is haram.'

Before providing tips on halal dating, he stressed that it was important to give a wide berth to the temptations of the devil. There were many. For example, the devil was always present where free mixing and free mingling were taking place. When a woman left her house, the devil *always* followed her, no matter what she was planning to do. He gave the example of two sisters leaving their home just to go to the parking lot outside. If some boys saw them from their windows, they would follow the girls no matter what, because the devil would sow a seed of desire in their hearts. When the young men passed by, the devil had already planted a craving in their bodies. Imagine if nine or ten men passed by them, just think how much desire that would amount to, and all because two girls went out the door! The preacher grew serious. He implored women to be on their guard and not to venture out unnecessarily. The best thing was to stay indoors. That was always best, he emphasized.

If women had to go out, it was important that they not walk in the middle of the road. Muhammad said, 'Women should walk on the sides of the road, close to the walls, so close that the jilbab scratches against the thorns growing there.' This ensured safety, at least from one side. Furthermore, it was important to avoid crowds, because the devil was always present in throngs of people.

The devil was also close at hand, explained the preacher, when a man and a woman who were not married found themselves in the same room. In that case, there would always be a third presence, the devil's. 'Even over the telephone! The devil will ignite that feeling, you all know this! You think, nobody sees us – let's go. The devil enters you and the other person. So don't ring, don't chat, don't poke on Facebook!'

He then addressed the men among his listeners. How were they to deal with a situation where a married woman invited them into her home? They would hear the voice of the devil inside them saying, 'Nobody will know.' The preacher said he knew of 'many cases of divorce taking place because the wife thought no one will know.' But Allah would know. Allah was always watching.

The young preacher believed himself privy to people's motives. He told the young men in his audience that he knew it was the beauty of a woman they were on the lookout for. Women, on the other hand, were seeking a successful man. She could marry a man who looked like a monkey because she did not see *him* – she saw his cars, his house, the rings he could give her, yes, all the things he could lavish on her. Men would struggle, sweat, and toil, work double shifts in order to give a woman what she wanted, while her main concern was in maintaining her looks. So he warned them to be careful, because men and women had different agendas. Women tried to seduce men in this society, but that was also the fault of men, for giving compliments like 'You're so sexy,' which only resulted in the woman wearing something even more revealing the next day, and the day after that an outfit that even the devil himself would not be seen wearing in public!

Four of the five episodes were finished. In the last one he would divulge tips on how to date with God's approval. The same preacher, sitting in front of the same heaving bookshelves, gave the camera a smile. Finally he was going to reveal what halal dating was.

'*There is no such thing as halal dating in Islam!* The only halal dating is when you are married to that person. Then you can date that person as long as you want! You can take her to the movies, drive to the park, go to Niagara Falls, whatever you want. *Marriage* is the only halal dating.'

That was it. There was no shortage of comments beneath the video, predominantly by viewers exalted by the advice. Although there were a few critical voices: 'He said hel give tips, im really annoyed I watched it all n no tips grrrrrrrrr.'

A girl ventured to comment that the sheikh himself was pretty hot. She was called 'sick in the head' for writing something like that about a holy man who would have felt ashamed if he read 'what u said about him being hot. he's not here to impress u with his looks but to teach u with Allah's permission!'

Ayan saved another video by the same preacher, titled *Islamic Marriage*, also in five parts. The final episode was 'Which Part of a Woman Is Allowed to Be Seen.' The conclusion confirmed what she already knew: Best to wear a niqab. That kept the devil at bay. Following these, she went into another YouTube clip, 'Must-Watch Islamic Reminder: Can Guys and Girls Be Friends?' The conclusion was no.

Muslim Youth Movement had posted a talk called 'Get Married or Die Fasting . . . ,' stressing the importance of getting married at as young an age as possible; leaving it until later could offer the devil an opportunity of gaining a foothold within.

On the home page for *Pure Matrimony*, it read: 'If you are SINGLE and want to meet a PURE marriage partner in a HALAL way, click here!' What followed was an advertisement featuring a man who had found his wife through this very site, and an assurance that the website used scientific methods of connecting people.

Then Abdi showed up.

'We have to tidy the boys' room,' Sara said one day.

Their cousin from Canada was coming to stay. The boys had to move into their parents' room.

Abdi was tall, handsome, polite, the complete package. He spoke polished English and stuttering Somali. He was passing through Norway en route to Somaliland. His parents thought it would be a good idea for him to become more familiar with his own culture, and his own family. Ismael thought he was cool. Leila thought he was exciting. Ayan fell head over heels in love with him. As they were related, she did not need to cover up. She could be freer than she had been with a young man since her early teens, prior to her self-confinement behind a wall of rules.

Abdi was to stay for a month.

It was not long before the flat felt crowded.

Toward the end of his visit, he asked Sadiq for Ayan's hand in marriage. Sadiq called their relatives in Canada.

They were skeptical. After all, Abdi was on his way to Hargeisa to receive a religious education and learn proper Somali, which he would need in adult life. Ayan was still in secondary school. Would it not be better to see how things developed? Was all this not a little hasty? Both sets of parents seemed to be of the view that their child could do better.

It was decided that the two of them would have to finish their educations first. Abdi and Ayan begged their parents to change their minds. *Get married or die fasting.*

14

Paragraphs

Geir Lie, the school's religion teacher, hurried along the footpath leading from Dønski school. He wanted to catch the bus into town.

On the main road he saw a woman draped in black approaching, the clothes fluttering around her body. Her face was concealed by a black veil. He moved to the right of the footpath, looking down in respect, because he presumed that when a woman covered herself, she was indicating the discomfort she felt at the male gaze. When the figure was almost alongside, he heard a voice say, 'Hi, Geir!'

He recognized the eyes. A feeling of relief washed over him. Ayan had been absent from school lately, and he had feared she had either dropped out or been sent to Somalia against her will. He had been concerned enough to call her several times, but she had not answered. He had considered ringing her parents but decided against it. She was of age, so he had no right; moreover, perhaps it was the parents who were the problem.

'I've been worried about you,' he said. 'I've tried to reach you by phone . . .'

'Everything is fine with me,' Ayan replied.

'Great, then I'll see you in class,' Lie said, a hint of uncertainty in his voice.

She looked straight at him.

'Oh, by the way, I've decided that from today I'm going to wear a niqab all the time.'

'I see,' Lie said. He did not like playing things by ear and looked at his watch. 'I need to get a move on if I want to catch my bus.'

She was one of his favorite students. Engaged, liked discussion and debate, and was knowledgeable. She could be a little weird at times, like when she had refused to go on the school trip to the nearby Catholic church or to a Buddhist temple. What he had found most odd was her unwillingness to come along to the mosque close to the school. She said their teachings were heresy. Ayan was very clear in her own mind about right and wrong and often expressed her views in class.

Her religious self-confidence was something he had not witnessed in any pupil previously. She spoke candidly about her faith. For Geir Lie, the fact she always mumbled 'peace be with him' every time she mentioned the Prophet's name was a genuine religious act. To put it simply, he was impressed and more than somewhat taken by his Somali pupil, not because he liked everything she came out with – on the contrary – but because she believed in it so strongly, a lighthouse in a sea of apathy.

It was a difficult class, troublesome, with a lot of absenteeism and loud, unruly boys. Many of these were Muslims, several of whom wanted to 'catch him out' and get the better of him. They raised objections and quibbled at his teaching, but on the whole their knowledge was superficial, so it was mostly nagging and clamor that gave way to demonstrative passivity. While Ayan was eager for good grades, many of her male counterparts did not seem to think they needed a diploma. Geir Lie was well-meaning and not given to excessive reprimands. Only infrequently did he take someone to task. Once he had asked a pupil to leave the classroom because of the trouble he was causing. At least then the others might learn something. When the pupil refused to budge, Lie approached his desk. The pupil shouted, 'Don't come near me, *kafir*!'

Geir Lie exploded. 'Out! Get out!'

'Don't touch me!' the boy shouted.

'OUT!' Lie roared.

Afterward the boy rounded up a few classmates and went to the principal to complain. They wanted to get rid of the religion teacher. When Ayan got wind of this, she marched up to the principal's office with a couple of girlfriends in tow to protest the complaint.

What was interesting, Lie thought, was that Ayan had authority in the class; no one made a noise when she spoke. She had a commanding personality and was impervious to criticism. One time, each pupil was to give a talk on a topic of his or her choice. She had presented an enthusiastic, albeit naïve, depiction of Islam. He let pass some comments about Christianity that were not quite correct and awarded her top marks.

The bus into the city center came into view around the corner. Lie stepped aboard. He wanted to make it to the Latin American Pentecostal church – Restauracion de Dios – before noon.

Ayan left the footpath and entered the school building, passing the 'Welcome' sign written in Arabic, Persian, Urdu, and French, and continuing on down the corridors. Without removing her niqab, she walked into the classroom and sat down at her desk.

She has been married off. That was the Norwegian teacher's first thought on entering the classroom and seeing the shrouded figure after her long absence. As she rounded the rows of desks and came to the front of the class, she saw that the pupil's face was completely covered.

The outfit, which included long black gloves, reinforced the teacher's suspicion that her parents had forced her into marriage. It was probably how their married women had to dress – to ensure that no other man could look upon them. There had been a special focus on forced marriages and genital mutilation at the schools in the Oslo region that year. The teachers had been sent material with information on the phenomena.

The Norwegian teacher was a slight, fair-haired woman in her fifties who preferred the pupils of yesteryear. She found herself constantly explaining words that seemed to be disappearing from the language: *livestock* was *cattle*, *sap* ran in spring, a *pasture* was where animals ate. What a *demesne* was and what *gentry* meant. She'd had pupils who did not know what a *troll* was. Was it possible to go through the Norwegian school system and never have heard of one? It certainly seemed so.

It was also lamentable when Knut Hamsun no longer stirred the emotions of the young. When the naturalist and feminist author Amalie Skram no longer brought a tear to the eye. Had literature lost its hold over young minds? At times the pupils could remind you of *Dead Souls*, they were so faraway in class. But not all the pupils were bad; some of them still wanted to engage in discussion, relate the works to their own lives, their own feelings, seek a convergence between literature and reality.

One of these was Ayan. She was an asset in class, whether the discussion was about nineteenth-century literature, the printing of caricatures, or freedom of expression. At the same time, conflicts rose around her. As form teacher, the Norwegian instructor was the one who had to have a word with Ayan the time the school was collecting donations for its annual fund-raising event. She had convinced several of her fellow pupils not to participate because the money was earmarked for Norwegian Church Aid. On another occasion, in an essay she submitted, she wrote that she viewed people who were not Muslims as weeds.

'What kind of view of humanity is this?' the teacher had asked. Or had Ayan not understood the concept of weeds?

Pupils from an immigrant background could have a weak and imprecise grasp of concepts. Perhaps she meant to say something else? Like how in a garden you needed many different types of plants – *diversity*?

The teacher asked Ayan to stay after class.

'Have you been married off?'

'No,' Ayan replied.

'Then why are you dressed like that?'

'I'm practicing.'

'For what?'

Ayan did not answer.

'To get married?'

'I didn't say that.'

'Are they sending you to Somalia?'

'I didn't say that.'

'Dressing this way, you'll only shut yourself off from society from people, from working life . . . '

'Who said I wanted to work in Norway?'

'You'll close the door on so many opportunities . . . '

'Who says I want to live here?'

Where had she learned to respond in this manner? Answering a question with a rhetorical question, so cocksure and rude. No matter, the rules forbade covering up in class.

'Here in Norway we have to show our faces.'

'You can't prevent me from dressing how I want,' Ayan replied.

'Yes I can, there are clear rules about it.'

'Show me the rules,' Ayan said brusquely. 'Where is it written?'

The teacher was nonplussed. Now that she thought about it, she could not remember seeing anything about covering up. She became uncertain.

'I'm going to have to take this up with the principal,' she said.

'Dressing like this is an important part of my religion,' Ayan declared, and before turning to leave she added, 'and this is a free country, isn't it?'

Hanne Rud had become the principal of Dønski Upper Secondary School the same autumn that Ayan had transferred from Nesbru. She had noticed the IB program pupil around and surmised that Ayan had wanted to change schools because she felt more at home here. Around half of the pupils had an immigrant background, many were Muslim, and a number of them dressed like her — in long skirts with wide capes or ponchos with hoods up. Clothes reflected identity and a common identity meant security. Groups of ethnic Norwegian pupils went around in ripped jeans and plaid shirts, all in muted tones. Hanne's uniform was skinny jeans and a blazer, and she usually wore heels.

This was her second post as principal. She had held the same position at Nadderud Secondary – the school in Bærum requiring the highest grades for admission – before coming back to Dønski, where she had previously taught. While many failed to get accepted at Nadderud, Dønski had plenty of unfilled places. By the application deadline the previous spring, barely four hundred pupils had applied and there was space for over five hundred. But Hanne did not shrink in the face of adversity, and her goal was to make the school more popular. She had applied for the job precisely because it was a school facing challenges. The dropout rate was high, particularly among boys.

She spent a good deal of time in the corridors. She wanted to get to know as many of the students as possible and thought it important they knew who she was, so that they could approach her if something was up.

The presence of several tough-looking groups of girls at the school had not escaped her notice. Many were from a minority background and had a need to assert themselves. It was a good thing, she thought, taking pride in their culture, their religion, and having the courage to express their opinions. They did not shy away from participating in discussions in class and challenging the core values of Norwegian society. That meant they were doing their job right, thought Hanne. Promoting diversity.

She now sat listening to the Norwegian teacher.

'She wore a niqab in class today,' the teacher informed her. 'Personally, I don't think we should allow that. We need to be able to see our pupils.'

'You have my support on that,' Hanne replied.

Sunlight was flooding in through the floor-to-ceiling windows. From where they sat, there was a view over the entrance to the school and the parking lot.

Earlier that school year, Ayan had lodged a written request asking to be excused from taking PE with the rest of the class. She had gotten a form from Hanne and filled it out. The teenage girl had familiarized herself with the Norwegian Directorate for Education and Training's circular. According to paragraph 3.3 §1–12: 'The principal may upon request grant students in secondary education exemption from classes in physical exercise. The student must provide testimony from a doctor documenting that the class is injurious to the student and that adapted instruction is not possible.'

Her request was sent on to lawyers in the county administration. It could take some time, as there were many fundamental questions to clarify. Hanne had informed her of the consequences of high absenteeism. If Ayan did not turn up for gym class, she was risking not receiving a grade in that subject and thereby failing to get a diploma.

Ayan had previously been very active. She used to go jogging in the local park with Ela and Ivana, and she had worked out for free at the Friskis&Svettis fitness center in return for working at the reception desk with Dilal. After numerous complaints were made about her disappearing to pray, her employers warned her she would be let go if it continued. She chose to quit instead.

The problems around physical exercise had begun that same autumn.

Ayan had complained to the PE teacher about not feeling comfortable showering with the other girls. The teacher, a young woman only slightly older than her pupils, offered her the use of her own changing room. She did not mind showering later, she told Ayan. After using the teacher's facilities once, Ayan said there was another issue: She could not take part in a gym class with boys. When the teacher asked why, she said her religion did not permit it. The teacher suggested this might be something Ayan could control herself – perhaps she could avoid tackling and close contact?

The following week Ayan said that she could not take part if music was played. Then there was the issue of her clothes – she found it strenuous to train in the tunics her religion obliged her to wear.

There were many Muslims in the class, and the young teacher always took this into consideration, checking, for example, which month Ramadan fell on when she set up the annual plan. During that period she saw to it the sessions were at low intensity. The teacher believed that one of the most important goals of the class was to bolster the desire to be active. She certainly did not want Ayan to have cause to abstain from physical activity, so she allowed her to cycle on an exercise bike in long skirts and putter around as she wanted.

Eventually she suggested that Ayan train on her own. Dønski ran a top sports studies program, including cross-country and downhill skiing, hockey, and football, and it housed an up-to-date gym with treadmills, bicycles, exercise machines, and free weights. These facilities were reserved for sports studies pupils, but the school made an exception for Ayan. She was allowed to put together her own training program. It was to focus on strength and endurance, and she was to follow it and record the results.

Ayan drew up a program, but after a few weeks she announced she could not use the gym room after all. Someone might see her while she was there! She could agree to work out there only if she was given a guarantee that *nobody* would come in while she was training.

'There are three doors into the room,' Ayan complained. 'Someone could walk in at any time!'

This was not a simple opposition to physical activity but something deeper, the PE teacher thought. It was obviously new, since Ayan, as opposed to many other Muslim girls she had seen, had excellent motor skills. She must have been very active as a child, the teacher figured.

Ayan then made a suggestion. She said she had some contacts at Friskis&Svettis, having previously worked as a receptionist there. She could ask them to open the gym to her after closing time and the teacher could come and observe her.

Now the teacher was wondering: Was something not quite right with Ayan?

The day after Ayan's niqab debut in the classroom, she came to school wearing it and refused to take it off.

Again the Norwegian teacher complained to the principal.

A few days passed. Was it to be on or off?

On February 25, 2013, Hanne Rud received an e-mail.

'Hi, I have begun wearing a niqab, clothing that covers my face apart from my eyes, and I was wondering what the rules were for this in the county. I have searched a little online but have not found anything saying it is not allowed and I wondered if maybe you knew something more about it. Yours sincerely, Ayan, Islam Net.'

Hanne was quick to respond. 'In my view it is important we are able to identify our pupils at all times. Therefore I do not want to encourage any form of clothing that makes this difficult.'

Ayan's reply came in a matter of minutes. 'I understand that it might be problematic in class or during tests, but otherwise wearing it on school property should not cause anybody a problem. If someone does want to identify me, then all they have to do is simply take me aside and talk to me.'

The student also requested that the other matter be speeded up. 'With regard to PE my taking part in regular sessions with the rest of the class is out of the question. Taking this into account, there must be some way I can be assessed and graded. It would be unreasonable for this to cost me my diploma.'

Hanne offered to forward the pupil's inquiries about the niqab higher up in the system, to the lawyers at the county government level. 'But along with the recommendation that this is not something desirable on our part.'

'That's fine,' Ayan quickly wrote back. 'But in the meantime I'll wear it in school and take it off in class if a teacher asks me.'

Hanne's answer came right away. 'You are not to do that. You are to follow my interpretation of the regulations until such time as another decision is made.'

Ayan took a couple of minutes to consider the matter. 'Then I would like to see these regulations you are interpreting.'

Hanne asked her to look at the school rules, specifically paragraph four. She also wrote that expecting each teacher to ask Ayan to remove an item of clothing would be a needless waste of time.

It would lead to unnecessary disruptions. The school's employees had to be able to identify a pupil without having to take her aside and speak to her.

'I will read the paragraph inshallah. Individual teachers already have to ask pupils to take down their hoods or remove their caps, so why should they not use as much time on me as they do other pupils? I only want to wear it in the corridors and I do not see what difficulty this can cause,' Ayan wrote. Hanne had left for a meeting by this time and wrote a short reply to Ayan's e-mail just before she left work for the day. 'We're not going to make much headway with this. My instructions remain the same. The county authorities should get back to me before too long, but for the time being you are to act according to my instructions.'

That afternoon Ayan found the school rules and checked out paragraph four. Under the heading 'Orderliness and Behavior,' it stated that 'pupils are to be punctual, turn up prepared and actively participate in class, schoolwork is to be carried out within the stip-ulated time, all pupils are to act in a respectful and polite manner, contribute to a work-conducive environment and display regard and respect to fellow students and others. Bad language, violence, offen-sive or threatening behavior or other breaches of generally accepted norms of behavior are not acceptable, nor are pornographic, racist or other material of an offensive nature permitted at school.'

It made no mention of clothing.

The next morning she copied and pasted the entire text into an e-mail to the principal. 'Is this the paragraph you were talking about? Because as far as I can see there is nothing here allowing you to dictate what I can wear as I am neither causing offense to anybody nor exposing them to danger.'

'Your familiarizing yourself with the school rules is commend-able,' Hanne replied. 'I was referring to the following sentence: "Pupils shall follow the directives of the school and its employees."' She added that she had already got word back from the county direc-tor supporting her opinion with regard to the niqab.

Ayan's reply was swift. 'I had taken that sentence into

consideration, and the school employees can ask me to take my feet down off a chair or lower my voice, but what business is it of theirs what I wear, when it is not something that has been legally determined. I would like to read the grounds on which the county director based this decision, it cannot merely be based upon your recommendation.'

Hanne sent a brief reply that, pending the decision of the lawyers, Ayan had to do as the principal decided. 'You need to act in accordance with that,' she concluded.

The final-year pupil's tone conveyed a deep distrust not only of Hanne's authority as principal, but of the entire system. Ayan wanted to make her own rules, challenge the old ones. Deep down, Hanne could not help being a tad impressed. After all, this was exactly how she encouraged her students to act. Think for yourself! Beat your own path. Seek out information, find things out, read, check up.

The principal was anxious to see if Ayan would follow her instructions. She hoped the self-confident young woman would see sense and not sabotage her education.

15

Strange Bird

Ayan's sister, Leila, was now fifteen years old. On her first day at lower secondary two years earlier, she had turned up in bright green pants and a red sweater, and wearing large round glasses. The other girls were wearing pastel colors and light tones.

She came across as tough and a little rough at the edges, someone who demanded respect – and got it. She played football in PE class and dived in swimming, and her Facebook profile looked like any other girl's. Still, she was different. When she wore a short white dress just like the others did for the Constitution Day celebrations, she received praise for her looks from the other girls for the first time.

'You look lovely!' exclaimed her classmates when she finally dressed like them.

'That's, eh . . . lovely!' they said when she turned up with intricate copper henna patterns on her hands and running up her arms after Muslim feasts.

She was an exotic bird, accepted, at times admired, but mostly overlooked. The important things took place outside and away from her; she was not in on anything. She was like Teflon. None of the other girls attached themselves to her. None of them let her in on their secrets. And what is a teenage existence without shared confidences?

She started a blog that no one read. She scrapped it and began a new one, which she called Pumpkinface. 'I'm going to continue blogging as usual the last one didn't go that well sooo I'm going to concentrate my efforts on this one hahahahahaahahaha sorry I just realized that . . . nope I've forgotten . . . . . . buuuuut I've been thinking that I should blog more sooo I'm going to blog exactly what I'm thinking about unless I forget it because that can happen, my cousin calls me goldfish brain because I forget things so quickly.' No one read that blog either.

Cliques formed quickly among the girls in the class, and these set the agenda for what and who was cool and trendy, what was noteworthy and what ridiculous, who was classy and who was not.

Leila did not fit into any gang. On rare occasions, like when they had group homework, she did go to other pupils' homes. Then they would have to keep the dog locked up if they had one, because Leila could not be near dogs, it was *haram*, a word the rest of the class learned early on. Haram = not allowed. Halal = allowed. Leila knew a lot, because she went to Koran school, and she was also in some Muslim organization or other in Oslo together with her sister. She carried a little red book in her bag with hadith sayings and stories about Muhammad. So passed the first year of lower secondary school.

Then summer came. While the rest of the class returned slightly more tanned and slightly taller than before, Leila had changed completely. The summer vacation she had spent with her extended family in Somaliland had led to her discarding the green trousers and red sweaters, and she turned up at school in a long skirt. Soon she began wearing a long cape and a matching hijab in colors blending with the autumn around.

'Why do you wear that?' a girl asked.

'It was given to me,' she replied.

The congregation bought it for her, the girl told her classmates.

Those who knew Leila's sister, Ayan, had noticed a similar change. Everything was dark, plain, and dull. In autumn, Leila wore athletic shoes in muted tones; in winter, she switched to hiking boots, like the boys in the class wore, except that hers were in fake leather. Not exactly the nicest type either, the girls agreed.

In cooking class, she was excused from making anything containing pork and exempted from eating meat that was not halal. The pupils in her group always made two desserts if the one on the menu contained gelatin. The stiffener was made from the skin, bones, and tissue of pig, which was not halal, the class learned.

One time the group she was in received good marks for their work and the boy sitting next to her raised his hand for a high five. Leila stared fixedly at him. He understood. Of course, palm against palm was haram.

On another occasion a boy who had forgotten his pencil case asked to borrow a pen. She said, 'All right, but then I can't ever use it again.'

He did not quite understand. Before she tossed it to him, she said, 'Just keep it. I can't touch anything you've handled.'

Another time a classmate, overjoyed at something, had hugged the person closest to him – who happened to be Leila – and she had broken free and shouted, 'Don't ever do that again!'

'Oh, sorry, I'm really sorry . . .' he stammered. He had not meant to offend her.

'If a boy touches me here,' Leila pointed, 'it is like getting a nail through my arm. If someone hugs me, it is like getting ten nails through my head.'

When the bell rang, she had to make it to her next class early to avoid the throng, so as not to risk bumping into a boy.

She no longer took part in extracurricular activities. Although she turned up for gym class, she refused to take part in ball games where there was a chance of her being tackled by a boy. She also rejected swimming, as she could not show herself in that state of undress, and dance and gymnastics, as they were haram.

So passed the second year of lower secondary school.

On the first day of their final year, her classmates returned more tanned and with sun-bleached hair. Leila arrived in a niqab.

Some of the boys laughed. When she went to the back of the classroom to pray, they took photos of her. 'She's not right in the head,' one said. They started calling her the Phantom Blot.

Nobody had seen her praying at school the year before. Now she was preoccupied with respecting prayer times and wore an alarm clock on a belt that vibrated when it was time to pray. If it went off during class, she put her hand up and asked permission to go out.

The teachers were uncertain how to tackle this newfound piety: Some allowed her to leave the room when she asked, while others did not. The school's attitude was that it was important to accommodate diversity. After a while she was designated a place to pray, a supply closet in the corridor. She was loaned a key to unlock the door and came back when she was finished. Sometimes she just went to the back of the classroom, faced Mecca, rolled out her prayer mat, kneeled, and mumbled her supplications. She followed the clock slavishly and interrupted both pupil presentations and tests in order to pray.

If music was played, she would leave the classroom. If a film was shown, she went out too. When they were role-playing, she declined to participate because she could not pretend to be someone other than who she was. That was also haram. She deleted the account she'd set up as Leila on Facebook and established a new profile, calling herself Bintu Sadiq – Sadiq's daughter – and posted exclusively religious texts.

A staff meeting was held. The principal was very much in favor of inclusivity: 'That has always been our focus here.' There was a desire to display tolerance and cultural understanding, and discrimination was the last thing anyone wanted to be party to, but eventually it was decided the situation could not continue.

Leila was summoned to the principal's office. She was informed she was not allowed to leave the classroom to pray. Doing so caused undue disruption and meant she'd miss out on lessons. Could she not just pray at break times instead?

Leila had no respect for the new requirements and continued putting up her hand when her alarm clock vibrated. At other times, she just walked out when it went off.

Arguments with teachers were not uncommon, and she didn't hesitate to speak her mind when she felt offended or misunderstood. Beyond that, she did not show much concern for school, and her grades sank from quite good to average.

The unfamiliar terms she used in religion class either impressed her classmates or provoked them. In their final year of lower secondary, the pupils were to deliver a talk on a topic of their choice. Sofie had picked 'religious headgear in school.' She was well prepared, having gathered material from newspaper articles and books. The talk sparked a heated discussion, as the issue of women's headwear often does, creating a front line in the debate on Islam.

'I can understand you wanting to wear it,' Sofie said. 'But when you do, you are submitting to the man!'

'Allah has created us differently and has ordered women to cover themselves!' Leila retorted.

Sofie continued to argue that it served to make women invisible and represented a desire to hand over hard-earned power. It wasn't long before Leila had the whole class against her.

'Allah distinguishes between two types of people,' Leila said. 'Those who obey and those who don't. The punishment for those who do not do as he commands is harsh!' she said in conclusion, fighting back tears.

'I think we'll leave the discussion there,' the religion teacher said.

'Do you think she's lonely?' Sofie asked Emilie one time when they were talking about how Leila was on her own so much, even during break times. 'God, imagine,' Sofie added, 'just standing on my own for a second makes me feel self-conscious.'

They decided to talk to her. But that didn't happen often. The two friends had so much else to discuss.

On the whole, the rest of the class knew little about Leila. They never saw her outside of school and did not miss her if she was not there. Prior to the first lesson in the morning, she sat alone at her desk while the others hung around in groups talking. On Monday mornings people rarely inquired how her weekend had been because she was never where it was all happening, where the teenagers had begun testing out adult life: Parties. Sex. Alcohol.

Now and again Leila spent break time with a girl from a different classroom in the same year. Amal was also Somali and had known Leila since they were small. Their mothers were acquaintances, although they were quite different. Amal's mother was quick on her feet, slender, and muscular. She had begun working in Norway as soon as she could, often juggling two jobs. Mostly manual labor, cleaning, heavy lifting. She was now taking long shifts as an auxiliary nurse at a residential care home.

'Amal, you know you live two lives?' Leila said during a break. 'This life and the afterlife. This life is a test. You either pass or fail. Every night God takes your soul, an angel comes, then God decides whether or not to give you a new chance. In a sense every time you fall asleep you're dying. You are blessed to wake up each day, remember that, you have been given a fresh chance, but you have to be prepared to die at any time.'

Amal accompanied Leila and Ayan to meetings at Islam Net and was influenced by Leila's constant appeals. 'Amal, you need to wake up! You need to open your eyes! You have to get closer to Allah,' she urged.

Amal began to immerse herself in the Koran, not just learning it by rote, as she had at Koran school, but reading and understanding it in a new way. It was as though Allah were speaking to her directly. She clicked on links Leila sent to her – about Islam being the right path, the only path, and about how harsh the punishment would be for those who did not follow the message of Allah. She stopped wearing trousers.

At home, Amal had begun criticizing all things Norwegian. 'Racism and discrimination is rife in this country, Muslims are constantly being harassed,' she told her mother. She put less effort into schoolwork, opting instead to read the Koran or watch videos on YouTube. Finally she announced she wanted to quit school because she was being bullied.

'What is going on? You're with the same kids as before, the same teachers, why would they suddenly be bullying you? If someone is bothering you, then tell me or let the teachers know and we can sort it out.'

But all Amal would say was that she hated school.

'Sweetheart, please, this is the final year. You can't drop out now!'

'I want an exemption from gym at the very least.'

Her mother, whom Amal had outstripped in height and build long ago, lost her temper.

'Here I am, running around for you, killing myself with work, taking care of all of you from primary school to secondary and on so that you can have a future here! And you want to drop out! What is wrong with you? I'm phoning your teacher.'

The telephone conversation gave Amal's mother more to think about, as the teacher was also concerned. The change in Amal's behavior had coincided with her spending more time with Leila. The two of them kept to themselves, had become difficult to relate to, and habitually denounced anything Norwegian.

'I hate Norway' became a constant refrain, along with 'Norwegians don't like Muslims.' Amal spoke about feeling trapped in a society where she did not belong.

'Norway is not trapping you!' her mother shouted at her only daughter. 'As long as you don't bother anyone, then Norway won't bother you!'

Amal was caught between her mother, who watched her every move like a hawk, and Leila, who coaxed her with thoughts of what paradise had to offer.

But Amal could also be embarrassed by Leila's need to assert herself. One morning on the bus, Leila was more covered up than usual, wearing a black gossamer veil over her niqab. It was sufficiently thick that no one could see through it but thin enough for Leila to discern the world around her. Leila received some oblique looks from Bærum's blue rinse brigade, who, in addition to schoolchildren, were the ones whose rides kept the county buses running. Leila grew exasperated with them gawking and stood up in the aisle and said, 'You think I can't see you! Well I can, I see you staring.

And what's more, I see a lot clearer than any of you!' Then she sat down in a window seat. Amal wanted the bus floor to open up and swallow her.

Leila had frequently expressed the desire to live in a Muslim country. She and Ayan had begged their parents to allow them to move to their grandmother's in Somalia, because they could not live how they wanted to in Norway. Their parents had told them they had to finish their education first.

Leila could not care less about her education, it was worthless. She had other dreams, she told her friend.

'I want to get married as soon as possible,' she said when she turned fifteen. 'As soon as I am married I'll have completed half of my *deen*, half of the righteous way of life, my good deeds,' she explained.

'You're too young!' Amal protested.

'I'm enough of a grown-up. I want to get married and have children now.'

'With who?' Amal asked.

'Whoever, as long as he's a practicing Muslim.'

Amal was taken aback.

'I want to have eight children,' Leila said one day.

'I want to move to a desert,' she said the next. 'I want to live where nothing grows, where there is only wilderness. I'll live on sand and water. Get closer to God. Prove that I don't need anything else.'

'Hmm. Right,' Amal responded.

16

Separation

Dilal rarely went out, but on this evening a bazaar was being held on behalf of Al-Furqan in an apartment near Grønland Square. The women of the ummah could not stand on the street with collection boxes, so they sold clothes and jewelry to one another. They were to meet at the home of a Norwegian convert married to a Moroccan. Dilal had thought about her appearance and had chosen to wear a Pakistani outfit given to her by her new mother-in-law. She had applied makeup, fixed her hair, and put on her favorite perfume. She was going to be out among people.

She was welcomed with reverence. *That's Ubaydullah's wife,* women whispered. Everyone knew about his secret marriage, although few had seen his bride. People turned their heads to look. Now she was there, in the flesh, the scandal.

Was she actually a proper Muslim? How is it possible that the wife of Ubaydullah does not wear a hijab? Muttered questions and comments abounded. Surely a more modest wife would better suit the spokesman for the Prophet's Ummah.

The women in the apartment were a mix of Islam Net members and wives of men in the Prophet's Ummah, or had a crush on them, or simply sympathized with the organization. Aisha, heavily pregnant, headed straight toward Dilal, clearing her way through the crowded apartment.

'Still? I figured you must have changed your style by now.'

But Aisha did not belabor the point. She was preoccupied with another scandal: that before leaving, Bastian and Emira had embezzled the collection money for Syria, the cash intended to alleviate the plight of victims of the war.

Ubaydullah had also been incensed about Bastian helping himself to the funds and betraying them, Dilal told her. It was nice to see eye to eye on something.

'So, what's it like being married to Ubaydullah, then?' Aisha asked. It was a year since she herself had proposed to him, then gotten married to Arfan and divorced from him. Now she was expecting his child. And was back alone.

As soon as the women heard the question, Dilal sensed them drawing closer to her. She was soon facing a barrage of questions.

'How can a Kurd be married to a Pakistani?'

'What does he think about you going outside dressed like that?'

'What's he like?'

Later on that evening, Ayan arrived with Leila. Ayan rushed over and embraced Dilal. It had been so long since they had seen each other!

'Tell me! Tell me everything that's going on in your life!'

Dilal obliged, then asked, 'What about you?'

Ayan looked perplexed. 'Dilal, I've met a man I want to marry.'

'That's great!'

'But my father won't accept him.'

'Who is he?' Dilal asked.

'His name is Abdi. A relation, from Canada, he's gorgeous, but my parents won't allow us to marry. He's gone now, but I want so much to go after him, get married, live in Somaliland, in a country where I feel at home, a Muslim country. I can't take much more of Norway.'

After buying some jewelry in aid of Syrian children and widows, they sat down to draw up a plan. Dilal had several ideas about how

Ayan could persuade her father. If she just persevered, he would eventually see it was true love and give in.

'Love is greater than anything. Where love is concerned, anything is possible,' Dilal said.

'Maybe you could ask Ubaydullah to talk to my dad? Perhaps he'd listen to him? After all, you chose someone your family was opposed to and have shown it can work . . .'

They discussed at length what Ubaydullah could say to convince her father.

Being in love. Having things your way. This was what they tossed around the entire evening.

'I don't have time to sit around and wait. I want to get married now! I want to get away from here,' Ayan groaned.

Dilal said she would see what she could do, but she did not think Ubaydullah was the best person to talk Ayan's father into coming around. He had not even managed to convince *her* father of their marriage. On the other hand, she had never let him try. She had just left and never gone back. Broken off contact with her family. Maybe Ayan could do the same?

'Maybe,' Ayan mumbled.

Unhappy love was the theme that Ayan chose to write about for her special report in Norwegian, which was to be inspired by art and literature.

'Many in modern society do not believe there is one true love out there for them even though so much of contemporary culture is dedicated to that very thing,' she wrote in the introduction.

'I too have my doubts, because we do not see much of it these days. Is no one willing to struggle valiantly for their beloved, or for a moment beneath the moonlight? For a Somali brought up in Norway, this is a difficult subject. The topic of love is practically taboo and the romantic love between a man and a woman is certainly not talked about. You seldom hear the words "I love you" exchanged between a Somali man and wife. Although parents say it to their children, their children would be shocked if they heard their parents say it to one another. In spite of this I adore love and unhappy love in particular, as it seems so genuine to me, so realistic. After all, not everything can have a happy ending.'

To shed light on unhappy love she chose Edvard Munch's *Separation* from 1896. The painting, which she included on the front of her assignment, showed a gloomy-looking man in a dark suit stooped over with eyes downcast while holding a hand over his bleeding heart. A blond woman in a white dress stood turned away, looking out to sea.

'I thought it was such an intense painting that I began to read up on it and then came across a text by the painter about the subject of the picture.' Ayan quoted Munch: 'So she left. I do not know why. She moved slowly away, toward the sea, farther and farther away. Then a strange thing happened. I felt as though there were invisible threads between us. As though invisible threads of her hair were still twined around me. And even though she completely disappeared across the sea I felt the pain where my heart was bleeding, because the threads could not be severed.'

In order to understand why unhappy love has such an effect on us, we need to understand the part love plays and how significant it is, she explained. 'Knut Hamsun actually opens the novel *Victoria* with an explanation of love. I have chosen to leave it out as I consider it blasphemous,' she continued. 'As human beings we are always striving for what we cannot have. Our hearts suffer in the pursuit but we suffer even more if we give up and leave. Those fleeting moments where we breathe easily and look our beloved in the eyes without fate coming between us, are the ones that keep us alive and almost drive us crazy. I think such ardent passion is a wonderful thing. It gives us hope in spite of hopelessness.' She ended by saying that the obstacles standing in the way of love 'were all too evident in many societies nowadays but you can choose to break with convention and go your own way.'

The consequences could be many, she wrote in conclusion, 'from honor killing to a cold shoulder.'

17

Fraud in the Name of God

'Once the Muslims were a people who loved death just as much as you love life,' Ayan wrote on Twitter. It was something Osama bin Laden had said, and it had become the refrain of jihadist bloggers the world over. A martyr's death was what was longed for, the acceptable way to salvation. This was intended to scare the infidels, those who denied God, because an enemy who does not fear death is a dangerous one.

Ayan had found a better world. A higher heaven. She listened to Koran readings recited by beautiful male voices. She watched videos on Peace TV, Talk Islam, and Quran Weekly. This was not the real life, the next one was. Death was only a transition to it.

At school she spent most of her time in the library. She often disappeared into the small book depository at the back. The room was without windows. By the door, class sets of *Animal Farm* and *Of Mice and Men* lay stacked. There were plastic boxes on the floor containing Bibles with pale yellow covers. German dictionaries for advanced learners lined a shelf.

Sometimes she went there alone, other times in the company of a couple of friends. Once, when the librarian had entered by chance, she saw the girls lying on green mats and praying. So that was what they were using the room for. She went back out quietly. On occasion the librarian saw Ayan's head disappear behind the sofa in the corner and then reemerge when she was finished praying. The librarian had bought the sofa at a jumble sale. The material had struck her as Middle Eastern looking and she thought it would liven up the featureless library.

Ayan's routine of practicing her faith in the middle of the chaos of the lunch break fascinated the middle-aged librarian. Youngsters sat in groups all around, eating and talking, but Ayan did not pay the least bit of attention. She sat calmly on the sofa with a book. Her ability to shut out the rest of the world was impressive.

Abdi was a distant memory.

After he left, Ayan had found several shortcomings with him. He was not really a proper Muslim.

She had devised a new plan. There was no reason to hang around waiting.

Ayan smiled scornfully when al-Qaida came up in a debate during a class on politics and human rights. The topic was the attacks on September 11. She had begun to reject discussions instead of participating in them, and this time she kept her input to a few comments and some condescending looks. Her classmate Ole Martin asked her afterward why she had scoffed at the victims, and she replied, 'The Americans got what they deserved.'

She held a similar view about the capture of Western vessels by Somali pirates in the Gulf of Aden. 'The West has dumped toxic waste off the coast of Somalia to break us, forcing us to engage in piracy to defend our country.'

She was happy about soldiers being killed in Afghanistan, she said. NATO forces were subduing the population and were guilty of mass murder. In Iraq, it was the Americans who were the real terrorists.

The teacher of politics and human rights had once considered Ayan a credit to the class. Yes, her views were extreme, but that promoted discussion because they were also consistent, and rational to a degree, even though he thought she had a penchant for conspiracy theories. Throughout the spring of 2013 the tone became harder.

Ayan was of the opinion that sharia should be introduced in Norway. It would put a stop to problems like criminality, drug abuse, and social distinctions, she argued. Changing the school rules would be a step on the way. She launched a petition.

'Give me the opportunity to prove that the niqab does not create problems for communication between people! Give me the opportunity to express myself!' the heading read, and then in a slightly thicker font: 'Is that too much to ask?'

'Yes, Ayan!' one person replied, alongside a drawing of a reconciliatory heart.

Ayan collected almost 150 signatures.

Part of her wanted to change the rules to suit her, another part did not give a damn. From January in her final year, she consistently broke another social contract: paying your bills.

It began with some clothes she ordered at the start of the year, items to wear beneath her niqab. On the receipt it said *Seductive Comfort Bra. Femme Lace Top. Davida Deep Plunge. Frib Top. Lea Slipper.* The alluring names were reprinted again and again, on every payment reminder.

In addition to the lace underwear, she ordered a waterproof first aid kit from the Red Cross and creams and soaps from Yves Rocher. The products came as ordered, and the invoices were all tossed aside.

Reminders. Final demands. Notices of debt collection. The charges quickly stacked up.

They haunted her only slightly.

Ayan had taken on the status of leader for a group of Somali girls. They met regularly at a room above the Gunerius shopping center in Storgata. The room was leased by a Somali association. They ate halal pizza, chatted, and schooled one another. One of them introduced the word 'whoreway' about Norway, and thereafter they referred to it as that.

Ayan was quick to criticize those who were not as strict in their beliefs as she was, and some, even like-minded people, perceived her to be a bit of a bully. She had gone from being open and approachable to sarcastic, patronizing, and loud. She was persuasive, was good at organizing, and liked to be in charge. Now and again the girls gave talks to the group. Ayan wanted to talk about Norwegians' views of Islam. Her premise was that Norwegians hated Muslims. She demonstrated her theory with selected quotations from critics of Islam. Norway wanted to destroy Islam, she explained, and read aloud extracts from Islam critics' blogs. How could the girls live in a country that did not respect them?

The parents had little idea what their daughters were up to. The mothers stayed at home for the most part, looking after large broods, and had seldom been out in working life; their fathers were often absent.

One of the girls inspired by Ayan was Samira, a Somali from one of the inner-city areas of Oslo. She had, like Ayan, been a rebel in lower secondary school and an advocate for women's liberation and rights. The writer Camilla Collett, who had described the aimless existence of bourgeois women in the nineteenth century, had been a particular heroine of hers.

Samira's mother, one of the people behind the initiative for Muslim primary schools in Oslo, had believed her daughter was becoming too Norwegian, and following the summer holidays after Samira's first year in secondary school she had left Samira behind with some relatives in Hargeisa while the rest of the family returned to Oslo. Samira had cried and begged to go back home to Norway with them, but to no avail; her mother had taken her passport and left. She received no schooling in Hargeisa other than intensive Koran studies, and there was nowhere to run away to. When, after two years in Somaliland, she was allowed to return to Oslo, she was neatly gathered into the fold. Her mother breathed a sigh of relief. Now it was time to marry her off.

The voice of Camilla Collett, from a time that was not yet over, echoed: *Our destiny is to be married, not to be happy.*

*

'Come on, Samira,' Ayan urged.

The one who had inspired her to put a foot forward was the Koran teacher. He was said to have close ties to al-Shabaab, a terrorist organization that had carried out a series of attacks in Somalia and other parts of Africa. In 2012 the group had pledged allegiance to al-Qaida. Mustafa knew many of the Norwegians who had gone to Syria, and he was rumored to help those who wanted to travel there. People said he was discreet; the initiative had to come from the other party, never from him. He hinted at things, avoided being explicit, but the people he met and the students he taught understood that if they wished to approach him, they would not be rejected.

The notion of Syria had grown in Ayan's mind. That was where they were going to create a caliphate – an ideal Islamic state. That was where she could live freely.

She wanted the lot of them to travel there. They would help Syrian children, she said. And they would live their lives exactly as Allah wanted, in the proper Muslim way. But there was a war going on there, was Ayan not worried about that? a girl asked.

No, they were in God's hands. Besides, the day they would die had been preordained from the time they were in the womb.

Several girls wanted to go. Samira was warming to the idea. Ayan was fired up. 'And we have to get married there. All of us,' she insisted. 'I can fix us up with Norwegian husbands.' She said she knew of many single Norwegian fighters who were there at the moment and listed them. *Him* and *him* and *him*. She told them they would all get lovely houses, much nicer than the local authority housing they were living in now.

'I really want to go, Ayan, but I'd like to see what it's like to live there for a year first,' Samira said, after a time.

Ayan looked at her. 'A year?!'

Her friend nodded.

Ayan shook her head. 'If you travel to Syria, you're going there to die.'

Samira swallowed. That was out of the question. Never to see her little brothers and sisters again? Her mother? Or her big sister?

At the same time, she really did want to help Syrian children, do what was right.

Ayan would not let up. They would just have to talk about it again later. She drummed into Samira the instructions the organizers of the Syria journeys had given her. They must never talk about this online, not on Facebook, over e-mail, or on chat. Only face-to-face, in places that were not bugged.

'Samira, it's high time we got engaged anyway. Isn't it?'

Ayan had the plan all ready: *Flee. Marry. Die.*

Most of the foreign fighters raised money for a little travel fund before setting out. Ayan had been given a pointer by those who had gone, or were about to go, about how to make some money. She needed to keep her eyes out for offers along the lines of 'get a mobile phone for 1 krone' and sign up for a fixed-period subscription where you paid later. She could then sell the telephone and the subscription. The bill would be sent to her but was to be left unpaid. Whoever bought the phone would be sure to make as many foreign calls as possible before the service was disconnected and the SIM card could be tossed.

Beginning in February and throughout spring, Ayan signed up for subscriptions with seven mobile operators: Netcom, Tele2, OneCall, Lycamobile, Chess, Talkmore, and Chilimobil. She sold the SIM cards and telephones she received in each package, making several thousand kroner in cash.

'Failure to pay may result in extra costs and legal action,' warned the letter from the debt collection agency acting on behalf of Talkmore. The biggest charge was for international calls. On the Netcom bill, a couple of hundred minutes had been logged as *zone World* in March, and by April the figure had risen to six hundred. 'OneCall wishes you a happy national day on the 17th and a wonderful month of May,' was written on one payment reminder. *Principal. Late fee. Interest. Extrajudicial costs. Legal remuneration. Court costs.*

She was issued three credit cards. One from Bank Norwegian,

one MasterCard for students, and one from an online clothing retailer. It was important everything happened at more or less the same time, as it would not take long before her credit rating was affected. She cashed out where she could. Her credit card debt increased, in step with the notices of debt collection. Ten thousand, twenty thousand, thirty thousand, forty, fifty, sixty. One hundred thousand kroner. More than half of the amount was for overseas calls. The window envelopes piled up. She tossed them, unopened, into a plastic storage box at the top of the wardrobe.

The fraud was easy to justify. It was God's will that she travel to Syria. She needed money to get there. God had offered this opportunity to her. Not settling up with companies that had their base of operations in a state that attacked Muslims could be regarded as a form of economic jihad.

Ayan continued to go to school so as to avoid complications while she planned her journey. But her attendance was poor. Sometimes she just took the bus into the city instead. Rules governing the maximum permissible absenteeism in secondary schools had recently been scrapped, so she was free to come and go as she pleased, without fear of losing her place. The only communication she had received was a letter warning her she was in danger of receiving lower grades for orderliness due to all her absences.

Ayan no longer wrote on social media. She had been advised to stay clear of the net. PST was monitoring it. All communications with those helping her to organize her journey were to be by handwritten letter, delivered face-to-face, or over Skype.

How to raise money. The travel route. Possible husbands. She could not live in Syria as a single woman. There, in the ideal Islamic state, it was a woman's purpose to marry.

Time was running out. Ayan had to leave the country before the creditors turned up at the door, before her swindle came to light, before her parents found out anything. She met up with her friends. Samira was not ready. Neither for Syria nor marriage. She wanted to hold off on deciding for as long as she could.

*

Aisha gave birth to a son. She named him Salahuddin. Ayan and Leila went to visit her in the basement apartment she shared with her mother.

Dilal also came, together with Ubaydullah.

'He looks like Arfan!' the spokesman for the Prophet's Ummah exclaimed, taking the boy in his arms and cradling him. 'The eyes, the smile, the whole face, in fact,' he said, chuckling.

The child's father was in prison in Pakistan and had not seen his son. Ubaydullah, now the main recruiter to Syria, was not able to travel and fight himself. He had Crohn's disease, an intestinal illness requiring regular injections.

Ubaydullah operated like a travel agent. People who wanted to journey to Syria would call and he would arrange a meeting in a place where no one could eavesdrop, whether a parking lot, a gas station, or a rest stop. Dilal witnessed boys go from being mildly curious to thoroughly convinced, devoted Islamists. At times she quarreled with him about whether these young men actually understood what they were getting themselves into.

'They could die down there!'

'You're worse than the infidels!' Ubaydullah complained.

Sometimes she accompanied him when he went to offer travel advice. She remained in the car, watching them work out plans and decide on the best route to take. The boys were instructed to shave their beards and dress in Western clothes to avoid arousing suspicion. Their friends and acquaintances were often enthusiastic about the trips. There was competition to be the one driving the fighters-to-be to the airport, with cars often packed with well-wishers from the Prophet's Ummah eager to see them off. When Egzon left, several of his friends accompanied him to Albania on the first leg of his journey. Traveling to Syria to fight would not be proscribed under any specific domestic terrorism law until June 2013.

After a while Dilal listened with half an ear, *brother such-and-such* got in touch, Ubaydullah called up *brother so-and-so*, and there were code phrases: *the bird has flown* and *the nest is ready*.

At times Dilal did have doubts about the whole thing, about

them, their feelings for each other, the marriage, but Ubaydullah would talk her into coming around. 'Remember! Your family will never take you back, and if they did, it would only be to kill you.' One night after an argument he disappeared and returned with a cat. 'This is all you need,' he said. 'What do you want with a family who want you dead when you have me?'

When Ubaydullah began to talk about having children, the reality of her situation started to sink in. *No, I can't bring a child into this*, she thought. *It's madness. I have to get out. Get away. I need to go home.* Talk of a child made things seem so tangible, so final.

But the trees turned green and she was still with him. She looked out at the street. They lived on the thirteenth floor. It was a long way down. The miniature people below went in and out of shops, got into cars, drove off. All she had to do was sneak out while he was asleep. But where would she go? She had no home any longer, she had broken contact with her family. She had nowhere to go. Oslo had become a scary place.

So she stayed.

In early May 2013, the Akershus County Authority made their decision. Headwear covering the face was forbidden on school premises, both indoors and on the grounds.

The principal informed Ayan of the resolution in an e-mail. 'I can understand if you are disappointed, but we have to abide by the decisions made by our politicians. That applies to you and me both.'

Ayan's response was immediate. 'This pathetic show of friendliness won't do you any good at all. I have showed you ample respect and tolerance by contacting you in the first place and doing as you requested afterward. Do not expect the same friendliness or respect from me in the future.'

Hanne Rud stared at the screen. The tone was harsh, the message uncompromising.

She stood up and looked out the window. Some pupils ambled past. Others sat in groups on the grass. Exam time was just around the corner, summer after that. The e-mail had stirred her up. She sat back down. Then she forwarded it to the school's liaison at the Asker and Bærum police station. The police sent it on to PST.

In a neighborhood on the east side of Oslo, Hisham's wife was becoming increasingly unwell. She was spending more and more time in bed. She took no interest in life around her, hardly had anything to do with the baby, and was prone to sudden panic attacks.

Her father believed that supernatural forces were at work, that she had been possessed by *jinn* – small demons. He got in touch with a man at the Rabita Mosque. The Algerian who sometimes called the faithful to prayer was known to be able to exorcise spirits. They agreed that he would recite some verses of the Koran over her. These verses were believed to have a blessed, healing effect.

Several members of the mosque were inclined to explain illnesses by evil spirits taking control of a person's body, especially if the illness was psychological. You read from the Koran, placed hands on the afflicted, sometimes holding the person down forcibly, and sometimes striking the individual, because the struggle the demons put up was powerful. But the devils would eventually be driven out by the words of the Koran. Because God was almighty.

Rabita Mosque is one of the largest in Norway, with more than twenty-four hundred members. It is open from morning to night, and surveillance cameras are in place at all the entrances and exits. Some sections are reserved for women, others for men. The mosque spreads out over four floors. It also houses common areas and rooms that can be locked. It was to one such room that Hisham's wife was brought in the middle of May 2013.

She was instructed to sit on the floor. The Algerian began to read from the Koran. He thought he heard her call out in a deep, diabolical voice, far too low pitched to be that of a woman. He read. She groaned. He continued to read. She shouted something. As though the devil was talking through her, the Algerian believed. Then he began hitting her. The spirit fought. He struck her across the back. The spirit would not give in. He took off his plastic sandal and beat her. Eventually the girl was silent.

Basim Ghozlan, the leader of the congregation, was at home when he received a telephone call that a girl at the mosque required help and that an ambulance had been called.

The paramedics found that the patient had undergone cardiac arrest. The twenty-year-old woman was declared dead on arrival at the hospital.

Rumors began to circulate. Had she been beaten so hard that her heart had given out? Had he shaken her? Someone said he had held her down while she writhed like a snake. Violent spasms had given way to her suddenly going limp and her body landing with a thud on the floor, according to the rumors.

The exorcist, for his part, had little doubt about what had killed her. The demon had seeped into her heart and body, had become desperate upon hearing the words of the Koran, and in its final death throes had coiled itself around the girl's heart and cut off her blood circulation. She would have died sooner or later anyway, he told a friend. Better for her to die here in the mosque, the man who cast out devils maintained, than face further torment.

The girl's parents were devastated. Her father had been the one who engaged the exorcist and thought the fault lay in his inexperience. He claimed his daughter would still be alive and rid of demonic influence if only they had entrusted the task to someone who knew what he was doing.

Hisham received word of his wife's death in Syria. Several members of the Prophet's Ummah attended the funeral in his absence. Later, when a dispute arose between his Eritrean uncles and the parents of Hisham's deceased wife about who should raise the six-month-old baby, his relatives appealed to him to return home. According to Muslim tradition, a child followed his father. With the mother now dead, it was in their opinion only right and proper that the uncles acting on his behalf took custody.

The jihadist asked a friend to investigate the possibility of flying back, but under what name would he travel? On what passport? He was wanted by the police in Norway and would have to travel incognito to be safe from PST.

There was no going back. Hisham had rejected a normal life, a wife, and his responsibilities as a father. He fought for Allah. Everything else paled in significance.

A plain gravestone stood in Oslo's Høybråten cemetery.

A tiny infant would never know her mother. She had never had a father.

'Here,' Ubaydullah said to Dilal one day, returning her mobile phone.

It took her time to gather courage.

She mulled it over at length. Breaking out of the prison she was living in, a prison she herself had helped construct. She hadn't dared to call either her brothers or her parents. But she could not go on living like this, she had to take her chances.

Early one morning at the end of May, Dilal lay in bed looking over at the man sleeping next to her.

I'm leaving you today, she said to herself. *Just so you know, today's the day.* She waited until he left the apartment before calling her sister-in-law.

'Can I come home?' she asked meekly.

Her sister-in-law gasped, then began to cry.

'Please!' Dilal implored.

'Yes! Come, come now!'

Immediately afterward a text message ticked in from her brother: 'The door is open.'

Dilal did not waste any time. She packed a little bag, put the cat in a cage, placed it under her arm, and left. The heavy front door banged shut behind her and she began to hurry down the street before realizing she needed to calm down, had to avoid attracting any attention. Just as she hailed a taxi, she remembered Ubaydullah had a large number of taxi drivers in his social circle. But by then it was too late.

The driver turned to her, and her heart pounded when she saw he was Pakistani.

'Oslo Central Station, the seafront entrance,' she said. That was where her brother and sister-in-law had arranged to pick her up.

The driver asked her questions along the way.

'Where are you from?'

'I'm Kurdish,' she replied. 'And you?'

'Pakistani. I thought you were Pakistani too,' he said, turning his head slightly to look at her. 'A foreigner in any case!' He chuckled.

They began talking about how it was to live as a foreigner in Norway. The taxi driver told her how much he liked it, how well his children were doing, how nice everything was.

'Norway offers us a lot of opportunities,' he said, turning off by the opera house and toward the station.

'Yes,' she mumbled.

Looking out the car window, she saw her brother already waiting. She gathered her bag and the cat and ran toward him.

They drove west. Ensconced in the backseat, Dilal dried her tears and opened her handbag. She held up a pocket mirror and did her makeup as they sped along the highway. She could not go home to her parents looking like she did, could not turn up looking the way she felt, so she put on concealer, rouge, powder, and eye shadow. Using a kohl pencil, she lined her eyes, then applied mascara and finished with lipstick. She brushed her hair and styled it with a thin layer of mousse. She turned to look out the window with her chin raised.

Soon they arrived at the family home in Bærum.

Her mother flung open the door. Then flung her arms wide.

Her father stood behind her. They pulled her in, held her close, swayed from side to side, not wanting to let go, tears running down their faces. Their only daughter was home again. The nightmare was over.

'Our princess,' her father sniffled.

'Our child,' her mother wept.

Before long her mobile phone buzzed with a text.

'Where are you???!'

'I've gone home. I'm never coming back.'

A half hour later, uniformed police arrived at the Kurdish family's front door. Several patrol cars stood parked outside. They said they were acting on a tip-off they had received about a planned honor killing and were treating the information very seriously.

Her father was apoplectic. Her eldest brother felt so humiliated he began to cry. 'How could we harm our own sister?'

Patrol cars turned up several times over the following days, the police acting on tips from Ubaydullah Hussain. Finally Dilal was called in to the Sandvika police station. Following a lengthy interview, the inspector in charge declared the case closed. 'That's the last time the police will be around to your house,' he said.

But Ubaydullah would not give up. He called, sent texts, and left messages. She never responded. Then his mother rang. 'Dilal, take him back, he can't live without you! He loves you!' *Still, she gets it,* Dilal thought. She remembered her mother-in-law once saying she could not understand how Dilal could put up with her son.

There were no formalities to be taken care of. They had been married in a Muslim ceremony, a union not recognized by the Norwegian authorities.

He had almost completely brainwashed her and filled up her mind afresh. Dilal had managed to escape from a prison constructed in her own head. The Kurdish girl made up her mind never to allow herself to be manipulated again. She was going to resume her training as a nurse, continue where she left off. Life was here and now.

June arrived, the sun shone from early morning to late at night and the school year was drawing to an end. The sixteen-year-olds at Gjettum had applied to different upper secondary schools. Which one was actually the best? Would their grades be good enough for the school of their choice? Leila, at least to her classmates, seemed like she could not have cared less, maybe she didn't want to continue with school at all, they thought. After all, she had made clear her hatred of everything about it. However, right before the deadline, she applied for a place in the health and social curriculum at Rud Upper Secondary, a school not far from Dønski.

The spring before the end of school was warm and sunny, with the girls displaying thighs and cleavage, the boys their arms and chests.

'Isn't it hot underneath all that?' a classmate asked Leila as the two of them walked out the school gates. Leila was busy putting on her niqab, like she always did upon leaving the grounds of the school.

'It's hotter in hell,' Leila retorted.

The summer holidays were approaching, and tests and exams were over. During a break, a few girls sat on the grass talking about their plans for the holidays. Sofie asked if Leila was going to visit her family in Somaliland as she usually did. She was not. She was going to teach Islamic history and give Koran lessons to children at the mosque in Sandvika. Leila wore a black jilbab and white trainers. Since they were on school property, she had removed her veil. The others sat around in sandals, shorts, and sleeveless tops.

'Would they give you dirty looks in Somalia if you wore shorts?' a classmate asked.

'They'd kill you,' Leila replied matter-of-factly.

The girls rolled their eyes when she left. 'She's really starting to creep me out . . . '

Then they turned their attention back to tanning.

Just before school ended, Bintu Sadiq updated her profile picture on Facebook. She changed it to a black flag with the Islamic creed in Arabic. She also changed her background picture to a black-and-white photograph of a fighter in a turban. Only his eyes were visible, his body was in shadow. He held a Kalashnikov, raised and ready to fire.

Graduation was approaching. The only venue large enough to accommodate the entire year was the local church, and the school leadership discussed at length whether this might prove objectionable to Muslim pupils. It was decided that if all the religious symbols – the altarpiece, baptismal font, pulpit, and representations of Jesus – were covered, it should be all right.

By the time the church was ready for the presentation of academic transcripts and the pupils filed in for the ceremony, there was not a crucifix in sight.

Leila was conspicuous by her absence.

'Just mail it,' she had said on the last day of school.

Her friend Amal, on the other hand, had chosen to collect her diploma in person as well as attend the celebration afterward. Following the ceremony, the whole student body was invited to a party at Ulrik's house. Amal, unlike Leila, had kept Norwegian friends all through school, ensuring she had a foothold in the country she grew up in. As far as her mother was concerned, this was where her daughter's future lay. 'Norway lets you live your life how you want to,' she would say, before repeating her mantra: 'If you don't bother Norway, then Norway won't bother you!'

Amal had begun to distance herself from Leila. Her interpretation of Islam was too dark, too strict and narrow. In the end, a trivial argument had led to a final parting of the ways. Trivial matters had become existential ones.

Right before summer holiday, Amal was planning to see a romantic comedy. Leila had grimaced in disgust when the word 'movie' came up.

'That's sinful.'

'Why is it sinful?'

'It's haram.'

'That depends on the film . . . '

'Why sully yourself and pay for the privilege to boot? Why watch someone kiss or have sex when you could spend the time reading hadith?'

'Leila, you're one to talk! You sit watching people getting their heads chopped off and being stoned to death on YouTube. Is that not haram?'

'It's God's punishment. And fitting.'

Amal had had enough. She couldn't take any more of Leila's yearnings for death, her talk of martyrdom.

'Death is at hand,' Leila often said.

It's waving to you. Death is near. Accept it.

Amal did not wave back.

Ayan had kept away from upper secondary during the end of the school year. She showed up again for the exams, as usual taking off her niqab as she entered the school gate. After the written tests, she went to see if she had been selected to do an oral exam. She had, in Norwegian.

At nine o'clock in the morning they were informed of the topic. 'Explain the concept of modernism. Set modernism in a historic context. Specify the characteristics of modernism.' They were to analyze five examples, including *Angst* by Edvard Munch and an extract from Kafka's *The Trial*.

The pupils had two days to prepare. They were to give an oral presentation before answering questions posed by an examiner. Ayan went home to read. She made notes, studied, memorized, and ticked off each text as she went through it. Two days later she answered the examiner's questions correctly and without hesitation. *Modernism emphasized new and transgressive ideas, broke with traditional forms, and was characterized by experimentation, artistic liberation, and belief in progress.*

She received top marks. In Norwegian. Allah had been merciful.

A few days later she ran into her Norwegian teacher on the street in Sandvika.

'Congratulations, Ayan!' the teacher said, smiling. 'Make sure you put those grades to good use now!'

Ayan nodded beneath her niqab.

Graduation took place shortly afterward. Each class was invited to take its place on the stage, where a teacher waited with an armful of roses. As their names were called out and they stepped forward, the headmaster presented each pupil with a rose, wishing them 'Good luck in the future!' and telling them to 'have a great summer!'

Ayan's class was called to the stage. Hanne had been wondering if Ayan would show up and was happy when she caught sight of her among the crowd. *She must have enjoyed some of her time here, then,* she thought, in spite of the conflicts and the uncompromising tone of that last e-mail. Ayan went up onstage with the rest of the class.

It was getting to her letter of the alphabet. Would she stand demonstratively, refuse to approach when her name was called? No, the graduate walked over to Hanne, accepted the rose, and returned to her seat.

Ayan received no diploma, only an academic transcript. Among the Bs and Cs, and the A+ in oral Norwegian, NA – not assessed – was printed in the space for physical education. A failing grade, in other words. Her refusal to take part in gym class was the demise of her diploma. Until she repeated and passed phys ed, her other grades were worth nothing. Her certification was insufficient for further education at a college or university.

Two years earlier she had harbored ambitions of being the first person in her family to further herself academically. Now she was finished with second-level education, without any qualifications.

On her way out of the school building for the last time, she passed the wall with quotations. One was attributed to Nelson Mandela, even though it was by an English poet in Victorian times. *I am the master of my fate. I am the captain of my soul.*

She had made up her mind.

I am the master of my fate.

18

The October Revolution

One morning, at the start of the school year in autumn 2013, one of the department heads at Rud Upper Secondary was looking out the window. From his office he could easily survey the entrance the pupils were now crowding in. A female figure in black approached. She looked as if someone had thrown a black sheet over her and fastened a schoolbag on her back. He hurried down the stairs and intercepted the black-clad figure as she came in the door.

'Hi,' he said. 'My name's Totto Skrede. Who are you?'

Leila introduced herself.

'You'll have to remove that.' He pointed to her niqab.

'No problem,' Leila replied, and took it off.

'Yes, that's the way we want it here.' Skrede nodded. The recent county school administration committee meeting was fresh in his mind, and he remembered Hanne Rud, the principal at Dønski, informing them in detail about the decision reached by Akershus county. Covering up at school was not permitted. Everyone's face had to be visible.

The following day he was again sitting by the window. The same thing happened! The girl entered the building wearing the niqab. He went down to head her off.

'That has to be removed.'

'I was just about to take it off,' Leila replied.

'It's to be removed on the pavement outside. It has to be off before you set foot on the steps to the school,' Skrede stressed.

That year, IMDi – the Directorate of Integration and Diversity – was raising awareness about genital mutilation and forced marriage. The county authority had employed an adviser who, as it happened, had an office right there at Rud Secondary School. Perhaps the girl should be considered at risk in some way?

Leila's form teacher called her parents in for a meeting. They did not come.

She decided to leave it for the time being, get in touch with them again later. The teacher thought Leila was interesting, a pupil displaying more maturity than the others in the health care, child and youth development curriculum, which this year was composed solely of females. The girl came across as being comfortable in her own skin and confident, bordering perhaps on overconfident, always seeming to think she was right.

The teacher had also noticed she did not socialize with her classmates. She made no attempt at small talk, didn't hang around with any of the others, preferring to go pray in a room at the disposal of those who wished to use it. Sometimes she did not turn up at all. That was a worrying sign. In the teacher's experience, absenteeism increased as the year progressed. Taking that as a basis, Leila was off to a bad start.

But it wasn't a bad start, it was a cover-up.

Despite the smokescreen, Leila did leave a few clues about what was really occupying her. After only a week at Rud, she changed her profile picture on Facebook. The new one paid tribute to Anwar al-Awlaki, a man known as the 'bin Laden of the internet.' In a lecture titled 'Call to Jihad,' he explains in detail why it is every Muslim's religious duty to kill Americans. In another online video, in an almost placid tone, he instructs al-Qaida militants how to mix chemicals to make bombs. He calmly reminds them to tape screws and nails around the device to render it even more effective. Red-hot metal shrapnel will then bore itself into the bodies around where the bomb detonates.

Barack Obama had placed al-Awlaki on a list of people who could be killed by the CIA, which he was, in a drone attack in Yemen in 2011. He was the first American citizen in recent history executed without judicial supervision by his own president. In the wake of the drone strike, Obama stated that al-Awlaki had been 'removed from the battlefield.' But the terrorist leader had in no way been removed from the virtual battlefield.

While Leila was at school, Ayan spent her days online. In addition to religious sites, she had begun checking out new types of videos. *Laura in the Kitchen* presented recipes for fatty American fare, from mac and cheese to peanut brownies and cinnamon rolls. Make popsicles from Nutella, Laura said, laughing. Bake a meat pie, the brunette suggested as she smiled and licked her lips. *Show Me the Curry* demonstrated how to make Asian dishes. *Somali Food* described cuisine from her parents' homeland. On one site, Ayan studied cooking suited to simple conditions: *NoSpoonsHereCooking* – how to make food without measuring or weighing.

She also spent a good deal of time seeking out tips for house-keeping, visiting sites with names like Decorate Your House, Learn to Sew, Create Magic in Your Home. She sat at the computer and hungered, for magic, for real life to begin.

On Twitter, her profile was more political than before. Her first tweet that autumn, after a considerable hiatus, concerned *jihad al-nikah* – sex jihad. The phrase incensed Ayan. 'By now you have probably already heard of the harem of Tunisian sex-warrior slaves heading to Syria in order to give up their young bodies to the appe-tites of ravenous rebels . . . and coming back to the country with bellies full of jihadi babies,' the website muslimmatters.org noted, reassuringly adding: 'There is no evidence!'

Ayan was outraged that the pure intentions of these women were dragged through the mud. By making *hijra*, emigration, you were washing away your previous sins, and here it was being presented as if you were traveling to Syria to commit fresh ones!

The story drew attention when a Lebanese TV channel reported that the Saudi Arabian preacher Muhammad al-Arefe, who had several million followers, had issued a fatwa allowing the gang rape of Syrian women. An Arabian website followed up; the same man had encouraged Muslim women to travel to Syria and have sex with the fighters to keep morale up. The Tunisian minister of the interior said women were being tricked into going to Syria and returning pregnant.

The sheikh denied having issued the fatwa. No human rights groups found any evidence that women had traveled on jihad al-nikah. The minister did, however, have a motive for circulating the story. In terms of percentage of the population, Tunisia was the country with the most young people traveling to join the ranks of the jihadists. Perhaps fewer would be tempted if they were branded as whores.

The majority of Ayan's posts were still Islamic words of wisdom. She petitioned God for protection with the hashtag #Pray4Syria. 'If all you can do is pray, then pray hard!'

For her part, she was going to do more than pray, and she was not going to do it alone. She'd have to bring along Leila, who slept on the bunk over her. 'Above all other things, the one thing that I found to benefit a person most is a suitable companion,' she retweeted from greatmuslimquotes.com.

One by one, her friends had pulled out. For her it was beginning to be a matter of urgency. All the unopened bills and reminders were stacking up in the box at the top of the wardrobe. Ayan had received letters from several banks, from all the mobile operators she had subscriptions with, then finally from the execution and enforcement commissioner containing a summons to appear before the arbitration board. All she had to do was leave the letters unopened, not show up in court. But sooner or later someone would turn up on the doorstep.

One week after her sixteenth birthday, a day before boarding a flight to Turkey, Leila changed her Facebook profile picture one last time. In red writing it now read: 'MUJAHIDAH: A caring wife for a mujahid today, and loving mother of the mujahid tomorrow.'

Ayan had also found a suitable companion in Syria. It turned out he had been living just up the road from her all these years:

The Eritrean, the Dønski boy, the widower – Hisham.

After the death of his wife at the Rabita Mosque, his child's maternal grandparents had been looking after Hisham's infant. It was only now, in October 2013, five months after the death, that the police had launched an investigation to establish whether there was any connection between the exorcism and the cardiac arrest. But by now all the recordings from the cameras had been erased and no one could say what had taken place prior to or during the incident.

The case would be dropped.

Anyhow, the widower was again engaged.

There's no such thing as halal dating, it's called marriage. As soon as Ayan arrived, they were to be wed.

The Skype ringtone sounded on her laptop. She clicked on the telephone receiver symbol. They never talked with the camera on.

'*Salam aleikum.*'

'*Aleikum salam . . .* '

Hisham told her about his house and car, life among the other fighters. He asked her to click on the camera icon. She put on her niqab and placed her finger on the symbol. She saw him. He saw her eyes.

'So how did you become "radicalized," then?' he asked, in a flirty way. He chuckled softly. 'Aren't you actually an Islam Net girl?' In other words, a girl who did not go all the way, one who halted at the threshold.

'No, I am not! I'll show you,' Ayan replied.

'Lift your veil, then,' he said.

She raised it and showed him her face.

'Take it off,' he challenged.

She took it off.

Part III

MASHA: It seems to me that one must have faith, or must search for a faith, otherwise life is just empty, empty . . . To live and not to know why the cranes fly, why babies are born, why there are stars in the sky . . . Either you must know why you live, or everything is trivial, not worth a straw.

—Anton Chekov, *Three Sisters*, 1901

19

Danse Macabre

*My daughters would never have left. My daughters always asked permission.
They would never try to fool me.* These were the thoughts going around
and around in Sara's mind.

But then they were brainwashed.

Somebody brainwashed them.

It was not the girls' fault.

It was not their parents' fault.

Someone or something out there was to blame.

The internet?

An aquaintance?

Because *her* daughters would never have left.

Two weeks had passed since Sadiq had gone after them, first to
Turkey, then on to Syria. It was a muddle to her. On TV she saw
bombs, war, shooting, houses in ruins, people fleeing. She had been
a teenager herself when the civil war in Somalia raged around her.
She had fled, had rescued her daughters from war, and now they had,
what, returned willingly? No, it was impossible.

Sara had fled to Norway for them. *For them!*

Had it been up to her, she would have lived at home in Hargeisa.
Yes, she had friends here, in Bærum too, but it was not the same as

having your family, your relations, your sisters around you. She was acutely aware of that.

For the first time in her life she had to tackle everything on her own. Sadiq had always taken care of things. Sara had never so much as opened a letter. Money matters were her husband's responsibility. The family often lived beyond their means. It was not uncommon for Sadiq to go to the social welfare office toward the end of the month to ask for extra money.

She rang her husband several times a day. *Have you found the girls? Heard anything? Haven't they called?*

They were lifelines for each other. She needed to hear his voice and he hers. They had to be together on this.

The days grew shorter. Darkness fell earlier. The most everyday things upset her, like seeing the girls' toothbrushes in the bathroom, finding hair ties under the sofa, going into their room where their shawls lay folded. Sniffing their scent on them . . .

She had not heard from her daughters since the day they left. They had made a huge mistake, but she had already forgiven them. They had to come home, then they could talk about it.

The verdict within the Somali community was harsh. They were critical of Sadiq as a father and Sara as a mother. The opinion in Somali chat rooms was that their daughters had taken off to Syria because he was too liberal and she was too stupid. Their leaving was a punishment from God.

Sara was in the kitchen preparing dinner when the telephone rang.

'Mom!'

'Ayan!'

'We're in Syria!'

'I know! Your father's there too!'

'What? Why?'

'Because of you!'

'How did he get in? Why has he come?'

'To get the two of you!'

'Oh . . . '

'Ayan, come home with him, bring your little sister, come back.

I'll give you his number. Please, I beg of you, do as I ask, call him and come back home with him!'

'Wallahi, he's crazy!' her daughter groaned.

Sara gave her his number. Then she called Sadiq.

'The girls rang me! They will ring you now!'

Sadiq, who was sitting in Osman's backyard smoking, jumped to his feet, embraced his host, and shouted. 'The girls are about to call me now!'

But they did not call.

Not that day, not the next one, nor the day after that. Sara was the only one who rang him, over and over.

As Sadiq was not there to drive the boys to school, she was taking the bus with them every morning and picking them up in the afternoon. It was wearing her out and keeping her going. When the refrigerator began to empty and the dry goods ran out, she and a friend went to NAV and explained the situation. She was granted a payout to cover the immediate necessities and an extra allowance for food in November, in addition to benefits for rent and electricity.

Sara had attended a few Norwegian-language classes but never learned much. On her certificate she had almost two hundred hours of 'unauthorized absence.' She had never put any effort into learning Norwegian, had never looked at a lesson plan, didn't understand what the letters from the school said, couldn't read the notes sent home from Isaq's kindergarten or from the kids' schools. If there was something she was interested in on the news, she asked the children or her husband to translate for her.

Sadiq, who had been tenacious in learning Norwegian, claimed to know the reason Sara had never bothered to learn the language. 'Sara comes from an arrogant family,' he said. 'To learn a new language, you need to be willing to make mistakes, and Sara could not countenance that. Her arrogance is like a membrane against knowledge. It's beneath her dignity to strive.'

Three years earlier, NAV had organized a job for her at a discount store, in order for her to gain the relevant work experience to enter the job market. The job description was 'customer service, cash register, stocking, tidying, and keeping the premises clean.' Upon returning from her first day she complained to Sadiq.

'They're treating me like a slave, giving me the most demanding tasks. They have me standing on a ladder stacking shelves.'

Sadiq replied that if she learned Norwegian she could work the till.

'I don't like the till,' she responded. 'I don't like numbers.' She was exhausted after each working day and cursed the job. One bright night in June, the chain store's warehouse was gutted by fire, causing the temporary closure of the shop, prompting Sadiq to joke that Sara had been behind it.

'You had it in for that place,' he teased. Sara was never called back after her apprenticeship ended.

She sat on the sofa looking out at the terrace. The junk silhouetted like a ramshackle ruin against the dim sky. Piles of boxes with things they might one day need lay on top of one another, collecting autumn leaves and bird droppings. The pains in her body were no longer diffuse. They were concentrated in her chest. In her stomach. In her heart. Loss. Sorrow. Deceit. She longed to feel the warmth of her daughters' cheeks. The Somali sun. Life as it had been.

The doorbell sounded. Two women stood outside. Sara invited them in.

When they left, she had no idea who they had been or what their names were, but they had looked kind and she thought they might be teachers. They had told her to let them know if there was any way they could help. She had asked for money.

A few days later they returned and handed her an envelope. There were 9,000 kroner inside. The teachers from Rud Upper Secondary had managed to find some money in the budget for social measures. Leila had left the school but Ismael was still a pupil there. They did not want to leave him in the lurch.

Osman's backyard was always filled with men. There were soft chairs and low tables in the shadow of the grapevines, and mattresses lay flat along the wall with cushions to rest your back against.

Smugglers and militia leaders sat around gossiping, smoking, drinking tea, and making plans.

The house lay behind a blue gate with sharpened spikes, and the cement top of the high wall surrounding the yard was covered with shards of glass. The stiff desert wind carried anything lying loose along with it, and plastic bags, string, lengths of rope, and all manner of lightweight litter were blown onto the wall and impaled.

It was calm at the eye of the storm. A few villages over, the jihadists were in control. A couple of hours away Assad was bombing Aleppo. The Kurds were a few miles west, and directly north lay Turkey.

The shifting alliances formed a perfect backdrop for profit. Wads of cash were counted. Ammunition, rifles, cars, two sisters – everything had a price in this cross between a military camp and a gangsters' lair.

Apart from Osman's mother, Sadiq had never seen any women in the house. He had heard voices; one he assumed belonged to Osman's wife and others he guessed to be those of his sisters. But he did not know what they were called. Osman never mentioned them by name, and it did not seem appropriate to ask.

In the evenings, when Sadiq lay in the guesthouse, Osman's voice dominated. He was no henpecked husband, that was for sure. He yelled and told people off, was quick-tempered and impatient. Osman and his wife had two daughters. Four-year-old Randa had the same auburn hair as her father, the same eyes, fair skin, and energy. She took after him in every way. She was boisterous and brave – to his despair; he didn't view her behavior as appropriate for a girl. Sadiq never saw Osman play with his daughter. When she approached him, he usually sent her away with, 'Go in to your mother!' One time she clambered up on his shoulders while he sat in the shade talking. He pulled her off and told her never to do that again, and another time when she was running around the yard with a neighbor boy and knocked over a glass of tea, her father slapped her hard across the cheek. He shouted to his wife, 'Don't let her out here anymore!'

'She's too active, that girl,' he sighed afterward. 'I don't know what I'll do with her. It will only get her into trouble if she continues on like this.'

Sadiq, who had allowed his daughters to climb, swim, and play ball, cheered for Randa when she saw her chance and snuck out. He would kick the ball her cousin always forgot in the backyard back and forth with her. She squealed with delight. Osman scowled at them but did not say anything.

Arabs have some odd ideas when it comes to women, Sadiq thought. How long would it be before Randa's spirit was broken?

The search went slowly. Osman had undertaken new jobs, some of which were lucrative. He was tasked with smuggling a bunch of jihadists across the border from Turkey and spent a long time planning the operation. There were bribes, middlemen, and drivers to think of. The fighters were to be picked up at the airport in Hatay, driven to a house in one of the villages near the Turkish side of the border, before being transported over when the Turks looked the other way, and delivered to an ISIS base. With Osman's help, the jihadists would get their reinforcements.

There was no sign of life from the girls. No one had seen them, no one even thought they *might* have seen them.

One day when Sadiq and Osman were waiting for lunch, Sadiq's mobile phone rang.

'Hi, Dad.'

It was Leila.

Sadiq got to his feet and went to a corner. *Don't scare her off, don't scare her away*, he told himself. He did his best to speak calmly.

'Leila, darling, where are you?'

'Dad, stop looking for us. Just return to Norway, go back home to Mom and the others.'

'I need to see you. Where are you?'

His daughter failed to answer. He told her where he was.

'I'm in Atmeh. Right next to the Turkish border. Why don't you both come here, or tell me where you are, then I can come and get you.'

The line went dead. He remained standing, waiting for her to call back.

Grilled chicken with raw onion and bread was placed on the table. He sat down without uttering a word; he had to take this in on his own. The other men were absorbed in their meal. Afterward they smoked and drank tea.

Then he turned to Osman. 'The girls called me!'

While his father was waiting in the afternoon sun in Atmeh, Ismael received a text from Fatima Abdallah. He had just gotten home from school. It was three weeks since his sisters had left.

'We have spoken to Dad, we're going to meet him soon, everything is still fine with us.' The message continued point by point.

1. We have not been kidnapped and are not being held against our will.
2. We aka Leila and I planned everything from the itinerary to money. Leila inspired me and encouraged me to go. So stop blaming everyone else. We were planning this for almost a year.
3. We did this 100% for Allah's sake. Not for any boyfriends or anyone else. So fear Allah and do not listen to the lies of the kuffar aka media.

The tone was familiar – his sister, the know-it-all – had not changed. He replied sarcastically, 'Nice! Lovely to hear from you.'

'We really want to stay in touch, unfortunately we cannot tell you anything if it's all going to end up in the media.'

Ismael did not reply.

'We love you all loads,' the girls added.

Behind the blue gate in Atmeh, the men paced back and forth waiting for the phone to ring again. Between the yard and the living room, in and out again.

The soft chairs in the backyard gave no rest, the shade was not cool.

Sadiq's telephone began to vibrate.

'Daddy, we're on our way to Atmeh.'

Osman leaped up from the mattress.

'The roundabout! Tell them to go to the roundabout!' he shouted and began marshaling the men. He would negotiate the girls' release, he promised.

Sadiq made ready to leave, but Osman refused to take him along. 'You'll only mess it up,' he said. 'You're the father. Too much emotion involved.' Negotiations were his area of expertise.

'I'll go and check it out,' he said.

Sadiq insisted on coming along, but then Abu Omar, Osman's father, butted in. 'My son will secure your daughters' release.'

Osman left. Sadiq immediately regretted letting him go without him. They were his daughters! He sat waiting. He smoked a cigarette. Called Osman. Lit another. Smoked. Called again. Lit one more. He pressed his palms together, drummed the fingers of one hand against the other. He got to his feet, sat back down. He heard shooting and went out into the yard. He listened, attempting to gauge where it was coming from. The crackling sound suggested multiple weapons. He had grown accustomed to the exchange of gunfire here due to the many militias competing for control of the smuggling route. It could flare into skirmishes that moved the front line from house to house, from one street to the next. The roads in and out of town, the highways and bridges were important points of control, but whoever controlled the roundabout controlled Atmeh. The shots were coming from the center of town, he surmised, as he walked in circles around the backyard.

A car skidded to a stop outside. He heard the squeal of tires as it braked and he recognized the sound of the pickup. The door flew open. Osman stormed in, sweaty and red in the face.

'Come on!'

As Sadiq clambered in, Osman jumped behind the wheel and began relating what had happened in snatches.

'More than one car. A black man. Two men in front. The girls in the backseat! They're with ISIS! ISIS has them!'

The driver of the lead car had entered the al-Nusra area without stopping at the checkpoint, a clear breach of the agreement between the local militias. The car had turned onto the roundabout. The man behind the wheel then made a complete circuit, as a show of power to prove he had the girls before exiting. But he was forced to stop by al-Nusra this time, and the commander, an older, experienced man, had approached the vehicle.

As he drew close, the black man had put the car in reverse and then hit the accelerator, but he'd lost control and driven straight into some roadside vendors selling smuggled fuel in glass jars.

The commander had made out two niqab-clad figures in the backseat. He had guessed who they were.

'The girls' father is in Atmeh,' he told the man behind the wheel. 'He is under our protection. Which means the girls are also under our protection.'

The driver had again put the car in reverse and driven from the roundabout at full speed while the Nusra soldiers fired after it. They had been aiming at the tires but several shots pierced the hood and the side of the vehicle, which eventually made it over to the ISIS-controlled area a few streets away.

'We didn't follow them,' Osman told him. 'Daesh are in control there. But . . . there is something else . . . I heard . . . someone said . . . that your younger daughter was hit!'

It was as if his heart stopped beating. Leila was shot!

'She's at the hospital here in Atmeh,' Osman said.

'We need to go there!'

The Orian hospital was under ISIS control, and armed men stood outside. Sadiq and Osman were refused entry. Sadiq attempted to force his way in but was pushed back, eventually being thrown to the ground. He walked around the building, hoping to find another way to get inside.

Osman begged him to be careful.

'We have to tread carefully in our little town. We're

tiptoeing around one another, sounding each other out all the time. Remember that.'

Sadiq, exhausted, slumped by the hospital wall. He wanted a cigarette, but that was not possible in front of the ISIS guards. Hours passed. The sun was beginning to go down. They sat on the ground with their backs to the wall in the wilted garden of the hospital. Flowers are not looked after in wartime.

'The situation is unsettled,' Osman mumbled. 'Everything is unsettled.'

The young guards were hungry. Sadiq gave a wad of cash to Osman, who counted off some banknotes and handed them over. The boys soon returned with shawarma, large chunks of spicy lamb in a wrap. Sadiq chewed on one, the fresh chili burning his mouth.

Afterward they sat drowsily, waiting for the hospital guards to change their minds, for Leila to come out. At midnight, the youths asked, 'Can we lie down for a while?'

They soon fell asleep on the ground with their weapons beneath their heads. Their features relaxed, loosened, their tense expressions disappearing. Only Sadiq remained sitting stiffly, alert, on watch.

At one in the morning Osman's wife called. She ordered her husband to return home.

'Bring Sadiq with you!'

'I want to be here when they decide to let us in,' Sadiq said.

'Come home. We don't want a head-on clash with ISIS now,' Osman insisted. 'We've already been through that once already today. Look how that ended!'

'You're a father. My youngest daughter is in there,' Sadiq said, pointing. 'I'm staying.'

But what they did not know was that Leila was no longer inside. She had arrived with a bullet lodged in her leg, just above the ankle. It was an ugly wound, and several nerves and tendons had been severed. The bullet had been removed by a young doctor named Firas. While he was dressing the wound, a gang of masked men entered.

Firas asked Leila in English how she felt. Was she feeling nauseous from the sedative, was she . . . ?

'Don't speak to my wife!' a man had shouted.

He was well built and in good shape, not particularly tall, with an African appearance and the biggest, whitest set of teeth Firas had ever seen. The doctor straightened up, and bandaged Leila in silence while the men stood watching.

'I'll take her now,' the black man said when Firas had finished.

'She should . . . ,' Firas began. He looked at the masked gang, then at the white-as-chalk teeth. 'She'll need to have it looked at again. Bring her back in a week so I can check if the wound is healing all right.'

The man had lifted Leila up without replying and carried her out. He placed her in the backseat of a silver-colored Land Rover and sped off.

Sadiq, unaware of this, sat well into the night waiting for permission to enter. Eventually Osman left without him. Finally Sadiq also staggered home. He knew the way and walked alone through the streets of Atmeh, a weapon over his shoulder and ammunition around his waist.

That day he had found his daughters, only to lose them again. They had called. They had come. Now they were gone.

It was unreal. He did not call Sara.

In the little guesthouse in Osman's backyard, he could not settle down to rest. They were here, someplace nearby, but where?

For what little was left of the night he twisted and turned in nightmares. He heard shots, hails of gunfire rained down upon him. ISIS soldiers took aim and fired, war raged all around him. He defended himself, returned fire, feeling a bullet enter his left shoulder, where the crate of Coca-Cola had injured him. He woke up drenched in sweat. Tried to get back to sleep but his thoughts would not let up. Was Leila badly wounded?

An hour before sunrise, the muezzin called the faithful to prayer. *Allahu Akbar*. He got out of bed. *There is no other god but Allah and Muhammad is his messenger.* Finally he fell into a peaceful sleep.

'We won't get them out by force, we can't start a war over your daughters,' Osman said. The sun had been up awhile and once again they were standing outside the hospital. Still they were denied entry.

'Let's go to the Islamic court, we can ask for a ruling that you have authority over them. We have to get a move on before they take them away with them,' Osman suggested.

The girls had traveled to Syria without the permission of their father, who was their wali. It should, according to sharia, be a straightforward case, in Osman's view. If the Koran and the hadith were to be complied with, Sadiq had authority over his daughters. If the Islamic court ruled in their favor, then the Islamists would have to obey the verdict. Nobody was above sharia.

On arrival at the local Islamic court they were informed the matter would have to be determined by the court in al-Dana, an hour's drive away.

There they were met by a man dressed in the traditional tunic and ankle-length trousers. Sadiq told him why they had come and they were told to wait for the judge. Time passed. Maybe the court wanted money? A ransom?

They were served tea before being shown in to Abu Qadim al-Tunisi. Sadiq put forward his arguments to the Tunisian judge, making reference to whatever he could remember the Prophet had said about children and parents.

'They left without my permission. I have, therefore, the right to get them back,' he stated as calmly as he could. 'According to the Koran, a father has authority over his daughters.'

The Tunisian gave him a look of slight surprise from beneath his turban.

'Well, the husband has authority now.'

'Neither of my daughters are married,' Sadiq objected.

'Yes . . .'

Sadiq stared at the judge, dumbfounded.

'Your elder daughter pledged her word in this courtroom,' the Tunisian went on. 'The marriage is sealed by a sharia contract.'

She must have been forced into it, Sadiq thought.

'It has to be annulled,' Sadiq protested. 'The Prophet says there can be no nikah without a wali,' he argued. This was the same as eloping, since when had that been allowed?

The judge pondered the matter, then nodded. 'There is no higher authority than the word of God as written in the Koran.'

Reason had triumphed. When could he fetch his daughters?

The judge continued in a calm voice. 'This is jihad. It is the duty of every Muslim to take part. It is fard al-ayn, meaning she does not need your permission. God has granted her permission.'

Sadiq shook his head vigorously. Was this supposed to be true Islam?

A man entered. He too wore a tunic and ankle-length trousers. He sat down across from Sadiq. A group of men with headbands bearing the Islamic creed stood around them.

ISIS had taken Muhammad's seal as its own. A white, slightly uneven circle with the Arabic symbols in black: *There is no other god than Allah and Muhammad is his messenger.*

'We're at war,' the man said. 'We need all the help we can get. What about becoming one of us? You can live here together with your daughters, and the rest of your family can come and join you. We can offer you a good life, a house. Everything you need.'

'That's good to know,' Sadiq replied curtly. 'But not now . . .'

'All you have to do is swear baya to Abu Bakr al-Baghdadi, then you'll be one of us. That's all you need to do. An oath of allegiance. In time we will build a state, just wait, based on Islamic law, on the Koran and Allah.'

Sadiq grew impatient.

'I don't have time for this. I didn't come here as a mujahid but as a father. I've come out of paternal love. My goal is to bring my daughters home to their mother. All I want now is to see them.'

The man across the table looked at him.

'Very well, as you wish,' he said, keeping his eyes on him.

Sadiq was left to sit and wait. After a while some soldiers came in to get him. They escorted him out of the building, across a yard, and into a large tent with mattresses, tinned goods, and sacks of rice stacked up inside.

Ayan entered, straight as a ramrod, swathed in a niqab covering everything except her eyes.

As Sadiq approached her, one of the guards told him, 'You have five minutes.'

He embraced his daughter, touched her covered head, feeling the curly hair beneath the veil. When she was little, he used to put his hand on her forehead and run his fingers over her hair, stroking her until she was calmed enough to tell him whatever the matter was. Now she pulled away.

Four minutes.

This was not the time to tell her off. Right now he needed to console her.

'Everything is going to be all right, relax, you're coming with me now. They can't keep you here. Don't be afraid. I'm here to bring both of you back.'

'But, Dad, this is our home now.'

'Ayan, you're confused . . . '

'Listen to me, we want to live here.'

Three minutes.

'Ayan, you . . . you've both been fooled. Leila's been shot. You're—'

The mobile phone in his pocket vibrated. It was Sara.

'Have you heard from the girls?' she asked.

'Ayan is here!'

He handed the phone to his daughter. 'Talk to your mom!'

Two minutes.

'Ayan!' he heard Sara say. She was crying into the receiver. 'Come back! Come home with your dad!'

Ayan just stood there.

Her mother continued talking: 'Go with your father!'

Ayan took a deep breath. 'I can't, Mom . . . '

'Yes, you can!'

One minute.

'I can't, Mom, it's not possible . . . I've married!'

Sara gasped.

The guards began to move toward them.

Ayan handed her father the phone.

Sadiq looked at her. 'You can't get married without . . . You listen to me! Do you know what the punishment is for that?'

His daughter stood staring at him.

'We've made our choice, Dad. Please respect that. We have the support of the sheikhs here,' she said in a calm voice.

He wanted to pull her close, hold her, but she had already turned to leave.

Time was up.

The guards escorted her out. She disappeared across the floor like a black wave.

She had deceived them, betrayed them, she had given herself to some man he did not even know. Whom had she married? He had not had the chance to ask her.

He took a moment to think things through. Ayan was a prisoner. Leila was wounded. They had to go back to the hospital to get her, then return here tomorrow to sort things out.

Sadiq was given back his weapon and ammunition belt. He left with Osman, who had been waiting outside. The Syrian was relieved to see him again. The court had scared them all.

At dawn the following day, Osman suggested bringing along his friend Hamza, a commander in al-Nusra, to negotiate. Hamza went by the nickname 'the Lion.' The young man had a big beard, a mane to rival his namesake, and moved like a youthful predator, vigilant and lissome. He was the one who usually livened up the atmosphere in Osman's backyard. Now he sat silently in the car. Shrewdness was what was called for at the moment. They had already been to the hospital earlier that morning and failed to gain admission.

'We have to prevent this from becoming a matter of prestige, avoid them losing face,' he said to Sadiq, and impressed upon him the need to come across as humble.

Only then would he get his daughters. ISIS had to feel like the dominant party; they bridled at the first sign of opposition. Although Osman was a big-time smuggler in Atmeh and respected in al-Nusra, he meant nothing to ISIS. These men had come from all around the world and taken over portions of his and Hamza's country, and now acted as if they owned it.

When they reached the court, his Syrian companions were told to wait outside, Sadiq was the only one invited in. He was ordered to leave his weapon with Hamza and Osman.

'I don't like this,' Osman mumbled.

'Sadiq, you're under our protection. It'll be fine,' Hamza promised. Osman turned in his seat. 'Just go in. See this through!' Hamza insisted. 'Nothing can happen to you as long as we're here.'

Inside, Sadiq was offered a chair and a glass of tea.

Once again he was asked to enlist in the Islamic State in Iraq and Syria. Were they so lacking for people?

Sadiq, as on the previous occasion, tried to sidestep the question, responding that it was a possibility, not something he would rule out, but first he wanted to see his girls.

Time dragged on, people came and went, until eventually a man motioned to him to get to his feet. The man, who spoke in a Tunisian dialect and was accompanied by a couple of others, led him outside. They halted in a yard.

A masked man approached them. 'Your son-in-law wants to meet you.'

'Who?'

'Your son-in-law.'

'Where?'

The man pointed to a vehicle a little way off. It was a pickup, silver-gray. It was some twenty yards away, parked by the wall surrounding the yard.

'Your son-in-law is in the car. He's from Norway. He wants to speak to you.'

Sadiq looked in the direction of the pickup, thought about it for a moment, then said, 'If he wants to meet me, he should come over here.'

The guard walked over to the vehicle and exchanged a few words with the occupant through the window. He insisted that Sadiq go to him.

Sadiq was indignant. This was not how a woman was supposed to wed. A suitor should ask for her hand, not just take her. This son-in-law had come on the scene without even introducing himself. Sadiq did not know his name or the first thing about his family, and now this young man wanted him – the father, the wali, the guardian, the head of the family – to go to him!

He forced himself to remain calm. He was on foreign soil and had to do as Osman said, be humble, walk over and say, *Do you love my daughter? Does she love you? Let me sit down with her and talk things out properly. If you are truly the one she wants, then I can be a father to you as well.* He could say that.

He wavered. Should he? No, it was out of the question! If this man wanted Ayan, he had to ask for her! Or ask his own father to do it on his behalf. There was a protocol to follow, even in a war zone. Ayan had been in Syria only a matter of weeks and now she was suddenly married!

The Somali's pride triumphed. He would not take Osman's advice to display deference. He straightened up. 'I have no son-in-law,' he told the guard.

'As you wish.' The man went back to the car and exchanged a few words with the driver.

Sadiq remained standing in the courtyard. A pair of masked men kept him under observation.

It was growing dark. A voice said, 'Come, you can meet with your daughters. Follow me.'

They entered a building, walked down a corridor, and exited into another yard.

'Move, move!' the guard told him. The masked men followed. Sadiq felt an AK-47 in his back.

He received a blow to the head. Then another. Followed by one more. He felt his head swim. He fell to the ground, where they kicked, spat, and swore at him. *Spy!* he heard. *Traitor!* Then they hauled him up, covered his eyes, bound his arms and legs, and threw him into a car. He lay on the floor in the back, between the feet of the men. At times they stamped their boots on him or kicked his head. The car drove quickly. He was nauseous, felt like he was about to pass out. A stinging pain spread across the back of his neck, prompting him to try to turn over. He received a kick on the jaw. 'We know your type, we've killed a lot like you,' a voice said. His head bounced up and down at their feet. He had no control over his body, he was squeezed into a position he could not adjust. *I need to protect my head*, he thought.

They drove for a long time. The blows abated, occurring intermittently, to his head, his neck, his sore shoulder. A kick in the thigh, the shins.

The car stopped. This is where they would kill him, he thought. They dragged him out. The ropes around his ankles were loosened and, still blindfolded, he was ordered to walk. He was led into a house and down a flight of stairs. A door was opened and he was thrown forward, a terrible stench hitting his nostrils. The door slammed shut. He pulled the rag from over his eyes. It was just as black without it. He managed to get up from the floor, felt his way along the walls – rough brickwork, peeling paint, some pipes, he made out the frame of a window that was battened shut. The walls were damp, the floor was wet, the stink was coming from below. He stretched out his legs, swept a foot across the floor. Part of the floor was slightly raised and in the middle was a hole. He was in a toilet.

He put his back to the wall, a thumping pain in his body, a searing in his head. He collapsed onto his side. The sewage soaked into the seat of his pants, seeped up his back and down his thighs.

Exhausted, he nodded off, or passed out.

When he woke, he managed to get up, to stand on his feet. After a couple of steps, he reached a wall. He tried to orient himself. His body ached all over.

He needed a strategy, he told himself. In order to survive. *Number one: Breathe through your nose, not your mouth. Number two: Save your strength.*

He guessed it was morning. Outside, he heard people talking, doors opening and closing. His door remained shut. He dozed off and woke up again. Everything in his mouth seemed enlarged, his tongue was swollen and pressed against his palate, his lips were cracked. He was thirsty but did not dare knock on the door to ask for water. The voices outside were louder. Were they planning to just leave him here? Maybe there had been a changing of the guard and the new ones weren't aware he was here. He felt woozy, his mind was fuddled. *Water! Water!* Everything faded again.

He was awakened by shouts and screams and doors slamming. He tried to find his voice but could not. He struggled into a crouching position but lacked the strength to stand up and so lay down on his side. Stretching out was not an option, the cell was not long enough.

The door opened. Light filtered in from the corridor. Three men entered. They kicked him to his feet, a military boot in the shoulder sending him against the wall. They set upon him, giving each other elbow room. He heard the click of a handgun. One man stood pointing it at him.

'We are happy Allah wants us closer to Him by spilling the blood of a traitor,' he said in poor Arabic. 'Allahu Akbar.' The other two joined in like a chorus. The echo was frightening. His mind was whirling.

Then they left. He collapsed. Putting his hand to his face, he noticed it was wet. He sucked on his own blood.

Something landed on him. It was wet, heavy, warm – a person.

For a moment he just lay there, with a man on top of him. Then he heaved him aside and nodded off again. Two men entered – were they the same ones who had beaten him up, or some others? They grabbed hold of the man, hauled him up, and pounded him with the butts of their weapons. Sadiq tried to get out of the way but could not escape blows to his own head, shoulders, and neck. The other man cried out, *'Ya ummi!'* Mother! He raised his hands to defend himself, fell, picked himself up, stood, before dropping to the ground and lying there motionless. The last of the kicks provoked no reaction.

A small, thickset guy with broad features and an unkempt beard lifted the man's arm and let it go. The man's hand thumped lifelessly onto the floor, and the torturer said, 'Our prey is all set.'

They took one foot each and pulled, hauling the man like a sack. His head thudded against the floor as they dragged him over the threshold. Streaks of blood were left behind down the corridor.

'Lock the door on that other piece of shit!' the little stocky one with the beard shouted in broken Arabic.

The guard slammed the door shut. The lock clicked. Sadiq was alone.

He lay dazed, hollowed out, and feeble. How long had he been here, without food or water? One day, two days, three? Faint with thirst, he dozed off, awoke again. He felt like he was sinking, trapped in quicksand. Blindly, he descended ever deeper, went under, his mouth filled up, his nose, his throat. He lost all air. Choked. Sank into the depths.

His enfeebled body went on high alert as the door jerked open and light was let in. He saw the outline of a man in the doorway. He was tall and well built. Sadiq crouched in the corner, readying himself for the blows. They had come to get him. It was his turn. His time was up.

The man handed him a cup of lentil soup. Sadiq drank slowly. It was the best thing he had ever tasted. When the cup was empty, he licked around the inside, as far as his tongue could reach, before running his fingers over the bottom to get the last drops. Then he licked his fingers until no taste of the soup remained.

The guard returned. With water and a crust of bread. Why was he being given food all of a sudden, what did that mean? Was it a good sign? A bad sign? A last meal?

When the guard came back to collect the cup, Sadiq asked what had happened to the man who had been taken out.

'You don't want to know,' the guard replied in a local dialect and slammed the door shut.

That evening, or that night, or whatever it was, the three men returned. The guard had screwed a lightbulb in the ceiling, so now Sadiq was better able to make them out. He recognized one of them: The orchestrator of the beating from the night before was short, compact, with a black beard spreading high up his plump cheeks, almost reaching his eyes. His face was broad, his hair tousled. The other man was tall, maybe close to six feet, with pale skin and dark, sleek hair. By his dialect Sadiq guessed he was Libyan. The last man was slender, with a golden tinge to his black skin, he could have been from the Horn of Africa, Eritrea perhaps.

The broad-faced, well-built one squatted in front of Sadiq. He did not say anything, merely stared right at him, his eyes fixed on Sadiq's. The two others stood behind him. They all had handguns. No one said a word.

They stared at him in silence.

They're trying to break me, Sadiq thought. The burly one remained squatting in front of him, the weight of his pistol making a pouch in the tunic. Sadiq decided to meet his gaze, to fight back: *I'm not so easy to crush, just try.*

He shifted position. His thickset counterpart did not. The man was younger than he had first thought, in his early twenties perhaps. Sadiq continued to eyeball him: *I'm an older wolf than you. I would beat you in a fair fight.*

He felt his heart beating and tried to breathe evenly. He used the technique he had learned as a sharpshooter to calm his pulse. But his heart would not allow itself to be mastered.

The bearded one got to his feet abruptly without saying anything, kicked Sadiq, and walked out. The other two followed.

'Why are you here?' the guard asked him the next morning.

'I don't know,' Sadiq answered.

'You ought to know,' the young men went on. 'Because this is death row.'

Sadiq felt a jolt pass through him.

'What have you done?'

'I'm innocent,' Sadiq said. 'Let me explain, let me see a judge!'

'Impossible,' the guard replied. 'The judge has had his say.'

'I'm here to find my daughters, to take them back home . . . '

'You're a traitor!'

'I'm a father!'

The guard spat in his face. '*Kazab!*' Liar! He spat again. 'You're spying for Western intelligence.'

Sadiq wiped off the clot of spit and looked right at the guard.

'My daughters just up and left and . . . now . . . I . . . am . . . searching . . . '

'You're lying. *Kazab, kazab!*' The guard left.

A dark feeling spread.

After a time the guard returned with a copy of the Koran.

'Can you swear on the Koran?' he asked, looking Sadiq in the eye.

'No,' Sadiq replied, 'I cannot. I'm covered in shit. I can't touch God's book like this.'

The guard went out, with the book in hand. When he returned, he led Sadiq into the backyard, turned on a tap, and hosed him down. A rush of life gushed through him and he gulped greedily at the water washing over him. Blood, shit, and sweat ran down his body, it was as though the cold water whipped him back to life. *Drink! Drink!* went the refrain in his mind.

Once he was back in the cell, the guard returned with the Koran. Sadiq placed his hand on it and repeated the words the guard said aloud.

'*Wallahi bi'l Qur'an . . .* ' I swear on the Koran . . .

That he was not a spy. That he was not a traitor. That he was not an infidel.

Then Sadiq said, 'I have only one mission in Syria – to find my daughters.'

The ISIS guard studied him for a time. 'I believe you,' he said. 'Call me Abu Ahmed.'

'My name is Abu Ismael,' Sadiq replied.

Abu Ahmed went out and returned with a dry blanket. 'I can't really help you, but I'll try. I don't want to meet Allah after making a big mistake. But if they come for you, there's nothing I can do.'

What would happen then, if *they* came? Who were they?

That night Sadiq was awakened again by a person being thrown into the cell. A heavy man, large and muscly, was dumped on top of him. His body was wet, and it was not from water or sweat; he was coated in blood.

The man tried to get up. He stepped on Sadiq, who pushed him off. There wasn't room for both of them.

'*Wish al-jahim hada?*' the man bawled. What kind of hell have I wound up in?

'Calm down!'

'Who are you?' the man asked.

Sadiq gave a dry laugh. 'There's no point asking me who I am.'

They stood, each with his back against a wall, facing each other.

'What sort of hell is this?' the man asked again.

'*Zinzanat al-qatl bi qisas,*' Sadiq said in Arabic.

The man took hold of Sadiq and pressed him against the cold, damp surface.

'What did you say?'

Qatl bi qisas was the term in sharia for the principle of retribution, an eye for an eye, a death sentence, in other words. *Zinzanat* meant 'cell.'

The man held him tightly. Sadiq managed to get his hand around the other man's throat and squeezed. He felt the strength in the man's young body, the sticky blood on his skin.

'Look me in the eyes,' Sadiq said.

The man gave a bitter laugh. 'What eyes?'

'Above where my voice is coming from,' Sadiq said.

The man released his grip.

'They can't kill me. I'm from here. I'm Syrian. But you, who fell from the sky, you they can kill, not me!'

'Pull yourself together and listen to me. You being from Syria or my falling from the sky makes no difference, we're in the death cell. That's how it is.'

'No! It can't be like that!'

He banged at the door with his foot, kicked at it with his heel, hammered with his fists. It opened.

'*Antum majanin?*' Are you crazy? It was Abu Ahmed. '*Khalas!*' Stop! Shut up! Keep it down and stay away from the door.

The young man gave one more kick, this time at the clammy wall.

'Where are you from?' Sadiq asked.

'From here. A village on the crest of the hill, a little west of here.'

'My name is Abu Ismael, I'm from Somalia.'

'Suleiman.'

'What did you do?'

The young man took a deep breath.

'My parents have an olive grove . . . '

He was silent for a time, then began to recount the story of the olive grove that his family had tended for generations. It was old; olive trees could live a thousand years. Their trees were hundreds of years old; if the trunk and the branches died, new shoots would grow, forming a new trunk, growing into new branches. The first olive trees took root right here in northern Syria, in the city-state of Ebla outside modern-day Aleppo. Thousand-year-old clay tablets show the boundaries of the farms, how many jars of oil were earmarked for the king and how many were allocated to the people.

Some time ago his family's olive grove had been divided by a road. Following the summer's fighting, land on one side of the road had wound up in ISIS-controlled territory, while the land on the other side was held by the Kurds. ISIS had warned him about going there. They would shoot him. It was enemy territory.

Summer passed. Suleiman tended only to the trees on the Islamists' side of the Karasi road. Over on the Kurdish side, the olives ripened just as well from sun and a little rain alone.

November was the harvest month. Last week he had cropped the olives on the ISIS land. When he was finished, he looked over at the other side. The trees were heavy with their fruit.

It is not easy for a farmer to see his crop go to waste.

At sunrise this same morning, he crossed the road. The crop was his and the year had been a good one. He placed a net on the ground and gave the branches a shake, before climbing a ladder with a basket around his waist to pluck the olives that had not fallen. On his way home he was discovered by an ISIS patrol, made up not of locals who knew him but of foreigners. They detained him, accused him of spying for the Kurds. He had grown angry, remonstrated, pointed at the olives. They had beaten him senseless. Now he was here.

The young man burst into tears.

'They took my sister and . . . she had come with me to help pluck today, to get it done quicker, since she is faster than any of us. My little sister . . . I've no idea where she is, where they took her, what they're doing to her!'

'*Awlad al haram!* Sons of bitches!' he shouted.

He got to his feet and pounded on the door. Sadiq attempted to restrain him, but Suleiman was like a raging young bull.

A gang of guards showed up.

Light fell on Suleiman. Sadiq had pictured a typical northern Syrian like Osman, pale-skinned, with brown hair, but he was dark, dark like Sadiq. His hair and beard were black, sleek and shiny. He stood, bloodied but unbowed, ready to take on ten men.

'Step aside,' they told Sadiq before grabbing hold of the young farmer, shoving him out and forcing him down the corridor.

Sadiq was angry at himself. He should not have said anything about the death cell, or made the young man talk at all. Why had he done that?

It had been so nice listening to him. He had quoted the Koran, a verse about olive trees. *God's light lit by the oil of a blessed tree, an olive tree . . . whose oil is well-nigh luminous though fire scarce touched it. Light upon light!*

A while later the door was opened again. They threw the young farmer on the floor. Sadiq ran his hand over him, felt his pulse. Was he alive? Yes. He continued to check his pulse at regular intervals. Is he alive? Yes. Sadiq tried to avoid his sewage-coated fingers coming into contact with the wounds. He must not do any more damage.

The night passed. The door was opened wide. The terrible trio. They dragged Suleiman out.

God's light lit by the oil of a blessed tree, an olive tree.

Morning came.

Abu Ahmed came in with tea.

Sadiq looked at him. 'Where is Suleiman?'

Abu Ahmad made no reply.

'What happened to him?' Sadiq persisted.

'You don't want to know.'

It was several hours before Sadiq came to himself again. He lay on the filthy floor, sobbing. He had never wept for anyone as he wept for Suleiman. A person he had known for only the briefest time. A person who should have lived but no longer did. A person with a vitality and strength he had scarcely seen the likes of, a farmer who should have had sons and daughters, a whole flock of children. A voice in Sadiq's head now took up and shouted what Suleiman had exclaimed upon being thrown into the stinking cell: *What sort of hell is this?*

A few hours later he was kneeling in the backyard, blindfolded, his hands tied behind his back. Two men held him down.

He felt the blade of a knife against his throat, the sharp edge pressed against his skin, barely cutting it. He was aware of a sharp pain, of blood trickling. He prepared himself mentally. He imagined the sensation of the knife edge slicing through skin, flesh, sinew, and finally the artery.

Poor Sara. His poor old mother. They were the ones he thought of most. The children would manage.

'We know you're a spy,' a voice above him said. 'Who are you working with here? Who's given you information?'

'I'm not a spy, I'm a father,' he repeated. 'If you're going to kill me, then kill me because I'm a father who refuses to abandon his daughters, but don't kill me because you suspect me of being a spy.'

Sadiq thought that if he admitted to spying, they would kill him. He told himself, *No matter how much they beat me, I must never say yes.*

The knife was taken from his throat. They began to beat him instead. He was still blindfolded. The worst beatings were when you could not see what was happening. You had no chance to tense your muscles before the blow landed, you were unprepared. He could easily take a beating with eyes open after this.

They threw him back in the cell. A little later Abu Ahmed came in. He brought water. Sadiq gulped it down. Then he got diarrhea.

He dragged himself back and forth the few steps to the hole in the floor. *I cannot be sick now*, he thought. *My situation is desperate, I am soon to be beheaded.*

The following day his diarrhea was gone. He and his body were attuned.

In the afternoon, a new prisoner was tossed into the cell. He could tell by the coughing, and by the voice, that he was an older man. Sadiq did not ask him anything. He did not want to know. The sorrow over Suleiman was too great.

Even so, unbidden, after a while the man began to speak in the darkness. He was a truck driver, his routes taking him all across Syria. He crossed the front lines and back several times a week. On his last trip he had been transporting a consignment of freshly plucked olives to be brined, preserved, or pressed into oil. He had driven from al-Nusra's area of control over to ISIS territory and had been stopped at a roadblock, where his vehicle had been searched. They had found several cartons of cigarettes among the freight. 'I had no idea they were there, no idea at all,' the man insisted.

Although cigarettes were not forbidden in the Koran, they were deemed haram by ISIS and looked on as a form of 'slow suicide' and pure pleasure. ISIS came down hard on people smoking on the sly, even in their own homes, and flogging was the usual punishment. Selling or smuggling was worse.

The next morning the older man was gone. Sadiq did not ask Abu Ahmed what had happened.

The trio returned.

'We know you're *shabiha*,' the bearded one said.

'My son, this is the first time I've heard that word, what is it?' Sadiq replied.

He had actually learned the word at Osman's. It meant 'ghost' in the Syrian dialect, and was used to refer to men in Assad's intelligence service. They appeared out of nowhere, capturing people, brutalizing and killing them before disappearing again. If the ghosts got hold of you, it was unlikely you would see the light of day again.

The bearded one got to his feet. 'Who's paying you? What did you tell them?'

'I'm just a father.' Sadiq kept to his mantra. 'I swear to you, if I was a spy I would tell you. I'm here as a father, I want to fetch my daughters home . . . '

'We're very fond of your daughters, they're good Muslims,' the younger one said. Sadiq gave a start. Did this guy know his daughters?

'And because we are fond of them, I'll make your last night taste that little bit sweeter, because tomorrow we're going to kill you.'

They tossed a bag of sweets to him.

Sadiq just stared at him.

'The sweets are from your son-in-law,' the one with the beard added. 'He asked me to give them to the old man. I promised to send his regards.'

He kicked a water bottle across the filthy floor. Sadiq shuddered. They left.

He did not drink the water. He did not touch the sweets. He had no desire to taste his own death sentence.

That night a young boy was thrown into the cell. Sadiq glimpsed him in the scant seconds the door was open and the light from outside came in – the silhouette of a boy not yet fully grown, with the face of a child. Sadiq did not utter a word. He could not bring himself to. He waited. And kept watch. And waited. He could not sleep when he knew one of them would be killed during the night. They came again just before dawn, pausing in the doorway for a moment before they hauled the boy out and disappeared.

Sadiq laid his head on the filthy floor. He had gotten used to the stench, the shit, the dankness. He thought about the guards, soldiers, torturers, and executioners he was surrounded by. What kind of people were they? How did their minds work? Sadiq believed himself a man who respected others, almost without exception, but he could not understand the men in this al-Dawla al-Islamiya. This had nothing to do with Islam, nothing to do with jihad. Least of all had it anything to do with God. Because God was merciful. They had forgotten that.

The next night he was the one they took out. He was handcuffed and blindfolded. Soft rain fell on his sweaty brow. Followed by a fist. He fell down, got mud on his face, in his mouth, all over. Then the blows ceased. Sadiq wondered what was coming. They removed his blindfold and turned him over.

'My father hasn't come here looking for me,' the fat one said. He pointed at the two others. 'Neither has the father of my brother from Eritrea, or my Libyan brother. Nobody comes here to fetch anyone. You're lying!'

He ordered Sadiq onto his knees. Drizzle was falling. The knife the man had pressed to his throat was wet.

They wanted a confession.

Sadiq answered on autopilot: 'I'm just a father.'

The knife was removed. While he kneeled in the mud, his hands tied behind his back, they debated whether or not to kill him there and then or let him live.

The rain continued to fall.

They forced him to his feet and back to his cell.

I have a small spark named Sadiq, he thought, as he lay dazed. *The rest of me is dead.* So far four people had shared the cell with him. All of them were gone.

He tried to put thoughts of them out of his head, empty his mind. He got to his feet, then slept in the fetal position, woke up, and got back to his feet. He did push-ups, knuckles resting on the wall, and performed squats to keep his blood circulating.

He had tried to keep count of the days, but become mixed up. Slowly, he grew accustomed to an existence in an area four yards square.

Occasional occurrences made life a little better. One day Abu Ahmed appeared with an empty bottle. Turned upside down and jammed into the hole in the floor, it reduced the stink.

One morning his warder brought him out into the backyard.

'*They* don't work on Fridays,' he said.

Friday. Day off. No beatings.

It was the first time he had seen the yard in daylight. Small light-pink flowers climbed up a wall, growing out of the compacted sandy earth. There were a few chairs and a lopsided table. A couple of cars took up the rest of the space. Beyond the wall, scattered olive trees grew. Sorrow welled up inside Sadiq. The thought of the vigorous young farmer. Syria was being drained of its best men.

A black flag with the seal of Muhammad flew above them. On a sign that no one had bothered to take down he saw where he actually was: Al-Dana Water Supply and Sewerage Treatment Plant. The Islamists were experts at making prisons of everything.

Sadiq swung his outstretched arms back and forth, enjoying the space and air around his body, the sun, the gentle breeze. 'I've spoken to someone . . . ' Abu Ahmed said. 'I told them about you. If you're lucky, he'll be here today.'

In the middle of the yard a group stood chatting. They had reddish beards and were light-skinned. Chechens, Abu Ahmed told him. They were reputed to be the best soldiers, brutal, disciplined, practiced in guerrilla tactics cultivated over centuries of warfare against the Russians.

'They want to see combat,' Abu Ahmed said, 'like everyone else who comes. A lot of people are disappointed when they are assigned to watch prisoners. They didn't enlist for that, not to hang around this shithole.'

Sadiq wanted to ask Abu Ahmed how he wound up here, what he was doing working for ISIS, but he did not. He remained stuck in his own thoughts, lacked the energy to contemplate those of others. He looked around. Prisoners and guards, executioners and victims. He drew in deep lungfuls of the autumn air. Oh, for a cigarette now!

A man came over to Abu Ahmed. He had a slight limp and stood resting his weight on one foot. The guard straightened up and pointed toward Sadiq. The man motioned him to follow and led Sadiq and Abu Ahmed inside the building. He showed them into one of the treatment plant's offices and introduced himself as Abu Sayaf.

'What brings you to Syria?' he asked Sadiq.

When he had heard Sadiq's story, he stood up and paced back and forth in the room, mumbling some verses from the Koran.

He turned and looked straight at Sadiq. 'If you remain in that cell, sooner or later you'll be killed.'

He left the room; Abu Ahmed and Sadiq sat and waited. When he returned, he had two of the Chechens with him. He instructed Sadiq to accompany them, and Sadiq found himself being led across the yard to another building, through a door, and down a corridor. He was shown into a large room with mats on the floor. 'Find an empty spot,' a guard told him.

A mattress! What bliss. He lay down on one of them. Just as he was stretching to his full length, the muezzin rang out: 'Allahu Akbar, Allahu Akbar!'

Voices from the minarets and mosques across the whole town mingled. It was beautiful, it felt sacred. Even in this hellhole, the call to worship was beautiful.

The afternoon prayer of *asr* was to be recited at a time defined by the length of any object's shadow. While in the toilet cell, Sadiq had not been able to make out the calls to prayer. Now they sounded like cries of freedom. He prepared to pray.

I bear witness that there is no god but Allah
I bear witness that Muhammad is the messenger of God
Hasten to prayer
Hasten to success
God is greatest, God is greatest
There is no God but Allah

When the calls died away, Sadiq made himself comfortable on the mattress. Beside him a man lay groaning. Sadiq looked around. The occupants of the room varied in age – there were boys and grown men – and several others were moaning and writhing in pain.

'What happened to you?' he asked the man beside him, who was trying to stifle a groan.

'You don't want to know.'

But Sadiq always wanted to know.

'They roasted our balls,' the man said, 'charred them.'

They had burned them black with a lighter, he told him. The pain had been out of this world. Several men had passed out. They had awoken to hellish pain. 'The agony!'

'What are you accused of?' Sadiq asked.

'I was guiding a man across the border, an IS fighter, he was killed and they accused me of betraying him . . . Wallahi, I'm innocent!'

Sadiq looked around. Again, the Syrians were the ones suffering the most, all those he had shared the death cell with were local Syrians. They were the ones dying.

The night seemed interminable. The mattress provided no succor. It was as though everyone in the room was inside his head wailing and crying.

The next morning Sadiq was taken to an office. When he saw the flags and placards bearing the seal of Muhammad, he lost hope.

There is no way out of here. They have already decided who will live and who will die.

Sadiq was told to sit and wait for the judge. An imperious man with a long gray beard entered. Abu Hafs an-Najdi was Saudi Arabian and responsible for the sharia court in al-Dana. He began the hearing.

Sadiq endeavored to use the correct words and phrases, as he had learned them in Saudi Arabia. He was careful to offer precise details in his story. The account of two daughters journeying to Syria without his permission. Of a father traveling after them.

The judge turned to some men and asked for the evidence in the case. Sadiq heard the words 'spy,' 'intelligence,' 'Norway,' 'Turkey.' One of the men held up Sadiq's mobile phone for the judge to see.

'This contains texts from his employers,' they said.

The accused was here on a mission at the behest of Western intelligence and this supposed search for his daughters was a cover story.

Abu Hafs asked to see the phone. He scrolled down the screen.

'What language are these texts in?' he asked.

'Norwegian.'

'Who here speaks Norwegian?'

There was a general shaking of heads. A Moroccan working at a garage was mentioned.

'Find him.'

Coffee was brought in for the judge and his men.

The Moroccan was finally tracked down.

'Do you understand both Arabic and Norwegian?' the Saudi Arabian asked when the court was again in session.

The man nodded. He was instructed to translate the messages on Sadiq's phone.

Sadiq knew that his fate depended on what the man said. He had to convince the Moroccan that he was telling the truth without using his voice. *I am just a father, I am not a traitor, I am just a father*, he said in his mind, hoping the message would reach the man, who suddenly turned to him.

'Who's Ismael?'

Sadiq was rudely awakened from his attempts at telepathy. He felt outside of himself, merely an observer of what was happening in the makeshift court.

'Who is Ismael?' the man repeated when Sadiq failed to answer.

Sadiq's mind was racing. What did Ismael have to do with this?

'I said "Ismael"! Can't you hear?'

'He's my son,' Sadiq replied meekly.

The Moroccan translated Ismael's message for Abu Hafs. *The police came today to question me. They asked where you were. I said I didn't know. Where are you?*

No one at home was aware of his imprisonment. He had, in their minds, simply vanished after the last conversation with Ayan. The texts on his phone had come while he was in ISIS custody.

The Moroccan continued to translate.

Dad, where are you?

Dad, call us!

Dad . . . ?

*

A few hours after the hearing, Abu Sayaf, the man who had led him from the prison yard the day before, stood over his mattress. When the Moroccan had clarified the contents of the texts from Ismael, Abu Hafs had asked the prosecutors if there was any other evidence that he was a spy. There was not. Sadiq had been sent back to the cell he shared with the other prisoners.

'You're being released,' Abu Sayaf told him. 'You're free to go, but you need a permit for the checkpoints and roadblocks. You'll get the papers tomorrow. Then you can leave.'

Sadiq felt like he was floating on air. He had survived! The blows, the kicks, the beatings – mock beheadings. He was free!

But it wasn't over. He was alive, but he hadn't accomplished what he came here for: his daughters.

His mind was cluttered, his thoughts crisscrossed and entangled with one another. He looked around at the men moaning in pain.

Abu Sayaf went on to tell him that the prison governor had opposed his release. Why had he done that? Sadiq was drained of strength, at the bottom, bewildered. This was not like being in the field in Somalia, this was unfamiliar terrain.

Still, for the first time since he had arrived at the water treatment plant he fell asleep with a sense of expectancy. He was awakened by the sound of a door being flung open.

He propped himself up on his elbows. It was the three men who usually beat him. A feeling of dread took hold, followed by relief. *You lost this time!*

A triumphant sensation coursed through him. The next day he would be leaving as a free man. The troika approached him. He heard the leader say, 'We're not done with you yet.'

20

Blueprint

Who was in charge here?

The judge had released him. The head of the prison had protested. Who decided his fate?

The young fighters were only pawns. The guards locked the doors. The torturers abused whoever they were given. The executioners beheaded on command.

Without these young men, the system would fall apart. It required brutality. Barbarism was the surface, the external face. Behind the façade, there was a strict hierarchy, and behind the hierarchy lay a carefully devised plan: the formula for a reign of terror, a machinery of violence lubricated with blood.

Not far away, a little farther to the east, close to the border in the north, sat the mastermind behind the system that held Sadiq prisoner. Samir Abd Muhammad al-Khlifawi was a lean man with a graying beard. He came across as polite and reserved, almost a little absentminded, but those who knew him were aware that he had an extraordinary memory and great logistical prowess.

In a small extension behind a house in the village of Tal Rifat in Aleppo province, beneath some boxes and a pile of blankets, lay a file of handwritten sheets: an organizational chart, pages of diagrams, and lists of names, along with instructions, guidelines, and a time-table. It was the blueprint of the Islamic State.

The man behind the plan had held one of the most trusted positions in Iraq's intelligence service. On March 17, 2003, when President George W. Bush gave Saddam Hussein forty-eight hours to relinquish power over his 'dying regime,' he also addressed Iraq's military forces in an attempt to get them to lay down their arms: 'It will be no defense to say, "I was just following orders."'

Over a quarter of a million U.S. soldiers were on standby in Kuwait, ready to invade Iraq. On March 20, they rolled across the border. Progress through the desert was swift. Many Iraqi forces had quit their bases before the Americans arrived. After a three-week campaign, they reached Baghdad. It took only a couple of hours to take control of the city. The Americans secured the Oil Ministry with a line of tanks and tore down the statue of Saddam outside the hotel where the foreign journalists were staying. Regime change could hardly have been choreographed and packaged for broadcast any quicker. Before a month had passed, Baath rule in Iraq had collapsed. On May 1, George Bush declared, *Mission Accomplished*.

Toward the end of the year, on a farm near his hometown of Tikrit, the fallen dictator was found in his spider hole, six feet belowground, along with two rifles, a pistol, and $750,000 in cash.

'You will not have to fear the rule of Saddam Hussein ever again,' George Bush said as images of the bearded, bloodied man were flashed around the world.

Saddam was finished. But his men were not.

Most of them were secular Sunni Muslims. Shifting alliances and the bargaining of loyalties were part and parcel of clan rule in Iraq. Many envisaged having a job under the new regime.

The Americans had other plans. When Paul Bremer, the top civil-ian administrator in Baghdad, dissolved the Iraqi army with the stroke of a pen, forbidding all those who had held leading positions under Saddam from seeking posts in the new Iraq, men like al-Khlifawi found themselves unemployed and banned from practicing their pro-fession. More than one hundred thousand well-trained Iraqi officers and bureaucrats were robbed of their positions and livelihoods. The Unites States had gotten a dangerous enemy – armed and aggrieved.

Colonel al-Khlifawi went underground in Sunni-dominated Anbar province in the west of the country. He changed his appearance and reemerged as Haji Bakr. The rejected officers sought a strategic alliance and found it with al-Qaida's men in Iraq, who were led by the Jordanian Abu Musab al-Zarqawi, a former troublemaker who had discovered radical Islam and sobered up. In the late 1980s, Zarqawi enlisted in the fight against Soviet forces in Afghanistan but realized, to his disappointment, that he had missed the war. The withdrawal was already under way when he arrived. In Afghanistan, Osama bin Laden took him under his wing while he built up al-Qaida, but he came to view Zarqawi as too extreme and did not support his enthusiasm for the mass killings of Shia Muslims.

Zarqawi fought loyally on the Taliban side when the United States attacked Afghanistan after September 11. Wounded in action, he left for Iran, traveling to Iraqi Kurdistan, where he joined the jihadist group Ansar al-Islam. Prior to the U.S. invasion of Iraq, Ansar al-Islam's enemy had been Saddam's regime, which they viewed as ungodly. Colin Powell, the United States secretary of state, had claimed that Saddam Hussein was in league with al-Qaida, that the Iraqis had trained the group in the use of weapons of mass destruction, and could cooperate with it on an attack against the West. It was a false accusation. In the wake of the U.S. invasion, it would ironically become truth.

For al-Qaida, the war in Iraq provided the opportunity to mobilize anew after the loss of its bases in Afghanistan dried up recruiting. Instead of the friendly society Bush had envisaged in Iraq, the country became the spearhead of a new wave of terror. Zarqawi himself was behind several attacks, including the bombing of the UN headquarters in Baghdad, followed by a series of attacks against American forces and Shia Muslim leaders and holy sites.

The Baathists and the Islamic extremists had one firm conviction in common: Control over the masses was to belong to a small elite who did not need to answer to anyone.

In 2004, al-Qaida in Iraq was formed with Zarqawi as its leader. AQI recruited from across the Arab world. Most came via smuggling routes through Syria. Assad allowed them safe passage – he wanted the U.S. mission in Iraq to fail, fearing that a successful outcome might tempt the superpower into a subsequent attempt to topple his own dictatorship. From his hideout in Pakistan, Osama bin Laden delighted in the attacks on the American forces but implored the rank and file on the ground to refrain from killing other Muslims. His appeal fell on deaf ears.

Anbar, where the terrorist leader Zarqawi and the strategist and former Saddam loyalist Haji Bakr were located, is the largest province in Iraq, barren and sparsely populated. Vast swaths of desert and seemingly endless stretches of road made the Americans vulnerable. One-third of the soldiers killed in Iraq lost their lives here. The insurrection grew. The Sunnis in Iraq felt themselves increasingly oppressed by the Shia-dominated and American-supported government in Baghdad. On top of this the Islamists promised a higher salary than the $300 a month offered by the authorities.

The Americans went to great lengths to put a stop to Zarqawi. In June 2006, a spy plane followed his spiritual mentor to a meeting with the terrorist leader. Two F-16 bombers dropped their payloads on the house he entered.

George Bush assured the world that 'Zarqawi will never kill again.'

From 2006, the name of a new resistance movement – ISI, the Islamic State in Iraq – began to circulate. Haji Bakr was one of its military strategists. The Americans tried to choke the growth of the network, and one mass arrest captured the former colonel.

The prisons were divided along sectarian lines; Sunnis served time with Sunnis, Shias with Shias. Experienced jihadists shared dormitories with youths who had never had anything to do with the insurgency. The Islamists doled out tough justice. Prisoners were tried in secret sharia courts and sentenced to beatings, having their eyes cut out, or death. The less their fellow prisoners knew about

Islam, the easier it was to convince them that jihad was a religious obligation.

The prison camps became sanctuaries for the resistance movement. Whereas their previous status as fugitives had meant that meeting with one another was fraught with danger, they were now free to sit in the shade of the walls, in places like Camp Bucca, to recruit and lay plans. As long as the prisoners did not make any trouble and followed the routines, the guards were not bothered by their machinations. On the contrary, they picked out prisoners who seemed to hold positions of authority to keep control of the others. One of those selected was Abu Bakr al-Baghdadi. The Americans gave the future ISIS chief a leadership role at Camp Bucca.

When they eventually understood what was going on, the Americans introduced secular education to offset radicalization. The inmates were taught to read and write, and moderate imams were brought in to preach about peaceful Islam. At the same time, the prison population was reduced by the release of those deemed less dangerous. Like Haji Bakr. After two years of incarceration, he was let out of Camp Bucca in 2008 and immediately went underground. A year later, Abu Bakr al-Baghdadi was set free, registered as a 'low-level prisoner.'

ISI's brutality had put them at loggerheads with several powerful Sunni tribes. The tribes wanted self-government, not submission to a dogmatic militia. With the help of the United States and local security forces, the tribes formed councils and militias called *sahwa*, meaning 'awakening.' These sahwa militias, deeply rooted in local areas, proved effective in the offensive against ISI and were well assisted by superior American weaponry.

When almost all of the ISI leadership was wiped out in an American air strike in April 2010, many predicted the end of the insurgence. Thirty-four of forty-two commanders were killed, and there were no qualified successors in sight. The organization badly needed a strong leader who could pick up the pieces and give it fresh legitimacy, and fast.

In May, the relatively unknown Abu Bakr al-Baghdadi was

appointed head of the organization, partly due to his training in sharia, because ISI had to rest on a solid religious foundation, but more importantly because he was a Qurayshi. According to Islamic tradition, the next caliph would come from the Quraysh tribe.

Abu Bakr al-Baghdadi was born in 1971 in Samarra into a family of teachers and preachers. As a teenager, he was passionate about playing football, a sport he would later prohibit. He lived a quiet life and shunned violence of any form. In the decade prior to the American invasion, he lived in a room adjoining a small mosque in a poor area on the outskirts of Baghdad. He spent most of his time reading, sometimes he led prayers, and he remained largely unnoticed.

The man who had been known as 'the invisible sheikh' quickly set his mark on the organization. Potential critics were eliminated and replaced with people he trusted, preferably men he had served time with in Camp Bucca. Under his leadership, ISI carried out a wave of well-coordinated suicide bombings in Baghdad and Mosul. Nevertheless, the Islamists were fighting a losing battle – people wanted peace, the tribes wanted to rule themselves. In spite of ISI preaching about the establishment of an Islamic state, the organization resembled a terror group more than a nation builder.

Then the event that would change the Arab world took place. In December 2010, a street vendor set fire to himself outside the governor's office in a rural Tunisian town. His cart had been confiscated by a police officer and the fruit seller attempted to bribe her, as was the custom, in order to get it back. She reportedly spat on him. His self-immolation led to unrest and rioting across Tunisia. A few weeks later, after more than twenty years in power, the dictator Zine el-Abidine Ben Ali fled to Saudi Arabia. The Arab Spring had begun.

The protests spread eastward to Egypt and Libya. In Syria, the burgeoning civil war created a power vacuum, a golden opportunity.

In late 2012, Haji Bakr and a small group crossed the border from Iraq into Syria. There, in the northern provinces, the government forces of Assad had for the most part been driven out, leaving a vast number of local brigades, military councils, and militias, at their height somewhere in the neighborhood of two thousand different groups, vying for power. It made for a vulnerable balance: No one was strong enough to seize power; everyone was strong enough to prevent another from taking it.

Perfect anarchy, which Haji Bakr knew how to exploit.

Syria was a means to achieving an end: Sunni-dominated control of Iraq. First, Syria was to be conquered bit by bit and appropriate territories put to use as bridgeheads into Iraq. In the village of Tal Rifat, Haji Bakr put the finishing touches to his plan. The key to success was a mix of strategic calculations and fanatical believers. The colonel himself was far from an Islamist; he was a nationalist and an opportunist.

In all the cities and towns that the Free Syrian Army or other rebels had captured, missionary, or dawa, offices were to be opened. These would serve as recruitment posts. Among those who came to listen to lectures and attend courses, a couple of men would be selected and instructed to spy.

'We will train them for a while and then dispatch them,' Haji Bakr wrote.

The spies were to do as follows:

Make lists of powerful families and their most important men
Find out their sources of income
Record activities forbidden according to sharia
Gather information on illicit affairs and homosexual activity
Provide details about rebel groups
Find out the identity and familial background of brigade leaders
Note political and religious orientation

In this way, ammunition for threats and blackmail would be stockpiled.

The spies would enable the structure of the local populations to be understood, who supported democratic ideas, who were loyal to the regime, which families were religious, which direction within Islam they followed, what kind of sermons the imam gave, what his views on jihad were, how much he was paid, who paid him, what other sources of income people had, how many wives a leader had, and how many children he had and their ages.

All this knowledge would provide an overview of where any cracks existed. Wedges could then be driven in, widening these cracks into cleavages, gradually fracturing the structure of the society until it split and fell apart. Even though the word of God was scarcely mentioned in Haji Bakr's detailed written plans, the colonel had a conviction that the faith of others could and should be exploited.

The intricate, thorough structure of Haji Bakr's method was created to spread fear. Each provincial council was to be led by an emir in charge of espionage, extortion, abduction, and murder. He was also in charge of all communication and its encryption. Meanwhile, another emir would monitor him and several other emirs 'in case they did not do their job properly.' Who was monitoring whom would not be clear to any of the individuals involved.

The provincial system was to be supervised by an intelligence department. This would in turn report to a security emir in each region, who was responsible for deputy emirs for individual districts. A head of secret spy cells reported to each deputy emir, sometimes bypassing several chains of command. At the local level, the spy cells would report to the district emir's deputy. Haji Bakr, who by now was nicknamed 'Lord of the Shadows,' had spun a sticky web, with the goal of everyone keeping an eye on everyone else.

From early 2013, a large number of dawa offices opened up in rebel-controlled towns across the whole of northern Syria. The offices could easily be mistaken for charitable organizations: Everyone was addressed as *brother*, and there was no mention of any Islamic State. Haji Bakr's men quietly rented rooms and lodgings. He had expressly forbidden any Iraqi soldiers from being among their number, and neither did he want to recruit too many Syrians. They might have strong local allegiances that could lead to a conflict of loyalties. The strategist wanted men from outside, and ISIS intensified their recruitment of *muhajirin*, foreign fighters. These newcomers knew no one outside their own camp, had no reason to show mercy, and could be quickly redeployed as needed. They were given a couple of months of training and religious instruction before being sent out to fight or being assigned a position within the state. Spies were also instructed to attempt to 'penetrate' the most powerful families by marrying into them.

The local militias seldom sought direct confrontation with ISIS. They had many more men than Daesh in total, but they did not want to risk opening a new front. The government was still the main enemy. ISIS's regional leaders were constantly kept up-to-date on weaknesses, splits, and signs of conflict by the spy network. This allowed them to enter into a crisscross of alliances with the different militias, without any of their 'allies' having knowledge of the deals they had made with others.

By winter 2013, the Syrian opposition had defeated the regime in large parts of northern Syria. But they had yet to take a large city. Rebel groups planned a surprise attack on the provincial capital of Raqqa.

The civil war had led to road closures and a lack of basic necessities. For the people in Raqqa, the situation was growing desperate. The city was located in a desert area, with the only fertile ground to the south along the Euphrates. There was a shortage of food and constant power outages. The cutting of supply lines was Assad's punishment against cities held by the opposition.

Early on the morning of March 3 the FSA, al-Nusra, and Ahrar al-Sham entered the city, first from the north, then from the east, finally from the west and south. By the end of the day they had taken control of most of the city center. There was jubilation as the golden statue of Hafez al-Assad was pulled down.

How could an entire city fall in a matter of hours?

Assad's forces on the east side of the city had left their positions before daybreak. The forces in the center retreated to the airport just outside the city limits. They were so badly coordinated that many of the rank and file had deserted. Only a few officers barricaded themselves and fought until they ran out of ammunition. When they surrendered, they were taken prisoner and executed. Their corpses were put on display in the central square.

The various rebel groups divided Raqqa among them. People streamed out onto the streets shouting, *Freedom! Democracy! Justice!*

Youth groups, women's groups, and theater troupes were formed. Uncensored newspapers were published. The revolution had reached the province before the capital; the people were blazing a trail. Lawyers came together, doctors organized, political parties were formed, and people imbibed the spirit of freedom. A number of dawa offices were opened. A revolutionary city council was set up to manage the expected anarchy. All that had not been allowed under Assad's rule was now to be tried.

Assad's vengeance was not long in coming. Scud missiles were launched, destroying residential areas, but the people merely cleared away the ruins, buried the dead, and persevered. The streets were cleaned on a voluntary basis, people organized services the authorities had ceased to offer long ago, power generators were run in alternation, shop shelves were stocked. The border to Turkey was open, and the best goods at the lowest prices in the whole of Syria were now available in Raqqa. The city council declared the city a duty-free zone, commodities people had never seen before began to arrive, a market for American cars was opened. It was a city of joy.

Until people started to disappear.

First some young activists. A newspaper columnist. Some youths who had painted the revolutionary flag on the city wall. An actor in a theater company. A priest. A lawyer. A doctor. A journalist. An author. In the middle of May, the leader of the Raqqa council was forced into a car by masked men and never seen again. A militia leader was killed in an ambush. Then another. Followed by a third. Who was behind it? There was growing unease, tensions rose, everyone blamed everyone else, and conflict broke out among al-Nusra, FSA, Ahrar al-Sham, al-Faruk, and ar-Rassul, which all held different parts of the city.

Nobody took responsibility for the disappearances and the murders. People had their suspicions, but few dared to voice them. Black flags began to fly in parts of the city.

The inhabitants had not foreseen anyone other than Assad's men suppressing and threatening them.

As soon as the regime's forces had been defeated, the extremists had begun to infiltrate Raqqa via their newly opened dawa offices. Haji Bakr kept his files well up-to-date. Some of those who spied for him had previously worked as intelligence agents for Assad, others were rebels who had fallen from favor with local militia leaders and desired revenge, and there were those who simply needed to make a living. Most of the men on his books were in their early twenties and some were only teenagers. As before, the older generation was wary.

As soon as the lists were complete, the process of elimination began. First the ones who had raised their voices in support of freedom and democracy, followed by all those who might do so.

Fear had returned.

When the Islamists had enough people to spy and sufficient fighters to defend their spies, Abu Bakr al-Baghdadi announced the expansion of ISI – the Islamic State in Iraq – into ISIS – the Islamic State in Iraq and Syria.

The summer of 2013 was a bloody one. The number of disappearances intensified in July, first by the dozens, then by the hundreds. Bodies were found tortured or with bullet holes through the back of their heads; others vanished without a trace. In August, suicide bombers attacked the FSA's headquarters in Raqqa.

None of the rebel groups helped one another when they were attacked in turn. As long as it did not affect them, they looked the other way. They all believed themselves to be immune from ISIS.

On October 17, 2013, the same day Ayan and Leila took the afternoon flight to Istanbul, ISIS summoned Raqqa's civilian leaders, clerics, teachers, and lawyers to what was understood to be a reconciliation meeting to discuss how Raqqa was to be governed. Of the three hundred in attendance, only two men dared to criticize the Islamists' insidious takeover, accusing them of being behind the abductions and the murders.

One of the men was found a few days later with a bullet hole through his head. His acquaintances received an e-mail with an image of the man's maltreated body and a single sentence: 'Do you mourn your friend?'

Then the other man disappeared. ISIS knew who was friends with whom, who had ties with whom, who did not have clean records in the Islamic sense, and who were organized or might offer resistance. Several opposition people fled to Turkey. The high brought about by the revolution in Raqqa had reached an end.

Control of northern Syria was now divided between ISIS and a multitude of militias. In Atmeh, ISIS was close to taking over completely.

In late November, Sadiq stood at a blue door in the town and knocked. He'd been released from the stinking pit at the waterworks some days earlier. Osman hugged him tightly, squeezing him between his powerful arms.

'Thank God, you've returned!'

Osman's mother also came running to embrace him. Her husband hobbled after her, with Randa behind him, while the other women stayed behind the door.

Sadiq had eventually been put in a vehicle and driven from al-Dana by the judge's men. These same men were now offered tea, figs, and biscuits. Only when they departed did the Nusra men make an appearance. Hamza, the brigade leader known as the Lion, had tears in his eyes.

'I was the one who left you with ISIS that day . . . '

Osman's men wanted to know all the details.

Sadiq told them everything. About the toilet cell. About the knife to his throat. About his acquittal and the night that followed it.

'Before dawn, while it was still dark and the prison was quiet,

I was awakened by the sound of hurried steps in the room. I heard low voices. What now? It was the trio of tormenters. Again? *They're going to beat those poor men with the injured balls*, I thought. Then I saw they were on their way toward me. They pulled me up and threw me against the wall. They handcuffed me and made to drag me from the room. I tried to resist, to cry out, but I was gagged. It was then I noticed that the Libyan was not only armed with a pistol as usual but also an AK-47. I was marched down the corridor, the muzzle of the rifle pressed between my shoulder blades. Then the Eritrean said something that really scared me. "No, this is wrong! I won't be a part of it!" he said, stopping in his tracks. That's when I realized I was in grave danger. They pulled me down the corridor. I could feel the rifle in my back and I hoped the other guards would hear my cries. I was flung into a vehicle, but not driven far, only to the next building. I feared that this was the place where they carry out beheadings, so the bodies would be easy to move and the yard not soiled with blood. "Your life is over," the Libyan whispered in my ear. "We usually let a condemned man pray before killing him, but not you, because you're no Muslim . . . kafir!" The one in charge, the fat one, said, "Look around. This is the last place you're ever going to see." Then he said, "I want to be pure when I meet Allah, so I'll grant you one final request. What do you want, traitor?" I told them, "I do not fear death, but please, treat me with respect. I do not want to die with my hands bound behind my back." I continued, "These handcuffs are painful. I'm not young like the two of you." The stocky one took a small key from his pocket, handed it to the Libyan, and said, "Give him his final request." The Libyan fumbled with the handcuffs, it was dark and he could not see very well. The handcuff on my right wrist came off but the manacle on my left wrist remained. Three words flashed inside my mind: *Save your life!'*

Sadiq paused for effect. 'I raised my arm. In one swift movement I hit the Libyan right in the face with the handcuffs. Reeling, he lost his balance but kept hold of me and we both fell to the ground. He got his hands to my throat and I fought to pry them free. But he was younger, stronger, I could not move, and I thought, *Now I'm finished.* He was on top of me. The fat one, standing about ten or fifteen yards away, opened fire. A couple of bullets ricocheted on the gravel right next to us, and the Libyan let out a howl. He had been hit in the thigh. He loosened his grip, wailed, and put his hand to the wound. The bullet had smashed his femur and blood was gushing out. He tried to stop the bleeding, and I snatched the rifle lying on the ground and made off. Once outside, I zigzagged across the ground. I ran, I just ran.'

Osman and his man sat on the mattresses, staring at him.

'And then what?'

Sadiq paused and asked for a cigarette. A soothing sensation coursed through him, the hit of the nicotine paralyzing him for a moment.

'I ran toward the olive grove, but the trees were too spread out, I would be easy to find, so I kept on running, but I was afraid I would run straight into an ISIS troop. I feared what daybreak would bring. The pitch darkness was already being replaced by a gray glow. I heard voices, and a little way off I discerned two figures. An older man and a younger one. They were dressed like farmers, one of them was carrying an old rifle. I had no choice but to trust them and began walking in their direction. When they saw me, they turned. I was still holding the Libyan's AK-47 and they must have taken me for an ISIS soldier. Then they noticed the handcuffs still hanging from my wrist and understood that I had escaped. Hesitantly, they motioned to me: *Come!* I followed them across some land, past a farm, and onto a scree at the foot of a hill. There was a small opening between the stones; at first glance it looked like a fox's den, but it widened almost to a cave a little farther in. "Hide here," they told me. I crept in feet first. *I can stay here*, I thought, as I lay on my stomach aiming out at my surroundings. You can trust us, they had said. They had not even asked if *they* could trust me. Two Syrians, the first people to suffer in this hell, when being asked for help, they helped.'

The men listening to him nodded.

'A little later in the day they returned. "Help me get to Abu Hafs," I asked them. The judge who had acquitted me was my only hope. A Somali on the run was never going to make it out of ISIS territory. I had to reach Abu Hafs and explain what had happened. The young man removed some of his clothes, typical Syrian farmer's garb worn in layers. He wrapped a red-and-white shawl around my face. Disguised as a local farmer, I left the scattered woodland, emerged onto the road, and traipsed the few miles toward al-Dana. Abu Hafs's base lay in the center of town, between the town hall and the market. It was like venturing into the lion's den, but facing up to those in power was better than being caught at a random roadblock. I could tell by the guards' dialects that they, like the judge, were Saudi Arabian. They led me into a waiting room of sorts, where a black flag hung on the wall. After a while a guard instructed me to follow him. Abu Hafs did not seem overly surprised to see me. "They're looking for you," he said. "The Libyan is dead." The fat one had shot him in a major artery and they had not been able to stop the bleeding. Afterward the fat ass told them that I had attacked them and escaped. *Now I am really in deep trouble*, I thought. But Abu Hafs merely shrugged and said everyone was replaceable. "You could take the Libyan's place," he suggested. "You've been a soldier. You know how to defend yourself. You should join us.' I made no reply. "Are you dubious?" he asked. I suddenly felt Abu Hafs's hand on my shoulder. He grabbed my waist and ran his hands down my legs, before gauging the width of my shoulders. "To check your size. For a uniform," he explained. He offered me money, a big house. I implored him to drive me here. Eventually he called in some drivers. We drove straight through all the roadblocks. And now I'm here.'

Sadiq asked for another cigarette. One of the youths laid a whole pack down in front of him. He continued, 'Do you know why I ended up in that hellhole? My son-in-law wanted me dead. He wanted me gone, so I wouldn't be able to save my daughters. Anyway, enough about what has been,' Sadiq said. 'Now we need to find a way to free my daughters.'

There was silence in the room, everyone waited for someone else to speak up.

'We need a good plan,' Osman said. 'In the meantime, you have to leave. This is not the right time to continue searching. These are troubled times and it is not safe for you here. ISIS has taken control of almost all of Atmeh . . . '

That same night a pickup pulled up outside the house to drive Sadiq to the border via the olive grove where he had crossed over the first time. As he was getting into the vehicle, Osman called out to him.

'You won't get into Turkey with that.' He smiled, pointing at the assault rifle Sadiq had over his shoulder.

Sadiq slung it off and handed it to Osman. 'It's a gift to you and your family. Take good care of it.'

He turned to the street, where two vehicles were approaching at full speed. They had black flags fixed to the roofs. The cars roared toward where they stood. *Finished*, Sadiq thought. *I'm finished. It's over.* All his strength deserted him.

The cars sped past, skidding to a stop at a gate farther along the street. Masked men jumped out, kicked the door in, and stormed inside.

Survey. Monitor. Abduct. Eliminate. The plan was working.

21

Home

'Did you send someone to kill Dad?'

Ismael typed in the question to his sister. He was shaken after his father told him about what had happened to him in captivity. Ayan's husband had been the one responsible for his imprisonment, torture, and attempted murder, according to his father.

There was no reply.

After crossing the border into Turkey, Sadiq had wandered about in Hatay for a couple of days contemplating whether to go back and make another attempt to rescue his daughters or to go home and gather his strength. He chose the latter.

When he landed in Oslo, he felt like being stretchered off the airplane, and as the airport train neared his stop in Sandvika, his emotions welled up. *Norwegians think we immigrants have no feelings for this country*, he thought, as he got into a taxi and gave the driver his address. But he, he loved Norway.

Sara. Ismael. Jibril. Isaq. They hugged him where he'd been beaten. When he cuddled up to Sara that night in bed, he felt like a small child who had finally found his mother.

Sara had been through the worst time of her life. Worse than during the civil war in Somalia, worse than when Sadiq went on ahead to Norway, worse than her arrival in that ice-cold country. Following her last conversation with Ayan, when she had pleaded with her daughter to return home with her father and had found out Ayan was married, her existence had become a blur. She had not heard any more from her daughters or from Sadiq. She feared the three of them were dead. Perhaps they had been shot, all of them together? Perhaps their bodies had been left in the desert to rot in the scorching sun? Had her boys become fatherless?

Every day, she was terrified that Child Welfare would turn up and take Jibril and Isaq. She had to make it look as though she was a mother who could handle her situation.

She felt a huge sense of relief when Sadiq finally phoned. *You're alive!*

But despair was quick to take hold again. He had made it out alone. The girls were still with that dangerous group.

'Turn on your TV!' Ela wrote.

It was early December and the evening news had just begun.

'Holy shit!!!!!' Ivana texted back. 'Wow, I actually realized it just now!'

'Me too. It's unbelievable. Should we drop in on her family tomorrow? Just to, you know, show our support?' Ela asked.

'I don't know. I've never really spoken to them that much. Not sure I want to pop by. Or if it's appropriate seeing as they're trying to keep everything on the down low.'

'Yeah, I get you,' Ela replied. 'I wouldn't know what to say anyway.'

They had been inseparable. Now Ela was singing in a pop band. Ivana was soon off to Australia to study. Ayan had gone to take part in a holy war.

Teenagers in their bedrooms in Bærum pored over the media coverage. On the Facebook page that Leila's class had retained, a new thread appeared.

Leila has been hurt
physically?

yeah, she's been shot

ohmygod

is it on the news?

yeah

Amal told me a week ago that Leila had been shot but I didn't
    believe it

VG reports that their father found them

thank god

their father found them, one of them had gunshot wounds
    and it was Leila

No! Are you serious?

What?!

Not exactly a bombshell

Play on words?

No . . . oh, shit

Soon after his arrival back in the country, Sadiq was debriefed
by the Police Security Service. They wanted to get an overview
of the different militias in Syria, of how and where they operated.
Sadiq had gained some insight in the time he spent with Osman, as
well as intimate knowledge of the conditions in an ISIS prison. PST
was particularly interested in Norwegian jihadists in Syria. Had he
spoken to any?

When the girls had left, Sadiq had sought advice from Geir
Lippestad, who had come into the public eye as defense counsel
for the right-wing terrorist Anders Behring Breivik. Lippestad was
the only lawyer Sadiq had heard of, so therefore he contacted him.
The lawyer now spoke to the media on behalf of the family. He told
NRK, the state broadcaster, that the girls would be leaving Syria as
soon as the younger one was on her feet again.

A young Somali, a good friend of Hisham, was surprised to
hear this. Was Ayan going to leave his friend after only a month of
marriage?

The young man knew both Ayan and Hisham well, and was also
a friend of the Koran teacher, Mustafa, who had exchanged letters

with Ayan before she had left, letters he assumed had been about the trip to Syria. Now, was Ayan and Leila's stay coming to an end already?

He called Hisham in Syria to ask if it was true.

'Chill out, brother,' Hisham replied. 'Don't believe everything you hear!'

'What happened?' his friend in Oslo asked. He had wanted to travel to Syria himself but had remained behind in Norway, first when Hisham left, and then when Ayan departed. He was among the few who had been privy to Ayan's plans and had urged her to reconsider. Not because he did not support jihad – he did – but because he believed women should not go until the fighting was over. War was no place for them. But Ayan had taken umbrage at that.

He told her, 'No matter how much I may want to go, I just can't do that to my mom.'

Ayan had merely smiled and said she was doing it as much *for* her parents as for herself.

Hisham's friend knew it would destroy his mother if he left. Like Sara, she was a traditional Somali woman, devout but not an extremist. The trip was Ayan's business, she was of age, but he had been caught off guard when it emerged that she had taken her younger sister along with her.

'Hisham, akhi, what happened? Tell me!'

'Her father came and began threatening her,' Hisham told him. 'If she didn't return with him, then this and that and the other were going to happen. Ayan had to tell him over and over that they *wanted* to stay in Syria and weren't coming back to Norway.'

'Oh, right.'

'So what he's coming out with now are lies.'

'Okay, good.'

'He lost it when she refused to go with him. He threatened to kill her. He said he'd strangle her with his own hands. The guards had to pull him away from her. Then he shouted that the punishment for disobeying your parents was death.'

'Whoa!' his friend said. 'So they're not coming back, then?'

'Not planning on it, no,' Hisham replied.
'Okay, have fun!'

In Atmeh, the young men in Osman's group were disappointed in Sadiq for going home without rescuing his daughters. How could he just leave them with ISIS? He should have stayed longer, tried harder, and not, as they saw it, given up. He had failed in his task, they thought.

In mid-November, just after Sadiq had been imprisoned, fighting had broken out in the border town. The bone of contention had been seven truckloads of weapons sent by the FSA general staff in Turkey. The trucks were to travel on from Atmeh and distribute the shipment across the whole region. But Suqur al-Islam, a moderate Islamist movement that had split from the FSA, demanded its share.

The skirmishes had lasted a few hours, until a solution was found. When the shooting died down and the various factions were licking their wounds, a group of ISIS soldiers drove quietly into town. They parked outside the headquarters of Suqur al-Islam, stormed inside, and following a brief exchange of fire, arrested the local militia leader along with a couple dozen of his men, then drove them to al-Dana, where Sadiq was imprisoned. In Atmeh, the heavily equipped ISIS fighters set about putting checkpoints in place.

Al-Nusra stood watching, because ISIS had seized only Suqur al-Islam territory. But then al-Nusra was attacked and soon ISIS had control of the routes in and out of Atmeh, including the roundabout, while al-Nusra was left in possession of unimportant parts of the town. For ISIS's rivals, Atmeh, which had been spared Assad's rockets due to its proximity to the Turkish border, was a big strategic loss.

After seizing control, the extreme Islamists began their purge. Men were arrested, women warned not to venture outside without a *mahram*, a male family member. ISIS trawled the shops for prohibited goods like cigarettes and alcohol. Everyone knew what these new authorities were capable of and bowed to their demands.

Only a few hours after taking control of the population, ISIS proceeded to take action against nature. An oak tree with a girth that exceeded the arm span of four men was a source of annoyance. The jihadists were of the opinion the tree seemed proud and over-bearing, and they accused the inhabitants of worshipping it. The same afternoon they took over the town, they felled the tree. The growth rings were counted at 150.

'Thank God, the Almighty, that this old tree is removed, after people were worshipping it instead of God,' a jihadist posted on the Our Call Is Our Jihad Twitter account. There was a picture of a masked man dressed in black posing proudly with a chain saw and the felled tree beneath. A black flag had been planted in the enormous stump.

Shortly after Sadiq arrived back in Bærum, a text appeared on the site Justpaste.it, written by one of the young men who had accom-panied him during his stay. The piece was titled 'The untold story of the 2 Somali-Norwegian girls who joined ISIS,' and it was attributed to Mujahid Jazrawi.

> You may have read in the media how two young Somali girls (who're sisters) from Norway left their family to join ISIS a few months ago, how their father went after them, how at one point we thought they were being held by gangs (well, they were, sort of, by gangs who use the cloak of Islam). Many questions were left unan-swered and details remained sketchy. However today we present to you the true untold story of their fate, and we hope that this serves as a warning and a wake-up call to ALL of our sisters insha' Allah.

The soldier wrote that Sadiq's daughters had left behind a note at home in Norway that read: 'You have taught us jihad in theory, we will now apply it in practice.'

'We began asking around, and the emirs of the battalions ordered their people to keep an eye out. The father told us the girls were being held hostage. After a while he received a telephone call from his daughter.'

Jazrawi wrote that the brothers, as he called his cosoldiers, had turned up at a prearranged location, thinking they were to negotiate a ransom for the release of the girls. They had been caught off guard when a black man – a Nigerian, the soldier wrote – turned up with the girls in the backseat of his vehicle. 'The brothers stopped him and a heated conversation ensued. The Nigerian turned his car around and the brothers opened fire. The car stopped at an ISIS checkpoint in Atmeh where the driver sought help as he was one of them. The ISIS fighters surrounded the brothers and the shooting began.'

After one of the daughters was hit in the leg, everyone went to the court in Atmeh, only to be told that the case would be heard at the court in al-Dana. 'Upon arriving at the court he was informed that his eldest daughter had married an ISIS fighter through a sharia contract at that very court! He was then put in prison for twelve days, nine of which he spent in solitary confinement and was also accused of being a spy for Turkey! He was humiliated and tortured and the director of the ISIS prison threatened to kill him.'

The Nusra soldier wrote that 'a judge called an-Najdi something or other' was to decide the father's fate.

'The judge asked the prosecutors to bring evidence against him but they were unable to show anything that proved his apostasy or that he was a spy. The judge ruled he was innocent and that he be released. This enraged the director of the prison and he protested the verdict!'

Back in Atmeh, the fighter had met Sadiq at Osman's.

'I asked, "What about your daughters?" He said, "I couldn't do anything for them, they even refused to let me sit with them!"'

'I tried to get him to change his mind, promised we would protect him and do everything in our power to secure his daughters' release, but he refused and insisted on leaving. Whereupon he left to save himself from being killed.'

The young soldier had later met the 'Nigerian.'

'We discussed his marriage to the elder daughter, and I said to him: "How can you marry a girl without permission from her father?" He responded: "Her father has no guardianship, al-Baghdadi is her guardian! And we were wed by legal sharia contract!" I wore myself out trying to make him understand the concept of paternal authority. I left the man, with the impression he lacked skill in the Arabic language and was quite simply ignorant.'

This incident was one of many. 'A result of the ISIS leaders inciting women to come here. Forcing them to leave the lands of the infidels to travel to "the house of Islam" and their headquarters in Raqqa, by saying it is one's duty.'

Christmas was drawing near.

Sadiq and Sara were living in a daze. Sadiq slept all day. Sara cried all night. They puttered around, shutting themselves off, each living in solitary sorrow. The days came to a standstill, they would go to the supermarket only to find themselves wondering, *What are we doing here?*

Their lives had fallen apart, the simplest things seemed insurmountable, and when they emerged now and again from the isolated chaos of their own minds, they were short-tempered. They had always pulled in the same direction, but now they were beginning to pull at either end.

Sara heard about some youths who had traveled to Syria and returned home. She heard about children being rescued. Her friends told her about parents in Sweden who had received assistance from the state to get their children out, been given money, tickets, passports. The Swedish authorities paid for the parents' stay in Turkey while they looked for their children, one of her friends said.

'I want to hand in my Norwegian passport and move to Sweden,' Sara announced, and blamed the state for not having done enough, the officials at border control for not stopping the girls, the police for being too passive.

Her daughters were blameless. Because her daughters would never have gone.

His body was in Norway, his mind in Syria. He was still on sick leave, still unable to work, and now not only on account of his shoulder.

He lay awake at night. He smoked. Sometimes he collapsed, only to snap awake drenched in sweat from a nightmare. He dreamed he was back in the cell, he felt the knife against his throat, or he was racing after his daughters as they ran away from him. Ikhlaque Chan, the integration officer for Bærum county, saw him standing in a corner at Sandvika shopping center talking to himself. Chan recognized Sadiq from meetings he had arranged for immigrant fathers and went over. Sadiq looked right through him as though he were glass, gazing instead at some point in the middle distance and continuing to talk to himself. He spoke in Somali, with a few Norwegian words peppering his mother tongue, before abruptly leaving the mall. A short time later, Chan ran into Sadiq in the parking lot. He was now himself again and gave Chan a friendly greeting. The integration officer stopped to ask him how things were going. Sadiq told him about the dramatic trip to Syria.

They went their separate ways. Chan told him not to hesitate to get in touch.

An acquaintance from the mosque in Sandvika approached Sadiq and praised his daughters' actions.

'Such a gift they have given you!' he said. 'Their sacrifice paves the way to paradise for your whole family.'

Sadiq exploded. 'Send your sons, then! Send them!'

The other man changed the subject, but Sadiq would not relent. 'Until you send your own children to Syria, keep your opinions to yourself!'

Snow started falling. A white blanket soon rested on the Kolsås ridge. The year was nearing an end, and Sadiq went into hibernation.

22

A Kind, Wonderful Man

'Ismael, no we did not. The whole thing was a misunderstanding. How are you and the rest of the family? We don't have much time so answer quickly!!!'

Two weeks had passed since Ismael had asked Ayan if she and Leila had sent someone to kill their father.

Finally she was online! Ismael sent another question. 'ARE YOU GETTING MARRIED?!!!! In Syria?'

Ayan replied right away. 'I am married ☺. Go on Skype! Where are you?'

'I'm at school. Don't know whether to feel happy or let down.'

'The problem is everyone knows about our situation.'

'What do you mean??'

'We didn't send anyone to kill Dad. He said he was cooperating with PST and the police on the news. The whole world knows. Espionage against Muslims is a very serious matter so the court here brought him in for a hearing. They asked him a lot of questions and tried to find out if he was a spy or not. It had nothing to do with us, we didn't send anyone. He was then acquitted and let go. No one was out to kill him. It's just like when the police in Norway take you in because they're investigating a case. It doesn't mean that they're

trying to lock you up or kill you. They thought he was a spy because
of all the messages between him and the police.'

'He said he was beaten, but anyway I don't care about that. I'm
more worried about you.'

'Did he tell you that Leila was shot because of him?'

'Yes, in the foot?'

'Because he said we had been kidnapped, which was a lie. In the
leg. Where was he beaten?'

'In the cell.'

'Where on his body? With what?'

'On his stomach, with rifle butts, why can't you just go to
Somalia?'

'We could but we don't want to go to a country where Islam isn't
practiced properly and where sharia doesn't exist. BTW you should
be happy I got married, he's a good man.'

'I knew this would happen.'

'What?'

'That you'd both get married down there.'

'Haha, listen, we had nothing to do with what happened to
Dad. Because of him my husband's car is wrecked, our clothes are
destroyed and Leila was shot, so it's only natural the authorities here
wanted to look into the matter.'

'To be honest, I'd be more than happy to go to Syria myself and
die for something I don't believe in if it meant you coming home.'

'I'm sorry it's so hard for you. How's school going?'

'Not good.'

'Why not?'

'I'm so distracted. Can't sleep. I want you home.'

'Concentrate, Ismael, we're fine here! We live in a nice big house
with a nice big garden. And I've learned how to drive. And you
mustn't believe that I or my husband want to kill Dad.'

'Who is your husband? Where did you meet him?'

'Through friends.'

'How could you get married, just like that?'

'He's a good man, that's why I married him.'

'Do Mom&Dad think it's okay?'

'No, unfortunately not.'

'Is he on Facebook? Is he from Syria?'

'No. From BÆRUM'

'Has he been married before?'

'No. He's here, do you want to talk to him?'

'What's his name?'

'Do you want to talk to him?'

'Did he go to Rabita Mosque? What's his ethnic background?'

'Do you want to talk to him?'

'Just ask him, I'm in class, can't talk.'

'Hisham is from Eritrea, and he didn't go to Rabita.'

'Hisham . . . ?'

'Yep.'

'Surname?'

'Hisham Abdiqadir. Is Mom unwell? How are things with her?'

'Both her wrists are injured, nothing else.'

'Have you any more questions about my husband?'

'Why the . . . are you in Syria and not Eritrea?'

'Because the jihad in Eritrea is finished hahaha.'

'Or Somalia?'

'I didn't come here to get married.'

'Yes you did.'

'Wallahi I did not.'

'I think you know the truth yourself . . . it's pretty obvious.'

'Believe what you want, the truth is I came here to be in the country of jihad.'

'Is your husband going to go out and wage jihad then? Eh?'

'He came long before I did.'

'Yes/no?'

'We're both engaged in jihad and he goes out to fight sometimes. It's very quiet where we're living but we can hear the fighting in the distance.'

'So you're pregnant . . . and he's off waging jihad part time. Sounds nice.'

'I'm not pregnant.'

'Imagine something happens to him, what then?'

'Then I'll wait until I can get married again.'

'You'll just marry the next mujahid? That sounds disgusting.'

'Don't people get married, divorced, and married again in Norway? Don't think of it as disgusting, Ismael, we're trying to live a normal life here.'

'They're going to die and you're going to satisfy the next one after this first one is dead.'

'I came here to die myself. Not to be anyone's whore. Don't insult me by calling me that!!'

'That's how it is, if you're not directly involved in the fighting yourself. If you live in a peaceful area. By the way, how is Leila?'

'Good, her wound is healing, it wasn't that serious.'

In the end Ayan summed up what she wanted to say in a series of numbered points: '1. We did not send anyone to kill Dad! 2. We did not come here to satisfy anyone other than ALLAH! 3. We are happy and well.'

'Just don't like the idea of you marrying again and again. I don't have anything against you tying the knot with one person, but when you know he's soon going to get killed in the war and you're planning to move quickly on to the next one,' Ismael wrote back.

'At the moment I'm married to a kind, wonderful man who I love dearly and inshallah he will be the only one I marry and grow old together with. Nobody knows when they will die. And I can't imagine living without him so forget about the whole remarrying thing.'

'I know he won't live for long if he goes off to fight on a regular basis.'

'It's not like that haha, they don't go off to fight that often, hehe.'

23

Spoils of War

Leila sent a picture to Ismael.

'Ha, I was shot first' was written beneath the photo of a foot in a cast.

It made Ismael shiver. His sister was such an idiot! How could she joke about something like that?

Later, over the phone, she told him that by the grace of Allah her foot had healed.

'Come home!' Ismael said to her.

'No, you come here,' his sister replied. 'We have a lovely big house, our own backyard, a garden . . . We have a black and white rabbit. As well as a gray one and a white one. They create havoc in the kitchen *and* eat our bread.'

'Dad risked his life for the two of you . . . and you accused him of being a spy and tried to have him killed.'

'Well, if he is a spy he should be punished,' Leila responded curtly.

'We want so much to help Muslims, and the only way we can really do that is by being with them in both suffering and joy,' the girls had written when they left. 'With this in mind we have decided to travel to Syria and help out down there as best we can.'

But they were not helping anybody. For a while Hisham had

allowed the sisters to volunteer at a hospital. He would drive them there and pick them up.

The Islamist hospital procedures had led to a large number of the employees leaving. Many had fled to Turkey. Doctors who had never taken prayer breaks were now obliged to pray five times a day. Nurses had to be fully covered while working, and male doctors were not to see their female patients' faces.

Ayan and Leila went around kind of helping out.

Then Hisham changed his mind. The hospital was not a good place for them to be. They were better off at home.

Because when a woman leaves the house, the devil always follows her.

A new thread had started up on the chat page of Leila's school class. The tabloid *VG* had reported that the girls most likely had travelled to Syria because of boyfriends. A boy asked if anyone knew more about this.

Camilla: She always said that because of her religion she did not and would not have a boyfriend, but you never know

Alexander: She was so unsociable. She probably didn't tell anyone other than her sister

Camilla: We don't actually know if she was unsociable or not, given that we had no idea what she was doing in her free time

Fridjof: hahahahahahahahahahahaaahahaha so true

Alexander: She was unsociable in class, didn't go on any school trips, didn't turn up at graduation or at Ulrik's party

Joakim: I don't think that had anything to do with how social she was, more to do with the religious aspect or whatever it's called. It did take place in a church after all

Fridjof: But hey, massive respect for her daring to go down there

Camilla: I agree completely, Fridjof, she really is a brave individual

Alexander: Are you kidding me?

> Fridjof: About what? Listen … it might be a stupid thing to do
>   but she did have the courage to do it. There's jihad and
>   shit down there
> Alexander: Yes, but she deserves ZERO respect. What good
>   has she done??
> Fridjof: She does deserve respect, even though it's a stupid
>   thing to do, she did leave everything she had to go and
>   help complete strangers
> Alexander: I get your point but I for one do not respect her

Her former classmates often spoke of her.

'The school actually treated her really well,' Emilie said to Sofie during a free period. They were now attending Nadderud, the most prestigious upper secondary school in Bærum. 'She may have felt left out, but then again she wasn't that easy to talk to either.'

'Wasn't exactly a ray of sunshine,' Sofie said. 'But neither was she a bitch.'

They agreed that it would probably have been easier for her if she had gone to a school where there were more people like her there, more Muslims.

The girls recalled what she had said about judgment day. 'It's like a crossroads,' she had told them. 'One way goes to paradise, the other leads to hell.'

'So where will I end up?' Emilie had asked.

'Because of how you dress, not covering your hair and the like, and as you're not Muslim, you're going to hell,' Leila had replied.

On seeing Emile's shocked look, Leila had wavered slightly. 'Maybe you'll be all right. We will sacrifice ourselves for all of you as well.'

Sofie contemplated those words. 'Is that what she's doing now, sacrificing herself for us?'

Emilie looked at her. 'Haven't a clue. What's she actually doing down there anyway?' She twiddled a strand of hair between her fingers and looked at Sofie. 'Do you think she went there to be a sex slave?'

*

The first couple of months in Syria, the girls lived in different locations, depending on where Hisham was working. They stayed in al-Dana and Tabaqa in Idlib province, then in Aleppo province. At the beginning of 2014, Hisham and Ayan moved to Raqqa, where ISIS had recently taken control. As a suitable husband had yet to be found for Leila, who was still recovering from her bullet wound, she accompanied them.

One militia after another had been defeated. The black flag was raised all across the city.

ISIS arrested whomever they pleased.

Whenever.

Wherever.

Charges were manifold.

Jeans were forbidden. Ornaments on women's clothing likewise. Smoking meant running the risk of losing the fingers you held the cigarette between. Long hair on men was prohibited, growth of beards was compulsory. Most of those harboring aspirations for freedom had either been killed or had fled.

The three youngsters from Bærum had taken possession of such a family's house. It was empty, insofar as it was without occupants, but was filled with everything one could need: bedclothes, towels, pots and pans, appliances, and electronics.

Those who did not support ISIS lay low and kept quiet, except one small group calling itself Raqqa Is Being Slaughtered Silently, which posted photographs online and reported what ISIS did not want the wider world to know. The leaders of Raqqa's most prominent tribes saw which way the wind was blowing and swore allegiance to Abu Bakr al-Baghdadi. The new force occupying the city replaced Assad's reign of terror with its own.

Everything had gone according to Haji Bakr's plan.

Hisham was one of the pawns. The pike angler had risen through the ranks and now commanded a squad of soldiers. He had arrived early in Syria, in autumn 2012, and was thus regarded as having seniority. Initially, he had joined al-Nusra but later defected to ISIS when the opportunity arose. Serving ISIS, on sacred soil, your thoughts required adjustment if you were to become a proper Muslim. If you hailed from a land of infidels, you were regarded as an infidel, no matter how well-read you were. Everyone began at the same level, as though hearing about Islam for the first time. For some it was familiar material; for others there was a lot that was new. Hisham did not understand much, as the lessons were held in Arabic and English. Prior to the religious instruction, the aspiring fighters had been subjected to a series of trials of patience, like being placed in a room with other newcomers to sit and stew. They could be left to themselves for days without any knowledge of what might happen or when. Some freaked out. It was an important grounding in life as a soldier, which in addition to going on the offensive involved staying calm, lying in wait, keeping your head down, and awaiting orders. A good fighter had ice water in his veins.

Only after weeks of patience training and religion classes did the new recruits begin weapons instruction.

The highest positions in ISIS were assigned to carefully chosen men. Like Abu Bakr al-Baghdadi, most of the top military leaders were Iraqi – ISIS was above all an Iraqi organization. Saudi Arabians held the uppermost positions in the courts, with Tunisians below them, and Arabians from the Gulf often worked in the intelligence services. Many Chechens, with their valuable guerrilla war experience, held midlevel ranks in the military.

There were opportunities for advancement, however, despite this consciously imposed hierarchy. Young men who had no experience of having people answer to them and had never so much as held jobs in the West could find themselves in command positions. Men like Hisham.

Young Muslim males had enlisted in holy war before. In Afghanistan. Iraq. Bosnia. Somalia. In that respect Hisham was part of a tradition. What was new was the speed at which it was happening and the flow of females, many in their teens. By autumn 2013, the number of Western migrants in Syria numbered around three thousand, several hundred of whom were women.

What made young women renounce their families, friends, and studies to travel to a war zone?

A group of researchers at the London-based Institute for Strategic Dialogue attempted to find an answer to this online, on Twitter, on blogs. These were the places the girls themselves chose to explain why they went. Three main reasons were offered.

The first was that the ummah was under attack. The West wanted to eliminate Islam and drive out Muslims.

The conflict was presented as a part of a larger war against Islam. The girls shared images of dead or wounded children from Palestine, Syria, and Afghanistan. A black-and-white perspective was typical. 'Either you are in the camp of iman – belief – or you are in the camp of kufr – unbelief, no in between,' declared Umm Khattab, one of the most active on Twitter in 2014. She, in common with the others, wrote under a nom de guerre, and many of the women used the prefix *umm* 'mother' in Arabic. She held the view that Muslims could not live in the West.

The second reason was the desire to establish the caliphate. Few women traveled with the purpose of fighting themselves. Those who did were disappointed. ISIS did not allow women near the front line, the privilege of the men. Only those charged with control of their sisters' morals in the female police brigade – al-Khansa – were given weapons training. They patrolled the streets of Raqqa with Kalashnikovs over their shoulders.

Female migrants traveled with the idea of building a new society based on the laws of Allah. An ideologically pure state. A paradise for fundamentalists. Some mentioned a call to help others, some wanted to be mothers and wives. Many of those who went there to marry had never had a boyfriend before.

The third main reason was individual duty and identity. Carrying out your religious duty while on earth secured you a place, perhaps even a good place, in paradise. Some wrote that they had no wish to live in this world at all and yearned for the hereafter. Umm Khattab, like Ayan, quoted the mantra of Jihadists the world over: *We love death more than you love life.*

The search for a sense of belonging went like a red thread through the Twitter messages. Many wrote about the sisterhood they felt in Syria, as opposed to the false, superficial friendships they had in the West.

Umm Irhab – Mother of Terror – wrote that seeking a better life had not been her intention. Her journey was rather a lesson in patience and hardship. The meaning of paradise would become clear through the trials she underwent and lead her to discover if she was worthy of entering. But it was not only in paradise that you reaped the rewards of following the way of God; you could also get what you wanted in this life – for example, being provided with a brave, noble husband. If Allah was willing, you might even be rewarded by becoming the wife of a martyr.

The unmarried women were known as *muhajirat* – migrants – and were first placed in a *maqqar*, a sort of hostel. They were not allowed outside without permission, and then only if it was strictly necessary, in which case they had to be chaperoned. If they needed something, they were to approach the administrator. Those who had already arrived explained the system to those who were planning to come. It was important to come with the right intentions, wrote Umm Layth – Mother of the Lion – one of the most active on social media. 'The reality is that to stay without a man here is really difficult.' She elaborated: 'I have stressed this before on Twitter but I really need sisters to stop dreaming about coming to Syria and not getting married. Wallahi, life is very difficult here for the muhajirat, and we depend heavily on the brothers for a lot of support. It is not like the West where you can casually go out to Walmart and drive home . . .'

When they married, which as a rule they quickly did, often immediately after arriving, they were given a place to live commensurate with the husband's status.

A Malaysian woman calling herself Bird of Paradise married a Moroccan she had never met prior to her wedding day and described life in the caliphate in terms of cost: '1. We don't pay rent here. Houses are given for free. 2. We pay neither electric nor water bills.

3. We are given monthly groceries. Spaghetti, pasta, canned foods, rice, eggs, etc. 4. Monthly allowances are given not only to husbands but also to wives and also for each child. 5. Medical check-up and medication are free – the Islamic State pays on your behalf.'

Mother of the Lion felt she deserved these benefits: 'In these lands we are rewarded for our sacrifice in migrating here, and receive *ghanimah* – war booty. Honestly there is something so pleasurable in knowing that what you have has been taken from the kuffar and handed to you personally by Allah as a gift. Some of the many things include kitchen appliances like fridges, cookers, ovens, microwaves, milkshake machines, vacuum cleaners, cleaning products, fans and most important – a house with free electricity and water provided to you by the caliphate and no rent, included.'

Umm Ubaydah shared her attitude: 'Alhamdulillah, God be praised, and they give food and clothes, mostly ghanimah, and today we received fresh bread.'

The electricity may have been free, but supply was intermittent, and as one woman explained, you could not always count on being able to charge your phone. It was important to have candles and flashlights available, and you had to learn how to wash your clothes by hand 'since you really cannot depend on a washing machine here.'

Leila and Ayan also were occupied with conveying a good impression of the caliphate. While Syrians fled their homes, Ayan wrote to Ismael, 'We get money without working here btw. Tee hee. The house costs nothing, electricity costs nothing, and water costs nothing.'

What, then, was expected from women in return for all this?

Umm Ubaydah could clarify: 'The best thing for a woman is to be a righteous wife and to raise righteous children.'

For some the whole experience was a disappointment. Even in one of the world's most infamous cities, where beheadings had become public entertainment, domestic life could be boring. But few admitted they had expected more of the caliphate than housework, and those who expressed criticism were swiftly put in their place by the sisters.

Umm Layth wrote: 'As mundane as some of the day-to-day tasks may get, still you truly value every minute here for the sake of Allah – wallahi, I swear to God I have come across such beautiful sisters who will spend mornings and nights in happiness because they are cooking the mujahideen food.'

Quite a few of the bloggers' texts were more akin to cooking blogs than war journals. One woman celebrated a cake she had baked, posting a photo of it with a grenade carefully positioned beside it: 'Oreo cheesecake à la @UmmMujahid 93 and me.' Daily life was described under the hashtag #SimplePleasures in #IS. Their references, which might include Disney movies, celebrities, and food products, revealed that many of the girls had, not long ago, lived ordinary teenage lives. For a while Nutella was all the rage – husbands posted pictures of the jar along with Kalashnikovs and grenades. Many of the young fighters had a sweet tooth and posted pictures of well-stocked shelves in the pastry shops of Raqqa.

Some websites specialized in recipes and snack tips for *jihadistas*. They were often basic and accompanied by simple illustrations. A recipe on the site of the al-Zorah women's group showed a sequence of photos: an egg in a bowl, sugar in a bowl, the egg and sugar being mixed, a spoonful of salt, a glass of milk, a glass of flour, a larger bowl with everything whisked together, and finally a frying pan. 'Sisters, you can make these pancakes and put them in the pockets of your fighter's fatigues when they're on their way into battle. We pray to God that this recipe is beneficial to our mujahid heroes!'

The pancakes could be served with honey, syrup, sugar, butter, jam, or – Nutella.

The women rarely expressed regret online for the choice they had made, although quite a few wrote about missing their families back home and displayed awareness of the worry they had caused. Fear of hurting their parents, particularly their mothers, was what had occasioned the most doubt when they were considering whether or not it was right to leave. One girl felt anguish for leaving her mother alone, since her siblings had already flown the nest: 'I ask myself if it was the right thing to do, but tell myself I would probably get married and leave her anyway.'

Umm Layth concludes: 'The family you get in exchange for the one left behind are like the pearl in comparison to the shell you throw away.'

Ayan and Leila displayed little emotion in the short conversations they had with their mother. They placed the blame for being unable to meet squarely on their parents.

'You made a big mistake reporting us to the police,' Ayan once told Sara over the phone. 'Now everyone knows who we are. We'll be arrested if we return to Norway.'

Sara sensed hope. Did that mean that the girls finally *wanted* to come home?

'We can help you—'

Ayan interrupted her. It certainly did not mean that.

'You can come here instead! You, the boys, and Dad. We'll welcome you with open arms. The Islamic State is soon going to take over the whole world, so it's best to get here sooner rather than later. Before everyone else comes.'

One day Sadiq received a call from a blocked number. As usual his heart missed a beat. It had been a long time since the girls had been in touch. When he heard a man's voice, his heart sank.

The man greeted him politely in slightly florid, broken Somali.

He introduced himself as Imran and sounded young, like a teenager.

He was in Raqqa, he said, and wanted to ask permission to marry Leila.

Sadiq got to his feet, unable to speak. His mind raced. A young man he did not know asking for his daughter's hand.

'Ask Leila to call me,' he said.

Leila called him almost immediately.

'Do you like him?' Sadiq asked.

'Yes.'

'Is he good for you? Do you love him?' her father continued.

'Yes,' Leila replied.

'If that's the case, ask his father to call me.'

Imran's mother was the one who called, as his father was dead.

'You will need to speak to my wife,' Sadiq told her.

Men were to negotiate with men, women with women. Certain rules had to be observed even when all others were broken.

Prior to Imran's mother's call, Leila had also spoken to Sara. She had only one question for her daughter.

'Are you sharing a bed with him now?' Sara asked.

'No, are you crazy!' Leila replied.

'Okay, fine. You can marry.'

Imran was British, of Somali descent. His mother told Sara he had excelled at school, being good at anything technical, a computer whiz. He was the youngest son in the family and had lived alone with his mother when his father died. One day the eighteen-year-old had stocked up his mother's fridge. He had made several trips up and down the stairs of their block of flats carrying forty-pound sacks of rice, bags of pasta, and a gallon of oil and put it all neatly away in the larder.

Then he had left for Syria.

Sara and Sadiq made up their minds to like Imran. Not least because he had actually asked for Leila's hand in marriage. Arrangements were made for Imran's brother to come to Norway as a representative for his younger brother. Sadiq was to be Leila's wali. The couple were married by proxy in Oslo by an imam.

Now Sara and Sadiq had two sons-in-law in the caliphate.

In early 2014, the militias in Atmeh and the rest of Idlib were planning a large offensive to retake the territory lost to ISIS the previous autumn. They had had enough. Disparate groups were constantly making deals and cooperating, but ISIS never intended to honor any arrangements they entered. They wanted to rule alone. When in December 2013 they had lured a popular rebel leader to negotiations only to torture him to death, they had gone too far. It was the final straw and it united the FSA and al-Nusra. By launching simultaneous attacks on several ISIS-held positions they robbed ISIS of its tactical advantage – the swift transfer of small units to where they were most needed.

In the space of a few weeks ISIS was driven out of Atmeh, most of Idlib, Hama, and the area east of Aleppo. When rebel forces attacked Tal Rifat outside Aleppo in late January, Haji Bakr decided to stay in the town incognito. He could have gained entrance to heavily guarded ISIS military camps if he had announced who he was, but the strategist chose to remain quietly in his home. The town was divided into two within a matter of hours. The Lord of the Shadows found himself sitting on the wrong side.

The master of surveillance and spying was eventually squealed on himself.

'There's a Daesh sheikh living next door,' a man called out to a contingent of rebel forces.

When the local commander knocked on the door, Haji Bakr opened it, wearing his pajamas. He said he wanted to get dressed but the commander ordered him out. Haji Bakr jumped backward, kicked the door shut, and shouted, 'I have a suicide belt!' He then came out with a Kalashnikov and was shot dead. The house was searched. Computers, mobile phones, books, and notes were confiscated. Underneath some dusty blankets they found it: the blueprint for the Islamic State.

Surrounded by low concrete slabs and red poppies growing wild, the Lord of the Shadows was buried in some parched earth outside the town, far from his beloved Iraq.

The ISIS capital was under strain. The rebels who had defeated the Islamists in Idlib were intent on taking Raqqa. ISIS deployed great numbers in defense of the city, which was subjected to intense rocket attack. Both sides suffered heavy losses, and there were many civilian deaths.

The Juma family heard nothing from the girls for several months. It was not until spring that Leila broke their silence.

'Broooother, how are things with all of you?' she wrote to Ismael in mid-March from the Fatima Abdallah account. 'Well, here's an update on what's been happening lately with us. We are well. We've been moving around a lot but are now settled again. We don't have a car anymore so it's hard to get to a place to go online. We don't have any mobile phone coverage so we can't ring you. It's been chaotic here lately but we're still alive. Tell Dad I'm sorry for hanging up on him last time we spoke, we were stressed out and in a real hurry. WE ARE NOT TRYING TO AVOID HIM, CIRCUMSTANCES HAVE NOT ALLOWED US TO SPEAK WITH HIM. You have to understand, we don't always have Internet access or telephone coverage and sometimes we can't talk even though we're able to go online. Btw the scar on my leg is soooooo badass. The plaster has come off and I'm learning to walk again, it's sooo hard, I don't know how I managed to do it before haha.'

Ismael had difficulty reconciling her breezy tone with the months of silence that had passed. It was as though his sisters had gone on a weekend trip and had been out of touch a little longer than they should.

'Talk to Mom&Dad, not to me,' he wrote back.

'What does that mean?' Ayan replied two days later.

She took up the thread where her sister had left off. It was not uncommon for the connection to be cut off and for answers to come several days or weeks later, as though the time in between was a vacuum.

'I can't face it to worry and care anymore. If you're not planning on ever meeting us again then I'd prefer you didn't talk to me. That's it,' Ismael replied.

'Get a grip. Of course we want to see you. People's parents have come from all over the world to visit.'

'We're not coming to Syria, I hope you realize that.'

'If you do want to come you're more than welcome.'

'To Syria?'

'Why not?'

'Because I have no plans on dying. You don't want to leave Syria, we don't want to go there.'

'Whatever, all in good time. How are things with You!'

'Ayan, I love you both very much. But you're a big depressing anchor weighing down my life.'

'Why?'

'I suggest you get in touch with Mom because I don't care anymore, bye bye, for good.'

'You're my little brother so don't dare try to break off contact. You have to care about me!'

'Do you want to say anything else before I block you and erase you from my life?'

'Ismael! That's enough! We're family, are you just going to throw us away? We'd love to go to Turkey and meet you but we can't risk being sent home! Consider visiting us, people have traveled here from Sweden and gone home safe. You're acting weak! This is not how you are, Ismael!'

'You're like random people in a crowd to me. You're nobody.'

'We really need your support.'

'I had two really nice sisters. What have I got now? *Fatima*?'

'You've got two even better sisters. Stronger and smarter than before.'

'I'll make sure that Jibril and Isaq don't follow in your footsteps. I used to respect religion but now I can't stand it.'

'Get hold of yourself. By the will of Allah both you and they will follow in our footsteps! Fear ALLAH and don't try to misguide small children.'

'Ranted the indoctrinated mouth. I believe in Allah about as much as I believe in the spaghetti monster, bye now.'

Something that had never been tested before was under way: the establishment of a caliphate in the modern world with people looking to the past for guidance. The Prophet Muhammad was the ideal, women sought inspiration from his wives. He had had twelve. 'The Prophet is more worthy of the believers than themselves, and his wives are their mothers,' it states in the Koran 33:6. If the project were to endure, women would play a key role. Without women there would be no descendants, without descendants there would be no viable state.

With the loss of territory in northwest Syria, ISIS expanded eastward, across the Syrian countryside. Black flags were planted where statues of Assad had stood, in the ruins of burned-out churches, on bombed-out Shia Muslim shrines.

The girls had moved from place to place within the caliphate as their husbands' postings required. However, their role in life had remained the same: housewives.

Their situation did not seem to weigh upon them. Ismael, on the other hand, felt increasingly trapped in a life that at times did not seem worth living. Winter had proved difficult, he had been frightened, angry, depressed, and frustrated. Every time he managed to pick himself up, put the thought of his sisters out of his mind, and live in the present, a new e-mail, an SMS, a call, or a demand to *Log on to Skype!* would arrive.

'So, are you ready for the exams. Have you applied for further education? Are you still working out?' Ayan asked, initiating a conversation at the start of May.

As usual there was no mention of anything to indicate she was residing in a war zone. Ismael wrote back to say his first exam was on Friday, he had applied to a technical college in the north of Norway, and his visits to the gym had gone to hell without the money for a bus pass.

'Watch out for wild reindeer,' Ayan wrote, adding that there were probably very few black people in the north, but lots of Sami.

Ismael ignored his sister's comment, choosing instead, as was often the case, to get straight to what was on his mind.

'The reason I want to break off contact is that I find it very hard to relate to sisters who in all likelihood I will never meet again.'

Ayan always dismissed talk of *never.*

'I like to be realistic,' Ismael continued. 'If you're not planning on leaving Syria and I'm not planning on going there, then we're never going to meet again, that's just the way it is. If we don't see each other within a year, I can't face any more cozy chats.'

Ayan's response took four days, coming again late at night.

'What makes you think this is a cozy chat, we're siblings and that's that. Doesn't Mom stay in touch with her siblings even though she only sees them every four years?'

As he trudged home from an end-of-school party at four in the morning, he typed in 'At least they meet!'

The conversations continued like this, intermittently. The sisters would write that life was great, apart from the heat. They were used to Norwegian summers and unprepared for the desert temperatures. They expressed their concerns about how Isaq, their youngest brother, was fitting in at school – 'Has he got any friends?' – or about his foot, which was slightly shorter than the other – 'Is it any better?' – or inquired if Jibril had been happy with the iPad they had given him, and if he was still going to karate. No, he was not, the family could no longer afford to pay for the lessons. All their money had been spent on trying to rescue *them*. The trip to Syria had put Sadiq in serious debt. They were unable to use the car, the EU roadworthiness test had been too expensive. The sisters responded by saying that they were sure Allah would sort that out too, along with everything else.

Ayan logged on erratically but at a regular time, between ten and eleven at night. She made contact one night in mid-May.

'You at home?'

'Yes. But I was going to bed.'

'Nooo, video chat, go online and wake the family!!!'

'Can't, have an exam to study for, anyway, good night!' Ismael sent her a thumbs-up symbol.

Three days later Ayan again requested a video chat.

'Why are you always logging on so late?' Ismael asked.

'I don't get the time to any earlier.'

'I have my math EXAM tomorrow. So I think I'd better get some sleep.'

'Soon inshallah I may have some exciting news.'

' . . . okay, good night.'

'You're such an idiot. Sleep tight!'

A week later, she got in touch again, between ten and eleven at night as usual.

'Hi. Hope the exam went okay!'

'Hi. Felt it went well.'

'Good. What other exams were you selected to sit for? What ones did you want to do?'

'It was good to get math. I wanted to sit for IT. But I always get the exams I don't want.'

'I hate that too, being picked to sit for exams in my weak subjects.'

'Oral and written Norwegian should go okay.'

'Inshallah, that's chill, let me know what subjects you need to take an oral exam in, maybe I can help you.'

'Will do.'

'Listen, is there something up with Dad?'

Now it was Ismael's turn not to respond. Yes, there was something up with Sadiq. He had become withdrawn, went about in his own world. He was present but showed little interest in what was around. None of what Ismael said or did seemed to mean much to him. He never asked his son about anything, school, friends, exams, plans for the summer, for next year. Ismael had not only lost two sisters, he had also lost a father. Sadiq spent all his time sitting at the computer looking at Arabic websites for news about Raqqa, about ISIS, about coalition bombing.

Ismael was merely air. The two who were not there were the ones who mattered.

Sadiq fantasized about different ways of rescuing the girls, but there was one problem: They did not want to be rescued.

Going to Raqqa, forcing them to come home against their will, no, that would not work.

The girls would first have to realize they had made a mistake.

'Can you put some serious thought into getting out of that hellhole soon?' he asked them when they called.

He bawled them out, until they hung up. Then silence. They had never given a number where they could be reached, the family could not get in touch, all contact was up to them.

As soon as the younger daughter's leg heals they will set out for home, he had instructed Lippestad to tell the media. They were being held against their will, Sadiq pointed out.

He told people he had been on his way to the library in Sandvika when Leila had called him out of the blue to say she had fled from her husband. Sadiq stormed into the library, looked up Raqqa on Google Earth, and found her position from what she told him she could see around her. From the library he had instructed her to wait by a mosque, where she found a bench to sit on, while he had called a Syrian friend and asked him to send someone to get her. Osman had done just that and now Leila was sheltering at the house of a young widow with two small children, Sadiq told people. After a while Ayan had also made it to the hideaway. They were now hiding from their husbands and awaiting rescue, their father assured those he told the story to. But in the spring the house they were holed up in had been bombed . . .

If anyone wanted to know more, Sadiq could provide details.

The little children had been playing outside in the yard when a helicopter, loaded with barrel bombs, began circling. The mother had rushed out, grabbed hold and lifted a child under each arm before running back toward the house. The helicopter was directly above them when it slipped its payload. There was an almighty explosion and the mother and her children were no more.

Two sisters, who were sitting in their room, were uninjured.

The gate had been blown open.

They could not remain there.

His daughters had rushed out.

Now he did not know their whereabouts.

The truth was: They had chosen a life without him.

They were making pancakes in Raqqa.

With sugar topping.

24

The End of Sykes-Picot

The days that shook the world came in early June. The time had come to realize the deceased Haji Bakr's primary objective – expansion eastward.

On the morning of June 5, 2014, a large convoy of military vehicles rolled over the border from Syria toward the Iraqi city of Samarra, situated on the banks of the Tigris, just over sixty miles from Baghdad. The former capital of the Abbasid caliphate was home to the al-Askari Shrine, one of Shia Islam's holiest sites, and its street layout and architecture dated from the ninth century; the war was putting world heritage in danger.

Suicide bombers cleared a path for tanks and infantry. A police station was blown up by a truck loaded with explosives, following which the Islamists fought their way toward the city center. That afternoon black flags were waving from Islamic architectural treasures. But the victory was temporary. Four Iraqi army brigades that had been equipped and placed on a war footing a few weeks before in order to defend Baghdad and the surrounding cities against the Sunni jihadists were readied for action. In the course of the afternoon, Iraqi helicopter attacks forced the Islamists to leave Samarra.

The following day, five suicide bombers attacked a large arms

depot in Mosul, the third-largest city in Iraq, allowing the jihadists to seize control of the materials inside. The assault was well
coordinated. ISIS had been infiltrating the metropolis for months
beforehand. Sleeper cells were activated and joined the offensive.
The suicide bombings, as well as the attacks coming from all sides,
from within their own ranks too, created the illusion of there being
many more jihadists than there were. In fact there were only just
over a thousand men, while Mosul, at least on paper, was held by
a force fifteen times larger. The Iraqi government had prioritized
the defense of the cities nearer Baghdad, and Prime Minister Nouri
al-Maliki had ignored Kurdish leaders' warnings of an imminent
attack on Mosul.

The international community watched in shock as American-
trained Iraqi soldiers discarded their uniforms and fled. The generals
were the first to abandon their posts, leaving their officers without
orders. Those at the top knew what a poor state the army was in,
since they had helped themselves to the funds that should have gone
to ammunition and had sent soldiers home with a small remuneration, pocketing their monthly salaries. Corruption pervaded Iraq
under al-Maliki, who implemented policies that granted all real
power in the country to the Shias, pushing away the Sunni tribes
and driving them into the open arms of the Islamists.

By June 9, the Islamists had taken control of the police headquarters, the airport, and numerous public buildings in Mosul. They
captured tanks, armored vehicles, pickups, and hundreds of weapons systems, many of them labeled MADE IN USA. Within a few
hours, the military booty had been safely driven across the border
into Syria. The city's largest prison was emptied of its inmates. Six
hundred Shia Muslims were executed in a nearby ravine; Sunnis
were offered the chance to fight alongside ISIS. The next day ISIS
had control over all of Mosul.

Within a few days, the Sunni jihadists were approaching Tikrit,
which up until the Middle Ages had been an important center of the
Syriac Orthodox Church. It was also the birthplace of the Kurdish
military commander Saladin, who had captured Jerusalem from the

Crusaders. And of Saddam Hussein. Many of his trusted men, both in the army and the party, bore the name al-Tikriti – members of his own tribe. Following the American invasion of Iraq in 2003, Tikrit had formed the northern angle of the so-called Sunni Triangle, where insurgency was at its most intense.

Here too the generals were the first to flee the battlefield. Lack of leadership led to panic among the soldiers at the local air base. Close to three thousand young men tore off their uniforms and fled on foot. They did not make it far before the Islamists caught up with them, calling out, 'Are you heading to Baghdad? We can drive you to the capital, hop in!' Those who did not come willingly were forced on board. The trucks stopped at a spot in the middle of the desert.

Eight hundred soldiers were executed over the next few days. ISIS posted video footage of rows of young men, all Shias, lying facedown in the sand. One after another, they were shot in the head. Some were placed on a bridge over the Tigris and shot through the back of the head before falling into the river. Others were forced to lie in freshly dug graves before being peppered with bullets, whereupon more of the young men were ordered to lie on their dead comrades to meet the same fate. Layer upon layer, in the same way that Saddam Hussein had ordered the Kurds shot a generation before in the purge that had been given the name al-Anfal after a chapter in the Koran describing God's order to Muhammad on fighting unbelievers.

Recordings of the mass killings were soon edited and publicized by ISIS's propaganda machine.

The same day as the massacre in Tikrit, Ayan was in Raqqa trying to access her bank account online. She made several attempts, without succeeding. She sent her brother a message.

'Important. Where are you?'

'At home. What's up?'

'I need you to log on to my bank account.'

'???????????????????'

'I can't log on to my current account or my savings account.'

She read out the passwords to Ismael, who entered them along with her personal password on his computer. When he saw the bank statements, he was shocked.

'You have a MEGA loan,' he wrote. 'Good luck with that!'

All her credit card loans were due and were listed as unpaid.

'Not a big deal. The state will take care of that,' his sister answered.

The state was indeed wealthy. Over the last few days, ISIS had conquered large areas of land and millions of new inhabitants. The money from the vault in the central bank in Mosul, several hundred million dollars, was now in the hands of the Islamists, as were oil installations, oil wells, and military materials.

Ismael then asked if his sister could do him a favor.

'Depends,' she answered.

'Can you and Leila make a video explaining why you left?'

'For the family?' Ayan asked.

'For the MEDIA! And soon, I need mon-nay! It would really help me out.'

Ayan told him she would have to discuss it with Leila first.

Ismael persisted. 'It would put both of you in a good light, you could show you aren't idiots being manipulated but that you're doing this for a reason.'

'That's true, I don't like people thinking we were fooled and that we're morons who came here to risk our lives.'

'$_$ now we're on the same page, girl,' Ismael replied.

'Quit thinking of me as cash, okay.'

ISIS continued its advance in the latter half of June. The group took control of a chemical factory, the country's largest oil refinery, and two border stations between Syria and Iraq. Sykes-Picot, the agreement drawn up by Britain and France in 1916, allocating 'spheres of influence' among Britain, France, and Russia, now existed only on paper – the Islamists held a single territory spanning Syria and Iraq. It was an enormous admission of failure for the government in Iraq to lose so much land – and an international border – to a nonstate actor. By the end of the month, the authorities in Baghdad had lost control over several more stretches of territory bordering Syria and Jordan.

June 29, 2014, was to be a memorable day for ISIS. Three important videos were posted via al-Hayat Media Center.

The first was fifteen minutes long and titled *The End of Sykes-Picot*. It showed a dark, bearded man swaggering around a captured Iraqi border station.

It was the Chilean from Norway, the enfant terrible of the Prophet's Ummah and the man who'd been charged with uploading the video threatening the Norwegian government: Bastian Vasquez.

He strutted casually around abandoned buildings, past torn-down signs, stopping now and again to show discarded emblems from uniforms or point out rows of SUVs.

'Keep sending vehicles,' he addressed Obama. 'They end up in our hands anyway!'

He displayed a row of prominent teeth with large gaps between them.

'And don't forget diapers for your soldiers,' laughed a man behind the wheel of a white pickup with IRAQI BORDER CONTROL still written on the side.

Bastian spoke relaxedly and confidently in English. He peppered his sentences with Arabic words, every statement ending in 'inshallah' or 'wallahi,' and he made small talk in Arabic with the ISIS fighters who had taken the border station. They were dressed in desert fatigues, whereas Bastian sauntered around in a long tunic over short Salafi trousers. With a faded baseball cap on his head, he resembled a young Fidel Castro. Toward the end of the video he entered a room where a dozen or so men were imprisoned.

'Yazidis,' he spat in the direction of the men on the floor. 'They worship Lucifer.' He looked briefly into the camera before leaving the room.

A viewer could assume the men were killed shortly afterward. ISIS did not keep prisoners of war. At the conclusion of the video, a police station near the border post is rigged with explosives and blown up. The dust settles and *nasheeds* – a cappella religious songs concerning battle and martyrdom – replace Bastian's guided tour.

Another video posted that day, *Breaking the Border*, showed American-made military vehicles that had been seized by ISIS passing freely over yet another stretch of border, while bulldozers leveled the sand heaps demarcating Syrian and Iraqi territory.

The most important video was a speech by ISIS spokesman Abu Muhammad al-Adnani, the sole Syrian in the upper leadership of the organization.

'The time has come for those generations that were drowning in oceans of disgrace, being nursed on the milk of humiliation, and being ruled by the vilest of all people, after their long slumber in the darkness of neglect – the time has come for them to rise,' he said. 'The sun of jihad has risen. The glad tidings of good are shining . . . Support your state, which grows every day!'

ISIS had become IS – the Islamic State.

'Listen to your caliph and obey him!' the Syrian urged. Abu Bakr al-Baghdadi was now the self-appointed leader of all the world's Muslims.

The caliphate had been declared.

The following day, Ayan called her mother in Somaliland. She made no mention of the newly declared caliphate. She only wanted to wish the family well with Ramadan.

Sara and her sons had arrived in Hargeisa at the start of the month of fasting. Its annual observance was one of the pillars of Islam, an activity all healthy adults had to carry out in order to call themselves practicing Muslims. Everyone in the family home was fasting, except Ismael. He also refused to attend the mosque. Nor would he pray at home.

Sara had wept. 'You're bringing shame upon us!'

She threatened him with the wrath of God and the torments of hell.

'I've already lost two daughters, am I to lose you as well?'

Apostasy in Islam is obvious due to the clear actions required in the practice of the religion; the pillars are the declaration of faith, prayer, charity, fasting, and the pilgrimage to Mecca. Sara threatened to disown him but could not follow through on her threat. Eventually she gave in and allowed him to eat with his little brothers, who were not yet required to fast.

The rumors had preceded their arrival. Everyone had found out, relatives, neighbors, the whole street: *Sara and Sadiq's daughters have joined IS.* In Somaliland, IS was considered a terrorist organization, spreading death and destruction like their own al-Shabaab. *Ayan and Leila had joined the terrorists.* The extended family mourned the 'little girls,' who for the first time did not accompany their mother on the summer holiday.

The fear of losing more children tormented Sara. It gnawed at her thoughts, requiring ever more space in her mind. Memories of her firstborn resurfaced. She had been a teenager, narrow-hipped, and had spent a day and a night in labor. Eventually he ran out of air and was buried the same day he was born. That was in February 1993. Ayan was born in December of the same year.

After her daughters had left, she had been overwhelmed by fear of losing her two youngest boys. She did not feel they were safe in Bærum. Someone might lead them astray and away from her at any time. If you grew up in Norway, you became either an extremist or an atheist, that was her experience. She had to save Isaq and Jibril. Give them a sense of belonging in a solid, Muslim culture. Give them a healthy Muslim upbringing.

Child Welfare Services was what she dreaded the most, an anxiety shared by her friends. Somalis were overrepresented in cases involving custody and care orders. You needed to watch out so the state did not come and take your children. They could take whomever whenever. At any hour of the day or night they could turn up and demand your child. They'd probably been keeping tabs on the family ever since the girls left, her circle of friends told her.

Horror stories abounded. Everybody knew somebody who'd had a child taken away. One boy, whose mother had refused him candy, had called Child Welfare to tell them his mother and father beat him. The next day the authorities came and took him into custody, Sara had been told. Families going on holidays to their home country had their daughters taken away from them because they were accused of traveling to have them circumcised. One ten-year-old had contacted the authorities because his parents had refused to buy him a computer game. 'Buy him the game!' Child Welfare had ordered them, but the parents could not afford to and then Child Welfare took him into care because children had a right to games. Child Welfare lurked online to make contact with children and ask if they had any problems. If a child, for a joke, replied that he or she was being beaten, Child Welfare and the police moved in. These kinds of stories circulated when Sara and her friends met on long afternoons when the children were in school or at kindergarten and the men were out. They themselves did not go anywhere.

Fear of Jibril and Isaq being next on the list made her feel faint.

When Sara was seven years old, her mother had died suddenly. Her father found a new wife, and the children from his first marriage were farmed out to different relations. She had been placed in the care of an uncle in Hargeisa who had room and needed help around the house. She was the only child in the home and was brought up to strictly observe Somali customs and practice. She was sent to the mosque several hours a week, where she studied Koran quotations by rote and was instilled with reverence for God and the Prophet, but she never learned to read or write.

Even though she had friends in the street and outlined games in the sand, she grew up with a great sense of longing. It was not viewed as natural for an uncle to hug a niece. Grief at the loss of a mother and the yearning for her siblings left a deep cut within.

After a few years she asked her uncle, 'Can my little brothers and sisters come and live here too?'

And so it was. One after one they arrived in Hargeisa. This was the first time she gathered her family. Her brothers and sisters were showered with kisses and affection, because if there was one thing Sara had plenty of, it was love.

She was fourteen when Sadiq first set eyes on her.

His marriage to a cousin had already been arranged.

Then he met Sara at a crossroads.

She came walking toward him, tall, thin as a rake, elegant and graceful, the most beautiful thing he had ever seen. He was fifteen, and he was sold.

The next day he knocked on the door of the girl Sara had been walking with to ask if the unknown beauty was promised to anyone. The girl said she would check. She returned and told him that Sara was free.

Sadiq went to talk to his mother.

'Mom, I like my cousin, but she's like a sister to me. And I've met someone else.'

'Who?'

'Her name's Sara.'

His mother mulled it over. She made some inquiries and decided to pay Sara's uncle a visit. She returned to her youngest son.

'Okay, my son, then that's how it will be.'

Serendipity. The year was 1990.

Then Sadiq enlisted in the war against the dictator. Sara waited.

Two years went by before he returned and they could marry; she was sixteen, and he was seventeen. He had never regretted it. Sara was everything to him.

Now, twenty-five years on, they struggled to pick themselves up, to heal, each in their own way.

Sara had found a new home for them in Hargeisa. 'Them' being sixteen people, and she asked Sadiq to send money for the rent.

The house was constructed so that the wind could blow through, making it airy even when the sun was at its strongest. The terrace, where a soft old armchair took pride of place, was north facing and tiled in a beautiful golden pattern. Flower tendrils wove together up the walls. The portico and fence looking over the yard were painted green. A large water tank stood in the corner.

Sara had gathered two of her sisters and their families, one brother and his wife, and some unmarried nephews and nieces. The nephews lived in a small dwelling in the corner of the yard, adjacent to the outside toilet, while each family had a room. Except for Sara, who had two. The largest bedroom was hers and there was another room for the boys. After all, she was the one paying the rent.

The rooms were large with mosquito nets at the windows and screens in front of the doors. Everything they needed lay open or was stacked in piles on the floor. There were no hooks on the wall to hang anything from, no closets to put anything in. Their suitcases lay on top of one another like a temporary wardrobe.

Both Sadiq and Sara were descended from nomads, their fore-fathers had had large flocks of animals. With your possessions in a suitcase you could always move on. Putting them away in a ward-robe meant you had decided to stay.

The parents disagreed on what to do when their daughters came home. They would need to go see a psychologist first, in Sadiq's opinion. Our family is all they need, Sara said. And an imam. Sadiq thought the girls were brainwashed, Sara called them misguided. They just needed to be led back onto the path of true Islam.

She had begun to give her husband dribs and drabs of her own plan.

'They want to live in a Muslim country,' she said over the phone from Somaliland. 'So when they leave, wouldn't it be better for them to move here instead of to Norway? Then we could all start afresh here?'

'And what are we going to LIVE on in Somaliland?' Sadiq inquired.

'You can find a job.'

Finding a job in Somaliland to support a family of seven to the standard they were used to in Norway was close to impossible. This discussion generally concluded with them agreeing: 'They need to get out first. We'll deal with the rest afterward.'

Sara pictured a life in Hargeisa for the whole family. For Sadiq, his home was in Bærum, in a flat at the foot of the Kolsås ridge. That was where he dreamed of bringing his family together again.

He had not accompanied the others to Somaliland. He had told

Sara he wanted to stay behind in Norway to look for work. The truth was that he wanted to make another attempt at getting the girls out. He could not tell his wife this because they disagreed on the best way to get them home.

If that dangerous group, as Sara referred to ISIS, got wind of them trying to get their girls back, they would only build higher walls around them and keep an even closer watch. It was better to allow some time to pass, give the girls the chance to realize that no, this life in the desert was not for them.

She had experience of war and had no doubt that the girls would not be able to persevere for long.

'They're used to a European standard of living,' she said. 'They'll soon grow weary and are more likely to come home if we don't nag.'

Whenever the girls called, their mother always pointed out that there were several paths to paradise. Jihad was not the only one, the Koran said. They could get there by helping others, by helping their mother, by being good daughters.

Sara accepted that they did not want to come home. That is, she accepted it as a fact. Sadiq did not.

He flew from Norway on the same day the caliphate was declared. At the airport in Hatay he met Mehmut, managed to cross the border, and moved back in with Osman. The situation had grown tense and the cost of bodyguards had risen to reflect that, as had the price of weapons and gasoline. The cost of everything had increased, because war is expensive.

He spent most of the time dozing in the backyard, because Osman said there were rumors that ISIS executioners had arrived in Atmeh to kill someone. Maybe he was the one they were looking for.

Sadiq fasted with Osman, and broke the fast with him, the two of them sometimes hiding like naughty boys to surreptitiously enjoy a bite to eat. He suffered a bout of illness, had stomach trouble, and spent days lying on his mattress. The pains came and went, followed by headaches. Then he ran out of money. He was not one step closer to anything, only more deeply in debt.

He wrote two identical notes, in Norwegian, which possible

rescuers could hand to his daughters so the girls would understand their father had sent them: 'This is Sadiq. Trust whoever gives you this. I love you.'

He gave them to Osman. The two notes were as far as they got.

On his return to Norway, life went on as before. His mind buzzed with constant thoughts of his daughters. He never found peace. When he awoke, the first thing to enter his mind was: I can't take any more. The second was: I feel like shit.

The start of the new school year in Bærum was approaching. Sara enrolled the boys at a school in Hargeisa.

Ismael was angry with his father for allowing his mother to decide his younger brothers' futures.

'The schooling they'll get in Hargeisa is worth nothing. No country in the world recognizes a Somali education!'

Sadiq was well aware of that – he had been required to repeat subjects at both the primary and secondary levels in Norway.

'But what can I do?' Sadiq asked.

'You can bring them back.'

'Your mother is making the decisions. You have to remember, she's a grief-stricken mother,' Sadiq told him.

Little by little, Sara had cleared the flat of the girls' possessions and her own. Every time she had come across clothes they had left behind it had broken her that bit more.

The girls had already purged their wardrobe themselves, anything tight-fitting, short, or with a low neckline had been thrown out long ago, anything see-through or diaphanous was long gone. But there had been enough left behind.

Before leaving for Somaliland, Sara had picked up a roll of garbage bags along with the groceries. On returning home, she had gone to the girls' room, gathered their clothes and shoes, and stuffed them into the bags. She tied the tops tightly and placed them at the front door. When Sadiq arrived home, she asked him to throw it all into the Salvation Army container in Sandvika.

Apart from a couple of beautiful hijabs and a white jacket she wanted to give to a niece in Somaliland, she had gotten rid of all their belongings. Toothbrushes, hair elastics, and underwear went into the rubbish.

'But the girls *will* be back!' a friend had protested.

'Right now there are others who need those clothes more than they do,' Sara had replied.

The wardrobe was empty. All that remained was a large plastic box on the top shelf. She had taken a look at its contents, unopened letters, of no interest to her.

The notes from the Arabic course hung on the walls. Happy. Sad. Young. Old. God is great. They were yellowed. The words had faded.

25

God Is Not Great

'I wish I had a big sister I could look up to, whose footsteps I could follow in and be proud of,' Ismael wrote to Ayan when he was back in Bærum after the summer holidays.

She did not answer.

He sent her a link to a lecture by the astrophysicist Lawrence Krauss titled 'A Universe from Nothing.' The topic was cosmology, the study of the origin of the universe, how it was expanding, changing all the time, and would eventually disappear. 'The universe is dynamic,' Krauss explained, and showed pictures of starry skies, galaxies, and supernovas – the fireworks of the universe. 'Scientists love mysteries. The excitement of learning about the universe. So different from the sterile aspect of religion where the excitement is in knowing everything, although clearly knowing nothing.' He added that all religion was a fairy tale. Ismael shared his opinion. Religions were made up of stories people had invented to try to explain naturally occurring phenomena.

Krauss explained that all the atoms in the human body came from exploded stars. 'We are all made of stardust, and the atoms in your left hand probably came from a different star than your right hand.'

Ismael was fascinated. This was the path he wanted to follow:

technology, physics, chemistry, the known and the unknown. He had sent Ayan the link to the lecture so she might also understand, yes, maybe even gradually realize what a mistake she and her sister had made and return home. Because if we understand what kind of universe we live in, Krauss had explained, then we'll also know how it will end. In a purely technical sense.

Ayan answered on August 19, the day ISIS broadcast the beheading of the first American hostage, the journalist James Foley. The video had been posted in the morning. It started with a clip of Barack Obama announcing air strikes in Iraq. The picture shifted to Foley kneeling in an orange jumpsuit in a desert landscape. A masked man dressed in black stood behind him with a knife in his hand. He made threats against America in a rough London accent.

Ayan did not mention the beheading, which photo analysts found out was filmed near the sand dunes south of Raqqa. She was stubbornly preoccupied with responding to her brother's accusation that he no longer had a big sister he could be proud of.

'Ismael, you know deep down in your heart that I am exactly the type of big sister you can look up to and be proud of! Tell me, if I had chosen to go to university, could I not have been whatever I wanted? Did I not have good grades at school? Was I not the one you woke up in the middle of the night to follow you to the toilet and lay awake with you afterward because you were frightened? Was I not the one who physically dragged you to school all these years? Haven't I always supported you and been there for you no matter what? So what makes you want to hurt me in this way now? Is it because I have made a choice you don't understand? Were you not the one who was so scared on the plane trip to Stavanger that you read the Koran? Were you not the one who read the Koran in your sleep? Are you not the one who is scared of jinn? You believe in Allah swt and are a Muslim deep down inside, don't allow yourself to be fooled by the kind of rubbish on that video, pick up the Holy Book and read it from cover to cover and then you will understand why you read it back when you were frightened and felt safe right away!'

It was soon midnight in Bærum, the August night was soft and mild.

'Ayan, I don't believe in God. The Koran has its good parts and its bad. God seems so limited. But you don't see that.'

In Raqqa it was still hot.

'God is anything but limited, did you know the sun has 365 points in its path? Allah swt swears by all of these points in the Koran. Btw where's Dad?'

Ismael did not answer the question about their father. It was too painful. Sadiq had entered a parallel universe, where dream and fantasy mingled with events around him. His hope reshaped reality into a fairy story of his own invention. Just like religion.

Instead Ismael argued against the omnipotence of God: '1. God cannot guide everyone to the right religion. 2. God cannot give me my sisters back. 3. God cannot create peace. 4. God cannot kill me right now. 5. He cannot = limited.'

Ayan protested: 'What about when death does come, who can stop it?'

'Death is not God,' Ismael replied.

'Your sisters are still alive. Wait a couple of years and you'll see there'll be peace. All that will be from God!'

'Nope.'

'Just read the Koran properly.'

'I don't view the Koran as sacred.'

'Read a translation of it and then you'll understand. You're just frightened.'

'No, I've lost any uncertainty I had. God is a dictator. He compels you to do things you might not want to. But he "loves" you. AND if you don't do as he asks, he punishes you for eternity. I have nothing against peaceful religions but unfortunately Islam is not one of them. You are indoctrinated to such a degree that you choose not to notice that, seeing as you're already in deep shit. STILL LOVE YOU. Just can't handle having a sister I'm not going to see again.'

Ismael concluded his statement with a red heart. He then sent her a link called 'Atheist & Muslim Debate,' which was a half-hour

discussion between a physics professor arguing against the existence of God and a Muslim student who believed he had proof that
He exists.

'I know that Islam is not a peaceful religion, but every living thing
has the right to defend itself,' Ayan replied.

'God seems so selfish. I don't like the idea of God. Creating man-
kind in order for them to worship him.'

His sister replied three nights later.

'Shut up you stupid little boy before the ground opens up and
swallows you. Never talk that way about God! Otherwise I'll have
nothing more to do with you.'

'Now you're on, finally!' Ismael typed. 'Before the ground opens
up and swallows you? When everyone interprets a holy book differently it's not so holy.'

'I feel sorry for you, you're so arrogant and think you have all the
answers,' Ayan wrote, adding, 'Where's our dad? Answer me that.'

Again he was reticent when it came to their father. He wanted to
be neither a spokesperson nor a messenger for their parents.

'You're the one who thinks you've found the truth,' he answered.

'Islam is the truth,' came the response from Raqqa.

'You accept so many things I never thought you would. How can
you believe it's morally correct to force people to convert or pay a
tax because they see things a different way?'

Ismael was referring to the system of *jizya*, a tax historically levied
by Islamic states on non-Muslim subjects residing in their land.

'People in Norway are made to pay taxes as well. The unbelievers
have to pay tax just as Muslims do, we pay zakat aka tax and they
pay jizya aka tax. It's fair and is just a tax by other names; I mean if
Muslims have to pay taxes, why shouldn't they pay too? How much
tax do you pay in Norway at the moment? You pay approximately
36%, almost half of what you earn, you're a slave without being
aware of it, especially with all the oil Norway has.'

'Do you know where your taxes are going?'

'Yes, but think about how much you pay compared to how little
we pay here. Do you know I get money from the state here?'

'Not working and being given money is not exactly something to brag about.'

'I don't lift a finger and I get everything I need, money, doctors, medicine, a house, water, electricity, the lot!!!'

'You're boasting about being handed everything on a silver platter. That's Somali logic. "I'm on welfare in Norway." Hard to beat free money.'

'I have a right to what I'm given, we're not demanding more than we're entitled to. We are given our share of the money coming into the state.'

'You're entitled to get things for free?'

'I'm entitled to have a share in the wealth of the Islamic State, yes. A proper welfare state.'

'You sound pretty spoiled if you ask me (nice to talk to you by the way).'

'Do you mean that or are you being sarcastic?'

'I mean it. Are you still married?'

'Yes, I'm still married hehe.'

'Same guy?'

'Yep. He's still alive. In case you were wondering.'

'All you hyper-religious types think life is an action film starring you in the main roles on a mission to accomplish what God wants.'

'Life is not a Facebook *like* or a movie, it's about what you choose to prioritize. You can view it in two ways, either live until you're 80 before you die and then nothing. Or live until you die and after that life begins.'

'That's so sweet,' Ismael replied.

'How was everything created? How did it all begin?' Ayan asked.

'That's the beauty of it. I don't believe the world was created for us but that we adapted to it. Let's drop this ☺. Do you think it's morally defensible to cut the hands off someone for stealing?'

Ayan suddenly disappeared, prompting a disappointed Ismael to ask, 'Do you not want to talk anymore?'

She turned up again a half hour later. 'Had to buy more internet access.'

Ismael repeated his question: 'Well?'

'I think so, yeah, because when people see what the punishment is for stealing they won't steal. We asked Syrians what they thought about life here now compared to before and they told us they feel safer. Crime has nosedived. Entire cities where drug use was endemic have become well-functioning societies. There are very few people here being punished now, I can promise you that,' she wrote, adding, 'shock therapy.'

'So you don't believe a person can change?'

'Of course they can change and you have no idea just how few people receive that punishment. What happens to people who break the law in Norway?'

'They're punished in a humane way.'

'Yes, they receive a sentence; actions here have consequences. In any case, these questions have nothing to do with the existence of God.'

'They have to do with sharia/Koran so I regard them as relevant. Can you walk around town on your own?'

'Yep. I often go shopping actually.'

'And do you have to be home by a specific time?'

'That depends on where my husband draws the line and has nothing to do with the state. All the women here can walk the streets ALONE.'

'So you can't do anything your husband doesn't want?'

'Of course I can.'

'Seeing as how you were created from his rib. Eh? You can?'

'Yes.'

'Are you punished? Can he strike you?'

'No and no! You know that my husband is from Norway, right?'

'Sure, but if it was written in sharia you would probably have accepted it, since you're going to heaven anyway ☺ right? Have women as many rights as men?'

'Yes.'

'Why don't men have to cover themselves?'

'They do. They have to cover parts of their bodies as well.'

'Their faces*. It seems very strange if you ask me. I find it offensive to men that women have to cover themselves up because men can't exercise self-control. What a load of bull.'

'It's for the sake of our honor, everyone shouldn't be made to look at my body. What good has it brought the world that people walk around half-naked?'

'Joy! But on a serious note, I think it's disrespectful to assume that I'm going to rape a girl just because she's half-naked.'

'Nobody assumes that.'

'Religion is so regional. People are born into the "right" religion and indoctrinated not to listen to what other people have to say.'

'Do I not know more about Christianity than many Christians? Eh . . . Don't I know a good deal about Judaism and the other world religions? Why did I choose Islam?'

'Because from the time you were small, innocent, and ignorant you were forced to believe in Islam. Right up until you liked it.'

'I was never forced.'

'You were forced, in the same way Jibril and Isaq are being now.'

As their three elder siblings had in Bærum, the youngest brothers now attended Koran school in Hargeisa. They learned verses from the holy book and to love and fear God. All summer long, Sara had tried everything to get Ismael to return to the path of religion. His apostasy pained her. She had taken him to see a well-known sheikh in Hargeisa for guidance. The two of them had met once a week in a mosque and sat on the cool floor of the holy building discussing matters. Ismael thought the sheikh a good man. He listened, presented his arguments, then allowed Ismael to expound his views before commenting on them. Ismael liked him. The sheikh often contradicted him but never pressured him to believe.

After Ismael had traveled home, they had continued to correspond. One argument Ismael had advanced to him, he now copied and pasted to his sister. 'We see something, we don't understand what it is; therefore: God,' he had written to the sheikh, calling it 'the argument of ignorance.' Vagueness provoked him. He wanted evidence. 'Can there be other explanations than the ones you offer me?' he had asked the sheikh. 'Is there anything besides scripture that can confirm what you say? There is no shame in not knowing something. But claiming to have knowledge of something you have no proof of is shameful. How was the universe created? We don't know. How did life come about? We're not certain. You say: picture a puddle on the road. It has a form, it has mass, it has edges, and the puddle fits the hole in the road PERFECTLY! The shape of the puddle, in all its uniqueness, fits exactly. GOD IS GREAT! This hole was PERFECTLY MADE to fit this puddle!!! What you call God I call evolution. We adapted to our surroundings, they were not created for us.'

'So thus far you've found out that religion is stupid?' Ayan replied.

'Yep. It's only personal opinions. I know you won't convince me nor I you, so all I have to say is I love you as a person. I'm happy to have shared 19 years of my life with you. But you have no idea how much I hate religion.'

'Then you're an atheist.'

'Exactly. I know religion took my sisters from me so I'm turning my back on it.'

'Don't you believe in anything? Are you still afraid of jinn?'

'Nope. I'm not even afraid of hell.'

'What is an atheist's solution to existence?'

'I take things as they come. I like to base my life on facts.'

'I need to go but write to me and I'll reply whenever I can! Btw where is our dad?'

'He went to an anti-IS demonstration.'

'Is he planning on coming down here again?'

'No, he says he doesn't want anything more to do with you. He has erased you from his life or some crap like that.'

'Oh dear.'

'What makes you think Dad would ever return to Syria? After all, he did say he was almost killed.'

'He's said he's going to come here to kill me and my husband and a load of other rubbish. Gotta go.'

'Dad is not himself.'

'I noticed. Sorry about that.' Ayan put in a sad emoji.

'You've destroyed my life actually. Bye. All my brothers and sisters have left me. Dad is crazy. Mom hates me. That's my life in a nutshell. I'm moving out ASAP to live my own life. Changing my name, cutting off contact with my family, moving to Jamaica and smoking weed.'

At the start of September 2014, two weeks after the video of the killing of James Foley was released, IS publicized its *Second Message to America*, a video showing the beheading of the American journalist Steven Sotloff. The murderer was the same, dressed in a black balaclava covering everything but his eyes and the bridge of his nose. He had been given the nickname 'Jihadi John.'

'I am back, Obama, and I am back because of your arrogant foreign policy toward the Islamic State, because of your insistence on continuing your bombings . . . just as your missiles continue to strike our people, our knife will continue to strike the necks of your people.'

Women didn't attend the public beheadings that took place in the square in Raqqa. Women and crowds were haram. But the wives of the fighters sometimes sat together watching videos of the beheadings that occurred at secret locations in the desert. They behaved just as bloodthirsty as their husbands and were happy to write about the killings on Twitter. 'So many beheadings at the same time, Allahu Akbar, this video is beautiful #DawlaMediaTeamDoingItRight.' One woman wrote that she would have liked to have been the one who cut off Steven Sotloff's head.

Umm Irhab – Mother of Terror – described the pleasure the gruesome details gave her. 'I was happy to see the beheading of that kafir, I just rewound to the cutting part. Allahu akbar! I wonder what he was thinking b4 the cut.' Another woman took delight in the eviction of a Syrian family from across the street. 'I'm pretty sure the men got beheaded, women chucked out,' she gloated. Umm Irhab requested more beheadings and was quick to dismiss those criticizing the use of violence. Another woman summed up the attitude: 'Beheading is halal. Go kill yourself if you say it's haram.'

Some of the women admitted not feeling fulfilled by having to sit and wait for the war to be won, and spoke of their desire to be on the actual battlefield. Umm Ubaydah wrote, 'My best friend is my grenade, it's an American one too, lol, May Allah allow me to kill their pig soldiers with their own weapons.' However, those wanting to fight were put in their place by their fellow sisters. 'You may gain more ajr – reward – by spending years of sleepless nights by being a mother and raising your children with the right intentions and for the sake of Allah than by doing a martyrdom operation,' wrote Umm Layth – Mother of the Lion. The women's brigades were a myth, she explained, there were even men who did not make it to the front, no matter how much they wanted, yes, there were men who grew so upset they wept because they were denied the opportunity of becoming martyrs in battle. 'For the sisters it's completely impossible for now. Inshallah in future.'

Shots and explosions often broke the silence of the night in Raqqa, and after hearing more shots than usual, Umm Khattab feared the state was under attack: 'Me and the sisters thought maybe murtads [apostates] were in the city lol I put the belt on and everything.'

She was referring to an explosive belt, a device anyone could utilize in the event of an attack. In so doing, you also ensured you were not taken as spoils of war, with the awful fate that could befall a female prisoner.

The rulers' thoughts became the ruling thoughts. At least online, the wives of the foreign fighters accepted what truth they were served. It was haram to question established truths.

The circle of friends back home that Ayan sometimes chatted with had diminished. Many had broken off contact with her. They were afraid of PST surveillance, but it was also due to how dogmatic she had become. One Iraqi classmate from Dønski continued to chat with her online, and on one occasion wrote how shocked she was by the rape of Yazidi and Kurdish women by IS. It was against Islam, she said.

Ayan interrupted her. 'They're not women, they're spoils of war.'

'What?'

'It says so in the Koran. It's allowed.'

'They're being abducted and used as sex slaves!'

'Spoils of war,' Ayan merely repeated.

'You're in favor of this??'

'The fighters need sexual release. They're men after all.'

Her friend had had enough. It was the last time they chatted.

On September 10, 2014, President Barack Obama gave a speech announcing that the fight against the Islamic State in Iraq and Syria was to be intensified. Referring to the organization as ISIL – the Islamic State in the Levant – he said:

'ISIL is not "Islamic." No religion condones the killing of innocents, and the vast majority of ISIL's victims have been Muslim . . . We will degrade and ultimately destroy ISIL through a comprehensive and sustained counterterrorism strategy.'

The strategy consisted of four parts: systematic air strikes, increased support to the forces fighting on the ground, counter-terrorist operations to prevent attacks, and humanitarian aid to displaced civilians. Secretary of State John Kerry met with Arab leaders in Jeddah in Saudi Arabia the following day, and within hours a coalition of ten states that would fight alongside the Americans had been formed.

In mid-September, three weeks after her brother had accused her of ruining his life, Ayan responded.

'Don't lay the blame on me, I found the truth, moved out ASAP and made a life for myself, as did Leila, and Mom. Dad has been nuts for a while, it just wasn't so obvious before. The only reason I can think of that Mom might hate you is that you have abandoned Islam. Move where you want and do what you please, but don't lose yourself. I didn't want to leave you but I had to go.'

'You did not have to go.'

Ayan's reply came ten days later, at two thirty in the morning. 'I did, I had to leave because we're at war with kuffar aka non-Muslims so continuing to live in a non-Muslim country can mean you go to hell. Btw there's a lot of bombing going on here, we're in more danger than before, so make sure to say a big hello to everyone from me and Leila.'

Ismael had been woken up by the accompanying *ping*.

'Wow. Thought you were dead. Do you really believe IS is going to take over the world?'

'Yes, I do, just look how much we have taken over in such a short time.'

'Be a little realistic, Ayan. I know you're smart. You're going to end up being killed in the bombing. You think it's a good way to die because then you'll feel you stood for something and took part in jihad. That's it.'

'How are things in your little world so?!'

'Sad to see my sisters offering their bodies to retards fighting to get killed, otherwise it's all good.'

'HAHAHHAHAHAHAHAHAHA better to die than to live life like a loser.'

'You're not a loser if you don't live like one.'

'Good to hear you're doing okay. Some people are successful in the next life and some are successful in this life, but I feel sorry for those who are in between.'

'I feel sorry for people who believe that kind of rubbish.'

'So what's happening in Norway? Did you get into college?'

'I'm taking a year out. Trying to get a job. Hoping to see you before you die.' Ismael typed in a sad emoji.

'Being a house cleaner is always an option, then again that requires schooling too. Hang in there! What's happening with Dad? Are you living with him?'

'Yep. At the moment we're pretty poooor.'

'We sure aren't.'

'Send me mon-nay pls hahaha.'

'Come here and work. You would have to follow the norms and rules in this country though.'

'Wouldn't dare.'

'But weren't you talking about going to Jamaica?'

'Hahaha then Mom really would commit suicide, her daughters went off to wage jihad and get married, Ismael left to get high with Jamaicans.'

The Syrian army intensified its air strikes on Raqqa in autumn 2014. When IS took control of Tabaqa air base in the first week of September, its revenge was merciless. Pilots and ground crew attempting to flee were shot. Soldiers who had surrendered were forced to strip down to their underwear. They were forced to run through the arid desert until they were ordered to stop and shot one by one at close range. The sand swiftly soaked up the blood.

IS was hungry to expand the caliphate, and by mid-September an offensive against the Kurdish-dominated city of Kobane in the north of Syria was under way.

On September 22, the United States and the coalition dropped their first bombs in Syria. Raqqa, targets in Idlib province, and military bases in the desert were struck by Tomahawk missiles.

The bombing led to an alteration in IS strategy, moving their operations to populated areas. The desert bases they abandoned offered little protection against bombs, but women and children did.

IS had grown overconfident. Its fortunes in the war had turned. The battle of Kobane had drained the organization of both men and resources. In spite of massive air strikes, IS had continued its assault on the city. Wave upon wave of jihadists were sent, thousands met their deaths, like lemmings off a cliff.

But new recruits arrived. Many came straight from the streets of European cities, were given a few weeks of indoctrination and military training, and then were posted to Kobane or instructed to carry out suicide missions. Some had second thoughts. They had come to fight against Assad and were disillusioned at being ordered to engage in hostilities against other Muslims. For the majority, their journey came with a one-way ticket. The punishment for desertion was death.

The largest contingent of fighters came from Saudi Arabia, followed by Tunisia, but new fighters also streamed in from Western countries, as did their future wives.

Aisha's relationship status on Facebook had changed that summer. In the end of July she had surprised many of her friends by posting a heart alongside the label 'married.'

'What?!?!?!?!?!?!?!?!?,' Umm Amira wrote.

'Chwat? Anyhow, *mubarak*. Congratulations! May Allah bestow the best of things upon you both in this life and the next!' Sølva wrote.

'For reallll?? *Mabrook!* Congratulations!' Kani responded.

'Think she needs to either deny or confirm this he he he,' commented Umm Bilal.

'Don't you have a child?' Hamidah asked.

Yes, Aisha had a child.

Salahuddin was one year old. And now that he was so big, she had begun talking once more about traveling to Syria. Dilal despaired.

'If you mention that one more time I'm calling Child Welfare. No, I'll call the police.'

She looked at her friend, who lay on the sofa moping.

'Why do you even want to go there?'

'I need to live in a Muslim country where they practice true Islam,' Aisha said. 'I don't want to raise my child here among the unbelievers.'

'Women aren't even allowed out! They're married off to random men!'

'I can't live in a non-Muslim country,' Aisha reiterated. 'It's unclean here.'

'But you can live your life exactly as you want to in Norway. You need to get a grip, pull yourself together, listen to your mother and take care of your son!'

Aisha posted photos on Facebook of women in niqabs with Kalashnikovs over their shoulders. In her everyday life she pushed the pram around Bærum, thinking life was colorless.

She said she wanted to collect money for women and children in Syria and asked Dilal to open a bank account for her.

'I'm on welfare so I can't do it because if they see money coming in they'll stop my payments,' she explained.

Dilal did as her friend requested, thought it was good she was getting involved in something.

Aisha and Dilal saw less and less of each other. When Aisha left the apartment, it was usually to go to the mosque or to attend meetings of the women's group of the Prophet's Ummah, while Dilal was busy training to be a nurse. Her visits to Aisha only got her down. It was Aisha's mother who looked after Salahuddin most of the time, feeding him, changing him, playing with him, putting him down for naps, while Aisha was being sucked farther into a life online, particularly by those tweeting from Syria.

Twitter accounts came and went. Blogs were started up and closed down. If the girls' accounts were suspended, they soon reappeared under new names. The migrants, as they called themselves, discussed what routes to take, how to conceal travel plans, and how to avoid arousing parental suspicion, and they reminded one another to be careful to erase all Islamic content on telephones and iPads before coming to the security gates at an airport.

Frequently asked questions concerned what items were available for purchase and what you needed to bring along. If you were fussy about particular brands or suffered from allergies, you should bring your favorite hair products or creams; otherwise everything was available, so carrying cosmetics just meant unnecessary extra weight, although it was emphasized that personal hygiene articles were not of the same quality as in the West. There was no point lugging along a load of books either, because everything could be downloaded, including the Koran. One woman offered some advice about what could be bought: 'Okay, listen. Say you want to buy a weapon or a car or anything at all, just bring extra cash. Used cars cost less than 10K. You can buy furniture, gold, whatever, even slaves. So if you have money it's no problem.'

The forums at times resembled schoolgirl chats prior to a camping trip. One know-it-all corrected them: 'Hello, you're going to live in a house, not a tent.' Practical advice was the most read, outstripping the sharing of religious poems, words of wisdom by Paulo Coelho, and news about the West's attacks on Muslims. The Malaysian Bird of Jannah was generous in sharing the details of her life. She told how she and her allotted Moroccan husband had each downloaded dictionary apps in order to communicate, as they did not share a common language. A qualified doctor, she was regarded as something of a veteran, having already spent a year in the caliphate, where she was now a stay-at-home mother with an infant son. To avoid answering repeated questions, she had compiled a season-based Suitcase Checklist.

Jacket (black or dark blue)
Waterproof warm boots (good for muddy, rainy days)
Fleece pajamas, as the nights can be very cold
Sweatpants (two)
Long-sleeved sweaters
Thick socks (three or four)
Wool underwear
Good-quality yoga pants/leggings (three or four)
Hat and thick scarf (for indoors, trust me, I wore these so much last winter) There are heaters here, Alhamdulillah, but you most likely won't have them in every room.
Good-quality undergarments, bras and underwear, and if you are married or plan to marry, you might want to bring things you would like to wear in private.
Clothes you can wear around your husband as well, maybe things that aren't so appropriate around sisters, for example short dresses etc. Whatever you prefer.

Aisha had first tried to get in touch with Arfan Bhatti in Pakistan. She wanted to live there with him. She sent him photos of his son. When he rejected her, and didn't want her to come, she announced she wanted to immigrate to Syria. 'Go wherever you like,' she told friends that her ex-husband had answered, 'as long as you don't take Salahuddin along.'

Emira, who had married Bastian, and was now in Raqqa with Ayan and Leila, made a suggestion. She could share her husband with Aisha. Bastian could take her as a second wife.

'You can't manage without a husband down here,' Emira told her. 'And it would be better to marry a Norwegian, wouldn't it?'

Marry Arfan's old friend?

Bastian had risen in the ranks. He had learned Arabic and was working on videos and websites for the propaganda department. A couple of years ago he had dreamed about designing the logo for the Prophet's Ummah, and now here he was, working for the man who was going to take over the world.

Aisha and Bastian were wed on Skype. Once again her parents were not informed their daughter was marrying. The Norwegian Chilean, who had left his daughter in Norway when she was a few months old, now got a stepson instead – Salahuddin.

Aisha also acted as a courier on her trip. She had been instructed to order some small parts on eBay to modify weapons. Some of these were the size of matchsticks and hardly weighed anything, so they were easy to conceal. She had ordered such items online previously but had sent them with others. Now she could take them herself to what she saw as her final destination.

Rumors had begun to circulate and she was afraid of being stopped, so a month after the wedding she posted on Facebook: 'I'm aware that some people have been asking about me and at the same time spreading gossip that I have journeyed to Syria. To the people in question: FEAR ALLAH! May Allah silence your tongues and forgive you! Even though it might be out of concern, you should all think before coming out with that type of talk. It cannot be that hard to understand what kind of a difficult situation you are putting me and my family in and how damaging it is to our safety and everyday life to spread those kind of FALSE rumors and gossip . . . I am not in Syria, just to make that clear! May Allah the Almighty and Righteous strike you gossipmongers dumb!'

She left for Turkey. Then she crossed the border.

Identity. Meaning. Rebellion. Being a part of something greater than oneself. Jihad rendered all personal problems small. For a time.

One day in autumn, Dilal received a message via WhatsApp.

'Hi Dilal, how's it going?'

'Aisha! Long time no see!'

'I'm on God's path.'

'Where are you?'

'You know where. I had to do it this way. Matter of urgency. Everything happened so fast.'

'Aisha . . . where is Salahuddin?'

'He's with me. He's here. He's safe. He likes it here. I'll send pictures. Dilal, I've married Bastian. Both Emira and I are married to him.'

'Aisha, you brought Salahuddin? To a war zone? You deceived me!'

'I had to!'

'And you've married not out of love for a second time. What are you thinking?'

'Can you send me the money in the aid account?' Aisha merely responded.

'Aisha, that's to go to relief work.'

'I'm going to use it to help people down here!'

'You said it yourself, remember, when Bastian and Emira used fund-raising money on themselves! Ubaydullah said it as well, that they couldn't be trusted? And now the three of you are together!'

'Dilal, just send me the money, and you're more than welcome to visit! I can find a husband for you!'

There was 30,000 kroner in the account. Dilal refused to send it.

'Can I have it as a loan then?' Aisha asked.

When she gave birth to her son, she had changed her name on Facebook to Umm Salahuddin. In Raqqa she changed her profile picture. The new one showed her son, who had just taken his first steps, in camouflage clothing with a Kalashnikov in his lap.

He was going to be one of the Cubs of the Caliphate, Aisha boasted.

Their arrival in Syria had coincided with a surge of foreign fighters coming into the country. According to American intelligence, approximately a thousand foreign fighters were arriving in the region every month. Quite a few of them brought children.

Boys who distinguished themselves from an early age were recruited into Ashbal al-khilafa – the Cubs of the Caliphate. They were taken from their parents when they were ten to live in camps and toughen up. They received systematic training and were subjected to harsh physical and psychological ordeals. Propaganda videos show the boys standing at attention while being struck with sticks. Others stand in the background, waiting their turn, while observing their friends' faces. They were trained in close combat and in the use of pistols, rifles, and knives. The ultimate test was to execute a prisoner.

The children were more than mere tools; they were to be building blocks. The goal of the Islamic State was not only to defeat the enemy and conquer the country but also to ensure its survival as a group.

Just before her son's second birthday, Aisha sent a picture of Salahuddin. The photograph gave Dilal the chills. His eyelid was swollen and purple, the blood vessels in his eyes were burst, and he had bruises on his cheeks.

Dilal tried to call. Aisha did not answer.

Part IV

PEER GYNT: Where was I, as myself, as the whole
man, the real?
Where was I, with my forehead stamped with
God's seal?
SOLVEIG: In my faith, in my hope, in my charity.

—Henrik Ibsen, *Peer Gynt*, 1867

26

Not Without My Daughters

Sadiq googled *Manbij*. Ayan and Hisham had moved again. The men went where IS ordered them, the women followed.

It was October 2014. The girls had been in Syria for one year. Maybe it would be easier to get them out of Manbij, which was in the Aleppo province, it occurred to Sadiq. His hopes soon turned to despair. The city was part of the caliphate, control was just as tight as in Raqqa. The Islamists had taken over the police forces, the ministries, the courts. The road between Manbij and Raqqa was a lifeline for IS, since Kurdish forces had destroyed, or taken control of, the bridges over the Euphrates from the Turkish border all the way south to Lake Assad. Although the majority of the population of Manbij was Arab, the Kurds viewed it as their land, having roots stretching back to the Middle Ages.

The Islamic State came as colonists, but not everybody was unhappy with the new rulers. This was not because of the popularity of their ideology but because the new state did not feel like the worst of evils. Justice was harsh, but it was predictable. The Islamists, for the most part, left ordinary people in peace, as long as they obeyed, dressed correctly, and prayed. Ordinary Syrians continued to persevere.

The IS-run administration was at times more efficient than people were used to. It was quicker to repair broken water pipes or fallen electricity cables, it cleaned up the parks, planted flowers, and swept the streets. Photographs of the tidying up were posted on Twitter. The caliphate was to gleam.

The eastern part of Aleppo province was a backwater. Most of its inhabitants made their living from agriculture and the only sign of industry was a single cement factory. Lawlessness had accompanied the civil war. Criminal gangs mixed with the rebel forces, plundering, kidnapping, raping, and killing. Crime fell when IS took control – the severity of punishments scared people: public flogging, the loss of your hand or your head, crucifixion.

Sadiq read online that the ruins of aqueducts and walls from ancient Hierapolis were to be found in Manbij. In another article he learned that there were as many refugees in the town at present as inhabitants. What if the girls could hide among the refugees, make an escape that way?

This is how he spent his days and nights, in front of the screen, reading and reflecting on everything that was happening where the girls were.

In mid-November, more Syrians and another American were ritually murdered. The IS video of the event, which they titled *Although the Disbelievers Dislike It*, showed the beheading of twenty-two Syrian soldiers and the decapitated head of Peter Kassig. The young aid worker was the fourth Western hostage that IS had killed. He had managed, some months previously, to get a letter to his parents in Indiana smuggled out: 'Don't worry Dad, if I do go down, I won't go thinking anything but what I know to be true. That you and mom love me more than the moon & the stars.'

The jihadi girls in the caliphate functioned as a fan club for the executioners. One of them described Kassig's beheading as 'gut-wrenchingly awesome, shariah = justice.'

Young men from both sides were falling at the front. Two days after Kassig was beheaded, two Norwegian IS terrorists were reported killed on Norwegian TV2.

The report began with a photograph of a smiling boy in a winter jacket, his skin dark against the snow.

'This is Hisham Hussain Ahmed,' the reporter said. The next picture showed the same boy holding a pike. 'He came to Norway as an unaccompanied minor in 2003 at age thirteen. In December 2012 he traveled to Syria,' the reporter went on. 'The Norwegian of Eritrean descent was said to have a leadership role in the Islamic State, IS.'

Hisham?

Sadiq felt relief coursing through him.

Hisham was dead!

Ayan was free!

A warm sensation of revenge surged through him. Hisham had humiliated him deeply, first by stealing Ayan away from her family and then by marrying her without asking permission. Finally Sadiq could put thoughts of him from his mind.

He rang Osman to break the good news.

'Great!' Osman said. 'She's sure to want to go home now.'

Hisham was out of the way. Ayan was a widow. All they had to do was await her call.

Osman had earned a tidy sum bringing foreign fighters in, now he could make money getting them out.

Ayan would probably reach out soon. Once the period of mourning had ended.

'I have the solution,' Osman announced one day when he called to see if Ayan had been in touch. 'There's a relative of mine. He has two faces, if you know what I mean. He's working for IS but is actually one of us.' The smuggler outlined the plan. 'Part of the road to Aleppo goes through a tunnel. At one end IS is in control, at the other al-Nusra. When he comes from Atmeh, he drives into the tunnel as a Nusra man and out the other end as an IS man. On his next trip to the caliphate he can stop off in Raqqa and Manbij on the way back, pick up the girls, hide them aboard, and drive through the tunnel and out. Very simple . . . also very dangerous.'

Osman would ring when 'the Double,' as they called him, was ready to carry out the job. In the meantime Sadiq was to wait.

'You'll soon get them back! But it's going to cost money.'

Later on that month Osman made contact again. 'The Double is ready. You just need to put him in touch with the girls.'

Sadiq called him. The Double answered in classical Arabic, struggling slightly with suffixes and some words. Nevertheless, his message was clear: It was a risky operation, both for him and the daughters, but it was possible.

'You have to get them to call me,' the Double told him. 'I have to be in direct contact with them.'

The deal had to be crystal clear. The girls needed to know exactly when and where to wait for their rescuer, and it all had to happen fast.

'Then I can drive them anywhere, to Turkey, wherever you want.'

'Yes, I'll have them call you,' Sadiq said.

Sadiq had been in contact with a Norwegian film crew about his attempts to rescue the girls. They had been following him since the summer. Their documentary had the working title *Only a Father.* That was how Sadiq had described himself in Syria when explaining who he was, and to IS when they accused him of being a spy.

The film crew had met Osman, Mehmut the driver, and Firas, the doctor who had bandaged up Leila and had since sought asylum in Sweden. They had also tracked down one of Sadiq's fellow inmates from the sewage plant, a Syrian from the last cell Sadiq had been held in. All they were missing now was the girls.

Veslemøy Hvidsteen, a reporter working for NRK, the Norwegian state broadcaster, was the one who had gotten in touch with Sadiq after seeing him on the news. His back was to the camera, but Veslemøy had recognized him. In 2006 he had appeared on an episode of *Migrapolis* – a series about the everyday lives of immigrants in Norway – she had made. Sadiq had been interviewed along with the psychologist who had helped him tackle his trauma and problems with aggression after the Somali civil war. The girls had also featured in the 2006 recordings, playing football with their father: Ayan, a lanky teenager dressed like a tomboy; Leila, still a child.

Veslemøy's husband, Styrk Jansen, was to direct the documentary. Sadiq had told him about the Double and that they were to meet him in a village near the border. First they'd have to hand over the agreed sum of money, then the girls would be transported out. He had told the documentary makers that the girls were in hiding, had run away from their husbands, were desperate, and had begged him to save them. When he had met Ayan in al-Dana the year before, he confided, she had grabbed hold of him like a cat bearing its claws out and whispered, 'Save us, Dad, if you can!'

In early November, the producer ordered plane tickets to Reyhanlı, a town in the south of Turkey, close to the village where they were to meet the Double. Styrk packed his camera, lenses, battery packs, and cash in dollars. Sadiq was allowing him to film the meeting with the Double, follow him to the frontier, if possible, and wait there until the girls came across. The embrace – the reunion between father and daughters – was to be captured on film.

The day before they were due to depart, Styrk received a call from Sadiq. He was breathing heavily and his voice was barely audible.

'I have terrible news . . .'

'What's happened?' the producer asked.

'I've received a picture . . . I've been sent a picture . . .'

Sadiq paused before saying in a grave tone, 'The Double has been killed.'

Styrk Jansen had to sit down.

'That's all I know,' Sadiq sobbed. It was Osman who had sent him the photograph, he said. 'He's been beheaded and crucified!'

Sadiq forwarded the image to Styrk. It showed a man tied to a fence, his body leaning into the barbed wire and his arms outstretched. His decapitated head, with a short dark beard and a round, heavyset face, was placed between his legs. There was a placard on his body with the words I AM A TRAITOR.

'Two nights ago he was on his way out of his apartment in Reyhanlı,' Sadiq explained. 'Outside the building, he was surrounded by several men in niqabs and bundled into a car. They drove him across the border into Syria. IS had uncovered his double-dealing. The local head of Nusra had been holding secret negotiations with IS in order to join forces. The meetings concluded with the Nusra commander swearing allegiance to Abu Bakr al-Baghdadi. The Islamists pooled weapons and men. The lists of personnel had given the game away. The same man appeared on both. It mattered little that they were now one group – if you've betrayed once, you can easily do it again. A spy is a spy. The sentence is death,' Sadiq related.

Styrk shivered.

'Are we the reason he was caught? Could it be because he was going to rescue the girls? Are we to blame for a man's death?'

'I don't know,' Sadiq replied. 'We'll have to wait until I get the full version from Osman. He's in mourning now. They were close relatives.'

Styrk canceled the airline tickets. Put the cameras back on the shelf.

Autumn brought darkness.

And it would get darker still. Osman texted Sadiq.

'Abu Siddiq is not dead.'

'Who?!'

The Syrian smuggler had made inquiries.

'Hisham! Your son-in-law. He used to call himself Abu Siddiq. Now he's changed his name again.'

'I'm sure he's dead,' Sadiq replied.

'He's alive. A guy that knows him has seen him twice. The second time was only two days ago.'

'Oh, no . . .'

'He was in the hospital. Wounded. Listen. Wait until you hear. The clinic where he was treated is underground. Several yards down. In a parking facility in Raqqa. And do you know who else was there? The leader! He was wounded in the same assault, or so they say. That's all I know.'

'How do you know he's alive?'

'The guy I know confirmed it.'

'So that bloody bastard was alive two days ago . . . '

'He had a Toyota 4×4 he wanted to sell, the same one he had in Atmeh! I saw pictures of it. His Arabic was really bad, by the way. He speaks the language like an idiot.'

Rumors flew this way and that. Rumors could take a life or they could bring people back from the dead. Osman knew people on all sides. When he got wind of a story, hearing various versions, he analyzed the pieces, added his own; his ability to patch the information together was his main currency as a smuggler.

Sadiq's daughters were unaware of their father's rescue attempts. In early December, after being out of contact with Ismael for several months, Ayan took up the thread of the conversation they had left off.

'Hey you! Have you bothered looking for answers or are you mucking about?'

'How are things?' Ismael answered.

'Alhamdulillah just fine.'

'Where are you now?'

'At an internet café.'

'What's happening?'

And there the conversation ceased. How he hated this! These messages from out of the blue that ended just as abruptly as they started. When he tried to make contact again, he was met with a wall of silence. Then a new message would pop up all of a sudden with a 'hi' and a smiley, and open up the wound afresh, then nothing more until his sisters saw fit.

Ismael had gotten a part-time job at a local supermarket, and he took all the extra shifts that came his way. When he was not working, he found himself with a lot of downtime, which he spent with friends, hanging out, going to the gym, and playing computer games.

He examined the prospectuses of a number of colleges and universities. The most prestigious courses, the ones requiring the highest grades, could be ruled out; he had not left school with particularly good grades. The previous year he'd looked at a petroleum-engineering program in the north, but then he discovered that unemployment within that sector was on the rise.

If he were to follow his heart, he'd learn about the universe, about atoms and physics and chemistry. He wanted to find out how the world worked.

At the same time, he wanted to forget it.

He had found it hard to focus in his final year at school, had been unable to apply himself. That was the reason his results had been so poor. He knew he had to pull himself together, but the application date for the next academic year was still a long way off. Next year he would do something with his life. Drag himself up from the trough, from the glum mornings, the bleak nights. Put his sisters behind him.

Advent, the darkest time of year, arrived, and still no snow fell to brighten up the Norwegian winter. One night in December he wrote to Ayan.

'I would sooner go to hell than worship God even if he exists. God is such a tyrant. He/She demands respect and subordination. Fuck that.'

He continued his nocturnal monologue.

'By the way, Ayan, I thought you were one of the smartest people I knew, I looked up to you, where did you lose all logic, do you really believe little ISIS/Daesh are going to take over the world? With their AK-47s and the equipment the Americans "left behind," ISIS and other small groups like them are only doing America's dirty work. ISIS is killing other religious groupings. Say ISIS takes over the Assad regime, do you know what will happen then? It would give the USA the excuse to send in forces and kill the rest. BUT HANG ON that's not the objective. There's oil there after all = less fatalities for the Americans – making Obama look good – America gets to pump oil ensuring their weapons industry continues to turn a profit. In the meantime IS soldiers sit around complaining that the USA won't send in ground troops just drones. "so unfair with drones, fight like a man"—Tards.'

Christmas was approaching and the shifts at the supermarket

increased. Ismael stocked the refrigerated counter with ribs, herring, and head cheese. He packed the biscuit aisle with ginger cookies, confectionary, and doughnuts. He filled up the fruit section with oranges, dates, and figs. Christmas beer. Mulled wine. Advent wreath candles for hope, peace, and joy. Lines of traditional marzipan pigs stretching from here to hell.

In the Juma household, neither father nor son lit any Advent candles. They never had. There was no calendar or decorations. There never had been. Sara had always made a point of not serving anything special at Christmas; it was important to make a distinction between Christian festivities and Islamic festivities. This year, she was in a Christmas-free zone in Somaliland anyway, and the blessed sisters were in a land purged of Christmas spirit.

From there, Ayan suddenly replied: 'I believe 110% that DAWLA is going to crush and humiliate this coalition that is in league against them if ALLAH SWT grants it.'

'Allah doesn't exist,' Ismael replied. 'I can also sit here and convince myself I am able to fly if I just believe hard enough. But it's still not going to happen.'

The wall of silence again, but Ismael continued. 'God is so great while at the same time he is such a self-obsessed asshole that he wants the people he "created" to pray to him five times a day and for those who don't believe in him to be killed. He is all-powerful and yet he's too lazy to send them straight to hell himself.'

Ayan started typing.

'You're playing with your life,' his sister wrote. 'Instead of talking crap and being offensive try finding the truth or shut up and respect other people's choices.'

'You. Are you here?' Ismael wrote.

'I refuse to speak to you when all you do is badmouth ALLAH swt. You may discuss, but with respect.'

'The truth isn't always as pretty as you think.'

'It's possible to express yourself with respect. Without deriding the other person's choices. Wondering whether or not God exists is something else entirely.'

'I don't believe God exists, but I find it odd your not realizing that dawla are going to lose in the long run and that it is not jihad but suicide. It's like lying down on a train track and saying "I'll survive if allah swt wills it" and you die. Nuff said.'

Silence from his sister.

Ismael logged off as well.

On Christmas Eve, he sent her a thumbs-up icon.

On Christmas Day, Ayan responded: 'Tell Mom that she must forgive me.'

She would never write to her brother again.

27

New Year, New Opportunities

Syria had become a dump, Osman complained. 'Nusra is squeezing me,' he wrote to Sadiq in January.

Osman had become entangled in the strings he had once pulled, as if someone was standing by to draw them taut, throttle him, and take over his business and operations. Being an independent player was no longer possible and even smugglers had to submit to circumstances. The war was brutalizing people, and the struggle for resources was becoming fiercer.

The traditional power structures from Assad's time, when Idlib province was ruled by a network of party careerists and local clan leaders, were gone. Atmeh had become a quagmire of organized crime, strict Islamic control – and anarchy. There was no authority with a monopoly on violence; it was the survival of the fittest. Many sank to the bottom and disappeared, first threatened and then killed. Abductions were rife, the victims often ordinary people, anyone, as long as they could pay. A nephew, a cousin, or a father might be kidnapped in an attempt to squeeze cash out of a family. Whether on the front line or in a dispute over a dollar, a life had little value.

Al-Qaida's Syrian arm had the most clout in the province and demanded others submit to it. Al-Nusra was attempting to establish a proto-emirate – putting its own area under strict Islamist rule and increasingly stealing features from IS. It engaged in extensive taxation of its territories, levying charges, tariffs, and fines for any infringement of the new rules. Smugglers were no exception. On the contrary, al-Nusra closely followed their activities and wanted a share of the profits.

'Things are tough. I'm exhausted. I feel like I'm at the end of my tether,' Osman wrote.

'No, brother, don't say that. What happened to Nusra?'

'Nusra has become like IS,' Osman replied. 'Any friends I had in Nusra are all martyrs now.'

'May God receive them. How did Nusra become like IS?'

Al-Nusra issued laws and decrees and sent them out to towns and villages under their control. Infidelity and homosexuality meant death by stoning, Assad loyalists could expect execution by gunshot to the head. 'All entertainment stores that feature billiards, table football, and computer games' were ordered closed, an edict read. The store owners were responsible for looking for another form of livelihood, which it was pointed out had to be legitimate according to sharia. Shops had to close during prayer time because God the Almighty had said, 'Bow with those who bow.' Written at the bottom of each edict were the words: 'And God is the one behind this intention.'

Al-Nusra was one of the wealthiest rebel groups in Syria. In the beginning, half of its resources had come directly from al-Qaida, the rest from donors abroad, mostly from the Gulf, and Qatar in particular. Over time the group captured military matériel from Assad and also financed its activities with income from the oil fields they had taken. They also earned millions from abducting people and holding them for ransom. If you were a foreigner who had the misfortune to be kidnapped in Syria, being taken by al-Nusra was a blessing in disguise. They were more interested in the money they could get for you than your head on a plate.

'Brother, have you spoken to your daughters? Is there any news?'

It was night. January had turned to February. Osman had logged on to Viber.

'The younger is four months pregnant.' Sadiq had just heard the news from Sara.

'The younger!' Osman exclaimed, and sent a crying emoji.

Sadiq just wrote KKKKKKKKKK, the Somali way of representing laughter in writing.

'Ah, you'll be a granddad, old man!' Osman wrote. 'You need to get her now, inshallah. The longer it goes, the more difficult it will become.'

That was just it. So many harsh words had passed between Sadiq and his daughters. They no longer spoke to him: They called Sara in Somaliland when they wanted to get in touch. When Sadiq had spoken to the Double prior to New Year, the Syrian had stressed that the assignment was extremely dangerous. The daughters had to cooperate.

Sadiq had been unable to admit to the smuggler that he could not even get in touch with them.

They must *want* to leave.

Sadiq had called the Double back after their initial conversation and reached his voice mail.

'Can you kidnap them?' he had asked.

A short time later it was the Double who left a message on Sadiq's voice mail. 'Sorry. If they don't want to get out then there's nothing I can do. That's not a job I'm willing to undertake. It's impossible.'

Sadiq had waited, hoping for a miracle: that the girls would call and say, *Save us*. Then he would have the plan ready: the rescuer, the vehicle, and the film crew. That was why he had let Styrk order the airplane tickets. Let him pack the equipment. They could still call and say: *Save us, Dad!*

But they didn't.

The day before he and Styrk were to travel to Reyhanlı via Istanbul, he had had to find a way to end the deception. It was too late to tell Styrk the plain truth – that the girls didn't want to leave the caliphate and that the Double had quite simply refused to take on the job.

It had been easier to make up a story about his beheading and crucifixion.

*

'When they have children they'll wake up and realize what kind of regime they're living under, that's what happens with the foreign women. Then they're forced to regret,' Osman wrote to him late one night. 'When the babies arrive they will focus all their emotions on them, then they'll want to flee Syria.'

Osman was the only one he had told about the girls not wanting to return home. The two of them could sit for hours chatting online.

'How are you planning to abduct them?' Sadiq asked.

'I haven't found the right people yet.'

'Try as hard as you can.'

'As long as there is blood in my veins and breath in my body I will not forget my sisters, your daughters, Abu Ismael. Don't worry, I'm your proxy in Syria.'

'You need to think up an exceptional plan. Think of it as the most outstanding operation you have ever carried out. And after that you and your family can be in Norway in a matter of days.'

Sadiq had promised Osman that he could get him asylum in Norway. 'Don't be afraid, my brother,' he added. 'Say hello to your dear wife, whose name you have yet to tell me.'

'Do the girls speak Arabic?' Osman inquired a few days later.

After a year and a half in Syria, surely they could make themselves understood? Sadiq had no idea whether the girls were in contact with local Syrians or just hung out with their European clique. The usual pattern of social intercourse was that the French fraternized with other French speakers, Germans with Germans, and Scandinavians with Scandinavians. Ayan spoke Norwegian with Hisham while Leila and Imran communicated in English.

Sadiq's nerves were on edge.

After a few days, Osman called. 'Listen. There are two kinds of people that can crisscross the front – from government-controlled areas into IS territory, over to the militias and rebel forces, and back again. Because everyone needs them. The mobile boys – the ones who repair telecommunications, the internet – and then there are those transporting fuel. The tank truck drivers. Without them the war stops.' When he got to the last part, he practically shouted: 'We send them out with the oil!'

Sadiq's role in the operation was to pay for it. But funds were non-existent. His friends had no more money to lend him. And he could not ask NAV for more. Sadiq toyed with an idea he thought might be lucrative: Very few foreign fighters from Norway had come forward in the media, the honor code of the milieu forbade it, you did not inform on one another or talk to the kuffar media. Sadiq thought he could sell information that Osman unearthed. They could start up a kind of joint information service, with Osman responsible for seeking it out and Sadiq for selling it.

Sadiq called a couple of journalists he had been in contact with previously and got a bite. He wrote to Osman. 'I have good news. I've made a deal with a Norwegian journalist. They'll give us money for every snippet we can get them on Norwegian foreign fighters, as long as there are photos or videos. Either ISIS or Nusra.'

'Perfect,' Osman replied on Viber, before sharing more details of his evolving plan for smuggling the girls out. 'I know a guy who has a wife in Raqqa. He delivers petrol to IS every third day. He can kidnap the girls and transport them back in the tank truck.'

'Excellent.'

'The vehicle first needs to be looked at by a welder and adapted so that the girls aren't injured. We'll partition the tank to make a six-foot-by-six-foot area and drill an air hole. The tank is very large. It holds 120 tons. He can take your son-in-law too. Did you understand all that? What do you say, Abu Ismael?'

'Get started.'

'Heads will roll . . . ' Osman continued. 'That's what worries me. I swear to God, if they discover what we're up to they'll throw us in the tank, pour petrol over us and burn us worse than that Jordanian pilot ☺.'

On Christmas Eve 2014, a Jordanian F-16 fighter plane had crashed outside of Raqqa. Twenty-six-year-old Muaz al-Kasasbeh ejected but came down in IS territory. The scenes of jubilant soldiers manhandling the captured pilot had been shown around the world.

IS began negotiations with Jordan to trade the aviator for the female terrorist Sajida al-Rishawi, whose suicide belt had failed to explode in an attack in Amman in 2005.

The leading jihadist ideologue Abu Muhammad al-Maqdisi was released from a Jordanian prison in order to act as an intermediary. Al-Maqdisi, who in the 1980s had been too extreme for Osama bin Laden, soon established contact. The Jordanian authorities required photographic evidence that the pilot was still alive before they would release Sajida. IS sent an electronic file to al-Maqdisi, but it was password protected. After several days of intense dialogue, he was sent the code to open the file. Once he received it the old Islamist understood he had been fooled. The password was 'Maqdisi is a pimp, the sole of the tyrant's shoe, son of the English whore.'

When he typed in the sentence, a video appeared on the screen. He watched as an IS soldier forced the pilot into a cage, doused him in gasoline, and set him alight. Osama bin Laden's old teacher was enraged. Fire could not be used as a punishment. That right was reserved by God exclusively for those who were condemned to eternal torment in hell.

IS posted the video online three hours later. The criticism of Islamist scholars was lost on them. The pilot had bombed a brick factory and his victims had been burned alive, they said, so he received the punishment he deserved, according to the sharia principle of *qisas* – retribution.

'I'm not afraid of my own group, they cannot betray me,' Osman wrote. 'But I am afraid of IS, they terrify me. Heads will roll . . . if we mess up.'

'I know, my dear friend.'

'And you need to find money,' the Syrian went on. 'A sponsor, someone to cover the costs. And soon. Remember – don't tell anyone the details, absolutely no one.'

'I would sooner risk my daughters' lives than risk the safety of you or other Syrians. If you want me to bring your entire family to Norway I will. I'm more than prepared to do it. I can guarantee you. You and Syria have become a part of my life and part of the very meaning of it.'

A couple of days later Sadiq sent him a reminder, not about the rescue operation but about the means of financing it – information on Norwegian jihadists.

'Find information for me, whatever you can on migrants from Norway. No matter how trivial. Please concentrate on that. It will yield a profit.'

'What kind of information do they need?' Osman asked.

'Their names or whereabouts for example, if they're leaders or ordinary foot soldiers. Any kind of information that can accompany a photo. We can sell the photos and buy what we need with the money.'

'Will I take pictures? Without talking to them?'

'It's not necessary to talk to them. Just the information, no matter how trivial. Confirmed or unconfirmed, with photos!'

'Will I take a picture on my mobile phone? The quality might not be the best.'

It would be good enough, Sadiq assured him.

The next day Osman went in search of Norwegian jihadists. He sent back word of what he had found.

'British mujahideen, from London, other foreigners, French, there are four Somalis staying nearby. Women. Their children are with them. I can take pictures of the kids. Do you want me to? They have a play area where the women take the children.'

'I just need the Norwegian ones!'

Osman did not get it. This was not really his thing.

'To be honest at the moment my mind is pretty occupied with the operation to rescue your girls. We were up until two last night planning, and now we're all set but you have to send us the money.'

'Seek out information, no matter how insignificant, about Norwegian foreign fighters, make that your focus, bit by bit. It will yield a profit,' Sadiq replied.

When it came to his son-in-law, other tipsters stole a march on him.

On February 16, 2015, the online edition of *Dagbladet* reported: 'IS leader from Bærum reported killed last autumn. But he was never dead. In actual fact he was badly wounded – but after receiving treatment at a hospital, where he managed to remain under the radar of Western authorities, *Dagbladet* can confirm that the twenty-four-year-old has been discharged and has returned to active service for IS.'

Sadiq's son-in-law had, according to the newspaper, been promoted to a 'midlevel command position, equivalent to the rank of sergeant in Norway.' According to the report, the twenty-four-year-old from Bærum, who went by the name Abu Siddiq in Syria, had been appointed to collect taxes on the Syrian oil IS exported via informal channels over the border into Turkey.

Sadiq had to pull himself together. He had known about this for a long time. Information was his new currency.

28

Housewives of Raqqa

A manifesto appeared that spring. It was distributed in the way jihadists in 2015 preferred – online. Posted by the women's brigade al-Khansa, it was titled 'Women in the Islamic State: Manifesto and Case Study.'

Usually articles and documents were quickly translated into English, French, and Russian, but the women's statement was published only in Arabic. Consequently, it escaped the notice of Western women considering a life in the Islamic State. It was aimed at women in the Arab world, particularly women in the Gulf, who were living lives not so dissimilar from what they could expect in the caliphate, minus the bombing. The manifesto urged all the women of Saudi Arabia to abandon that stronghold of hypocrisy in favor of the caliphate, in order to fulfill God's plan for women as wives and mothers. Living for her family was a woman's 'divine right.'

The manifesto echoed the sentiments expressed in *Halal Dating*: Always keep an eye out for the devil. He never let up, he would pierce a woman's heart, tempt her to undress in the sight of others, and encourage her to scorn God's creation by having surgery on her nose, ears, and cheeks – or 'hang things from her ears, . . . have hair in some places and not in others.' The devil's work flourished in clothing stores and beauty salons, the authors warned.

'Abide in your houses! Do not display yourselves as was the display of the former times of ignorance!' the Koran 33:33 decreed. This was God's command to the wives of the Prophet. For IS, the edict was to be obeyed by all women, only in some circumstances was it halal to go out. Doctors and teachers could work, but never more than three days a week. A woman could leave the home to study Islam, or if chosen to wage jihad, as long as she remained wary of the devil and was properly covered up.

This meant full niqab, ideally in three layers, and also covering the eyes. A woman being veiled and hidden from men was always preferable. But that did not take away her importance. A woman's role could be likened to that of director – 'the most important person in a production, who is behind the scenes organizing.'

The authors of the manifesto used the same rhetorical devices as the radical preachers Ayan had listened to prior to her departure: first ridicule, then threats. Western civilization was obsessed with science and carried out research on 'the brain cells of crows, grains of sand, and the arteries of fish,' a distraction from the fundamental purpose of humanity – to worship God. Everything that went against or took time from the praise and veneration of God led directly to hell. As the Prophet said, 'My prayer, my rites of sacrifice, my living and my dying are for God, Lord of the worlds.' The blame for women being forced out of their natural state was ascribed to feminism. This had caused both sexes to become confused and lose sight of their distinctive characteristics. Only in the caliphate were Real Men and Real Women to be found, because God had created woman 'of Adam and for Adam.' Women had forgotten their fundamental roles, and the destructive consequence of this 'was obvious to anyone who looked.' Modern society was the work of the devil, under the guise of words like 'development,' 'progress,' and 'culture.' The authors did, however, grant some latitude regarding the use of modern technology; sciences that 'helped facilitate the lives of Muslims and their affairs' were permissible.

The tone was a religious variation on Soviet propaganda texts. Everyone was enthusiastic, well fed, and strong in belief. 'Al-Khansa Media traveled these lands to check on the happy situation that Muslim women face on their return to what was there at the dawn of Islam. We saw the black robes that enrage the hypocrites and their friends and the progress that the state brings us. We are ascending to the summit of this glory through the expansion of the State of Muslims.'

The manifesto concluded with a call to rally for jihad: 'Despite the raging war and the continued coalition against the Islamic State, the bombers in the sky flying back and forth, despite all this destruction, we find continued, patient, and steadfast construction, thanks be to God.'

Onward!

In the caliphate, a man had the right to educate his wife if she was disobedient, and he defined what constituted disobedience. For a short time, Aisha had been the wife of Oslo's Alpha Islamist par excellence – Arfan Bhatti – the charismatic playboy possessing the X factor of power that Bastian had always felt he lacked. Now she was Bastian's property, his second wife. The transition was nothing like what Aisha had expected.

Bastian locked her indoors. He locked her out of the house. He hit her. Worst of all, he beat Salahuddin. He now had in his custody the son of Arfan Bhatti, the man he had always dreamed of impressing and resembling.

When Aisha attempted to protect her son, when she screamed at her new husband, he just pushed her aside.

He boasted that he was going to teach Bhatti's son how to be tough. Salahuddin was going to be a Cub of the Caliphate, and thus he needed to be disciplined from an early age. The boy was not yet two.

Aisha was forbidden from going out. Bastian told her he would kill her if she left the house. One day, needing something for Salahuddin, she had tried to sneak out.

Bastian found out and fired shots after her in the street, she later told a friend, forcing her to turn and go back.

Dilal had tried and tried but had not been able to get in touch with her since she had received the picture of the battered and bruised little boy. She didn't have a phone number for her, so she sent a message on WhatsApp.

'How are things with Salahuddin?' she asked. 'What's happened to him?? Answer me! Aisha, please!'

There was no reply from Raqqa.

Then one night she received a message from Aisha saying she needed the money in the aid account.

'What happened to Salahuddin?' Dilal asked.

Everything was fine with him now, Aisha answered, adding praise for the Islamic State. The system was fantastic, everything worked, they were very happy and were having a great time.

Dilal told her she had given the money to Save the Children, and inquired more about Salahuddin's blue marks in the photo she had been sent a few weeks earlier. Aisha did not respond. Then several hours later, shortly after midnight, when Dilal was about to doze off, she received a new message on WhatsApp.

'I have to tell you something,' it began.

Aisha was typing.

She and Bastian had argued, a couple of weeks back, she wrote. He had slapped her before throwing her into the backyard, locking the door, and beginning to hit Salahuddin. She had stood with her ear to the closed door, pleading for him to stop.

The child had screamed. Loudly, desperately. Gradually, only exhausted crying was audible. She heard a thump against the wall. The sobbing stopped. It was quiet.

Then she heard the sound of Emira gasping from inside, the key was turned and the door thrown open. Salahuddin lay lifeless in her friend's arms.

His face was swollen, covered in blood and vomit; his cartilage was smashed, the whites of his eyes were red, the blood vessels burst. Aisha tried to bring him around, shook him. His body was warm but limp. He had no pulse. No heartbeat. No breath.

Dilal sat in bed, shuddering.

The blows to Salahuddin's head must have caused him to throw up, she reasoned. He would then have lost consciousness and suffocated on his own vomit, or his respiratory tract might have filled with blood.

The student nurse sat looking at the words as they appeared on the screen.

'I held him in my arms. I carried him out to the backyard,' Aisha wrote. 'I went around the garden the whole night with my dead son in my arms.'

Dilal was numb.

She was also furious. At the child murderer, *and* at her friend. She was to blame for her son's death, she had taken him to a war zone filled with psychopaths, for her own damn sake. She was deranged!

'What about Emira?' Dilal asked. 'Couldn't she have stopped him?'

Emira, who had just given birth, sought refuge when Bastian became violent, tried to protect herself and her own child. Bastian never laid a hand on her, Aisha added.

Dilal received another picture.

It was a grave in sandy soil, some dry straws coming up through it. There was Arabic writing on the stone that Dilal could not read. Perhaps they were words of praise to Allah, perhaps it read *Salahuddin*. The light was yellowish, a breeze must have been blowing, filling the air with sand.

There, beneath the stone, beneath the thistles, beneath the sand, lay Salahuddin.

Just shy of his second birthday.

'He's in a better place now,' Aisha wrote. 'He is a martyr. He is with God.'

Children went straight to God, she emphasized. Their souls were carried by beautiful birds. In paradise, the children were free, they could fly anywhere they wanted, and when they grew tired they could rest in the lanterns hanging from God's throne, just like the martyrs.

'Can I ask you a favor?' Aisha continued. It was now late at night.

'Of course,' Dilal replied.

'Can you tell my mother that Salahuddin is dead?'

Dilal could not believe it. 'Have you not told your mother?!'

'I can't bring myself to . . . '

That night the student nurse wept for the boy she had kissed as a newborn but barely known. She was still married to Ubaydullah back then. He had held the boy and said he had Arfan's smile. Later, she had cuddled with him, pushed him in his stroller. What if she had reported Aisha to the police when she had started talking about traveling to Syria? She had threatened to contact Child Welfare but had not. She had been busy with her own life. The student nurse was at a loss. She might have been obliged to report it? Could she have saved Salahuddin's life? Would he still be alive now . . . ?

It turned out Aisha had approached several friends and asked them to tell her mother about Salahuddin. Three of them met to consider what to do.

'Every time I see a little Pakistani baby, my eyes well up with tears!' one of them said.

'What Bastian did was nothing short of torturing him to death,' said another.

They were angry at Aisha for viewing Syria as 'romantic,' for thinking it was 'cool' to wage a war against the West.

Aisha's mother lived in their neighborhood. Which of them would tell her? Should they all go together? It was unbearable. They agreed to seek the advice of an imam.

The imam told them it was not their responsibility to inform the mother of the terrible news. 'That's something your friend has to do herself,' he said.

The media beat Aisha to it. In late February, TV2 covered news of the death.

'A two-year-old Norwegian child, taken by his mother to Syria last year, where she planned to join the terrorist group Islamic State, has been killed,' the report began.

The only person named in the report was Bastian Vasquez. But the reporter made reference to having spoken to the father of the child, who claimed Vasquez was responsible for the child's death. Social media quickly identified Arfan Bhatti as the father.

No one had informed Aisha's mother of her grandson's death prior to the news item. She called and texted everyone in her list of contacts who could know anything. Eventually she reached one person who could confirm that yes, it was true.

She had not seen her daughter or her grandson since last summer. Aisha had left for Syria without saying goodbye after marrying Bastian on Skype. The last the grandmother had heard was a voice message in which Aisha had said that they were fine and she hoped everyone at home was well.

Her initial reaction was to travel to Syria and be with her daughter, but she had no idea where to find her.

The father of the child gathered the inner circle of the Prophet's Ummah to discuss how to avenge the murder. Should someone be dispatched to Syria, or could one of the Norwegian jihadists down there end the life of their former brother?

Bastian's blood was halal for them now, killing him was permissible. A life for a life.

'He's the one who held a knife to my throat,' Sadiq wrote to Osman. Bastian was the man who had wanted to kill him at the prison in al-Dana, he told friends in Oslo.

'Really?' Osman wrote back.

The Chilean was the man who had tortured him, Sadiq confirmed. He had recognized him from his photo. The same unkempt hair, the same crazed look on his face as the one who hit hardest in the prison, the fat one with the broken Arabic.

'Wow. I know him too. I've met him,' Osman wrote, but Sadiq was done talking about Bastian.

'Send me the photos of the Norwegians!' Sadiq urged.

'Calm down. I had an accident last night. It was raining a lot, I dropped my smartphone and now it's fucked.' Several weeping emojis followed. 'All my photographs were erased. The phone's IC was wiped.'

'How, how is that possible??'

'We're going to Tabaqa on Wednesday. That's near Raqqa. We'll try to get some new photos of the Norwegians then.'

'Inshallah.'

'But, my friend, what happened with wiring the money? Time is running out. The lads are waiting for you. They are waiting for me. It's time for both. I gave people my word. What am I to do, my dear friend? Seriously, Abu Ismael.'

'Just tell me what you need from me?'

'We have to buy a camera to take better pictures and I need a computer. I also have to pay for the trip to Raqqa. It's best if you come. Don't be late.'

Osman texted again around midnight to remind him.

'Are you sleeping, my dear friend? Time is running out. If you want to be here when we get the girls back you need to come quick as a flash.'

'When should I come?'

'Today!'

That same week a trial opened at Oslo District Court. Three men were accused of having participated in, planned to participate in, or supported hostilities in Syria. It was the first time a Norwegian court of law would try someone for suspected violation of section 147d of the General Civil Penal Code, which stated that 'imprisonment of up to six years shall be imposed on those who form, participate in, recruit members, or provide financial or other material support to a terrorist organization, when the organization has taken steps to realize their purpose by illegal means.'

Section 147 was known as the antiterror paragraph and was the basis for the conviction of Anders Behring Breivik. It was supplemented with part d in June 2013 in order to take account of those connected to international terror organizations. The prosecution claimed that the Kosovar Albanian brothers Valon and Visar Avdyli and Somalian Djibril Bashir had illegal ties to the Islamic State. All three denied the charges.

The court case revealed the three men's activities in Syria. It also shed light on friends of theirs, including Hisham and Bastian. Egzon, the third Avdyli brother, who once had brought Aisha home after she'd been thrown out into the staircase by Arfan, had been killed in combat the previous year. Evidence produced included photographs of the accused posing together with weapons. E-mails containing details of arms purchases were read aloud. PST had bugged their apartments and their cars, and set up listening equipment at their regular haunts. When the police overheard two of them discussing blowing up a kindergarten, they no longer dared allow them to walk around freely.

'You see, we can't come home anyway, we'll be put in prison if we do!' Leila said to her mother. Leila knew the wife of the eldest Avdyli brother; she had remained in Raqqa when her husband had returned to Oslo for a short visit.

Was the girls' hijra also deemed criminal? Would they face charges if they returned home? They had, after all, *taken part in, planned to take part in, and supported a terror organization.* Perhaps, Sadiq considered, it would help to say that they were brainwashed. Would a waiver of prosecution be granted on the grounds of someone being brainwashed?

A couple of days into the trial, Leila got in touch with her brother. It had been several months since he had heard from her.

'Hi,' she wrote.

'Oh my God!' Ismael replied, typing in a smiley and four red hearts.

'Long time no see,' his sister responded.

'Indeed.'

'What's happening?' Leila asked.

'You tell me. How's it going?'

'I'm pregnant!'

'Hahaha.'

'7 months! I have a big belly!'

Ismael sent a shocked emoji and asked, 'Everything else good?'

'I'm good Alhamdulillah, the cold is the only thing I can complain about otherwise things are fine, the man of the house was wounded a few months back, but maybe you heard about that. How are things with You?'

'Great. I've accepted the world as it is.'

'How is Mom getting on? And don't be so pessimistic! The world only seems like a bad place if you choose to view it like that, it's all about perspective.'

'Mom has gone to Somaliland. And taken the boys. Dad is here in Norway.'

'I know all that.'

'I've learned to accept that Mom doesn't love me and that my sisters are in Syria.'

'What do you mean she doesn't love you?'

'It's because I have no belief. I've been, like, disowned. Kinda.'

'Then we're in the same boat, Dad has done the same to me.'

'Not exactly the same boat. Same sea. Different boat nigga.'

'Fine I don't want your stupid boat anyway, mine cooler! IS**'

'Can I ask you a question?'

'Go for it.'

'Do you seriously believe IS will take over the world?'

'Yes.'

'Then I know how far down in the sand your head is buried. No offense.'

'I've lived here over a year now, I can see how things are headed.'

'IS is not a proper army, with ground forces and airplanes.'

'From a military viewpoint they have a really good army and FYI they have well-organized ground forces and are building up their air force.'

'They can't even fly. Or have I been misinformed? I have seen videos of the ground forces.'

'Ismael, the media make them out to be a gang of unprepared noobs living in a bubble who just want to pick a fight with the world. But that's far from the truth. They're taking over airports and military airstrips and there are many among them who can fly.'

'But not one plane in the air.'

'They have a national army and are prepared for an attack by the Americans, they've even invited them to try.'

'That's like me writing to John Cena saying "come and fight me, you coward, I'm ready for you." U feel the analogy.'

'When the Americans pulled out of Iraq after declaring "mission accomplished," IS promised to return bigger and stronger than before,' Leila responded.

'The USA annihilated the Iraqi army and killed Saddam. Because they could,' Ismael wrote back.

'Are you aware of what little effect their air strikes here have had?'

'Ground forces would accomplish more. But Obama isn't allowed to send them in.'

'He'll do it eventually. Trust me.'

'I promise you that IS will disappear from the Middle East.'

'And I promise you that they're here to stay. Ismael, this might seem a little random, but have you straightened your hair in your profile picture?'

'Hahahaha. Yeah. A bit. Nah. Lots of gel.'

'Not bad. Not bad.'

Ismael was a handsome young man. Golden skin, an open, still-childish face, and a big smile that competed with the new white sweater he was posing in. He pasted another picture of himself on the thread.

'Omg! You've grown!' Leila wrote.

Ismael sent her another, where he was wearing a black-and-white singlet, mirrored sunglasses, and headphones. In his profile picture he was sporting a navy blue jacket with a fur collar. Somali straight outta Bærum style.

'Send me some photos too. I miss your ugly face,' he wrote, adding a red heart.

'Haha. Some other time. Talk soon inshallah, it's getting late and I have a child that needs to sleep lol haha.'

'Remember to do it. You could be dead by tomorrow.'

'Okay, inshallah.'

'Sweet. Good night!'

Leila sent a photo all the same. A headless selfie showing a long, slim body dressed in black pants, a black sweater, with a shawl over her shoulders and a bulge on her stomach.

'Ur face woman!'

'Good night. Hahahaha. See ya don't wanna be ya . . . '

'Fuckin' nigger!'

'Hey, watch your language.'

'Sorry, meant sweetheart.'

'Hahaha, sure.'

'I'm only kidding. Bye.'

29

Boys from Norway

On Sunday, March 1, Sadiq and Styrk Jansen traveled to Hatay. The girls were finally to be rescued. The producer brought along $3,000, a laptop, and the telephoto lens Osman had requested. He was hoping to get a happy ending in the can so they could wrap up the documentary.

The film crew had become Sadiq's closest allies, helping with money, applications, and printouts, lending him a car when needed. They stuck by him every step of the way on his rescue plan, through thick and thin. They paid for his plane ticket now, just as they had for the flight to Reyhanlı back in November when they were supposed to meet the Double. They were still shaken by his crucifixion and murder, and hoped that their rescue plan had had nothing to do with it. They believed what Sadiq told them, that the girls were desperate to get out of Syria. That Hisham was the problem.

Styrk had booked rooms at the Antakya Huyuk, just by the Sugar Palace, arriving late at night during a torrential downpour. Osman came to the hotel the next morning to pick up the money, the laptop, and the camera equipment. Osman told Styrk he needed the camera in order to take better-quality photographs. The ones he took on his mobile phone were not so good.

The smuggler outlined the plan. The girls were to remain inside the tank truck as long as they were in IS territory. Once clear, they would get out of the tank, switch vehicles, and drive until they crossed the border into Turkey, where Sadiq would be waiting with a rented car at a prearranged spot.

Osman had contacts deep within the IS system, and he controlled a network of couriers and drivers known to him via family ties in the three northern provinces of Raqqa, Aleppo, and Idlib. Two of his nephews had recently married. The plan was for their wives to try to make contact with Sadiq's daughters and surreptitiously slip them the note their father had written: 'Trust whoever gives you this. I love you.'

Osman produced his telephone. He spoke into it clearly and concisely, issuing orders, making arrangements, and double-checking he had been understood. After his last call, he looked at them and said, 'The operation is under way.'

Osman crossed back over the border into Syria. Rain was teeming. The streets of Hatay were wet, cars shimmered, and the sky was gray. Sadiq and the documentary makers stayed indoors.

A carpet of fog covered the entire region, the spring rain had set in over all of northern Syria, subduing the war, quelling the fighting. At the Antakya Huyuk they waited for updates.

'The regime has closed the road,' Osman wrote the following evening.

At nine o'clock, Leila, unaware of everything that was going on, sent a message to Ismael.

'U Alive?'

'Yeah.'

It bore the hallmarks of a banal conversation, as though they no longer had anything to say to each other.

'How are you?'

Ismael, afraid of giving anything away, refrained from writing more. If the girls found out about the planned kidnapping, it would fail.

Sadiq received another message from Osman on Wednesday

evening: 'The road was re-opened this afternoon. The boys have left for Raqqa.'

Sadiq could not relax. On Thursday morning, he wrote back to Osman: 'Give me some encouraging news, what's going on?'

Osman rang him in the afternoon: 'We've run into difficulty.' The car was stuck in the mud and the continuing rain meant it would not be moving anytime soon. 'Be patient, my friend. There have been reports that al-Jolani has been killed in an air strike,' he added.

The head of al-Nusra was the last thing Sadiq cared about. He sat motionless in the room, browsing the internet on his phone. Later the same afternoon, Osman reported, 'I can't get hold of the boys. All telecommunications are down where they are. ISIS is communicating by walkie-talkie, we have to wait for the rain to stop and the net to be up and running.'

It was still bucketing down in the Turkish border town. Styrk Jansen was bored. He thought about something Sadiq had told him the previous night, about Hisham having taken two new wives since Ayan had run away from him. Chechens. Hisham had already forgotten Ayan, Sadiq had said.

Osman rang on Friday morning. The route they were planning to take out of Raqqa after picking up the girls had yet to be decided upon. 'I suggest going via As-Safirah, the road is longer but safer, we could also take a route through Kurdish-held territory, but the Kurds are troublesome, I don't trust them, and we run the risk of running into Ahrar al-Sham on the way, what do you think . . . ?'

'What?' Sadiq responded.

' . . . the Kurds are in Ain Issa, the truck is ready, the girls are . . . al-Nusra is fine . . . avoid IS . . . before it gets dark . . . ambush, danger of that . . . driving without lights on . . . what do you think, brother?'

Sadiq had no clue.

The shortest route was through the area under Kurdish control, by way of Kobane, which IS had lost in late January. If the road was clear, you could be in Turkey in a couple of hours. The other road, the long one, meant an eight-hour drive – assuming you did not run into any obstacles.

Kurdish forces were only a few miles outside Atmeh. They were vying for control of the important border area currently divided among themselves, IS, and al-Nusra. Osman had said that the Kurds owed him a favor. Some time ago he had found a dead Kurdish soldier on al-Nusra land. The common practice was to leave enemy combatants lying where they fell, throw them in an unmarked grave, or sell their remains back to the family. Osman had called the commander of the closest Kurdish battalion. 'I've found the body of one of yours. I can drive him to you.'

Now it was payback time. He got in touch with the Kurdish officer, reminded him that he had delivered the soldier's remains, and asked for free passage through his area of control.

His request was granted. With that, the last part of the plan fell into place – they would take the road through Kobane.

A scout car was to drive a few minutes ahead of the tank truck to check the road was safe, that no new checkpoints had been set up or fighting had broken out.

By the time Osman sent word that they would soon be leaving for Raqqa, Sadiq and the film crew had been waiting in Hatay for five days. 'They executed a man here in Atmeh after Friday prayers today because they believed him to be a spy,' he told them.

Sadiq waited. Styrk waited. Veslemøy had arrived from Iraqi Kurdistan and was preparing to film the girls. They had production meetings in Sadiq's room. Sadiq drummed his fingers on the table. He went in and out of the room. Paced up and down the corridor. Walked down to reception. Went outside to smoke. But never far away. His mobile phone stayed close to his heart in his breast pocket.

Osman did not ring until the early hours of Sunday morning.

The car had been approaching Raqqa. Then all hell had broken loose. There was an air raid, bombs had pounded the ground around them. Buildings and cars had been hit. The driver had put the car in reverse and sped back in the direction they came.

They had waited an hour and again driven in the direction of the city. The bombing started again. They turned around. They tried a third time. And beat a retreat for a third time.

'Get some sleep,' Osman wrote to Sadiq. 'We're headed into an area without mobile coverage. Save your strength, you'll need it when you have your girls back. You'll hear from me tomorrow.'

'Are the girls in the car??' Styrk asked while Sadiq texted with Osman. 'Are they in the car?'

'I don't know, I don't know!' Sadiq said, almost shouting.

'Ask him, then!' Styrk urged.

But by then Osman's phone had lost its signal.

The filmmakers said good night to Sadiq and left the room. Osman would be calling in the morning. It was best to get some rest; none of them had had much sleep. The waiting kept them high on adrenaline.

Back in their room, the camera bags were packed and ready. Extra battery packs were charging. Early in the morning Mehmut was going to pick them up and take them out to get some shots of the surrounding area, unless Osman let them know he was approaching the border with the girls. In that case, Mehmut would drive them all there.

It was just before midnight and the couple were already in bed when there was a knock on the door. Styrk got up.

'Who is it?' he asked.

A man's voice answered. 'Norwegian Police Security Service. PST. Can we come in?'

What was this? Styrk slid the door chain off its track.

Two men were standing outside. They were tall, broad shouldered. One of them had a shaved head and snus under his lip, the other was dark-haired with pale, almost white skin.

'Hope we didn't wake you,' one said.

'No, you didn't wake us,' Styrk replied, looking at the two Norwegians in surprise.

'The rescue plan is in the final phase and we're here to see it through,' the other one said.

'What?'

'We're cooperating with the Turkish authorities and are taking over from here.'

'Huh?'

'That means the two of you need to head home.'

Veslemøy, who had hurried from Kurdistan to get the girls' border crossing on film, reacted with anger.

'You don't have the authority to send us on our way!'

However, the Turkish authorities do, the policemen pointed out.

'If you fail to leave, it could put you in a very unpleasant situation.'

'The girls could be here tomorrow! We're filming it. We've arranged it all with Sadiq,' Styrk exclaimed. He stood, hands on his hips, glaring at the two policemen.

'Sadiq stays with us,' one of the policemen said. 'He's taken care of.'

The documentarists were told that filming at the border was anyway and under all circumstances out of the question.

'If you turn up at the border with cameras, you will be in serious trouble,' one of the policemen said.

'We've been planning this for months! Now you turn up and ruin it, just so you can take credit for saving little girls from IS!'

Veslemøy, still in her nightgown, saw the film, their final scene, slipping away.

'This is Turkey,' one of the policemen said. 'Turkish rules apply.'

The air went out of them. Fear set in. The Turkish authorities were not known for sympathetic treatment of journalists filming without a permit.

'So you do it, then!' Styrk said. 'You film it for us.' He held out a spare video camera.

'We'll see what we can do,' the policeman answered, taking the camera. 'Have a safe trip home!'

As soon as they left, Styrk rang Sadiq.

There was no answer. He sent a text. He tried calling again. Still no answer.

Styrk and Veslemøy stood in the room talking things over. The policemen had said something about Sadiq being taken into custody, hadn't he? That they had him under supervision. Was that how they had put it? The documentarists weren't sure. Taken into custody by the Turkish authorities? Was he under arrest?

The couple discussed what the best plan of action was. Should they stay and try to find out what had happened to Sadiq, was that the right thing to do? Or should they do as PST advised them and clear out?

At one in the morning Styrk texted a colleague in Oslo.

'We were just woken up in our hotel room by two PST men at the door. We have been requested to stay away. They are taking over the operation.'

After Styrk and Veslemøy had said good night and retired to their room earlier that evening, Sadiq had quickly packed his few possessions and left the hotel.

He had been in touch with the two policemen, whom he knew as Nils and Bjørn, the previous day.

Sadiq had sought assistance from them long ago. He had first asked if PST could help in getting the girls out of Syria. That was not something they were willing to take on. But following discussions at the top level, and since Leila was a minor, the decision was made to assist on Turkish soil, something they had not done with other jihadists. As far as PST was concerned, what happened in Syria was Sadiq's business, what they referred to as 'a private rescue operation.' The Norwegian police would make the Turkish authorities aware of the situation so the girls did not end up in prison for crossing the border illegally. Sadiq and the policemen, who were both from the local PST office in Asker and Bærum, had had several meetings over the course of the last year, and in February, Sadiq had informed them that the plan was soon to be put into action. He asked them to be prepared for the girls' impending extrication.

The Norwegian embassy in Ankara had also been involved for some time. Cooperating with Turkish intelligence had not been all smooth sailing; *in Turkey, do as the Turks say*. Everything was carried out in the strictest secrecy. The legal attaché at the embassy had worked hard to get assurances from the Turkish authorities that the girls would not face arrest when they got to the border. There was still paperwork to be taken care of.

When Nils and Bjørn had arrived in Hatay, they were notified by
the Turks that they would not facilitate matters unless the film team
left. PST had no knowledge of any film team. If the team neared the
border, the cooperation would be stopped, the Turks said.

'Do you have a camera crew along with you, Sadiq?' the policemen had asked when they met him on Saturday afternoon.

Sadiq confirmed that he had.

'They need to go home,' the PST men had said.

Sadiq had gulped down some water to calm himself. That was
the film down the tube. And what was he going to say to Styrk and
Veslemøy? He had to be careful not to rock the boat.

It was late at night, the sun would soon be up. Styrk and Veslemøy
were looking into flights to Oslo. Sadiq sat in his new hotel, in a
room provided by PST, looking at the telephone that lay charging.
It made a ticking sound for each new message coming from Styrk.

He did not pick it up.

What a mess. Mehmut would be coming to the Antakya Huyuk in
the morning as arranged. Should he call and tell him he had changed
his hotel, that PST and the Turkish security authorities had taken
over running things inside Turkey? No, best not complicate matters.
If he told Mehmut, he would relay the news to Osman and he might
call the whole thing off. He would just not turn up, not answer the
phone, lie low.

Sadiq had been caught unawares. Losing control was not something he had considered. He had believed he could handle it all, get
all the help offered by the Ministry of Foreign Affairs, from the
embassy, from PST, from the Turkish authorities, and still call the
shots. He had thought he could let Styrk or Veslemøy, who also paid
all his bills, film while he, in effect, was the director. Now all of a
sudden it was a police operation.

He lay in bed thinking about Osman on the other side, about the
driver who was going to pick up the girls in Raqqa, get them in the
vehicle, and drive them out. The secret operation had to be kept
under wraps. The driver might face arrest when they made it to

the border. The last thing Osman – a smuggler of weapons, ammunition, people, anything – wanted was to come to the attention of the Turkish police. Should he let him know? Or just let the driver be taken by the Turks?

He would have to see how it panned out.

He lay thinking about something he was constantly trying to put to the back of his mind: When the vehicle made it to Raqqa, how were they going to get the girls *in*?

The driver had asked Osman the same thing. The note from their father was not going to be of much use if they did not want to go home.

Osman had just replied, 'Figure it out.'

He switched on the TV, zapped to the al-Jazeera news channel. Aleppo. Civilians, children among them, lay dead after a rocket strike. The reporter said something about Raqqa being hit, but there were no pictures. Maybe the girls were killed before they got out?

He watched the footage of the war taking place just over the border. Syrians dying.

We want to help Muslims, his daughters had written. But there was only death in their wake.

Sadiq had told PST that it was now a matter of days. The policemen had passed the message on to the Norwegian embassy in Ankara. The following day the two PST men met with Sadiq for an update on how the rescue operation in Syria was proceeding. Were the girls en route?

Osman was impossible to reach. The day was spent waiting.

The PST men were in regular contact with their superiors back home, who in turn were in touch with the Turks. The embassy in Ankara had dispatched two employees to help in Hatay. Being mindful of the girls' attitudes toward interaction with men, they had taken care that one of them was a woman. Then, was homesickness the reason the girls wanted to leave, or were there others? The embassy had taken security precautions in that respect, but what was most important was to try to attend to the girls' needs; the diplomats had seen to it that an ambulance would be standing by just in case. After all, there was no way of knowing what state the girls would be in.

Sadiq had been very clear about the girls' wish to flee the Islamic State. Their situation was desperate. Now, the diplomats and the police were waiting. The paperwork was ready. Sadiq had signed papers saying he accepted the fine the girls would incur for illegally crossing the border. It was a formality, as the money would come from the embassy budget. He had also put his name to travel documents for Leila, who was under eighteen. The consular section had organized these documents, so-called laissez-passer, so that the girls could fly from Hatay to Oslo, and would not be arrested by the Turks.

Like the diplomats and the policemen, Sadiq sat around, got to his feet, sat down in a different chair, shifted position in his seat. He went out to smoke. His smartphone lay on the table. Nothing demands more attention than a telephone that is silent.

After much toing and froing, Styrk and Veslemøy had booked tickets on the earliest flight on Sunday morning; it was exactly a week since they had left Oslo. When they came down to the reception counter at dawn to check out, they were informed that Sadiq had left the hotel. They assumed he was arrested and settled his bill.

On Monday morning, back in Oslo, Styrk went to PST headquarters. Sadiq was not responding to his texts. Was he being held in custody? Had they taken his phone from him? Was he under arrest? The film director was fuming about missing the opportunity to get footage of the girls crossing the border, furious that PST would be the ones waiting to meet them, not him and Veslemøy.

At PST headquarters he was met with a wall of silence.

Nobody told him that PST had traveled to Hatay at Sadiq's request, that they had been cooperating on this for a long time, and that Sadiq had kept the film crew in the dark.

'Is he going to call soon?' Nils asked.

'About time he got in touch, isn't it?' Bjørn asked.

'I never know when Osman will ring,' Sadiq answered.

'Has he called?' they asked a little later. Sometimes one of them would go out and come back in again to hear if there was any news. 'Any word? Didn't he say he was going to ring this morning?'

'An agreed time isn't set in stone, not like in Norway,' Sadiq said. Everything was approximate, anything could happen, everything could change. Welcome to the real world.

Finally, Monday afternoon, the mobile phone lit up. It was a text from Osman. Sadiq read the messages aloud.

'Air strike. Today. They took out al-Nusra's HQ. Where you were. My friends are dead.'

'Oh . . . God!' Sadiq wrote in response. 'What about the girls, and the ones who were to get them? Have they left? Tell me about the operation!'

'I'm finding it hard to collect my thoughts, I'm talking to you but I'm not awake. It was a large strike. All the Nusra buildings were leveled. Thirty dead so far.'

'May God receive them . . . But what happened to the men who were to drive the girls?'

'Abu Ismael, we're burying the martyrs. I'm at the grave site now.'

Sadiq did not relent. 'I need the last confirmed information about our operation. Is it proceeding as planned or has there been any change? Have they left Raqqa or not? If they have left Raqqa, where are they now?'

'The father and brother of one of the drivers we sent to Raqqa have been martyred. I have not been able to reach the drivers.'

So the girls would not be coming today.

'Leila,' Ismael wrote.

'Yes?' she answered.

Ismael was wondering how the rescuers would manage to get his sisters to come along. He knew that Leila and Ayan lived in their own apartments, each with her husband. Would they be picked up when the men were out, or would they be coming along too? He tried to sound things out.

'How are things with Ayan?' he asked.

'Alhamdulillah.'

She was using *Praise be to Allah* as a sort of shorthand to refer to all being well with Ayan.

During their last conversation around Christmas, Ayan had written that she wouldn't talk to him until he stopped talking trash about Allah. But he had not believed she would make good on her threat and punish him, as if she had not ruined his life enough by going off to die. He had to fish for more information from Leila.

'Do you have any news about Ayan? When did you talk to her last?'

'Last week.'

'Is she pregnant?'

'Ask her.'

'You're lying. You met her last week?'

'Don't call me a liar, I chatted online with her last week.'

Ismael was fed up with the shadow play, the affected airs, the arrogance. Rescue operation or not, he wrote down some points he called 'Tutorial on how to get to Paradise':

FOR WOMEN:
1. Marry a guy who is most likely to die in war
2. Get pregnant
3. Husband dies
4. Profit
5. Repeat until you die for max profit

FOR MEN:
1. Go to place where it is Jihad
2. Get bitches pregnant cuz bitches love martyrs
3. Die in war
4. Profit
5. You are dead so there is no step 5

'Watch your blasphemy!' Leila replied. 'Please watch your language when you're talking to me. Do you really think it's nonsense? Or are you trying (and failing btw) to be funny?'

'It's a joke. Borderline blasphemic.'

'Well, drop it.'

Ismael contented himself with sending a picture of the three wise monkeys holding their hands over their eyes, ears, mouth. And typed in 'soon-to-be Uncle Ismael.'

The next morning Osman wrote to Sadiq.

'I haven't heard from the lads. I'm worried about them. I'm extremely anxious, and I'm dreading what to say to Hussam who lost both his father and brother. I want the girls, the men, and the vehicle back safely. In that order.'

Meanwhile, the diplomats and the PST men sat in Hatay waiting. Sadiq assured them that the girls were on their way and would soon reach the border.

As the week progressed, the texts from Osman grew gloomier.

'The lads have had an accident on the way to the girls,' he wrote. 'Hussam was driving. His wife was accompanying him to make it look like a family trip, they were both injured. They're in the hospital in Gaziantep.'

'I'll pray for them. How are you planning to proceed?' Sadiq asked.

A Kurdish soldier had come across Hussam and his wife and given them first aid, stopping the bleeding and thus saving their lives. He had taken their valuables and given them to the local Kurdish militia, the YPG. Their mobile phones had contained photos of the girls in Raqqa, taken from a distance, and the pictures Sadiq had sent so the kidnappers would recognize them, in addition to telephone numbers of people high up in Nusra. When Osman paid the Kurds a visit to reclaim the items, he learned that it was now they who wanted a favor in return.

'They wanted Hussam, they think he's a central figure in Jabhat al-Nusra,' Osman wrote. 'When I refused they demanded payment before they would hand over the belongings. Again I refused. Then they asked me for something that could land me in deep trouble. They wanted ammunition. If I get hold of it for them, and it comes to light, I'll be judged a traitor. Then I'm finished. Oh these Kurds, they've got me over a barrel!'

'Any other news?' Sadiq asked.

'The driver's brother died in the attack on al-Nusra's headquarters. His other brother is in a coma. My head feels like it's going to explode. I took five headache pills today.'

'Have a sixth!'

'At the moment it feels like I need Viagra to stand upright, my friend!'

In Hatay, Sadiq and the cops sat twiddling their thumbs. How long would the embassy keep their people there? How long would the police wait?

'Hussam is in a really bad state, both his father and brother were killed. I'm trying to find a new driver. But the repairs to the car are going to be costly. I don't know why all this misfortune and all these mishaps have befallen us! I really want to help you,' Osman assured him. 'But I'm terribly afraid of Daesh. They have spies everywhere. Believe me. Every time I solve one problem another one crops up.'

The tank truck had left Raqqa without the girls. They were going to make a fresh attempt, Osman informed him. 'But everything is changing all the time, first the road is open, then it's closed, only to be re-opened. We draw up a plan deciding what route to take and when the day dawns they have just set up roadblocks and diversions. We were in Manbij today, then without warning they closed the road, and although we wanted to head east we found ourselves going west. It's complicating everything. We constantly have to fine-tune the plan, examine every detail and look at it from different angles. Believe me, if I had my way I would take your daughters on my shoulders and carry them all the way to Norway. What have you heard from the girls?'

He hadn't had any contact with them.

The rescue team was in the hospital.

Osman was attending funerals.

The tank truck had been dispatched on other assignments.

While the girls, those damned girls, were sitting in Raqqa unaware of everything.

After another week, orders came from PST headquarters: Pack and return!

Sadiq did not have the money to stay. Styrk had financed his travel and hotel. The whole thing was supposed to take a couple of days, and he had been in Hatay for two weeks fooling himself, fooling the film crew, the secret police, and the diplomats in Ankara. They had believed in a rescue operation; Sadiq had believed in a miracle.

At the airport in Oslo, the two policemen shook his hand. 'See you.'

They walked off. Broad shouldered, straight backed, with long strides. They were headed home.

For them, the operation was finished.

Sadiq remained standing among the airport travelers. He looked around. People were waiting for their luggage. They were waiting for one another. They were buying beer and spirits. He went over to the self-service machine to buy a train ticket home. He keyed in his destination and his PIN. One way to Sandvika. The machine beeped. His card came back out. Rejected.

30

Shoot the Girls If You Want!

The days were long, the nights interminable.

'Let's put an end to this tragedy once and for all!' Sadiq wrote to Osman when he was back in Norway.

Osman had other things to think about. The militias in Idlib were planning to strike Assad a major blow. Although rebel forces had controlled most of Idlib province since 2012, Idlib city, the provincial capital, situated not far from the main road between Aleppo and Damascus, was still in Assad's hands. By late March the battle for the city raged for a fifth time. Seven factions, with Jabhat al-Nusra and Ahrar al-Sham at their head, had joined to form a coalition called Fatah, conquest. The inhabitants who had not managed to flee barricaded themselves indoors while the army of conquest attacked the city from three sides.

Syrian state television reported that the government army was beating back the attempts of 'terrorist groups to infiltrate Idlib.' But Assad's soldiers were driven south of the city and despite attempts to regroup found themselves overwhelmed. The city was encircled by thousands of enemy fighters.

After five days of fighting, Osman wrote to Sadiq: 'Idlib is free!'

'Brother, there will be a happy ending to our lives!' Sadiq responded.

The Nusra front celebrated on Twitter: 'Thanks be to God, the city of Idlib has been liberated!'

Bearded men embraced, wept, held communal prayers in the park, tore down the flags of the regime, and chipped out the eyes on the enormous golden statue of Hafez al-Assad.

Assad loyalists were lynched. People shot and killed their own relatives to cleanse their names, so they would not be dragged into the undertow of revenge. Before long the Fatah army set up local sharia courts in the different parts of the city. Raqqa was the first provincial capital Assad had lost. Idlib became the second.

Osman wrote to Sadiq: 'I've taken lots of pictures for you to sell to Norwegian journalists.'

One of the leaders of Assad's hated people's committees was beheaded, another was dragged alive behind a car, and a third was shot through the eyes. But that kind of wretchedness was already available to the Norwegian media from the news agencies. What they wanted were pictures of the *Norwegians.*

Osman sent several photographs of beheadings that fighters were circulating among themselves. One showed a thin older man in a gray tunic. His head was being held down on a chopping block. A burly man in brown ankle-length trousers and a *khamiis* stood over him. The executioner was masked and wore a black hat. The ax was resting on the back of the man's neck when the picture was taken.

Sorely in need of money, Sadiq made up a story to go with the picture and then went to *Dagbladet* with the 'scoop.' The man acting as executioner, he told them, was a Norwegian by the name of Abu Shahrazaad al-Narwegi and the victim was a sharia judge.

'I'm getting the car repaired now. Send the money,' Osman wrote on April 7.

'I've been trying to get hold of milk for my daughter for three days,' he wrote the following day.

'You can suckle from my breast!' Sadiq replied the next morning.

April 9: 'We're leaving for Raqqa in two days.'

April 10: 'The tank truck will stop at Deir al-Zour on the way to Raqqa. I'm going along myself. If you don't hear from me, read a blessing over my soul!'

April 11: 'The tank truck left Deir al-Zour this morning.'

April 12: 'Things are going according to plan.'

April 13: 'We're ready to make our move.'

April 14: 'We're standing by. They're bombing the roads.'

April 15: 'The tank truck is in Raqqa. But the girls aren't here. We're waiting for them to turn up.'

April 20: 'We're standing by to punch, punch, punch.'

April 21: 'The plan is being put into action in one hour.'

April 22: 'Raqqa here. Nothing to report. We're waiting to strike.'

April 23: 'My nerves are going to blow soon.'

The picture Sadiq had sold to *Dagbladet* covered the whole front page. 'IS source tells *Dagbladet* – Norwegian executioner beheads his victims' went the headline. '*Dagbladet* can today reveal the first picture of what sources say is a Norwegian involved in an execution in Syria. The executioner, said to be a Norwegian national, has resided in Syria for some time fighting for the terror group Islamic State.' The article went on to say that the man was born and raised in Norway and that the journalists were aware of Abu Shahrazaad al-Narwegi's Norwegian identity and that he was still 'listed in the National Registry under his Christian birth name.' Consequently, the man in question had to be a convert, reasoned those who followed the Islamist crowd. That narrowed the list of whom he could be. There was only a handful of Norwegian converts in Syria, none of whom resembled the man in the photograph, apart from Bastian Vasquez, who was in jail, something the journalists were not aware of. The newspaper also presented information about the victim: 'He had already got his wife and children safely out of the country and to Qatar. The plan was for the family to start a new life in the wealthy emirate in the Persian Gulf. But the alleged deserter was exposed before managing to make it out of Syria. He was arrested and a short time later executed in front of a large crowd. The sharia judge was condemned to death – because his former friends in the

Islamic State believed him to be a traitor.' The two journalists who had bylines on the story added that they had the information from 'several sources' – which meant Sadiq and Osman.

If the journalists had done a quick search online, they would have learned that the picture had been released by IS, and that the story of the execution had been picked up by the activist group Raqqa Is Being Slaughtered Silently. The man was no sharia judge but a villager accused of dabbling in black magic. The story of the sorcerer had two months earlier been reported by several media outlets from newspapers in the UK to television stations in the United States.

The accused sorcerer had become a sharia judge. The executioner had become Norwegian. Courtesy of Sadiq gabayaa – Sadiq the poet.

'Are we talking hours, weeks, or months before this happens?' Sadiq wrote to Osman in the wake of the front-page spread.

'Days,' Osman answered. 'The problem is your girls are well-guarded. They must be highly prized by their husbands. My lads have been on the cusp of going in four times, but there are always armed men outside the gate.'

One of Osman's men sent his wife in to check. They agreed beforehand that if she did not come back out within a half hour, they would make their move. The minutes ticked by, the men readied themselves. Just a few minutes before the half hour was up, she emerged.

'The girls were there but there was also seven IS soldiers and nine other women in the house. An attack was out of the question!' Osman wrote.

Ayan and Leila now lived with a group of girls in an old mansion. When Hisham or Imran was sent to the front, the sisters moved in with each other. No women could live alone in the caliphate.

'The girls are behind solid fortifications, a living fortress of IS soldiers,' Osman wrote.

'That's exactly what bothers me and makes me lose hope,' Sadiq replied.

'Your daughters never go out alone. They are always in a group,' Osman complained. 'One of the lads attempted to sneak in between them, but it was no good, there were too many of them, it was impossible. By the way, looks like Assad is on his last legs.'

'What about IS?'

'If Assad falls, IS will fall. That's for sure. Time will prove me right.'

Their conversation continued into the early hours.

'Have they silencers?' Sadiq asked.

'You can buy them for $2,000. Be patient.'

'I want the guards watching my girls out of the way.'

'I have five men on the job and two women. They have five rifles and two handguns. I've bought the ammunition and one of the handguns, the lads have their own weapons.'

'It's not enough for an operation like this.'

'My dear friend, we cannot open fire in the middle of IS territory . . . we can only strike on the sly.'

'Do whatever you have to, shoot the girls if you want, get rid of them, just put an end to this!'

'Your daughters are also my sisters!' Osman wrote back.

Around one in the morning Sadiq wrote, 'Put an end to this torment, this torture I'm going through. Concentrate, focus!'

'Cool down!' Osman answered.

Bærum was cool enough. The temperature hovered under 40°, did not rise above 50° at a stretch, and they called this spring?

Sadiq wore a winter coat, heavy boots, and a gray-flecked beanie with a black ribbed bottom. He felt the chill constantly but did not want to put on the heat too often, since he was the only one there. Ismael was out a lot. He had gotten a girlfriend during the spring and was at home even less. Sadiq had met her once; she was so pale she was almost translucent, with long blond, almost white, hair.

He could tackle the cold in winter, when he was prepared. But now in May, when the grass was green and the new leaves on the birch trees shimmered, no, that made him shiver. He slept with his hat on, but it did not help because without Sara the bed was cold.

He often got up at night to wander around the neighborhood. He walked a lot during the day as well. Ascending Kolsås ridge was a favorite. Struggling up the steep path. He enjoyed the view from the top, no matter how sad and frustrated he felt otherwise. But mostly he stayed in. Drummed his fingers on the table. Ethiopian rhythms. Eritrean rhythms. Somali rhythms. He found himself composing a few lines. Calling a friend. And then another. He sent texts. To Osman: *Has anything happened?* To Sara: *I miss you.* To Ismael: *Will you be home for dinner?* But not to the girls anymore. He had not heard anything from Ayan since November. It was also months since he had received a message from Leila. Osman replied: *Stop nagging.* Sara answered: *The boys miss you too.* Ismael answered: *I fix food myself.* Sadiq was being worn away inside.

It was as though fate was always one step ahead of him. Something or other with a fiendish temperament threw a monkey wrench in the works. Every time they were close to getting the girls out, something happened to thwart their plans. But if whatever it was, was of this world, he did not know.

'I'm in the hospital, in Dar al-Aisa, near Aleppo,' Osman wrote one day. 'There was an air strike. I was almost killed. My back is full of shrapnel.'

Two MiG fighters had roared above him. *As if the highways in heaven came crashing down*, he described the noise. These were the aircraft, purchased by Assad from the Russians, that had wrought the most destruction on Syria.

'I thought my number was up.'

Sadiq stayed cool. 'When are you going to get around to kidnapping those bloody girls?' he inquired.

Osman responded by sending him a picture from his hospital window of the Euphrates flowing gently past. 'I'm still bedridden, surviving on painkillers. My neighbor committed suicide yesterday. Threw himself down his well.'

'My younger daughter is soon in her ninth month. The elder in her seventh.'

Sara had told him about Ayan also being pregnant.

'The lads hinted at it, that she was expecting. With regard to the younger one, her husband is around her the whole time. But I've got wind of plans to send the husbands to the front. They'll be gone for a few weeks,' Osman wrote from his sickbed. 'Rumor has it the Americans are planning to bomb Atmeh, everyone has evacuated their headquarters. My Facebook account has been shut down btw. I have lost all my contacts. According to the message from the Facebook administrator because of "support of a terror organization, incitement to violence, and posting pictures containing violent images."'

On May 8, Sadiq wrote: 'I'm forty today. I love my mother. She's the one I'm thinking about today.'

'The IS men have still not left the house,' Osman wrote three days later. 'My boys are bored of hanging around and waiting. The girls are lucky, their soldier husbands are always around. These guys never go anywhere, what is it they actually do? The latest from Raqqa is there's a lot of internal squabbling in IS. Quite a few desertions. I think the situation will soon turn bloody, the tools are being put away and the weapons taken out.'

'Due date soon, this is our last chance!' Sadiq pestered.

Two nights later, Sadiq came home from the miserly spring, placed his phone on the living room table, sat down on the sofa, and stared at it. It was close to midnight. He picked it up and checked his messages and e-mail. Nothing new. He put it back down, took it up, and tapped on the messages from Leila. He wanted to write to her, even though she had stopped writing, stopped responding.

'It's Dad. I'm worried about both of you.'

Not a peep, as usual.

The house, on the other hand, made sounds. The refrigerator hummed, the stovetop emitted clicks now and again, the washing machine could suddenly gurgle, and the dishwasher swished, sounds he had never thought about before, but now, on his own, it was as though the bare apartment was trying to say something.

He sent another text.

'Salam aleikum. Have you given birth?'

Secondary school students were out celebrating the approaching end of their final semester. Horns from the buses and vans they painted and partied in could be heard. Rain was forecast for later that night and heavy drops were already beating upon the windowpanes. Leila would be eighteen in October. Next year she was supposed to be one of those students out enjoying life. He sighed. He was getting to his feet to find something to drink when the screen of the mobile phone lit up.

'Aleikum salam.'

Followed by: 'No, not yet.'

Then another peep: 'She's not due for a month.'

Then she logged off.

Sadiq sat stupefied on the sofa. Leila had replied as though they had seen each other just yesterday. *She* is not due. Did she know it would be a girl, or was she guessing?

Who is my daughter, actually?

This was a question he found himself asking more and more. Who was she? Did he ever really know her? And Ayan, people said they were birds of a feather, he thought he understood her so well. Did he actually know her at all?

He wrote a message to Osman: 'My younger daughter, the tall one, called me tonight, in four weeks she is giving birth to a daughter. This is our last chance. We only have a month.'

Exhausted, Sadiq fell asleep on the sofa in the early hours of the morning. It had been a restless night, spent toing and froing, looking at the internet, and smoking. He did not stir until late in the day. When he woke up, he thought about the Somali twins he had read about online the night before. The girls had called their parents in Bristol to say they had fled from the Islamic State and were in hiding. Their parents had gone to the police, and the British prime minister had appeared on television to say that if they were penitent, they would receive a pardon and face no punishment. The seventeen-year-olds had, however, been tracked down by IS, taken prisoner, and beheaded. Killed because of what they had said to their parents, punished because their parents had gone to the media, slaughtered by IS because that kafir David Cameron had shown support for them. They had been beheaded in the center of Raqqa. In the photo-graph they had looked so much like his daughters. He could picture it all so clearly, their pleas for mercy, the knife cutting their throats, the screams, before it went quiet. The thought of the blade against a throat made him feel nauseous.

But when he went to read the story again that Saturday morning, it was no longer online. Yet he had read the entire thing the previous night, even seen the photograph of the beheadings. He thought it had been on Al Arabiya's web pages, or maybe on Reuters. But it had disappeared from the net, as though it had never existed. He was confused. Had he imagined the whole thing?

He stared out at the gray morning. It looked chilly. Tomorrow was Constitution Day. People in Bærum were ironing the shirts of their national costumes. They were shining their shoes. Getting flags out. Placing sprigs of birch in vases. Shopping for the May 17 breakfast or buying flowers and champagne for the host. Final-year students were preparing for their last big party prior to exams.

Sadiq was not invited anywhere.

There were no small boys to accompany to the children's parade. No one to cheer on as they hopped along in a sack race, balanced on stilts, or threw balls at tin cans. All that would still happen, as usual, only without Isaq and Jibril.

The life around him no longer concerned him. He used to be happy, for the most part. He thought about that now, how cheer-ful he had been. Even during the civil war, even when he lost his father and brother. Now he was mainly indifferent. Nothing had any effect on him.

At the same time, he was becoming forgetful, unable to remem-ber things or words. Sometimes, like now, he wondered if he was imagining things; he believed he had read things he had thought up himself, things that really did take place, but only in his head, stories born of his own anxiety.

He decided to take a shower. It enlivened him a bit. While he was in the bathroom, his mobile phone on the living room table received a message.

'Abu Ismael, your younger daughter, the tall one, is in Atmeh.'

The hot water poured over him. He wondered if he was losing it. He pondered, had he read about the two girls or had he dreamed it? It had all been so clear to him: The Somali sisters from Bristol, Cameron making his statement, and now it was all gone. No sisters, no beheadings, no Cameron.

In Atmeh, Osman was growing impatient. 'Abu Ismael, are you asleep? Wake up!'

The mobile phone emitted its peeps into the empty room. Sadiq dried off, dressed, put on water for coffee, and checked his phone, as he routinely did several hundred times a day.

'I need to drive to al-Dana, won't have any signal, be back in two hours. Reply to me,' read the last message. Sadiq scrolled up the screen. And stiffened. Then everything loosened. Like an avalanche. Leila was rescued! A wave of relief washed over him. Tears ran down his cheeks. Then in the next moment he thought: *Only Leila? Why only her? Where is Ayan?*

He began frantically texting Osman. Tried to call him. But the Syrian had no coverage. Should he ring Sara? No, he had to wait.

So he waited.

Two hours passed. Leila was out! Three hours. A burden had been lifted off one shoulder. But the thought of Ayan still weighed upon him, casting a shadow on the news.

Osman finally got in touch again. 'Abu Ismael. Good news. Your daughter with a child is in Atmeh. Your tall daughter.'

With a child? Had she already given birth?

Osman was overcome with joy at having saved Leila. She had come out onto the street outside the house they lived in, dressed in a niqab, with the child on her arm. Osman's boys had driven slowly past her, pulled in, handed her the note, told her they could drive her out of Raqqa, whereupon she had jumped into the car and they had driven through all the roadblocks, all the checkpoints, just driven, driven, they had not been stopped anywhere along the way.

'A godsend,' Osman wrote. 'He showed us mercy today.'

Sadiq asked to speak to his daughter.

'Wait awhile. She is tired, wants to sleep.'

'I can fly down first thing tomorrow. Do not send her to Turkey before I am in Hatay.'

On receiving no answer, he tried to call. Osman's mobile phone merely made clicking sounds.

'This is good news, don't worry,' Osman wrote.

'I'm worried about everything,' Sadiq responded.

'She says she is tired, that she doesn't want to talk to you. Your grandchild is four weeks old.'

A four-week-old child? Leila had just written that she was due in four weeks. Had he misunderstood? Had she actually written that the child was four weeks old?

'I want to hear her voice.'

Was it someone else? Perhaps it was Emira, Bastian's wife. She had a child. She was also tall. Her father had said she wanted to travel home but had not been able. But she was Pakistani, not Somali. Osman could not have been so mistaken. On the other hand, Osman had not seen her face, only written that she was tall. His mother and wife were looking after the runaway and her child now.

Hours went by. Finally a message came: 'Dear brother. My best friend. The girl is in my house. Don't worry. Please. Calm down.'

11:20 p.m.: 'Eh . . . ? Who is she or who are they? Let me speak to her.'

11:21: 'Just wait, I don't want to pressure her.'

11:22: 'Have her send a recording on WhatsApp.'

11:22: 'The girl says she knows your daughters.'

Do not crack now. He was floating in another dimension. It was over.

She is the image of your daughter Leila. I'm sure it is her, she is just frightened. She told me lots of things at odds with one another. First she said she was from the UK, then she told me she was from South Africa.

11:24: 'A liar.'

11:25: 'She says she is not your daughter. She also said your daughters are twins.'

11:25: 'Tell God to send her to hell! She's lying. I don't care who she is. I won't waste time. Or energy. You've kidnapped the wrong girl.'

How long had it lasted, the joy at Leila being rescued? He went onto the balcony to have a smoke. Sensing hope and losing it came at a cost. Some sentences formed into a poem.

> *The leaves are quite still*
> *Not so my heart*
> *Nor my head*
> *They clamor*

When Ismael arrived home from a May 17 party, unaware of the drama of the last few hours, he sent a picture to Leila. It was of their mother, taken in Somaliland the previous summer. Sara was sitting on the floor with her legs tucked under her, looking into the camera. 'Don't u miss this face?' Ismael asked.

He had tried reasoning. Tried logic. He was exhausted by the whole thing and just wanted his sister to look at their mother and realize how much pain she had caused her. Leila remained silent. Ismael could not sleep. At four in the morning, he sent a picture of himself and asked, 'Why are you and IS in favor of suicide bombing?'

No response from Raqqa.

Only Osman wrote. The rescue team had seen a woman in a niqab leaving the large house with a small child, and they thought it was Leila and that she had given birth. They told her they could help her get out of Raqqa. The girl had hopped into the car and sat in silence for the entire journey.

'Are they staking out the wrong girls?? Have they been anywhere near my girls at all? Remember, my girls have skin like olive oil, if this girl is from South Africa then she's very black. My girls aren't that black.' Sadiq added, 'My wife will be upset when she finds out you thought the girls were so dark ☺.'

'Remember, we can only see their eyes,' Osman replied.

The girl had become a problem for him. He was fearful on several fronts – that she might blow his network, that she would give him away to the Turkish police and land him in trouble next time he crossed the border, that she might still have ties to IS. She knew where he lived, had seen the smugglers. He impressed upon her the importance of not exposing him. After a few days, the girl and her baby were dispatched across the border to Turkey. A family had their daughter returned to them, without having lifted a finger. Out of the war zone, delivered for free. Sadiq felt bitter. The girl had been rescued with the help of his network. The world was unfair. The pain unbearable. He had believed, though, if only for a brief time, that Leila was free . . .

Sadiq made no attempt to talk to the girl when he realized she was not Leila, even though she could have had valuable information about his daughters. He could not face it, as if he did not want to know how things actually were with them. Not knowing offers its own type of protection.

In Raqqa the heat had set in. The pregnancies were beginning to take a toll. When the girls were outside, they wore several layers, as well as material covering their nose and mouth. The power outages that had rendered the rooms freezing cold in the winter now stopped all the fans. For a few short weeks the sandy earth had a green tinge to it, now it was again brown, spring in the desert shifted quickly to baking heat.

But they never called home to gripe. In the caliphate everyone was happy and had faith in the future. Anything else testified to apostasy.

After a week, Leila answered Ismael's question from May 17.

'I have never said anything about suicide bombing,' was her terse reply.

Ismael wasted no time posing a follow-up question. 'What is the IS view on suicide bombers?'

'Why are you asking me about fiqh, when you don't even believe in it?'

Fiqh is Islamic jurisprudence and the interpretation of sharia as expressed in the Koran and tradition. In addition to dealing with ritual deeds like prayer, fasting, alms, and the pilgrimage, it covers civil law, criminal law, and the area concerned with Ismael's question: the law of war. As far as IS was concerned, God was the legislator and sharia a part of the revelation that could not be altered or adapted.

'I just want to know.'

'I don't see the point.'

'Too difficult a question?'

'No, just don't understand why you're asking me when you can easily find out on the net,' she answered after midnight.

'Don't want to read propaganda. Want to hear from you, since you're there,' Ismael wrote, and sent an image of an ear.

'What good is it to you to know these things when you neither believe in anything nor are looking for anything to believe in. I could understand if you were asking in order to get a better understanding of religion but it seems like you're asking merely for the sake of debate.'

'I just want to see if you share my values.'

'I really don't have the time or the inclination for a debate at the moment, starting with belief in God, because if you don't believe in God none of the answers I give you will be of any use.'

'Stop beating around the bush. Is IS for/against suicide bombers? It's not a debate. Merely a simple question. I'm not asking why. Just yes/no.'

After a few minutes the cursor began to move. It was one in the morning. An answer was on the way from Raqqa.

'Hey, it's Leila's husband . . . finally, mate, we get to speak.'

'Hey man. I asked my sister a question. Do you mind answering?'

'Yeah, I know, she's just feeling tired. Due to the pregnancy.'

'My dad respects you a lot for asking to marry her. So do I.'

'Thanks for telling me.'

'Take good care of her, bro.'

'Trust me, I will, Ismael. I wanted to speak with you for a long time coming. Aaww brotherly love, how cute.'

'Back to my question though?'

'I see you like fiqh. What madhab are you btw . . . don't tell me Shafi like all Somalis. FYI, electricity might cut out any second.'

Madhab is a school of thought within fiqh. There are four in Sunni Islam, including the Shafi in North and East Africa, while the Hanbali, the strictest, dominates in Saudi Arabia.

'Lol . . . I'm not looking for reasoning around it, just give me a plain answer, yes or no?' Ismael persisted.

'Dude, take it one step at a time. Lol.'

'So that's a yes. Right. I was not sure if the West were just shedding bad light on you guys or if you actually promote suicide bombing. So I would respect a simple answer from you. If that's not too much to ask.'

'We have just got to know each other, man, this topic needs a hot cup of tea. How about you come and I'll make us nice Somali tea, discuss things, like the older generation?'

'Haha, would I come back alive/in one piece?'

Imran changed the subject, wanted to engage in small talk.

But Ismael would not let up. 'Just answer me first. Since I asked so nicely.'

'Okay, this question is highly debatable. Some of the scholars in the Islamic State allow it and some don't, calling it suicide. However, the majority agrees with it due to the great damage it causes the enemy. All those who do it do it at their own will and are never forced. Funny enough there is a loooooooong list and this is what amazes many. Now my question to you is how is this benefiting you in any way?'

'I am just curious how the "true" religion can even be misinterpreted,' Ismael replied.

One Norwegian jihadist was sitting contemplating whether or not to carry out a suicide mission.

Eventually some of Bastian's compatriots in Syria had taken action and reported him to the sharia court in Raqqa. Following summary justice, Abu Safiyya was sentenced to death for the murder of his stepson, Salahuddin.

Bastian was waiting for his life in this world to come to an end. Time dragged on and he remained in the cell. One day he was brought before the judge again and confronted with a choice: Face being beheaded or carry out a suicide attack for the Islamic State.

Receive the punishment for treachery or die like a martyr.

'Oh, Allah destroy them, and let it be painful!' Bastian had urged on his video. 'Oh, Allah, take vengeance upon the transgressors,' he'd threatened the crown prince and the prime minister in Norway. 'Oh, Greatest One, show them your wrath! Oh, Powerful One, show them hell!'

When the border station that IS had just taken over exploded in a sea of flames, he had laughed.

Now it was his life that could end in a sea of flames. In the cause of Allah. He could get into a truck, with armor plating fitted to prevent the tires being hit. He could sit behind a windshield covered with welded metal with only a peephole cut so no one could shoot him. He could start the car when given the signal. And drive toward the target. The infidels and the apostate. Or seen from another perspective – toward paradise.

He could shout 'Allahu Akbar' right before he triggered the device and the vehicle exploded.

But he did not want to.

He wanted to live.

He had been up there. His videos had been viewed across the whole world. IS needed him for propaganda. He thought he would receive a reprieve.

He did not.

Sharia was carried out to the letter. *Kill he who has killed. A soul for a soul.* He who had sought paradise would instead end up in hell. That was the place for child killers.

Leila's due date was June 10, Sara told Sadiq.

'I've had an idea,' Osman wrote. 'Let's see if we can turn her visit to the hospital to our advantage. Let me chew on it.'

'15 days left. Just so you know. The clock is ticking,' Sadiq wrote.

'Three of the lads have been arrested!'

'What?'

'They were stopped at a Nusra checkpoint. The car was searched and their weapons were found. They were accused of passing information to the Kurds.'

'14 days left.'

'They're being held at al-Nusra headquarters, four miles from al-Dana. My nerves are gone, I'm so upset, I've sent a sheikh . . . '

'13 days left.'

'We have managed to infiltrate the hospital. Have made a deal with the obstetrician. When your daughter comes in to give birth, he will make sure he's the attending, and when the baby is delivered he will tell her the child is sick and needs follow-up. She will come to let him take a look at the baby every day. The more often she comes the better our chances of seizing her. The doctor will convince her that the baby needs to go to a special hospital in Turkey. The road goes through Atmeh. It's a golden opportunity. The lads are with you until death.'

'What about my elder daughter?'

'We'll need more money. We're running low on cash. We need money to buy the three boys back. None of them have earned anything on the operation, and we owe the owner of the tank truck. He also needs money to live. The boys have not complained yet, they are very understanding. Tell your daughter that giving birth in the hospital is safest. But don't make her suspicious. And find a way to send us more money!'

'I have to be up early in the morning, so I need to get some sleep now,' Sadiq wrote. He tended to bow out of their conversations when the issue of money was raised.

During the night he wrote, 'Troubled, very troubled. Demons are toying with me.'

Osman answered, 'I know you are going through hell. As am I.'

The Syrian smuggler had increasingly less room for maneuver. Kurdish militias were closing in on Atmeh and were now in control of several roads in the immediate vicinity. IS was on the offensive. Nusra was on the offensive. Assad was bombing.

The area under Islamic State control was larger than ever. In mid-May 2015, IS fighters had seized control of the ancient city of Palmyra. They had executed regime soldiers who had not managed to flee, emptied the dreaded Tadmur prison of inmates whom they then recruited, and planted explosives around the ancient monuments in the city. In addition, IS won a strategic victory when Ramadi, the capital of Anbar province in Iraq, fell.

The coalition could not beat IS solely by bombing and it lacked partners on the ground. Several of the more moderate groups the West had attempted to ally with were swept aside by IS, or joined the Islamists' ranks. There was also a lack of reliable intelligence. The coalition needed people to infiltrate, gather information, and indicate targets.

A year had passed since Barack Obama unveiled a plan to train and equip a five-thousand-man force to fight against IS. The plan, which had been budgeted at half a billion dollars, was quickly passed by Congress but was stranded from the start. The men, who were to undergo a six-week training course, were to be extracted from war zones in Iraq and Syria and trained in Jordan, and then reintroduced into the conflict and equipped with advanced weaponry. The Americans ended up preparing sixty men. A quarter of the weapons arsenal disappeared into the hands of other militias in exchange for access on the ground. In addition, there were divisions between the United States and some of the coalition partners. The main aim of Turkey and the Arab states was to depose Bashar al-Assad; the United States was focused on destroying IS.

The Americans, British, and Russians, as well as the Arab states, tried to acquire assets on the ground in Syria. British intelligence had put a lot of resources into both infiltration and training. MI5 attempted to infiltrate mosques, Salafist organizations, and extremist groups to find people to act as informants on IS. Psychologists were used to find the right kind of individuals. Those enlisted underwent comprehensive personality tests to determine if they were the type who could easily slip over to the other side and in so doing become the most dangerous type of all – double agents with a stronger loyalty to IS than to the UK.

The men on Osman's rescue team complained that they felt they were under surveillance. Someone was watching them, they believed. The two Norwegian girls had become a heavy burden on the shoulders of many.

Recently, numerous activists had been arrested and killed. They were paraded on video as traitors before being shot on camera. If IS could not find an activist, it took a relative in his place. One of the most prominent citizen journalists behind the group Raqqa Is Being Slaughtered Silently, who'd managed to flee to Turkey, had to watch his own father being tied to a tree and shot, the entire scene professionally lit and filmed by a camera crew from the terror state's communications department.

On June 1, Osman sent a picture of a snake and wrote: 'IS is very close to Atmeh. Do you know what blood type your daughter has, A minus, A positive, B minus? Please try to put some pressure on the newspaper, we need money. People at the hospital need to be paid.'

On June 2, he sent a picture of a beheading. 'An engineer from Jabal al-Zawiya.'

On June 5, he sent a reminder. 'I need to pay the doctors at the hospital.'

On June 7, he sent a fresh reminder: 'Where are you? What's happened? Save us!'

Sadiq pleaded that he was trying. 'I'm furious with the newspaper people. They haven't sent me any money. They're awaiting more information on the Norwegians, they're particularly interested in a Norwegian sniper.'

At four in the morning, two days before his daughter was due to give birth, Sadiq wrote: 'My life is turned upside down since the girls left. From bad to worse. They're still brainwashed. They still want to be there. They're happy living life in a place like that. I have no job, can't find any work, my wife has gone to Somalia, I live with Ismael. Those who have helped me cannot help me for all eternity. No one can help me forever. Norway has helped me. I am broken, I don't know what to do, everyone is fleeing Raqqa, and my daughters want to stay! How can we help them if they don't realize themselves the huge mistake they've made? That is the problem. My daughters are not awake.'

The following night Osman responded: 'ISIS has closed all the roads, everyone must stay in Raqqa.'

On June 10, Sadiq replied: 'I have decided to take more care of my son, Ismael.'

June 12: 'The roads are still blocked, the route out of Raqqa is closed, there are snipers everywhere. FSA has declared war on IS. They have ceased their attacks on Assad and have opened a front against IS. Oil is not coming out, gasoline costs a dollar per quart, prices have shot up, wages have been cut, aid organizations have stopped sending food supplies, the farmers can't ship their produce, there are no vegetables. Raqqa is under siege. Patience is called for. Pray that the birth is delayed.'

June 15: 'My younger daughter called me. She has not had the baby yet.'

Osman replied: 'Things in Raqqa are turning worse for my boys. The chances of getting your girls out are worsening by the day. But we won't give up. We'll get to them before the birth.'

But the child came first.

On June 18, seventeen-year-old Leila became a mother. When the contractions became stronger, Imran had taken her to the hospital. Twelve hours after the birth, she had called her mother in Hargeisa to tell her everything had gone well. The baby was a girl, as she expected.

Sara had been jittery prior to the birth. Leila was narrow-hipped, as she herself had been, a build that had proved fatal for Sara and Sadiq's firstborn.

Now they were grandparents.

They could rejoice in that when everything was over.

On June 20, Sadiq wrote to Osman: 'My daughter has given birth to a daughter.'

June 21: 'I have become a grandfather.'

June 22: Osman sent a video of a beheading he thought Sadiq might be able to sell.

31

Ramadan

'Dad is here! *Aboo!* Daddy!'

The boys rushed to meet him. The sensation of their little bodies crashing into him, how he had missed it! They leaped into his arms, let him throw them in the air. A year had passed since he had seen them. Sara stood smiling at him. Beautiful, warm, happy.

She was a different woman in Somalia from the one she had been in Norway, where, devastated by the loss of her daughters, she had become an old lady of thirty-eight years.

She no longer cried every day. In Hargeisa she had two sisters, a younger brother and his wife, and children everywhere. Small nieces and nephews often came to the big house and stayed. Relations came before anything else. Sara had brought clothes from Norway that Isaq and Jibril had grown out of, and the daughter of her deceased sister, who was the same age as Ayan, had been given the one garment that had avoided the trash bags – the white jacket she had not been able to throw out.

The walls resounded with laughter and there was a smell of perfume in the hall. It was Sara's house. She ruled the roost. All she needed from Sadiq was $300 a month in rent and money for a household of sixteen.

In the kitchen, there was a brick bench with two holes where the women placed charcoal and lit a fire every morning. Pots and pans were placed directly on the embers. Early in the day the aroma of sweet tea with cardamom seeds filled the air, later on the smell of bean stew, porridge, or pancakes. During the course of the day they mixed dough for samosas, then kneaded and rolled it. Spices were rinsed of pebbles, straw, and soil, the amount needed was transferred to two trays, and a small girl was tasked with picking out everything not going in the mortar. The women chopped the filling, sautéed it, put it in the dough packets, sealed them, and deep-fried them in oil.

Feeding the large household took most of the day, there was always someone in the kitchen. Sara was never alone. That was how she wanted it. She had lost her family twice and brought it together again. Now she had lost it for a third time. All she wanted was to have them all gathered under one roof. Preferably here, under the sun.

Sadiq had been ordered to Hargeisa by his mother. 'My son, you must gather your family,' she had told him over the telephone. She'd had mixed feelings about Sara moving from Norway. Married couples should not be apart. No, either he had to move to Hargeisa, or Sara had to return to Norway, said the matriarch.

His head was thumping. His thoughts emptied of meaning. His mouth dry. His body drained of energy. Ramadan enforced its own rhythm. A month to feel the pain of the poor. A month of pure suffering. A month to come closer to God.

It was more than 100° in the shade. The air was still. Neither food nor drink was to pass their lips from before the sun came up until it went down – from around four in the morning until seven in the evening. At midday everyone was knocked out, even the children calmed down.

Sadiq solved some of the unpleasantness by turning the days around. He stayed up at night and slept during the day, usually from around noon until the early evening, getting up an hour or so before dinner.

There were obligations to attend to in Hargeisa that did not exist in Bærum. They were called relatives. All members of the extended family had to be paid a visit. Everyone requiring help had to receive it. Everyone who wanted to talk had to be listened to. Sadiq shifted into another mode. He dispensed with trousers and tied a *macawiis*, a sarong, around his waist. He swapped his shoes for sandals. He even dispensed with his phone at times, when he had no credit and could not be reached anyway.

Life ran its course. There were flies, cockroaches, and scorpions indoors. Donkeys, camels, and goats outside. No word from the girls.

A calm of sorts descended upon the family. Sadiq's mother was bedridden and he spent a lot of time at her place. Her granddaughters' hijra had affected her deeply and she could not refrain from talking about it while other relatives preferred not to. After almost two years, it was as if the girls had ceased to exist. As though the relatives did not want to stir a bad memory. The previous year the wound had been open, and everyone wanted to know all the facts, discuss them, wonder, and express hope. Now a heavy stone lay over the girls, a stone no one could face rolling off.

'She never leaves the house!'

Osman was frustrated.

'Your granddaughter is fifteen days old.'

Pretending the infant had an illness had not worked. Leila and Imran had left the hospital before the doctor Osman had made a deal with even knew they had been there.

Asiyah – pronounced with a long *a* and an aspirated last syllable – was named after the pharaoh's wife who found baby Moses in a basket in the bulrushes. She, as opposed to her husband, believed in the existence of one God, and he ended her life, torturing her to death. A true heroine revered by Muslims, Christians, and Jews.

Sara received three pictures of the little girl. She looked like Leila when she was a baby, with lots of dark hair and full lips. Pink cheeks shone in the pale brown face, which would soon darken. Her eyes were closed in all the photographs. In one she was lying on her side, curved into an S shape, as she had been in the womb. She was lying on a green blanket with Arab writing on it that was impossible to make out. Sara recognized Leila's glasses, narrow with plain black frames, nearby on the blanket. They had gone to the optician in Sandvika together to get them. Leila had wanted as discreet a pair as possible.

Asiyah was dressed in different outfits in the three photographs, in white and baby pink, all white, and all pink, there were teddy bears, rabbits, and bows on the clothes. In the background was a tray with mineral water and mango juice. Where was Leila getting her hands on all this baby equipment? All shiny and brand-new, there, in a war zone?

Allahu Akbar, Allah!

The call to prayer sounded from several minarets in the town. Powerful and booming from those closest; deeper, with a more distant echo, from the ones farther away. There was something soothing about the beautiful male voices lifted in praise of Allah: the drawn-out *a*, then the sustained *ll*, followed by the second *a*, an octave higher. The voice quivering for a time before fading into *akbar* – and then a new *Aaaaaallaaaaah.*

Following *iftar*, the evening meal at sundown that concluded the day's fasting, Sadiq usually went to a local café. The women of the house remained sitting on large carpets in the yard. The evening breeze roused them and they drank tea, ate sweets, and looked at the stars. Sometimes a visitor dropped by, a relative or neighbor. Some came to ask a favor, or to offer something, or simply to chat.

Sadiq went out the gate. The house Sara had found was the last one on the street with a wall around it. The next dwelling was made of corrugated iron, tarpaulins, old carpets, sticks, twigs, and plastic bags. The road was of earth and sand, deep potholes making it impassable for cars, allowing the children to play safely in the streets.

There were tents and shacks lining the street farther on. And goats, always goats, lots of goats, their emaciated forms drinking rainwater and grazing on husks. Any vegetation on the ground was soon forced up by tongues and teeth and clamped between their jaws. The few trees that did grow in the city center were fenced off with chicken wire to keep the goats from them.

Sadiq passed the tarpaulins on his way to the main street.

The heat had subsided. He was looking forward to an espresso and a smoke, maybe there would be someone there to have a chat with. Whether it was due to his age or the years spent in Norway, he could not cope with the heat like before.

As he savored the strong coffee, his mind began to settle after the long day of fasting. His mobile phone beeped: a text from Osman. The screen lit up. The night was dark and starry. No one used unnecessary light in Somaliland.

'I have terrible news, my dear brother,' the message began. 'We fled Raqqa. Thank God, the lads and I are safe and sound. We had to get away . . . the Eritrean found out about us. He has control over your daughters. I am so sorry. I cannot help your daughters now. Pray to God for us.'

Sadiq's head began to swim. His hands shook. It was as if the girls were dying within him. Here he was, sitting in the dust, a continent away, powerless, staring into space.

He took the long way home.

Ramadan was nearing an end. The others were looking forward to Eid al-Fitr, the feast marking the end of the month of fasting. Lamb, birds, and fish would be baked with herbs, fried with vegetables, boiled and mixed with rice and pasta. The house was to shine, as were its occupants. The little boys washed one another in a large tub filled with water in the backyard. The largest mirror in the house was brought outside. It was the inside of a cupboard door, the sill of which was broken off. One by one the boys sat in a chair in front of the mirror, getting their hair cut by the family member most skilled in the use of a scissors and razor. The hair at the back of the neck was scraped short with a razor blade. The hair was to end in a defined line, straight across the nape of the neck and curved over the ears toward the forehead and afterward glazed with black Brylcreem. A steady stream of boys flocked to and from the mirror under the banisters. They turned and tilted their heads, looking at themselves from different angles, admiring the shine, studied themselves in profile, and turned to look over their shoulders to check if their newly purchased jeans looked all right from behind.

Sara was in bed. She lay in a daze, hot and hungry. The afternoon was the warmest time of the day. Her mouth was dry. Not a drop of water until the sun went down. A week had passed since Osman had sent word that he and his men had left Raqqa. She could not face going out to see the bustling preparations.

The telephone beside her on the bed rang. She registered a crackle on the other end of the line before she jolted awake.

'Eid Mubarak! Blessed Eid!'

'Leila!'

'Happy Eid al-Fitr!'

'My little girl! We've been so worried about you!'

Leila continued on, seemingly unaffected by her mother's expression of concern.

'We're going to celebrate Eid at some friends'. Imran is on leave. Everything's fine with Asiyah.'

'And Ayan?'

'She's not here and doesn't have internet where she is. Asiyah is one month old tomorrow, we'll be celebrating her aqeeqah and I promise to send pictures! I have to go. Bye, Mom!'

Hearing her daughter's voice had been like receiving electric shocks. She and Sadiq had feared both Leila and Ayan could be beheaded on account of Hisham discovering their dad's rescue plan. But now to hear, *We're going to celebrate Eid at some friends'* – as though she were calling from an ordinary life, in an ordinary town, in an ordinary country.

Toward the end of July, Sadiq received a text from Leila.

'Ali ibn Abi Talib said: if you wish to know where the true believers are, look where the arrows of the kuffar point. Things have been a bit hectic here with Asiyah's aqeeqah and all the preparations around it. You should know that we are happy and well, we are safe and ALLAH has provided us with plentiful rizq. HE gave us both husbands who take good care of us and HE has blessed us with children, do not believe everything you see and hear on the news because the media have done nothing but twist the truth and mislead people.'

Sadiq read the message aloud to Sara. They looked at each other in silence.

'That was written by Hisham,' Sadiq said.

Sara shook her head. 'That's how she talks now.'

Aqeeqah was a sacrifice. Two goats were slaughtered for the birth of a baby boy and one goat for a girl. *Rizq* meant gifts or provisions. Sadiq read the text aloud again to see if there was anything between the lines. The preparations for their granddaughter's feast had been hectic. As though they came from an existence filled with parties.

A second part to the text message followed: 'God has taken us from the heathens and led us to a Muslim country. A land where people love us and we love them for the sake of God. Keep in mind that God has ordained that our reward is here. Wallahi, fa wallahi, thumma wallahi, know by God, and again by God, and yet again by God that we are not brainless girls just running around aimlessly. God knows the number of books we read, the number of lectures we listened to, and the number of learned men we sought advice from prior to our departure.'

The last part, although similar in tone, was written in Somali. Which meant Hisham could not have written it after all. But he still might have dictated it, Sadiq insisted.

He had made his son-in-law out to be a monster that had captured, brainwashed, and gagged his daughters. Thus the girls were to be pitied, as were the parents.

He could not admit that what he wanted was not what his daughters wanted.

Sara opened the photographs of Asiyah in the freshly ironed baby clothes. So they were probably gifts, which Leila had written were so plentiful.

Self-satisfied, the seventeen-year-old had told them: *Keep in mind that God has ordained our reward here.*

The Islamic State's version of: because I deserve it.

Part V

Hell is other people.

—Jean-Paul Sartre,
No Exit, 1944

32

A Different Life

Sadiq entered the apartment. The smell of old dust and unoccupied rooms hit him. Everything was just as he had left it, the dishes dirty and the place untidy. He stopped in the entranceway. Except for the hum of the refrigerator, the one with the sticker that read ALLAH SEES YOUR HEART AND YOUR DEEDS, everything was quiet.

If Allah looked into Sadiq's heart, he would see a hard lump.

He wandered around the empty apartment, jet-lagged after the flight from Hargeisa, shivering in Norway's late-summer temperature. He had to adjust his circadian rhythms after Ramadan, after all the irregular hours he had been keeping. He had to, he really did, he needed to sort out his life.

He made yet another plan. Or a life buoy. 1. Put the girls out of his mind. 2. Find a job. 3. Pay off his debts. 4. Everything else would fall into place. Sara would return home with the boys. Life would continue as before, only without the girls. They had made their choice. They had left. They were never coming back.

He had to adjust to a life without them.

A life without them.

A different life.

*

The mail had piled up over the summer. There were letters for him, for Sara, some final demands for Ayan and Leila. They would eventually be written off as bad debts by the creditors. He opened the letters to Sara. They were bills and a demand for reimbursement from NAV. She had failed to inform them about moving to Somaliland and had therefore continued to receive child benefits. When the school reported the boys' nonattendance, the welfare office had investigated the matter and found that Sara had broken the rules. Taking the children out of Norway meant losing the right to child support. Bærum county was demanding that the incorrect payments be refunded.

Sadiq was informed his job seeker's allowance was going to be stopped. Support was dependent upon his making use of follow-up assistance from NAV in order to 'be in a position to gain or keep suitable employment.' The agency explained: 'The recipient has to be active, is required to arrive at NAV when called in for appointments, and collaborate on a plan of activity as well as follow up on it.' The background for the warning was that 'it has come to the attention of NAV that you have taken repeated trips abroad during the period when you were in receipt of job seeker's allowance without having applied for these trips or having them approved.' The payments were dependent on 'residency in Norway.'

He also received word from Bærum county that he would have to move. There was a waiting list for larger family apartments.

He was called in for an appointment the following week.

At the meeting, the caseworker told him he did not need the four-room apartment. He was the only one living there, after all, now that Ismael had left for college.

He nodded. What could they offer him?

A one-bedroom apartment.

He received notice of a date to move out. He had to clear out the girls' half-empty closets and drawers. Go through their papers. Pack Sara's clothes. His own. The boys'. Sheets and bedding. Towels. Pots and pans, saucers and bowls, knives and forks, kitchen utensils. He had to take down the framed poster of Mecca. The notes in Arabic. The remnants of a family life.

Essay assignments. School reports. Science books. A whole box of unopened letters addressed to Ayan. He did not throw away any papers. He hardly threw anything out – that would require an estimation of value, is this important or not? He stuffed everything into a couple of boxes and fled. To bars and cafés. Played the drums, met friends. Sometimes Sara's friends called him up to check if he was behaving himself. Now and then they dropped by. When people asked him how it was going, he told them he was working on a new rescue plan. That he would soon succeed.

The plans he had made for a new life on his return were on hold. The dashed expectations, the betrayal, the loss, the ever-increasing debt weighed upon him. The spark that was Sadiq was in danger of being extinguished.

He was broke and had borrowed money from friends for two years. He had sent a text to a couple of them when he was in Hargeisa saying he had been admitted to a hospital and needed treatment. One of them had sent him a small sum. The money had dwindled away, new clothes for the boys, food for Eid, money for school, gas, and the upkeep of the car. He owed Osman money for the last, unsuccessful rescue attempt. Expenses had accrued despite the negative outcome.

'Come to Hatay!' Osman told him. 'There's a market for everything!' He suggested a range of ways for Sadiq to make money, and listed Sadiq's advantages; he had a European passport, contacts in Somaliland, and access to Osman's network in Syria.

In Hatay, he would be closer to the girls. He would be just around the corner if they wished to get out. He could meet them at the border, in Atmeh, or he could go to Raqqa. Bring them home or die trying.

One day Osman called him and proposed a deal. He had contacts in Syria who had gotten hold of an extremely rare and valuable substance: red mercury. It could fetch a sky-high price. The profit would be huge. Supposedly, the stuff had almost magical properties and could be used in the manufacture of dirty bombs and suitcase nuclear devices. But it was also dangerous, he warned: It was forbidden everywhere and had to be smuggled; dealers and distributors operated in the shadows.

Sadiq weighed his options. Should he seize the opportunity to do business in Hatay, or struggle to get his old life in Norway back in order?

He had only bad memories of that town, and what Osman was suggesting involved great risk. Besides, he had taken his first step toward securing a steady income. He had signed up for a taxi driver's course.

'That's wonderful!' the caseworker in Bærum county had said. 'Really great that you're taking the initiative to find work.'

The course was starting the Monday after next and would last three weeks. This time he *would* take the taxi license test, he *wanted* a job, yes, he wanted *two* jobs, *three* jobs, he was going to apply for a train conductor course, or be a tram driver, earn money and pay back all that he had borrowed. He couldn't let everything continue collapsing around him any longer. No, he had to tell Osman that he would not travel to Hatay. Not now, not ever.

NAV in Bærum had extended his job seeker's allowance after all, and he would still receive housing support, even though the children no longer lived with him. Social services was aware of the difficulty of his situation. He did not think it unreasonable to have to move, since he no longer needed accommodation for seven people. After Ismael moved out to study nanotechnology, he no longer had children at home. He was *single*. Damn it, what was he sitting at home for? It was Friday night. No one to look after, no one to support. He called a friend.

Sara lay in the large double bed with just a sheet over her. The August heat was sticky, the air heavy. There was not a breath of wind.

The house was finally quiet. One by one they had all fallen asleep. The children. Her sisters. Their husbands. Now it was Sara's turn.

The telephone rang. *Sadiq*. He was the only one who called at this hour. He knew the house was quiet and he could have Sara to himself. She pressed Accept.

'Mom . . . '

'Ayan?! . . . '

Sara pressed the telephone against her ear. She had not heard her elder daughter's voice since winter.

'Mom . . . ' Ayan repeated, her voice was weak.

'Ayan, my girl!'

'I've given birth to a daughter . . . '

'God be praised!'

'She's beautiful. She was delivered here at home. It took soooo long, and was so painful, I've lost a lot of blood.'

'Ayan, dear . . . '

'I'm very tired . . . I need to go, just wanted to let you know: She's fine, healthy.'

Sara rang Sadiq. The call went straight to voice mail. At the tone, she couldn't gather her thoughts to say anything. She rang a second time and left a message but was cut off before finishing because her credit ran out.

Sadiq was sitting on the metro into Oslo. The city was bathed in a sudden late-summer warmth. It was still light and the air was sultry as he exited the train.

The battery on his mobile phone was empty, so the news of a new life did not reach him while he was in the downtown bars.

Not until the following day, when he got home and charged his phone, did he receive the message. Another granddaughter.

Named Sara.

A storm was brewing. Sudden gusts of wind caused branches to break and fall to the ground, the last of the petals were blown from the stalks, summer was over. Water streamed down the hillside, raindrops beat upon the decking outside the living room where Sadiq sat alone. All day. All afternoon. All evening. Then the night began. He sat awake through it, smoking, with a glass in his hand. He thought about Sara, about little Sara, and about the two girls who had betrayed him.

I cannot take any more of this, he thought. *Waiting for texts. The disappointment of failed rescue attempts. I want my normal life back, my normal, boring life. I want my wife on the sofa, Ismael at a party, and the girls at the mosque. I want to take the boys to the pool, without having anything on my mind except that we are going swimming. Then we can all meet here in the apartment, eat dinner, and talk. Like we used to do.*

He was hardly out of one tunnel before he was plunged into a new one. They divided, turning labyrinthine, he was walking into dead ends at every turn.

He looked out.

Osman logged on.

'Anything new?' Sadiq asked.

'Yeahyeahyeahyeah.'

'What's happened?'

There was a ticking sound on the line.

'Atmeh is under attack!'

'What's going on?'

'Five rockets came down. Here, in the middle of town! It's burning!'

It was a smaller war within the larger one. The war in Syria consisted of hundreds of minor conflicts, many of them centuries old. They all concerned the same things: land, soil, resources. One conflict was taking place right outside Osman's blue gate.

The five rockets had been launched by Kurdish YPG guerrillas in reprisal for an attack. Two of them had come down near a hospital, two in a residential area, and one in the middle of the roundabout. On Twitter, Jabhat al-Nusra promised revenge.

The Kurds and the Islamists had been quarreling over control of the border areas since the beginning of the civil war. The Kurds wanted a coherent territory, not scattered cantons within Sunni-Arab land. The problems had intensified in early August when YPG erected a lookout tower near Atmeh, viewed by the Islamists as a violation of a local agreement forbidding forts. They accused the Kurds of shooting from the tower and launched an attack.

According to the deal, the Kurds were to keep east of the

Euphrates and the rebel forces to stay west. But one of the Kurdish cantons lay on the west of the river, in the same little pocket of land as Atmeh, and this had led to repeated clashes. Each side blamed the other for reneging on the agreement.

Atmeh had become a more dangerous place. Coalition forces were bombing, IS was waiting for an opportunity to take over the town, and the Kurds were exerting pressure only a mile or so away. The border areas, with their supply lines and smuggling routes, were the locations of a lot of death.

Things were better under Assad, Osman now opined. When Assad was in power, you could get on with your life, things were predictable and not all bad, as long as you did not get mixed up in anything. Arrests were not made at random; people knew the score. No one was taken without a reason. Osman recalled the opposition to the war among the businessmen in Aleppo before he left there. The trading town had long refused to join in the revolt against Assad. People had feared the consequences; they had, after all, seen what had happened in Iraq, a long and drawn-out fight to the death between Sunnis and Shias. Syria could only be worse. Aleppo had held back, tried to stay out of it, until that was no longer possible. The city was now an inferno.

'Rockets will rain upon the Kurds,' Osman threatened. 'Are you coming down?'

Osman knew two arms dealers in Dubai. They could meet him in Hatay. They wanted a sample of the red mercury to check its quality. Osman had responded that his suppliers were willing to send a drop of the substance for them to take a look at, but only on payment of a $10,000 advance. The price per pound was, after all, $1 million.

Sadiq could find no peace. He felt an acute urge to do something. One last heist.

It was early September. If he did not leave this week, it would be too late, the taxi course was due to start and failing to show up would mean losing his job seeker's allowance.

He boarded the afternoon flight to Istanbul.

'I'm in Hatay!' he texted to Osman when he landed. 'Come and meet me!'

It was hot and sunny, with a drowsy atmosphere prevailing in the town. Sadiq walked the same streets he had previously walked searching for his daughters, waiting for a call from the middlemen and his Syrian network. He dropped by his favorite places, first the breakfast café that served the best beans, after that Gulp, the bar on the corner by the modest Sugar Palace. He called Osman. No answer. He felt alone. He had made the trip on impulse. Madness. They were going to be fooled, he thought. Before leaving, he'd been told by someone that there was no such thing as red mercury, that any trade in it was a pure con.

Most of the tables at Gulp were empty. The only customer besides Sadiq was an older man. He was dressed in shorts and a faded T-shirt and was halfway through a large glass of beer. He had a reddish-gray complexion and looked tired, like an old laborer. The skin on his hands was coarse. He smoked, took a sip, sighed, and took another. Late morning turned into afternoon. Sadiq noticed the man's identity card on the floor beneath his chair, together with several Turkish lire bills. He drew the man's attention to it and the man picked up both the card and the money.

'Monthly salary,' he slurred. 'If I drink any more, I'll probably lose my trousers as well.' He laughed hoarsely. He had a Syrian dialect.

Sadiq drummed his fingers on the tabletop. Another hard-luck story was the last thing he needed.

On the pavement outside, a Syrian family was having a heated discussion. The father was angry and the mother was in tears. The father had bought a kebab for each of the children. One of his sons had asked for another.

'And who's going to pay? Who's going to pay? Who?!' the man shouted. '*WHO is going to PAY?*' He emptied his pockets, throwing small change on the ground in front of his son before turning to go while calling out: 'I'm not hungry, I'm not hungry, you all go ahead and eat!'

The man rounded the corner. His family quickly gathered up the coins and hurried after him, out of Sadiq's field of vision.

Suffering wherever you looked.

He had to get hold of a Turkish SIM card. Using the Norwegian one was expensive. Sadiq always had two telephones in Turkey, a smartphone with a Norwegian subscription so he could go online where there was Wi-Fi, and an older model he could use with a Turkish SIM card. The telephone shop he had usually used, which also sold crocheted baby clothes and slippers, was just up the street.

When he got there, an older man and a younger woman were in front of him in the queue. Judging by their dress, they were poor, the man was wearing a white tunic and a keffiyeh, the woman a black abaya and hijab.

'It's not possible,' the man behind the counter said. 'We can't register you.'

The father and daughter were stateless refugees from Syria. They had lived at a refugee camp outside Damascus for thirty years and never received Syrian citizenship. Therefore, they had no national identification or social security number for the shop assistant to enter into the system, meaning he could not sell them a SIM card.

'No matter how much I want, it will not go through the system,' he explained.

For Turkcell the man and his daughter did not exist.

Then it was Sadiq's turn.

Nationality?

Norwegian.

ID?

Sadiq handed him his passport.

He was deemed worthy of a Turkish SIM card.

He called Osman from the new number. Still no answer. It was 100° in the shade. He went to the same old juice presser who had always served him and ordered an avocado juice with pistachio seeds. Osman still didn't answer.

He continued on to Four Friends, where the kitchen was open twenty-four hours a day. The waiters came over and greeted him.

'How's it going?' they asked.

'Good,' Sadiq replied.

But things were far from good.

At sunset he made his way down to the empty, air-conditioned dining room in the hotel and ordered a bottle of ice-cold water. They had Wi-Fi there and he could try to raise Osman on Viber and WhatsApp. He found a socket and sat down to charge the phone. There was some activity at least – the screen lit up, the battery percentage rose.

The smoking ban had made it to Hatay, so he had to go outside for a cigarette. The foyer doors were open. He stood on the street inhaling nicotine until he was dizzy. He felt a light breeze on his back, between the material of his shirt, clammy with sweat, and his skin. A tickling sensation. He had the wind at his back now, did he not?

He went back in to his telephone. Eventually he received a text message.

'Hang tight,' Osman wrote. 'Await message!'

Sadiq made his way to a hipster bar across the street from the hotel. A bowl of popcorn accompanied the beer he ordered. It occurred to him that he needed salt. That's probably the reason he was so exhausted, he thought. He finished the bowl.

His telephone rang. It was the middlemen from Dubai. He went to meet them, but nothing came of it. They traded in all kinds of things, he gathered. But they were on different planets. His mind was elsewhere. The night was heavy.

His head was pounding when he awoke the next day. He texted Osman. The border was closed for the time being, so he was not coming.

Was Sadiq supposed to sell the mercury on his own?

No, no, Osman replied, he would back him up from Atmeh.

The next day Sadiq walked around aimlessly. The middlemen did not show up in the evening. He went to bed. The night was hot and clammy. His head hurt. The only air getting into the room was through a little opening high up under the ceiling, it was impossible to breathe. He cursed himself for making the trip. Gloom began to take hold.

'What are you waiting for? Answer me!' Sadiq shouted into the phone the next morning. The promise of easy money had not materialized.

'Okay okay,' Osman replied. 'I was driving south toward Al-Harem yesterday . . . then there was a load of shooting. Chaos! Many killed. Sadiq . . . ?'

But Sadiq was no longer listening.

He had no more space in his head.

33

Voices in the Mind

Sadiq was having a hard time focusing.

Streets, roads, squares, culs-de-sac, rules, regulations, taxi meter, weekend rates.

He was spending most of the day at the library in Sandvika. He looked at Arab news sites. He checked mail and messages. He did his homework. He went back online. Osman called him about the middlemen in Dubai. He fantasized. Wrote poetry. Studied. Recalled. Forgot. Hospitals, schools, embassies, churches, mosques. Graveyards, parks, sports arenas.

He was supposed to memorize every single little street in Oslo. Tors Gate, Odins Gate, Løvenskiolds Gate, Gyldenløves Gate. He learned about traffic management systems, outpatient transport, credit management, first aid, customer service, and safety procedures. Can you drop off passengers at a bus stop? Are you required to have a child seat in the car?

'How are things with you?' Osman asked him one morning.

'Ah, this taxi course, you know,' Sadiq answered.

'Ha ha, I should send Mehmut to Norway to give you some competition!'

'I have a load of Mehmuts to compete with. This country is

already crawling with foreigners,' Sadiq wrote back. 'Lots of Syrians now too. You should come over, bring your family.'

Osman paused before responding.

'Yes, I might. I don't know how life is going to be from now on. Both al-Nusra and IS want me working exclusively for them . . . I'm running a huge risk. I should get my family out, my wife and daughters at least, but then there's my parents to think of, I don't know, you're going to have to help me, promise me that, if I have to get out . . . '

Sadiq promised.

September 30 was the date for the exam.

The candidates were issued fifty questions along the lines of 'Which route would you take from the Central Station to Ekeberghallen sports arena?'

At the same time as the new batch of prospective taxi drivers were filling in answers in Oslo, the Federation Council in Moscow was approving the deployment of Russian air power in Syria. Mere hours after the decision, Russia dropped its first bombs over Homs.

After handing in his exam papers, Sadiq took the train to Sandvika, traipsed up to the library, and turned on a PC. A weight had been lifted. The first exam was over. Then he read the day's main news and a heavier burden took its place. The war had escalated. It would be even more difficult to get his daughters out. According to the Russian Ministry of Defense, the attack had targeted IS, and their missiles had hit military installations, vehicles, munitions stores, communications centers, and supply lines.

The Russian media rejoiced in Vladimir Putin finally tidying up Syria. Russia would show the world how to win a war and how to crush terrorists.

Over the following few days, the Russians bombed everything but IS. Only one Russian strike out of ten affected the terrorist organization. Most of the damage was done to the FSA – the only secular force in Syria – and Jabhat al-Nusra, al-Qaida's Syrian arm, along with several other militias linked by their opposition to Assad.

The goal was clear: to keep their ally in the Middle East in power.

The bombs were dropped on the peripheries of territory held by the rebel forces. The tactic was to weaken them sufficiently for government troops to retake lost ground. Several of the American-backed groups, some trained by the CIA, were also bombed.

The militias were quick to regroup, find cover, or conceal themselves, while the civilian population remained unprotected against death from above. Moscow insisted their attacks were surgical strikes against terrorists, but many of the bombs were dropped far behind the front line, often in areas Syrian government forces intended to attack. Hospitals, residential areas, and schools in rebel-controlled towns were hit. No target was too soft.

Thus far in the war, the Syrian air force had been responsible for the greatest loss of life. It had used imprecise weapons like barrel bombs – oil barrels or similar receptacles packed with high explosives and metal shrapnel. These were dropped at a height just out of range of the rebel forces' antiaircraft defenses. Even a gust of wind could determine where they actually landed. They were unguided; they hit where they hit, detonating with devastating force. A red-hot, flying metal fragment could sever a child's arm, or cut the child in two. When you saw a barrel being dropped from above, you had thirty seconds before it hit the ground.

Thirty seconds.

While Assad's pilots were dependent upon clear weather to drop their explosives, the Russians' airplanes were far more advanced. Protection was no longer to be found in a layer of fog or clouds.

Even though the Russian attacks were heavy, it was impossible to win the war from the air. By autumn 2015, there were approximately 150,000 rebel soldiers on the ground in Syria, excluding IS. Many were convinced Islamists with a strong belief in paradise and what it had to offer. No militias, none whatsoever, planned to give in.

Russia wanted to weaken the forces the West could conceivably work or negotiate or bargain with. Putin wanted the world to be left with one choice: Assad or IS.

The West was in a more difficult position. It was looking for someone to take over from the Islamic State if it was bombed out of existence. They found no one.

'Hell is raining down upon us! Hell is landing on our heads!'

'Calm down, talk to me, my heart is dry, I'm listening . . . ' Sadiq responded.

'The Russians are slaughtering us! They're only targeting civilians! They're bombing children! It's us, us they're hitting. We, who are against IS! They let IS carry on, while we die!'

Osman sent new reports daily. October was filled with atrocities.

'They're blowing our ashes across the country. We're sinking deeper and deeper. The chaos is also in our minds. We don't know what to do.'

One night he rang in tears.

'The building was completely destroyed, a deep hole, a crater, it was hit by two rockets. One to open it up, the other to kill. They want to get every one of us. In the end only IS and Assad will be left!'

'Who was hit?'

'Our friends! They have children, they have families!'

'May Allah welcome them,' Sadiq said.

'If I had to take the devil by the hand to beat the Russians and Assad, I would do it. I swear to Allah, I'm ready . . . but I'm very tired, it's chaos here . . . '

Sadiq stayed up late every night. His dread was intensified by the fear that Raqqa, where the girls lived, would be carpet-bombed. He alternated between giving up on the girls one day and being overwhelmed by a desperate urge to rescue them the next.

He heard more strange sounds in the apartment. Was that from the stairwell? Outside the window? All these noises were making him jump. Were they also audible when the family was here? Was there an explanation for each of them, the refrigerator, the dishwasher, a pipe, a cupboard door, a branch against the window, someone outside, someone in the apartment above, an echo in the entranceway? Or was it that damned jinn, half a step ahead of him, laughing?

He tried to calm himself. He tried to think straight. No, he was not afraid, he was not. He had always been viewed as having ice in his veins. But the October night was so dark, he could not shake his unease. His thoughts turned to the Syrians who had been killed. Where were their souls now? Why did they not come and speak to him? Tell him whether they had entered paradise or hell, so he could know how it actually was. Imagine if those on the other side could let him know what steps to take. Those who had left this world, had they managed to say goodbye before the bomb fell? He thought about Osman's friends. Children killed in their beds. Mothers rocking babies to sleep. Death from above, had it come suddenly, without warning? Or had they heard the airplanes first? Had they managed to call out 'Allahu Akbar'?

He thought about his dead friends from the war in Somalia. There were so many. Why did they not come to him now and ask: *How are things with you?* They never did that. He often thought of a childhood friend, a boy who would forever remain a teenager. Sadiq had been the watch commander and was informed of a man who wanted to come into the camp but did not know the password. 'Shoot him,' Sadiq, only a teenager himself, had said. The next morning he saw the body.

Oh, these blasted sounds. They were around him the entire time. While all he wanted was to hear Sara breathing next to him.

The second week in October, a few days after the missile strike that had wiped out the building with Osman's friends inside, the Syrian told Sadiq that IS had withdrawn from a large area it held close to Hama.

It took only a few hours to realize why. Osman described the first coordinated attack by Russian airplanes and Syrian ground forces.

'At four this afternoon Russian planes began bombing the territory al-Nusra and FSA control in Hama. Oh God, this is so terrible!'

The next day: 'At six this morning regime forces entered the area.'

The Russians were bombing the way for Assad to take back control of the country step by step. The IS retreat prior to the operation testified to a trade-off: *Pull out if you want to avoid casualties, we're taking over.* IS and Assad were perfect enemies. Unlike the local militias, which desired regime change, it was all the same to IS who sat in Damascus – as long as they could run the caliphate as they liked. The Islamists had no intention of taking over all of Syria now.

'A dirty game,' Osman hammered into the telephone.

One day he wrote: 'NATO air-dropped twenty tons of ammunition, provisions and fresh water to the FSA.'

It was sorely needed. The opposition forces were running low on supplies now that the roads were impassable.

'They dropped a further thirty tons, but in the wrong location, it all landed in ISIS hands! I'm not kidding, NATO gifted the supplies to ISIS!'

Osman believed the world was conspiring against the Syrian people – that Russia, Assad, and NATO were together against the ordinary Syrian. At least that was how it looked on the ground.

The next message Sadiq received was a picture of a corpse. He had no trouble recognizing the man. It was Hamza, Osman's best friend, the one they had called the Lion. He lay outstretched, a red mark on his face, like a bruise. His face was framed by black curly hair and an unkempt beard that was dusty looking, or perhaps he had begun to go gray.

'Aaaaa I am hardly able to write this. Hamza, you remember him? The Lion in al-Nusra, killed north of Hama. He was with us when we went to the court in al-Dana. May Allah accept him as a martyr. Console me! I'm crying. My family is crying. He left behind two wives and seven children.'

Sadiq remembered Hamza as a force of nature; like Osman, in his early thirties.

He wrote back, 'God accepted him into paradise. How was he killed? A sniper? Regime air strike? The Russians?'

'Russian air force.'

'May Allah raze the house of the pilot.'

'He wouldn't listen to me. He never did, there was nothing I could do. Life has become miserable for us. For me and my family . . . our circumstances worsen by the day.'

*

The only woman in the Norwegian IS contingent maintaining a presence on social media was Aisha. While the sisters had not shared anything publicly, she published updates with reports on life in Raqqa on Facebook. The first post came in the middle of October 2015.

'I've noticed there are numerous people who want to know what it's actually like living in IS so I've decided to write about it a little, in order to give a more genuine perspective.'

She wrote in Norwegian. The posts seemed intended for Norwegian girls considering traveling and were a sort of *IS for Dummies*. She had titled the initial post 'Life and the Building of a Society in the Islamic State' and described how every district had its own administration, schools, court, police force, hospital, and welfare system.

'The criteria in order to receive assistance is of course in accordance with Islamic guidelines,' she emphasized. All that was not good in the state was the fault of the enemy: 'The enemy's brutal bombing of the civilian population and the hospitals is the reason for the lack of resources and equipment.' Enemy attack was also to blame for schools not functioning. The descriptions that followed were similar to what other IS girls had posted online. You were given a house or an apartment 'dependent on availability,' everything was free, the refrigerator, microwave, washing machine, air-conditioning, and TV.

The portrayal of the caliphate was almost becoming a genre all of its own: Welcome to the lovely life where everything is free and, moreover, helps you get to paradise.

Sadiq had first promised he would vacate the apartment by October 1, then he'd been granted an extension to November 1. But October turned to November and his possessions still lay strewn about.

He awoke to hoarfrost and a chill in the air; the temperature would drop below freezing at night, and the white shimmering layer covering the ground would then melt in the course of the day. Autumn was at its most beautiful, with colors in bright yellow and red, and a breeze that cleared the air. One day, when he finally forced himself to start packing, he came across the gray-flecked beanie he had put away in May. It was time to pull it back down over his ears.

One evening in early November, as darkness fell outside, he was sitting at the computer. He heard a voice in his head: 'Here's some advice. Get the girls out! It's going to get worse. This is only the beginning. This war will not quiet down for a long time. The girls must get out.'

The voice continued, 'To think straight you have to forget they're alive. You have to imagine you will ship two corpses home.'

He got to his feet. He had to leave. He had to get them out now. Everything but the war had been emptied of meaning. At five in the morning, he sent a text to a friend. 'I have to travel to Hatay, then on to Dubai, before returning to Hatay, then . . . . into Syria . . . If I survive I'll see you again, if not just try to do what you can for my children. Best regards, Sadiq Abdallah Juma.'

A few hours later he sent a new text: 'I'm going to sleep now. Think about it for eight hours and get back to me.'

His friend texted back as soon as he woke up: 'Traveling to Raqqa now sounds ***extremely dangerous.'

Sadiq wrote back saying MI6 had requested he come. That the British were going to help him with the rescue operation. Four agents from Dubai were going to assist. British Intelligence wanted to recruit him.

A few days later he got in touch again. 'I'm in Raqqa. Unbelievable.'

'You're joking!' his friend replied.

'I'm serious.'

'Keep your head down!'

Later that day his friend heard that a mutual acquaintance had run into Sadiq at the local Oslo shopping center.

Sadiq the poet had taken hold of his mind.

He had met MI6 in Hatay, he said. Four agents had flown in from

Dubai to meet him. They had outlined a plan on a grand scale for extracting his daughters, he revealed.

He said he had passed the taxi driver's exam. Now all he needed was a written statement from the police stating he had no criminal record and a certificate of health from a doctor, and he could start applying for jobs. But he spent his days at the computer.

In the wake of the terror attacks on Paris in mid-November, the president of France, François Hollande, vowed vengeance on IS. Two days later, French fighters struck twenty targets, including command centers, recruitment bases, munitions depots, and training camps. But the problem for France, and for the coalition, was that there were still four hundred thousand civilians in Raqqa who were not allowed to leave. The hospitals were in danger of running out of blood.

As the situation for the girls, and their babies, seemed increasingly perilous and life in Bærum lacked direction, Sadiq became more focused on traveling again. The rescue operations he rehearsed in his head grew ever more spectacular. British and Somali intelligence services were involved, as well as French counterterrorist units. He also featured. 'I have to go in myself to save my daughters. That's just how it is,' he told friends. But he needed to get some money together.

He was broke. The refrigerator was empty. He sent the bulk of each welfare payment to Sara and the household in Somalia every month. He had already alienated friends by borrowing too much; he could not ask them for more.

The newspaper was his only option. His contacts in Raqqa had tipped him off about a big story, he told them, and promised photographs. Bingo, 3,000 kroner in his hand.

Dagbladet ran the story on December 18, 2015. 'Exclusive – 272 IS fighters lying low in Europe. 150 more terrorists on the way.' Sadiq's inventions had again led to front-page news.

'*Dagbladet* can reveal details of two waves of IS terrorists specially trained to strike at targets in Europe. The first wave is reportedly in place. The second contingent remains for the moment with IS in Syria, having completed training at a camp situated between Sinjar and Mosul in Iraq.' *Dagbladet* wrote that the information had come from 'a source with intimate knowledge of IS activities.'

The journalists could also relate, based on what Sadiq had told them, that the first wave had originally numbered 300 but 28 of these had lost their lives in Syria, in bombings, and other acts of war. This left 272, who were under 'instructions to lie low.'

The second wave was for the moment in Syria: '112 have completed their training' and the terrorists were traveling 'in 11 cars.' The article did not lack details. 'One group has been trained to martyr themselves by carrying out suicide attacks. The individuals have been described to *Dagbladet* as "completely brainwashed." The other type of terrorists have been drilled in performing acts of terror using firearms and fitted with suicide belts.' The journalists added, 'Both methods were utilized in the terrorist attacks in Paris on November 13.'

The journalists wrote that 'PST confirm that the information was known to them prior to *Dagbladet* contacting them.'

This was incorrect. PST had denied any knowledge of the story. The journalist who had been in touch with them had been so doubtful about the veracity of the information that he revealed the source of the story to PST: the father from Bærum.

The newspaper decided to run the story all the same. The spread gave the impression of *Dagbladet* being well-informed, of almost being on the ground in Syria, and being privy to IS terror plans. And it sold newspapers, as playing on fear often does. Terrorism experts in Oslo shrugged. The details were too precise to be true. It was not uncommon in the Arab world to use precise, preferably irregular numbers, to grant a dubious news story credibility: 300 terrorists, minus 28 killed, 272 left. A photograph of a building and a large crater accompanied the text. The caption read: 'A source, who has previously given reliable information, claims that planning related to the attack in Europe took place at this building in Raqqa. Photo: private.'

Sadiq and Osman had delivered to order: something about jihad-ists, preferably Norwegian, with pictures.

The third holiday season without the girls was drawing close.

Ismael returned home from Vestfold University College. He had changed his major midway through the semester. Nanotechnology was not the right fit after all. He was now aiming to become an automation engineer, designing, creating, developing, and managing automated systems, which the prospectus stated meant 'systems collecting data from sensors, supervising, controlling, and regulating processes according to given rules and purposes.'

Concrete. Tangible. Verifiable. Ismael had found his niche.

Just before Christmas, after several months without a word, Leila got in touch. It took its customary form, as though nothing in particular was happening around her.

'Hi, Ismael, what's happening, no more messages?'

She went on. 'Can I ask you a question, and you promise to answer totally honestly? You say you don't believe in Islam, right? Are you at least searching for something to believe in? Like, seriously, because if you don't believe Islam is the truth then there must be a truth out there, right? Are you looking for it? Your niece is doing fine . . . thanks for asking, 4 months old now.'

'Can't take more of this,' Ismael wrote back. 'Whenever you get in touch I'm reminded of 2 sisters I'm never going to meet again. So congrats on the child but just stop contacting me. I believe I will revert to whatever I was BEFORE I was born when I die. That's it.'

'Ismael . . . I never thought of you as a pessimist, what do you mean we'll never see each other again? Never say never. I asked if you were searching for the truth because that's what you told me last time (how you wanted to find something to believe in) because as people we need "something" to believe in no matter what it may be. "I believe I will revert to whatever I was BEFORE I was born when I die." Do you mean to tell me that you're living and have ambitions to become nothing?'

Ismael replied after an hour. 'Yep. I think you misunderstand, nothingness is neither good nor bad, nothingness is perfect harmony. Think about how beautiful nothing actually is.'

Leila did not respond.

After an hour, Ismael asked, 'Are you being bombed?'

A week later he wrote: '?'

Then he noticed Leila had deactivated her account.

There was nothing more after that.

34

Legacy

The brain is built up of experiences. They start in the womb.

A newborn can recognize her mother's voice. After a week she recognizes her smell, after a few more her face. At two months a child can raise her head when lying on her stomach. She can distinguish between herself and her surroundings. At three months a baby can signal when she wants to be cuddled. At four months she can interact visually. By five months she is able to interpret the feelings behind facial expressions. A six-month-old baby will begin to show interest in other babies. She will be able to sit by herself, in some cases will have begun to crawl.

At seven months she has formed a bond with her parents, if she has been given the opportunity. The world develops fast. The brain is quickly furnished. Experiences will figure into language, logic, and systems. At eight months old she will learn to be skeptical of strangers and to check with her parents to learn if the newcomer is *one of us*. Thoughts will begin to form, which in time will turn into beliefs and convictions. At nine months old she is able to stand.

That was when Leila called. 'Asiyah just stood up on her feet!'

Sara cried, 'Oh, how wonderful!'

When the girls called their mother, it was to update her about the babies' progress. Asiyah had been through several bouts of illness, but Leila was now confident she had fully recovered. Little Sara did not have much of an appetite. But things were much improved.

In autumn 2016, the two sisters, their little girls, and their husbands were living together in a large collective, with Norwegian, Swedish, and British couples. Along with an increasing number of children.

'It's so nice, Mom,' Leila told Sara. 'We're never alone.'

The women made food, watched each other's children, ran errands or cleaned the house, while the men carried out the tasks the Islamic State ordered them to. The sense of sisterhood seemed strong. If one of them had a headache, another one did the dishes, if one of them had a toothache, another would fetch her painkillers, the girls told their mother. They cared for one another's children, washing them, changing them, feeding them, and putting them to bed.

Cousins Asiyah and Sara lived a life like their mothers, indoors.

Their grandmother asked about the bombing.

'Mom, it's not a problem. We live in a solid house, and we have a really good basement, a proper bomb shelter, don't worry.'

When they heard the airplanes, they just went down, they assured her, plain and simple, an everyday occurrence.

On social media IS girls were preoccupied with appearing unafraid. The bombing was more an irritation than anything else. 'Three bombs already in the space of an hour. What kind of animals bomb people at nine in the morning. I hate America,' wrote one British girl. Umm Jihad shrugged it off: 'A bomb landed literally right behind me as I was walking home. Bombs are noisy is all I can say.'

Three winters, three springs. Without them.

The girls hardly got in touch throughout 2016. They called on Muslim holy days and that was it. Was that the only times they were allowed? Sara wondered. But she did not ask. She never asked anything that might annoy that dangerous group who were no doubt listening in.

Sadiq and Sara had been prepared for the worst for a long time. Readying themselves mentally for the day when the news came that their daughters were dead. Sometimes Sadiq thought it would be for the best. It would give them closure. They could then get on with their lives. Sara could return home.

When she rang from Hargeisa and said she missed him, he cut her off.

'You know where I am. If you miss me, then come home.' She was the one who had chosen to move, now she wanted sympathy and to be consoled for making that choice. She knew what he meant, that she should come home, enroll the boys in school.

Find the girls! That was what Sara had said from day one. *Save them!* For Sadiq that had become the meaning of life.

He was diminished in Sara's eyes, he knew that. He had failed as a father, as a man, as the head of the family. This was the punishment. They had left him. His daughters. His wife. His youngest sons. Ismael. He was alone.

'Your wife will soon return,' his friends said, to comfort him. 'Your daughters too.'

There was little sign of that happening.

But his sons wanted to come home. In Hargeisa they spent most of their time in front of the PlayStation in the living room. Or they played football using a dented plastic bottle. Their parents had argued the previous summer about where they should live. Sadiq had been prepared to compromise. One more year, then they had to come home, in plenty of time for the next school year. *Fine*, Sara had said.

She kept her word. A month before school finished for the summer, she and the boys landed at Oslo airport. The very next day Isaq and Jibril were back at school in their old classes. They were given close follow-up from the school and Child Welfare. The goal was for them to continue at their age level.

Ismael returned from college and took a summer job at a local supermarket. The three boys shared the bedroom while Sara and Sadiq slept in the living room. Ismael whispered to his little brothers at night: 'Norway is where we belong.' Isaq and Jibril nodded in the darkness.

Ismael had no contact with his sisters any longer. The last time he had heard from Leila was the message before New Year, when he had sent back a question mark. And received no response. From Ayan he hadn't had any news for a year.

In August he took a break from his supermarket job. He had been picked as one of a hundred participants in Emax, an entrepreneurial program for young people organized by Innovation Norway. The program aimed to inspire and enable 'young entrepreneurs to continue developing their dreams and striving to realize their goals and visions.' The course concluded with a weekend in Lillehammer, where the young people would get the 'tools to develop themselves and create their own, and Norway's, future.' The hundred who were picked out were divided into ten groups to undertake tasks set by different companies. Their ideas and their development would be evaluated and a winner chosen; previous winners had been invited to London, Silicon Valley, and Shanghai to 'network and learn more about building and scaling a business.'

Ismael's group did not win, but it had been a memorable weekend. He posted a photograph of his new friends on Facebook, all of them standing with their arms around one another. Ismael was dressed in the same style as the blond boys with him, in a light blue shirt and jeans, looking the part of a young businessman. '@emaxnorway fantastic experience!' he wrote.

When summer was over, he boarded the train back to college to start the second year of his automation engineering course. When he got back, he changed the background picture on his iPhone. The white writing on a gray background summed up his situation: *Be willing to walk alone. Many who started with you, won't finish with you.*

Being back together again as mother, father, and children was not all rosy. They had lost the old and spacious apartment, and the one-bedroom unit that Sadiq had been allocated by the county when he was alone was overcrowded. Neither was Sara happy with the location or the neighbors. The apartment was in a block of flats for social welfare clients and most of the residents were single. There were alcoholics, drug addicts, and a lot of noise. People could be heard making dinner at three in the morning, playing loud music all night, or arguing. Sara complained to a friend that there were syringes and broken bottles everywhere. 'It's no place for children,' she stressed. She went to NAV and asked for a new apartment. The family was told to look for one themselves. The local authority could subsidize the rent, but they would be responsible for finding a place themselves. Sadiq searched online and they went to viewings, but they were refused as tenants at each turn. *Norwegians* don't like Somalis, Sara concluded.

But Somalis like Somalis, and as soon as Sara returned to Norway she got back in touch with her circle of friends in Bærum. After fifteen years in the country, she had built up a large network of female compatriots, many of whom were members of the Somali Women's Association.

On her return, Sara had wanted to lance the boil. Sadiq had made the Somali community aware of his anger at Mustafa, the young Koran teacher, whom he held responsible for the radicalization of his daughters. 'He is the start of our nightmare,' he used to say. The association viewed Sadiq's accusations against Mustafa as criticism of them. They were the ones who had hired him, after all, and had chosen to keep him on as a teacher – even after the girls left. If their radicalization and journey to Syria had anything to do with him, then surely others would also have departed, they argued.

Sara had attempted to get hold of Mustafa after the girls left, but the young man, whose salary had been partly financed by her household budget, refused to meet her.

Eventually he sent her a message via one of her friends saying, "I had nothing to do with their journey to Syria. Their leaving came as a shock to me. May God protect you all.'

Well, so it wasn't him, then, Sara concluded.

Sadiq, on the other hand, was reprimanded on social media for having accused the Koran teacher of terror recruitment, thereby bringing shame on all Somalis. It was time to close ranks.

Rumors abounded. When the criticism in the media had come out, the Tawfiiq Mosque had asked Mustafa to stay away for a while. The religious leaders were worried. The mosque, like others in Oslo, was occupied with fronting the fight against radicalization. They dispatched a young religious leader named Abdibasid Ali Mohammed, a handsome, well-spoken, well-educated Somali, to participate in panel discussions on how to combat extremism. He was a willing participant, as long as he did not have to shake the hands of any female members on a panel.

Mustafa was interrogated by PST because of the sisters' trip. PST had received tip-offs about his alleged ties to al-Shabaab, to IS, and terror recruitment activity. His friends were also called in for questioning.

One of them, a teenager closely involved with the Prophet's Ummah, was first asked some questions of a general nature before being asked if he knew Mustafa.

'Mustafa . . . ? No . . . '

'So how come you've stayed the night at his place, then?' the policeman responded.

The young man realized that they must have been in possession of a lot of information, as he had spent the night on Mustafa's sofa only a single time. Halfway through the interview, a man entered the room, a tall, fair-haired Norwegian who spoke fluent Somali and had detailed knowledge of clans, ethnic groupings, and movements in Somalia. The teenager was impressed. Sometime later, following a visit from PST to his parents' home and a subsequent dressing-down from his father for ruining the opportunities Norway had given him, he made the decision to withdraw from the extremist network.

Teaching the Koran was not his main source of income. He also had a job as a security guard. Long after the sisters had left, the young Islamist was employed at the University of Oslo at its Blindern campus. In his dark blue uniform adorned with NOKAS, the name of the security company, he made the rounds of the faculty buildings at night.

PST searched but found no evidence against Mustafa.

He merely gave Koran lessons, everyone said. He was a good Muslim, he collected money for war victims, spent time with troubled youths. He sometimes drove around picking up boys who needed guidance. He might go to a bar and offer an inebriated Somali a lift home. They could have a chat on the way. Did the boy need help? Did he have problems?

Mustafa came across as a brother. He *was* a brother. He stood with open arms and a ready ear. Then things would come full circle, the helping hand would tighten its grip. It was time to give something back.

One who was eventually taken in, arrested, and charged was Ubaydullah Hussain – 'Allah's little slave' and Dilal's former husband.

In September 2016, he became the first Norwegian to be charged with terror recruitment. The Director of Public Prosecutions believed there was sufficient evidence to prove he had recruited and facilitated the travel of would-be terrorists to Syria. Several of those he had helped had later been killed in action, according to the indictment. He had made travel arrangements, purchased clothing and equipment, helped procure tickets, and put the departed in touch with other contacts. 'He was in direct communication with individuals with ties to ISIS in order to ensure that those traveling were picked up and transported across the border in Turkey,' the charges stated. PST believed him to be in effect a member of IS until his imprisonment.

The Prophet's Ummah lay with a broken spine. Ubaydullah was in custody, Bastian and several others were dead, most of the other members were in Syria. Arfan Bhatti, who Aisha had called 'the glue of the group,' was still a godfather of sorts, but the Prophet's Ummah no longer arranged demonstrations and the Facebook group was no more. They still met over a meal, preferably at one another's homes.

Arfan Bhatti was among those who had kept in close contact with Hisham in Syria. Many no longer dared chat with the Norwegians

waging jihad, wary of coming to the attention of the security services. Because PST hounded the young Islamists, paying visits to
their families, uncovering other activities of a criminal nature they
were involved in, activities that could more easily lead to a conviction than terror recruitment. It appeared to have an effect. In 2016,
as far as PST knew, no one left Norway for Syria. While the way to
paradise no longer went through Syria, the radicalization continued.

For young women, the pious wave continued too. There were
girls in different parts of Oslo who had considered traveling at the
same time as Ayan and Leila but had remained behind. Many now
agreed that IS was not true Islam. Only in the event of a state being
created that really was proper Islam would they journey down.

One of the mosques the strict teenage practitioners were drawn
to was Tawfiiq. 'Going to the mosque twice a week used to be
enough,' one of the girls in the Tawfiiq Sisterhood related. 'Learn
about the Koran on the weekends, behave correctly, and wear
a shawl, or at least have one on when you arrived at the mosque
and take it off on the way out. Now the girls practically live in the
mosque, kids in their early teens.'

What were they looking for?

Sisterhood. A place to belong. Paradise. To follow the Prophet. To
marry young, because 'marriage was half the religion.' Many parents
were proud when their daughters began practicing their religion
with more enthusiasm, but the line between this increased activity
and radicalization was thin. You did not suddenly wake up one day
a fanatic; it was a direction you grew in. The girls in the extremist
networks influenced one another, supported one another when the
world opposed them. They excluded those who disagreed with them,
dismissing them as either kuffar or friends of kuffar. They lent their
ears to preachers claiming the West would not be satisfied until there
were no Muslims left. And why would they not, when the West was
becoming increasingly preoccupied with what Muslims should and
should not do, what they could and could not wear? There was fear
and ignorance on both sides, the more moderate stated.

Ayan and Leila had sailed on the early wave of radicalization that led them to Syria. They left precisely when the doors were wide open, both out of Norway and into Syria. Had they waited a year or two, they might not have been borne along but been content to be among these pious new practitioners, living in and at the same time parallel to Norwegian society.

Leila called to wish the family a happy Eid al-Fitr in September. She complained about her leg hurting and being in pain when walking. Getting to the internet café to call was a trial, she told Sara. The foot she had been shot in had never healed properly. Otherwise everything was good.

Sara had accepted that the girls did not want to return home. She was not interested in digging any more into it or finding out who was to blame. She believed her daughters had misunderstood something or other in Islam. That was all.

In Sadiq's mind, there was no room for acceptance. Anxiety had taken root in him body and soul. He had dreamed of getting his old boring life back – of the boys returning, of Sara returning – but now that they were back, he thought his life was just that, boring.

Osman and he continued their nightly conversations and indulgence in daydreams. 'They're getting out, whether they want to or not,' he told his Syrian helper.

'It's out of my hands,' Osman admitted.

Sadiq could no longer rely on his assistance. Smuggling had become harder. Everything had become difficult. Turkey had partially closed its borders. Where there had been barbed-wire fencing with holes in it there was now in places a seven-foot-high concrete wall. The border station of Bab al-Hawa where Osman used to cross had been damaged by a missile. At the other frontier posts, he did not have a permit to cross, or else they were under Kurdish control. Osman was stranded in Syria.

They went back and forth analyzing who and when and how and what would happen in Raqqa. How long would Raqqa hold out? Who would take the city? How long would IS survive? And if IS was driven out, who would take its place?

Many of the local groups that were cooperating in the fight against IS had little in common; they were enemies who had entered a tactical alliance. When IS was defeated, new wars would break out. There were so many competing interests on the ground that any solution seemed far off. Turkey, the United States, Russia, Iran, Iraq, and Saudi Arabia; Hezbollah, Kurdish guerrillas, Iranian Shia Muslims, and a multitude of Salafists, Wahabists, Islamists, and jihadists were all fighting for their own interests on an ever more bloody battlefield. And then there was Assad.

Five years of international impotence had passed. There had been negotiations and condemnations, diplomats and politicians were hamstrung. There was only one thing that never let up: death from the skies.

Assad was left in peace to massacre his own people. The images were shared on social media: people who were alive yesterday but not today.

It was primarily the rebel-controlled areas that Assad bombed. In autumn 2016, the inhabitants of the caliphate still lived in relative security. Attitudes became reinforced. Only one truth existed and it was never opposed. The jihadist wives shared a mentality and influenced one another. Girls from modest backgrounds could brag of their slaves on Twitter: 'My house help (slave) showed me how to bake Syrian bread. Today I finally made my own,' Muslimah4Life wrote.

Access to open sources about daily life in Raqqa had diminished. Twitter had put an effective monitoring system in place to quickly close IS accounts. In addition, the caliphate placed its own restrictions on use of the internet.

The good times were long gone. The standard of living sank, even for the foreign fighters. From late summer 2016, IS no longer shared a border with Turkey. At the start of the year, the Islamic State had announced a 50 percent cut in soldiers' salaries. The reason was 'extraordinary circumstances.' Local fighters now received $200 a month while their foreign counterparts could expect $400. The foreigners had constituted an overclass of sorts in Raqqa. They had moved into the best neighborhoods. Some of them, like Ayan, had brought money along with them from home and could live better than the local population as long as the funds lasted.

Over the course of the autumn, several of the supply lines into Raqqa were shut. Prices soared. People lined up for hours for a pail of soup or a sack of rice, in queues IS wanted to hide but that Raqqa Is Being Slaughtered Silently continued to report on.

Even though a woman was to remain in the home, there was a lot of work that could be imposed on her. For the girls in Raqqa, this meant making food from early in the morning until late at night. Ayan and the sisters prepared meals for the fighters in large cooking pots. Rice, meat, and vegetables. Potatoes in deep fryers. Chicken casseroles. Fried fish from the Euphrates.

The food was made at home or in large communal kitchens. At dinnertime the freshly prepared food was trucked out to soldiers defending the state at the front or at checkpoints.

The sisters had completely embraced Islamic State ideology concerning obedience to one's husband. Ayan, who back in Norway had been such an advocate of gender equality, told a friend from home she chatted with that she was open to Hisham taking another wife.

'Wouldn't you be jealous?' her friend asked.

'No, we need to make more babies,' Ayan replied. 'If the war is a long one we'll need new soldiers.'

Personally, she was hoping God would bless her with sons.

Both Aisha and Emira had remarried after Bastian was killed. Aisha had given birth to a son after Salahuddin's death.

'What more could you want than to be able to raise the next generation of lions the in Islamic State who will go on to spread Islam?' Umm Muthanna wrote on Twitter. According to the counterterrorism research foundation Quilliam, there were now just over thirty thousand pregnant women in the caliphate.

From a young age children were taught to revere the state and hate nonbelievers. Intensive study of the Koran was required from early on. School, which started at age six, was an instrument to teach them to obey. The children were to be indoctrinated to be loyal subjects, to become the new preachers, the new fighters. History, philosophy, and civics, referred to as 'the methodology of atheism,' were removed from the curricula, as were art and music. In geography, they learned solely about the Islamic world, while physical education was replaced with 'jihad training,' which focused on martial arts and shooting.

The teachers had also to be reeducated. All the laws of physics and chemistry originated with God when he created the world. All evolutionary teaching was out. Darwin's name was taboo. The instructions were detailed, the word *watan*, 'homeland,' and all appellations for Syria were to be replaced by 'the Islamic State,' 'Land of the Muslims,' or 'Al-Sham province.' Examples in mathematics that had anything to do with interest rates, democracy, or elections had to go, and units of calculation were now in tanks, artillery, and bullets. All images not in accordance with sharia were eliminated: women's faces, uncovered body parts, non-Islamic dress.

In order to achieve an ideal Islamic society, as Muhammad had outlined, you had to start with the children. The best boys in each age group were given special training. They watched people being stoned, crucified, and beheaded. Witnessing such events was presented as a privilege, and being allowed to participate was a greater privilege still. Small kids who distinguished themselves were granted the honor of handing the executioner the knife he would use to sever the head of victims; in some cases they were allowed to carry out the killing themselves. Children were trained to spy on their family and neighbors, to be messengers, fighters at the front, foot soldiers, suicide bombers, or snipers. Small hands were trained to make explosives and handle light weapons, rifles, submachine guns, and grenade launchers.

The extreme was becoming the ordinary.

Girls received their own special upbringing. They couldn't be Cubs of the Caliphate; instead they were to be Pearls of the Caliphate.

The Salafist rhetoric gleamed.

What is more precious than a pearl? If you owned one, would you leave it lying around, would you allow it to be soiled, would you leave it outside the door for people to touch, even steal?

No, you would wrap it up, place it in a jewelry case, on silk or velvet, and lock it away so as not to tempt thieves. You would take it out only on special occasions, when the circumstances were safe.

Women were pearls. So beautiful, so precious.

Best keep the box locked.

IS set a whole host of rules prescribing the upbringing of girls. They were to have some education but not too much. When very small, they were to stay close to their mothers, learning virtue by example. From the ages of seven to nine, a girl was to study the Koran, mathematics, and Islamic natural sciences. From ten to twelve, she was to learn the fundamentals of Islamic law, particularly the parts concerning women. She was to learn to sew, knit, and cook. From thirteen to fifteen, she was to study sharia, Islamic history, the life and doctrine of Muhammad in depth, as well as housework and child rearing. Marriage should not occur too late in life, possibly at nine years of age, which was the lower limit, while sixteen was viewed as the ideal.

Young girls were to be raised to 'build our ummah, produce men, and send them to do fierce battle,' according to the IS publication *Dabiq*. The children of the caliph were to be drilled from an early age to obey the caliph and despise nonbelievers, to be inured to violence and ready for war.

'I know someone . . . they could rescue them . . . they could drive in . . . '

It was Osman. 'Hide them in the car . . . drive them out . . . over the border . . . let me speak to them.'

Osman warned Sadiq not to get ahead of himself. 'If the Kurds take Raqqa they're done for. The Kurds are like devils . . . they won't spare two black women in niqabs. Nor their children . . . now, listen . . . '

Their children.

Two little girls experiencing things for the first time. They toddled around. Held on to the edges of tables. They laughed. Cried. They had both turned one over the summer.

Humans are social animals. From birth a child seeks out human contact. In the very first weeks of life, a child's brain begins storing expectations, while the mother produces hormones reinforcing her capacity to offer care, intimacy, and attention.

Osman had written to Sadiq: 'When they have children they will come to their senses.'

But not Ayan and Leila.

In the eye of the storm, life went on. When the men were at the front, the women stayed at home. At mealtimes they sat around large plastic sheets, eating from the same platter, with children playing around them.

For infants and toddlers it is the small world around them that matters. Even under extreme conditions, children can feel safe as long as their routines are maintained, as long as the grown-ups are not out of whack.

At the same time, a child's brain is vulnerable. Dramatic events and fear are stored in the mind as fragmented images, scary pieces, which return as nightmares and trauma. Experience influences that part of the brain where thoughts and belief systems are formed, where reason is constructed.

For the time being the two cousins were living among their playmates.

But a stolen house is not a safe one. It would soon come to an end. The caliphate would be history.

Two cousins.

With a heavy legacy.

The jewelry box will break open, the silk will tear.

They will discover that hell is here. Hell is us.

If they survive.

The Basis of the Book

It was Sadiq Juma who wanted the story of his daughters told.

'I want people to recognize the danger signs,' he said. 'We were blind. We thought it would pass. Now we know better.'

He was seeking better cooperation among parents, schools, mosques, and the police.

For me, the most important question was: How could this happen?

The title came easily. Two sisters. Everything centered around them.

The first thing I did was listen to the family and write down their stories. I then interviewed friends and classmates, teachers, principals, and other adults whom the girls had been in contact with in early adolescence. I subsequently attempted to trace the path that led Ayan and Leila to radical Islam, to try to understand what inspired the two sisters to travel to Syria.

Their parents allowed me access to the papers the sisters left behind. From these I selected essays, report cards, and class photographs, as well as notes from Koran lessons and evening courses at Islam Net, in addition to the minutes of the committee meetings, the missionary instructions, the niqab petition, and printouts of e-mails. Ayan's orderliness was a benefit to me – she made lengthy lists of volunteers she had recruited to Islam Net, complete with telephone numbers and e-mail addresses. I was consequently able to contact a wide number of people who knew her. Similarly, I got in touch with all her friends on Facebook, all her followers on Twitter, some of those following her friend Aisha, and several of the people featured in the class photographs.

I went to meetings at mosques in Oslo, of Islam Net, and of other religious youth organizations, looking for traces of the girls. I got in touch with Somali associations and approached Muslim Facebook groups seeking information about the sisters.

In this way, a network of friends and acquaintances slowly emerged. Together with the parents, and written sources, it provided the most important basis for information.

Because the sisters did not contribute directly to the book, e-mail exchanges and written conversations they participated in proved invaluable. Not least, the logs of conversations between them and their brother on Messenger, Viber, and WhatsApp gave important insight into how the girls think and what judgments they made along the way. What they communicated was an echo of IS propaganda, but the sisters do not seem to have felt they were individually supervised. Had that been the case, a number of things told in confidence, not featured in the book, would have been excluded. I view their words as the picture the sisters wished to paint of the caliphate.

I sent several requests to the girls asking them to provide background of their own on their decision to journey to Syria and to present how life is there. I received no answer. I also attempted to reach them via other parties with contacts in Raqqa. The sisters responded with silence.

There may be any number of reasons for this. One is purely procedural: IS members were not allowed to be interviewed unless they cleared it with the communications department of the Islamic State. IS conveyed information either through spokesmen or by controlled interviews with representatives of the leadership. Interviews with rank-and-file members not approved by the leadership were carried out only anonymously. The sisters could not utilize anonymity; they were completely identifiable to IS.

When their father came to take his daughters home in November 2013, the sisters made a clear choice: They decided to remain in the Islamic State. They said they believed in the project and have since said, written, and demonstrated that they stand by that point of view.

Apart from their father's first rescue attempt, which they refused to join, they did not know of or participate in his plans. This is clearly evident from the log of communications between Sadiq and Osman. Kidnapping the daughters against their will was always the intention. On the logs with Ismael, the sisters also appear to stand completely behind the caliphate. They have never, either verbally or in writing, expressed any negative views of the Islamic State. They have, as is patently obvious from this book, broken with their father politically and religiously. His remarks about them or the Islamic State should therefore in no way be a burden for them in IS-controlled Syria.

How should you portray people you have never met, who do not want to tell you their side of a story?

One guiding rule is to begin with actions: What did they do? When? What do we know from written sources? What do people around them say they said, wrote, or did?

A book within the genre of literary journalism is composed of scenes that build upon one another. These scenes are reconstructions. The better the sources, the more accurate the scenes will be. Where I describe a person's thoughts, they are based on what that person said he or she was thinking in a given situation, or what people in the book told others that the individual was thinking.

I did my best to find as much information as I could about the lead-up to the sisters' departure and about life in Raqqa. But only they know their thoughts and motivations.

The names of the sisters have not appeared in the media and so I gave them fictitious ones. If they return to Norway, wishing to live a life here, they will have their names intact. I also changed the names of their brothers, while their parents, in accordance with their wishes, retained their true names.

Sadiq chose to reveal his name and picture to the media,

in addition to openly relating his family's story at talks and in interviews.

Several friends of the sisters who contributed did not want their real names to appear and themselves chose the names they are known by in the book. It became clear to me at an early stage that the sisters' decision to travel to Syria was a vulnerable subject for many of them. A number of the girls were also concerned they would be identified as holding extremist views or of having ties to a terror organization, which the Islamic State is defined as by Norwegian law.

With regard to the employees of the schools the sisters attended, some wished to appear under their full names, while others are simply referred to as 'the Norwegian teacher' or 'the math teacher.'

I made copies of their interviews available to all the individuals to allow them the opportunity to correct any errors.

When the sisters departed on October 17, 2013, the family first contacted Asker and Bærum police station. Parts of their case were subsequently transferred to PST. I was granted access to the police station log from the first days and got statements from PST on how they handled the case.

In addition, I used sources in the diplomatic services regarding the consular assistance provided in Turkey in March 2015.

Is it ethically defensible to focus on the lives of two girls when they have not granted their consent?

My answer is yes. The entire world is trying to understand the reasons for radicalization among Muslim youth. Researchers, politicians, and youth workers are attempting to understand why some teenagers reject education and a life in peaceful surroundings to join a terror organization. There is no single explanation, but one can point to several factors, including the search for identity, meaning, and status; the desire to belong; the influence of others; excitement; the need to rebel; and romantic notions. In the girls' case, elements of a profound religious awakening can be added. Push-and-pull factors feature prominently when researchers talk about radicalization. Something pushed them out, something pulled them in.

An examination of those involved in extreme Islamist milieus found radicalization to be 'a multiethnic phenomenon, typified by young men with low education, criminal backgrounds, and lack of involvement in working life,' PST stated in a report in autumn 2016. Six of ten had immigrated to Norway in childhood or when they were young. The milieu was characterized by a high dropout rate from secondary schools and unemployment. As long as the same number of youths continued to live with these challenges, the potential for recruitment remained.

As a journalist, it is my task to put my finger on problematic aspects of our society. Confronted with this story, we must ask: Is this merely to do with them, or does it also have something to do with us?

I offer no explanation, neither of what attracted them to Islamic radicalism nor what propelled them out of Norway. I relate my findings. It is up to each reader to draw his or her own conclusions. Where did it start? What were the underlying reasons? When could they have taken different choices? How could an aspiring diplomat choose to become a housewife in Raqqa? Why did they become more interested in life *after* death than *this* life?

To understand the choices people make in their lives, we need to know something about those people. A religious choice is personal. It does not stand in isolation from a person's private life; on the contrary, it is closely tied up with what he or she has experienced, the circumstances in which the person has lived, and the environment the person grew up in.

I therefore also decided to focus upon individuals other than the sisters, as closely as I found justifiable.

Two Sisters introduces a number of Norwegian nationals who travel to Syria. The descriptions are dramatic. They deal with childhood, internal family relations, abuse, fraud, betrayal, murder – and love.

Allow me to present examples of choices I made concerning the publication of personal information. One important individual in the book is Aisha Shezadi. I used her full name, as she herself has opted to be in the public eye through her own texts and interviews prior to her departure for Syria, and afterward through Facebook posts open to the public about life in Raqqa. Neither she nor her parents have responded to my requests to talk to them. Aisha's story is written as related by her friends and written sources. I quoted the verdict against her father that was made by Oslo District Court in May 2016, which is accessible to the public and casts light on her childhood.

Research on those traveling to Syria, from both Norway and other European countries, shows that young men with backgrounds in violent or broken homes, and youths with an unstable childhood and a criminal past are overrepresented. It is during the vulnerable teenage years that most European foreign fighters are radicalized. With regard to the two sisters, I found that in addition to being a quest for meaning and identity, their actions were born of a religious awakening, a protest, and rebellion.

In order to shed light on all this, I focused more closely on some people than they themselves would want. One of these is Arfan Bhatti, who features in the book due to his marriage to one of the sisters' friends. He made it clear to me in person, both face-to-face and in writing, that he did not wish his private life to appear in print. I did not comply with that wish, on the basis that he has been, and remains, a central figure among radicalized Muslims in Norway. His personal actions cannot be viewed as distinct from his leadership role. As Aisha put it, he is 'the glue' of the Prophet's Ummah. In May 2017, he was arrested and accused of storing weapons, but he was released after a few months.

Ubaydullah Hussain likewise did not wish to contribute. I met him during Ramadan in summer 2015 to arrange an interview and was asked to contact him again after the fasting was over. I informed him, via messages and letters – the last two addressed to him in prison – about the topics I was interested in and requested his version of the story. He declined to respond. In April 2017, he was convicted of recruiting others to IS and received a sentence of nine years in prison.

The third man who appears in this book through marriage to the sisters' friends is now dead. I carefully trawled all the information on, and accusations against, Bastian Vasquez, given that he can no longer defend himself. The information I chose to use was confirmed by several sources in statements independent of one another. I also reviewed police documents and other case papers from the period prior to his departure for Syria.

Consequently, I based the portrayals of Bastian Vasquez, Arfan Bhatti, and Ubaydullah Hussain in their entirety on what others have said about them, in addition to written sources. I made my depictions of these individuals available to their lawyer, John Christian Elden.

The religious trail led to several places. First, to Islam Net.

The organization confirmed Ayan's central position in the organization in the years 2011 and 2012. Descriptions of Islam Net are based on observations made during conferences I attended and on recordings of debate meetings available on their website, as well as on written sources. I also interviewed members and the leader, Fahad Qureshi.

The trail led to the young Koran teacher in the Somali-dominated Tawfiiq Mosque in Oslo. He operates under the name Mustafa but is known to the police by another name, the moniker he has also used in his employment as a security guard. I know his real name but chose to use the name he goes by in the mosque milieu and among friends.

He repeatedly rejected all my approaches. On several occasions I informed him of my desire for his version of the content of his Koran lessons and to what degree he was involved in the sisters' trip to Syria.

In my attempts to track him down I also visited the Tawfiiq Mosque. On my initial meeting with the leader, Abdibasid Ali Mohammed, he told me he had never heard of any Koran teacher named Mustafa. Neither did he know him under his real name. When I mentioned the speculation in the media over the role of the

Koran teacher in the wake of the sisters' departure and expressed surprise at the name being unfamiliar to him, he informed me that 'this conversation can only continue with lawyers present.' When he later accepted to meet me at the mosque, a lawyer from the In Solidum law firm was present. The reason given was that I had made 'serious accusations' and had 'behaved aggressively' during our previous conversation. The answer was nevertheless the same: The leader had never heard of any Koran teacher named Mustafa. Even though he was a well-known figure in the mosque.

The appeal for information about Ayan and Leila that I posted on the mosque's open website for women – Tawfiiq Sisterhood – was deleted soon after.

I also interviewed Basim Ghozlan, leader of the Rabita Mosque, in relation to the death of a young woman on the mosque premises. He stressed that the mosque does not endorse exorcism and that it took place without the knowledge or permission of the leadership.

Sara and Sadiq's stories are based mainly on what they themselves related to me about their childhoods, youth, and lives in Norway. I have only Sadiq's version of large parts of his dramatic accounts of his trips to Syria. I went through the details of his story with him numerous times, double-checking and asking him to confirm earlier statements, and attempted to find secondary sources for times, places, and events. The accounts of the prison cell in al-Dana, torture, and interrogation are, in their entirety, Sadiq's version, as are the days he spent in Hatay prior to his initial entry into Syria. The story of the sisters as described by two al-Nusra fighters on the website Justpaste.it agrees with Sadiq's account. In addition, the filmmakers Styrk Jansen and Veslemøy Hvidsteen interviewed one of Sadiq's fellow captives, who confirmed the parts of the story he was witness to. Sadiq's experiences also follow a pattern consistent with what others have told of their own time in IS detention. Other people who have made the same journey across the border to search for their children, prior to Sadiq's trip and subsequent to it, also were asked to enlist in IS and then imprisoned as spies and tortured before their eventual release.

In order to gain insight into the various rescue plans, and the desperation Sadiq experienced as those plans either failed or were never put into action, the message logs between Sadiq and Osman were crucial. They gave a unique insight into the operations of a local smuggler in the ongoing war and how intertwined he is with the society around him. Osman is aware of the use of this information and has also agreed to be interviewed for the documentary *Only a Father*, albeit with his back to the camera. I changed his name.

The logs were written in Arabic and were translated by the writer and Arab Spring activist Iyad al-Baghdadi. He also translated voice messages from Osman and the so-called Double, and I drew heavily from his knowledge of Salafism and its appeal when new information came to light about the girls' radicalization, in turn prompting fresh discussion.

I benefited greatly from experts in the field, including the writer Charles Lister, the blogger Aymenn al-Tamimi, and Thomas Hegghammer of the Norwegian Defence Research Establishment, whom I constantly pestered with questions.

Lister's *The Syrian Jihad* is a work I often reached for to check the time line of events in Syria and for background on the conflict. Aymenn Al-Tamimi's blog provided up-to-date information about IS and matters concerning al-Nusra. Shiraz Maher's *Salafi-Jihadism* was an important reference. A list of other books that I found helpful is included at the back of the book. As regards women in IS, the literature in French is one step ahead of what is available in English, as is apparent from the reference list.

In addition, I was in contact with the activists behind Raqqa Is Being Slaughtered Silently and also discussed conditions there with representatives for organizations on the ground in Syria.

To a large degree I relied on articles and reports available online. My Norwegian sources include Marius Linge's in-depth study of Islam Net, Brynjar Lia's studies of the Prophet's Ummah, and Thomas Hegghammer's writings on jihadi culture and radicalization.

I made use of research reports from the Brookings Institution, King's College, Quilliam, and the Institute for Strategic Dialogue.

The information on the reaction of Aisha's mother came from the Norwegian daily newspaper *Vårt Land*. The account about Haji Bakr appeared in *Der Spiegel*, and Abu Muhammad al-Maqdisi's negotiations with IS were published in *The Guardian*. Sadiq showed me his income tax form for 2015 where DB Medialab, a company connected to the *Dagbladet* newspaper, was listed as one of his employers.

A complete list of links to reports and articles can be found on kagge.no using the search term *To søstre – kildeliste*.

This book would not have been possible without all those who contributed. I am impressed with and grateful to those who chose to speak when it would have been easier to keep silent and to those who set aside time to further illuminate matters so that they are as correct as possible.

Some of these people I spent hours, days, and weeks with; others I merely chatted with online or met for a brief interview. Together they created the images, scenes, and stories in this book.

I am deeply grateful to all those who spoke to me and responded to my inquiries.

Assistant Professor and Arabist Pernille Myrvold from the University of Bergen helped me with Arabic words and transcription. Likewise, the medical student Warsan Ismael helped with regard to Somali words and phrases.

I am grateful to those who unearthed material for me. Nasser Weddady found the al-Nusra soldier's text about the sisters, and the historian Tore Marius Løiten located relevant articles and research material. Ikhlaque Chan, employed by Bærum county, offered me interesting perspectives on radicalization from his work with youths from the area. I also am thankful to friends of the girls for sharing what they knew, as well as the teachers and principals at Dønski, Nesbru, and Rud secondary schools.

I am grateful to Styrk Jansen and Veslemøy Hvidsteen for their cooperation over the course of two years. We shared material we found and discussed each other's projects under way.

The author Trude Marstein tidied up my language, while the

editor in chief at Kagge, Tuva Ørbeck Sørheim, held things together to the last to ensure the book actually was published.

I thank the publishing director, Anne Gaathaug, who arranged my meeting with Sadiq Juma, and the publisher, Erling Kagge, who was there at every stage and at every twist and turn the book took. For the English version, I am grateful to the translator, Seán Kinsella, and the editor, Alex Star at Farrar, Straus and Giroux. They did a tremendous job of helping transfer my text into English.

Turning a story told into a book is demanding. Many choices need to be made along the way, many decisions considered. What ended up in this book is what I found most important to answer: What causes two girls, who are good students, who are ambitious, and who fled from war when young, to seek out war again and submit to the strict control of the Islamic State?

For her help throughout the process of making their story into a book, I thank Cathrine Sandnes from the Manifest think tank, who was there to discuss the choices taken along the way, and contributed to putting the manuscript together. Finally, I thank the editor Aslak Nore, who delved into the topic and met the problems around it with great knowledge and enthusiasm.

Together we arrived at how this story could best be told.

Two individuals deserve the most gratitude.

Sadiq and Sara.

Of approximately ninety sets of Norwegian parents whose children have traveled to Syria, only a handful have come forward. The rest have remained silent. There can be many reasons for this: to protect themselves, or to protect their children, perhaps in the hope that if their children return, they can continue their lives where they left off, without the stamp of being a jihadist.

Sara and Sadiq experienced one of the worst things imaginable to a parent: their children leaving them with no intention of ever returning. They invited me into their home in Bærum and to Hargeisa in Somaliland. In addition, I undertook a trip to Hatay with Sadiq.

They themselves decided where to draw the line; they established how open they would be. They both read the finished manuscript, or in Sara's case had it read out loud in translation by an interpreter. They had the opportunity to make corrections. They were not, as per our agreement, allowed to correct or change what others said about their daughters. In this respect, all the sources are independent, have been compared against one another, and were double-checked.

I am deeply humbled that Sara and Sadiq allowed me to study the dynamics and story of their family. What I included in the book is what I found most relevant to the question: Why did the daughters go?

Without the courage of Sadiq and Sara, there would not have been any book.

Åsne Seierstad
Oslo, October 4, 2016

Glossary

Arabic words often have various spellings in English.

abo	Father.
ajr	Reward in the hereafter.
akh	Brother.
akhi	My brother.
akhirah	The hereafter; life after death.
Alawites	Syrian religious minority.
Al-Dawla al-Islamiya	The Islamic State (IS).
Al-Dawla al-Islamiya fi al-Iraq wa al-Sham	The Islamic State of Iraq and Syria (ISIS).
Alhamdulillah	Praise be to God.
al-Khansa	IS women's police brigade.
Allah	God.
Allahu Akbar	God is greater.
al-salaf al-salih	The first three generations of Muslims after Muhammad.
al-Shabaab	Islamic terror group on the horn of Africa.
al-Sham	Greater Syria.

aqeeqah	Animal sacrifice for a newborn.
Baath	Renaissance/resurrection; the ruling party in Syria and previously in Iraq.
baya	Loyalty; oath of allegiance.
caliph	A religious successor of the Prophet Muhammad.
caliphate	A geographical area ruled by a caliph.
Daesh	Arabic acronym for the Islamic State.
dawa	Literally, invitation; proselytizing of Islam.
deen	Righteous way of life; good deeds.
Dhu al-Hijjah	Pilgrimage month.
dunya	The world; earthly life.
Eid al-Fitr	Celebration marking the end of Ramadan.
emir	Leader, commander.
fard al-ayn	An individual's religious duties.
fard kifaya	Collective religious duty.
fatwa	Islamic decree.
fiqh	Islamic jurisprudence.
fi sabil Allah	The cause; the way of God.
Five Pillars of Islam	Faith, prayer, charity, fasting, pilgrimage to Mecca.
ghanimah	Spoils of war.
hadith	Descriptions of the word, actions, and habits of Muhammad.
hafiz	Someone who knows the Koran by heart.
hajj	Pilgrimage to Mecca and Medina.
halal	What Allah has permitted.

haqq	Right; Truth.
haram	Forbidden.
hijra	Emigration.
iftar	Evening meal at sundown during Ramadan.
imam	Leader of congregational prayer in a mosque.
iman	Belief in the metaphysical aspects of Islam.
inshallah	God willing.
Jabhat al-Nusra	People's front; Syrian militia, previously tied to al-Qaida.
Jannah	Paradise.
jihad	Struggle; holy war.
jihad al-nafs	Jihad of the soul; internal holy war.
jihad bi'l-sayf	Jihad of the sword; battle against infidels.
jilbab	Long, loose coat or garment with a hood.
jinn	Spirits, demons.
jizya	Tax on non-Muslims.
Kaaba	The cubelike building at the center of Islam's most sacred mosque in Mecca.
kafir	Nonbeliever; infidel (singular); **kuffar** (plural).
kazab	Liar.
keffiyeh	Men's scarf worn around the neck and head.
kufi	Prayer cap.
madhab	School of thought within Islamic jurisprudence.

maqqar	A hostel for women.
muhajirat	Female emigrants.
mujahideen	Participants in jihad; holy warriors.
muntadayat	Forums, gatherings.
mutah	Joy, pleasure.
nikah	Marriage conducted according to Muslim law.
nikah al-mut'	A temporary marriage.
niqab	A woman's garment covering the entire face except the eyes.
qami	Tunic.
qatl bi qisas	Principle of retribution in sharia, a life for a life.
Quraysh	Powerful tribe in the Arabian Peninsula in the time of Muhammad.
Ramadan	The ninth month in the Islamic calendar, the fasting month.
ridda	Apostasy; abandonment of Islam.
sabr	Perseverance, patience.
salam aleikum	Peace be with you.
shabiha	Ghost, applied to agents of Syrian security services.
Shahada	Declaration of faith, one of the Five Pillars of Islam.
sharia	Islamic law.
Shaytan	Satan.
shura	Ruling council.
sunna	Muslim law based on the teachings and practices of Muhammad.
sura	Chapter of the Koran.

swt	Abbreviation of Subhanahu wa ta'ala: May He [Allah] be glorified and exalted.
talaq	Islamic divorce.
ulama	Islamic legal scholars (plural); **alim** (singular).
umm	Mother.
ummah	Society; the Muslim community throughout the world.
ummati	My people.
wali	Guardian.
wallahi	By Allah; I swear to God.
wudu	Ritual washing before prayer.
Yahudi	Jew (singular); **Yahud** (plural).
zakat	Alms, charity, taxes; one of the Five Pillars of Islam.

References

Ahmed, Leila. *Kvinder og køn i islam — Historisk rødder til en modern debat*. Forlaget Vandkunsten, 2008.

Akerhaug, Lars. *Norsk jihad — muslimske extremister blant oss*. Kagge Forlag, 2013.

Armstrong, Karen. *Muhammad: A Biography of the Prophet*. San Francisco: Harper, 1992.

Azzam, Abdullah. *Defense of the Muslim Lands*. 1987. www.ayyaz.com.pk/Books/Shaykh.Abdullah.Azzam/Defence.of.the.Muslim.Lands.-the.First.Obligation.After.Iman.pdf.

Bouzar, Dounia. *Désamorcer l'islam radical*. Ivry-sur-Seine: Éditions de l'Atelier, 2014.

———. *Ils cherchent le paradis, ils on trouvé l'enfer*. Ivry-sur-Seine: Éditions de l'Atelier, 2014.

Brown, Jonathan A. C. *Hadith: Muhammad's Legacy in the Medieval and Modern World*. London: Oneworld, 2009.

Erelle, Anna. *Dans la peau d'une djihadiste*. Paris: Robert Laffont, 2015.

Farah, Nuruddin. *From a Crooked Rib*. New York: Penguin, 2006.

Filieu, Jean-Pierre. *From Deep State to Islamic State*. London: Hurst & Company, 2015.

Hénin, Nicolas. *Jihad Academy: Nos erreurs face à l'État islamique*. Paris: Fayard, 2015.

Kasiki, Sophie. *Dans la nuit de Daesh: Confession d'une repentie*. Paris: Robert Laffont, 2016.

Kepel, Gilles. *Terreur dans l'Hexagone*. Paris: Gallimard, 2015.

Khan-Østrem, Nazneen and Mahmona Khan. *Utilslørt. Muslimske Råtekster*. Oslo: Aschehoug, 2011.

The Koran. Norwegian translation. Einar Berg. Oslo: Universitetsforlaget, 1989.

Lawrence, Bruce. *The Qur'an: A Biography.* New York: Grove Press, 2006.

Lewis, Ioan M. *Understanding Somalia and Somaliland.* New York: Columbia University Press, 2008.

Lister, Charles R. *The Syrian Jihad: al-Qaeda, the Islamic State and the Evolution of an Insurgency.* New York: Oxford University Press, 2016.

Littell, Jonathan. *Syrian Notebooks: Inside the Homs Uprising.* New York: Verso Books, 2015.

Maher, Shiraz. *Salifi-Jihadism: The History of an Idea.* London: Hurst & Company, 2016.

McCants, William. *The ISIS Apocalypse: The History, Strategy, and Doomsday Vision of the Islamic State.* New York: St Martin's Press, 2015.

Nesser, Petter. *Islamist Terrorism in Europe: A History.* New York: Oxford University Press, 2015.

Oberlé, Thierry. *Jinan – Esclave de Daesh.* Paris: Fayard, 2015.

Sheikh, Jakob. *Danmarks børn i hellige krig.* Copenhagen: Leonhardt and Ringhof, 2015.

Sidea, Emanuel. *Mannen från Harem. Reportage.* Stockholm: Natur & Kultur, 2016.

Soei, Aydin. *Vrede unge mænd.* Copenhagen: Tiderne skifter, 2011.

Stern, Jessica, and J. M. Berger. *ISIS: The State of Terror.* New York: Harper, 2015.

Thomson, David. *Les français jihadistes.* Paris: Les Arènes, 2014.

Trévidic, Marc. *Terroristes: Les 7 pilliers de la déraison.* Paris: Lattès, 2013.

Weiss, Michael, and Hassan Hassan. *ISIS: Inside the Army of Terror.* New York: Regan Arts, 2015.

Åsne Seierstad was born in 1970 and studied Russian, Spanish and the History of Philosophy at Oslo University. An internationally bestselling author, she has also received numerous awards for her journalism. In 2000 she published her first book, *With Their Backs to the World: Portraits from Serbia*.

After 11 September 2001 she went to Afghanistan, reporting for a number of major Scandinavian newspapers. The following year she went back to live with an Afghan family and wrote *The Bookseller of Kabul*. It went on to sell over two million copies. In Spring 2003 she reported on the war in Iraq from Baghdad and later released *A Hundred and One Days: A Baghdad Journal*. In 2007 she published *The Angel of Grozny: Life Inside Chechnya*. Following the atrocities in Oslo and Utøya in July 2011, she reported on Anders Breivik's trial and later published her extraordinary, universally acclaimed book on the massacre and its aftermath, *One of Us*.

Two Sisters is her sixth book. Released in Norway in November 2016, it became the bestselling book of the year, and won the prestigious Brageprisen.